The Enduring Impact of the Gospel of John

The Enduring Impact of the Gospel of John

Interdisciplinary Studies

Edited by **Robert A. Derrenbacker Jr., Dorothy A. Lee,** *and* **Muriel Porter**

Foreword by Francis J. Moloney, SDB

WIPF & STOCK · Eugene, Oregon

THE ENDURING IMPACT OF THE GOSPEL OF JOHN
Interdisciplinary Studies

Copyright © 2022 Wipf and Stock Publishers. All rights reserved. Except for brief quotations in critical publications or reviews, no part of this book may be reproduced in any manner without prior written permission from the publisher. Write: Permissions, Wipf and Stock Publishers, 199 W. 8th Ave., Suite 3, Eugene, OR 97401.

Wipf & Stock
An Imprint of Wipf and Stock Publishers
199 W. 8th Ave., Suite 3
Eugene, OR 97401

www.wipfandstock.com

PAPERBACK ISBN: 978-1-6667-3869-8
HARDCOVER ISBN: 978-1-6667-9972-9
EBOOK ISBN: 978-1-6667-9973-6

AUGUST 17, 2022 1:45 PM

New International Version:
Scriptures taken from the Holy Bible, New International Version®, NIV®. Copyright © 1973, 1978, 1984, 2011 by Biblica, Inc.™ Used by permission of Zondervan. All rights reserved worldwide. www.zondervan.com The "NIV" and "New International Version" are trademarks registered in the United States Patent and Trademark Office by Biblica, Inc.®

New Revised Standard Version:
Scripture quotations from Revised Standard Version of the Bible, copyright © 1946, 1952, and 1971 National Council of the Churches of Christ in the United States of America. Used by permission. All rights reserved worldwide.

To our students, past and present,
at Trinity College Theological School

Jesus said: "Very truly, I tell you, anyone who hears my word and believes the One who sent me has eternal life" (Jn 5:24)

Contents

List of Illustrations or Tables | ix

Foreword | xi
    Francis J. Moloney SDB

Abbreviations | xvii

Introduction | xxiii

Part I: The Johannine Text

1   Echoes of Luke in John 20–21 | 3
    Robert A. Derrenbacker Jr

2   Friends, Foes, or Rivals?
    John Among the Philosophers | 21
    Fergus J. King

3   The Fourth Gospel as Ancient Literary Artefact | 43
    Dorothy A. Lee

4   Will the Real Ἰουδαῖοι Please Stand Up? | 62
    Christopher A. Porter

5   Vines and Wines in First-Century Galilee | 81
    Tamara Lewit

Part II: Historical Interpretations

6   The Interpretation of John through Key Moments of
    Church History | 105
    Mark R. Lindsay

7   "Come, Holy Ghost, our souls inspire:"
The Musical Inspiration of John's Gospel | 124
       Peter Campbell

8   Johannine Glory in Bach's John Passion:
"In deepest lowliness made noble" | 144
       Katherine Firth and Andreas Loewe

9   Dostoevsky's Use of the Gospel of John
in *Crime and Punishment* | 161
       Scott A. Kirkland

10   Women in John's Gospel and the Women's
Ordination Debate | 175
       Muriel Porter

Part III: Contemporary Readings

11   "Walking on the Sea?" : A Moana Intertextual Reading of
John 6 in Light of Climate Change in Pasifika | 195
       Brian Fiu Kolia

12   A Sign of the Times: John's Gospel
and the Contemporary Anglican Communion | 212
       Alexander Ross

13   "In Spirit and in Truth": The Meeting of Lectionary
and Liturgy in the Gospel of John | 229
       Colleen O'Reilly

14   Encountering God: Preaching an Incarnate Word | 249
       Raewynne J. Whiteley

15   From Text to Life: A Pastoral Reading of the Gospel of
John | 263
       Gary Heard

16   Losing Ourselves to Gain Ourselves for Justice:
An Address on John 17:20-26 | 278
       Garry Worete Deverell

Contributors | 285

List of Illustrations or Tables

Chapter 5

Figure 1

Sixth-century CE mosaic from the pilgrim Church of Saints Lot and Procopius, Mount Nebo, Khirbet al-Mukhayyat, Jordan.

Figure 2

Third-century CE mosaic from the House of the Amphitheatre, Mérida, Spain.

Figure 3

A reconstructed oil press of a type used from the Hellenistic to late antique period, at Maresha, near Jerusalem, Israel.

Figure 4

Limestone press weight stone of a type used from the Hellenistic to late antique period, probably from the Galilee.

Figure 5

Wine being transported in amphorae. Late antique church mosaic, Samuel and Saidye Bronfman Archaeology Wing in the Israel Museum in Jerusalem.

Chapter 8

Example 1.

The opening of the Superius (highest) part of Byrd's setting for three voices from the Gradualia ac cantiones sacrae (1605), showing the text "Jesum Nazarenum" (Jn 18:7b) and "Nunquid et tu ex discipulis eius es" (Jn 18:17b).

Chapter 13

Table 1

Readings from the Gospel according to John in the Eucharist

Table 2

Saints Days or Commemorations

Foreword
Francis J. Moloney SDB

ENGLISH LANGUAGE GOSPEL SCHOLARSHIP has always had a fascination with the Gospel of John. Listing only major contributions that have come from the United Kingdom during the modern and contemporary era, the number and the quality of commentators on the Johannine story is remarkable: J. B. Lightfoot (1879),[1] B. F. Westcott (1881), J. H. Bernard (1928), G. H. C. Macgregor (1933), E. C. Hoskyns (1947), R. H. Lightfoot (1956), C. H. Dodd (1953, 1963), John Marsh (1968), Barnabas Lindars (1972), C. K. Barrett (1978), Mark W. G. Stibbe (1993), Leon Morris (1995), and Andrew Lincoln (2005).[2]

Necessarily, major trends in Johannine scholarship are reflected in this series of essays, from the era of careful historical and philological analysis (Lightfoot, Westcott, Bernard, Macgregor), to studies radically challenged by the appearance of the first (German) edition of Rudolf Bultmann's epoch-making commentary in 1943, down to contemporary, more literary and reader-oriented studies.

Bultmann raised the question of sources, and traced stages in the development of the Gospel as we now have it. Bernard had already made

---

1. The date represents Lightfoot's appointment as the Bishop of Durham, at which time he apparently assembled his unpublished Cambridge lecture notes on John 1–12. They were discovered by Ben Witherington III in 2013 in a bookcase located in a part of the Cathedral Library that had formerly served as the monks' dormitory. For their publication, see J. B. Lightfoot, *The Gospel of St. John*. On the story of their discovery, see 21–24.

2. This list is limited to the UK. For bibliographical details, see the Bibliography below; also Moloney, *The Gospel of John*, 25–26. Lincoln, *Saint John*, appeared after my commentary. The list could be greatly lengthened by adding English-speaking scholars from the USA (e.g., R. E. Brown [1966–1970]) or Australia (e.g., Mary L. Coloe, *John* [2021]). They continue and enrich the British tradition.

important suggestions along these lines well before 1943. But Bultmann's attribution of the Johannine discourse material to early Mandean Gnosticism raised acute theological issues. He read the Gospel of John as the Gnostic revealer's revelation of authentic living. He rightly claimed: Jesus is not simply the revealer ... he is the revelation.

Despite concerns over his source theory which is nowadays largely abandoned (or modified), Bultmann's turn toward the theological was a milestone in the history of the interpretation of the Fourth Gospel.[3] As I have insisted with my students over the years: "Ignore Bultmann at your peril!" Hoskyns (especially), R. H. Lightfoot, Dodd, and Marsh represent British reactions to Bultmann's Gnostic and existentialist reading, as did, for example, Rudolf Schnackenburg in Germany (1965–1975) and Raymond Brown in the USA. Paradoxically, largely because of Bultmann's profound contribution, all post-Bultmannian commentators saw the need for a decisive turn to a theological reading of the text. This is especially true of Hoskyns' work. At times his prose commentary almost matches the beauty of the original!

An increasing focus upon the Fourth Gospel as a carefully designed unified narrative followed the 1983 epoch-making study of R. Alan Culpepper.[4] His work was expanded and developed in British circles by Mark W. G. Stibbe,[5] and the fine commentary by Andrew Lincoln.[6] As well as tracing what the Johannine text might mean in and of itself, the issue of how that narrative can give (or not give) meaning to generations of hearing and reading audiences called for investigation. The door opened upon a new world of interpretation, more determined by the location and beliefs of those who received the text rather than those who may have stood at its origins.[7] *The Enduring Impact of the Gospel of John* is

---

3. Modified source approaches still appear in significant German scholarship. See, for example, Becker, *Das Evangelium*, and Haenchen, *John 1-2*, a translation of the 1980 German original.

4. Culpepper, *Anatomy*. Interestingly, this important study was written during sabbatical study leave at the University of Cambridge, under the eye of the British literary critic, Frank Kermode.

5. As well as his 1993 narrative commentary, see his timely and instructive monograph, *John as Storyteller*.

6. As well as his careful reading of the Gospel as a unified literary whole, Lincoln's commentary is ground-breaking in its nowadays unfashionable insistence that the author of the Fourth Gospel drew directly from the Synoptic Gospels.

7. It is beyond the scope of this Foreword to document this movement. For an overall presentation, see The Bible and Culture Collective, *The Postmodern Bible*. More

a significant Australian contribution to that new approach to our time-tested and inspired text.

Despite my compartmentalizing of the various "approaches" to the Gospel of John that have marked the past 150 years, I am always struck by the fact that we always stand on the shoulders of those who went before us. For example, a significant aspect of Hoskyns' commentary is his careful analysis of the reception of the Johannine text.[8] He was acutely aware of the enduring impact of the Gospel of John, as were many of his contemporaries.[9]

It is an exciting experience, as a senior Australian with a professional interest in the Gospel of John, to locate this volume and to indicate its significance. Its location is reasonably easy to identify. From what I have gathered from oral tradition, it had its beginnings in a meeting of the Faculty of the Theological School at Trinity College (University of Divinity). Encouraged by College leadership, and the Research Office of the University of Divinity, of which Trinity is a member college, the assembled members of the Faculty sensed that they shared a professional and pastoral interest in the Gospel of John.

This is not surprising, given that Trinity College is a college of the University of Melbourne and the University of Divinity and was established to prepare candidates for ordained ministry in the Anglican Church in Australia. Whether their academic formation had taken place in the great universities of Europe (including Oxford and Cambridge), the USA, or in Australia (national universities and the University of Divinity or its predecessor, the Melbourne College of Divinity) during their academic formation, they had all been exposed to the long history of British interest and expertise in the Gospel of John outlined above. The decision to work together on a volume of collected essays that circled around their shared interest in John came quickly and easily.

Perhaps the major significance of the volume is indicated in its subtitle. *Interdisciplinary Studies.* How have a variety of disciplines received

---

recently, and focused upon the Fourth Gospel, see Kitzberger, Interfigural Readings.

8. See "The Fourth Gospel in the Second Century"—the final version of which is the work of F. N. Davey, Hoskyns' editor, based upon fragmentary notes left by Hoskyns—(Fourth Gospel, 207–28), "The Use of the Fourth, Fifth and Ninth Chapters of Saint John's Gospel in the Early Lectionaries" (363–65), and "The Liturgical Use of the Pedilavium or the Washing of the Feet" (443–46).

9. The final version of this essay is the work of F. N. Davey, Hoskyns' editor, based upon fragmentary notes left by Hoskyns.

the Johannine text? The editors have done a sterling job to produce a work that, despite the variety of voices called for by "interdisciplinary studies," to generate three distinct but unified "Parts" for the presentation of their study: (1) the Johannine text; (2) historical interpretations, and (3) contemporary readings.

There would be no impact if there were no Fourth Gospel (Part I). What is its relationship to the broader Gospel-tradition? Has the cultural world within which it was developed and preached influenced its shape and message? How does it rate as a deliberately designed ancient literary artefact? Was there something going on within the dynamics of the community—rather than a rejection of non-members of the community—that might have generated John's problematic use of the expression "the Jews" (οἱ Ἰουδαῖοι)? Is first century viticulture reflected in the text?

Various "receptions" of the Fourth Gospel are illuminatingly illustrated (Part II) through the unforgettable presence of this Gospel across the history of Western music, especially Johann Sebastian Bach,[10] and the crucial literary and interpretative significance of John 11 for an understanding of Dostoyevsky's *Crime and Punishment*. The details of the Johannine text have also played a critical role in shaping the original articulation of the Christian faith-system, and the development of post-Reformation Christianity. It continues to play that role as the Churches are asked to accept the undeniable truth of the unconditional equality of women's and men's ministry with the unforgettable "woman-texts" in hand: the Mother of Jesus, the Samaritan woman, Martha and Mary of Bethany, and Mary Magdalene.

Although the variety of disciplines represented in the essays is the main feature of the work, the sample of contemporary readings offered (Part III) takes that variety into further fields. Rich studies form these concluding chapters: the possibility that the Christology and Theology of the Gospel of John provide a model for the "provisionality" of the

---

10. A personal note is in place here. I first experienced a live performance of Bach's Johannespassion while in Germany during my years of doctoral research (1973–1976). I recall being overwhelmed, in the light of my research into the Johannine use of "must be lifted up" (ὑψωθῆναι δεῖ. See John 3:13-14; 8:28; 12:32–33), by the combination of the words and music of the stirring opening chorus: "Daß du, der wahre Gottessohn, zu alle Zeit, auch in der größten Niedrichkeit, verherrlicht worden bist" ("that you, the true eternal Son of God, triumph even in the deepest humiliation"). Such experiences remain forever formative. The essay in the book focuses upon the Johannespassion. It could be extended into the Cantatas where Bach's sensitivity to the impact of the Word of God is one of the many signs of his genius.

Anglican communion itself, an illuminating study of the development of the widely used Common Lectionary, and the place of Johannine readings within it, and a sensitive use of the "story line" of the Fourth Gospel as a pastoral challenge to provide life and light to those in need.

Although not placed side by side, a powerful study of the challenge to preaching as communicating the incarnate word could also serve as commentary on two significant transcultural studies: a Pasifican reflection upon "walking on water" in John 6:16–21 and a powerful First Nations person's homily on John 17:22–26. They are eloquent culturally and Gospel-based appeals to protect our common home, and to the cruciform nature of the self-gift required for the dream of unity among all Australian peoples.

The Faculty of the Theological School at Trinity College, University of Divinity, and the editors of this volume, are to be congratulated on a significant contribution which has its roots in the traditional British love for the Gospel of John but has the courage to go further. Different disciplines and different cultures necessarily generate a variety of meanings from the same inspired and inspirational text. Christianity's future in our sedate and comfortable Western culture, especially as it can be experienced in Australia, depends upon an openness to all disciplines, and all cultures. Although not the final word on these crucial issues, *The Enduring Impact of the Gospel of John: Interdisciplinary Studies* shows that this was the case as the Fourth Gospel told a story of Jesus that both belonged to, yet transcended, its surrounding world. The process has continued since apostolic times; long may it last in the life of our contemporary Christian Churches and beyond.

Bibliography

Barrett, C. K. *The Gospel According to St John: An Introduction with Commentary and Notes on the Greek Text*. 2nd ed. London: SPCK, 1978.

Becker, Jürgen. *Das Evangelium des Johannes*. 2 vols. Ökumenischer Taschenbuch-Kommentar zum Neuen Testament 4/1-2. Gütersloh: Gerd Mohn, and Würzburg: Echter, 1979–1981.

Bernard, J. H. *A Critical and Exegetical Commentary on the Gospel According to St. John*. 2 vols. Edinburgh: T&T Clark, 1928.

Brown, R. E. *The Gospel According to John: Introduction, Translation, and Notes*. AB 29. 2 vols. Doubleday: Garden City, NY, 1966.

Bultmann, Rudolf. *The Gospel of John: A Commentary*. Translated by G. R. Beasley-Murray. Oxford: Blackwell, 1971.

Coloe, Mary L. *John*. 2 vols. WC. Collegeville, MN: Liturgical, 2021.

Culpepper, R. Alan. *Anatomy of the Fourth Gospel*. F&F. Philadelphia: Fortress, 1983.
Dodd, C. H. *Historical Tradition in the Fourth Gospel*. Cambridge: Cambridge University Press, 1963.
———. *The Interpretation of the Fourth Gospel*. Cambridge: Cambridge University Press, 1953.
Haenchen, Ernst. *John 1-2*. 2 vols. Hermen. Philadelphia: Fortress, 1984.
Hoskyns, Edwyn Clement and Francis Noel Davey. *The Fourth Gospel*. 2nd ed. London: Faber & Faber, 1947.
Kitzberger, Ingrid Rosa. *Interfigural Readings of the Gospel of John*. ECL 26. Atlanta: SBL, 2019.
Lightfoot, J. B. *The Gospel of St. John. A Newly Discovered Commentary*. Edited by Ben Witherington III & Todd Still. The Lightfoot Legacy Set 2. Downers Grove, IL: IVP Academic, 2015.
Lightfoot, R. H. *St John's Gospel: A Commentary*. Oxford: Clarendon, 1956.
Lincoln, Andrew T. *The Gospel According to Saint John*. BNT. London: Continuum, 2005.
Macgregor, G. H. C. *The Gospel of John*. London: Hodder & Stoughton, 1933.
Marsh, John. *The Gospel of Saint John*. London: Penguin, 1968.
Moloney, Francis J. *The Gospel of John*. Sacra Pagina 4. Collegeville, MN: Liturgical, 1998.
Morris, Leon. *The Gospel According to John*. Grand Rapids, MI: Eerdmans, 1971.
Schnackenburg, Rudolf. *The Gospel According to St John*. 3 vols. HTCNT IV/1-3. London: Burns & Oates; New York: Crossroad, 1968–1992.
Stibbe, Mark W. G. *John as Storyteller. Narrative Criticism and the Fourth Gospel*. SNTMS 73. Cambridge: Cambridge University Press, 1992.
The Bible and Cultural Collective. *The Postmodern Bible*. New Haven: Yale University Press, 1995.
Westcott, B. H. *The Gospel According to St John: The Greek Text with Introduction and Notes*. Grand Rapids, MI: Eerdmans, 1881.

Abbreviations

AAA&S	American Academy of the Arts & Sciences
AB	Anchor Bible
ABC	Australian Broadcasting Commission
ABR	Australian Biblical Review
AJP	The American Journal of Philology
AM&B	Applied Microbiology and Biotechnology
AP	Ancient Philosophies
ArgPhil	Arguments of the Philosophers
ASMS	American Society of Missiology Series
ATDC	Inter-Anglican Theological and Doctrinal Commission
BBC	Blackwell Bible Commentaries
B&CT	The Bible & Critical Theory
BCP	Book of Common Prayer
BETL	Bibliotheca Ephemeridum Theologicarum Lovaniensium
BIS	Biblical Interpretation Series
BJSP	British Journal of Social Psychology
BNT	Black's New Testament Commentaries
BTB	Biblical Theology Bulletin
BWV	Bach-Werke-Verzeichnis (Bach Works Catalogue)
BZNW	Beihefte zur Zeitschrift für die neutestamentliche Wissenschaft

CE	Cronache Ercolanesi
CIL	Corpus Inscriptionum Latinarum
CNT2	Commentaire du Nouveau Testament, deuxième série
C&L	Christianity and Literature
CRFSFS	Comprehensive Reviews in Food and Science Safety
CSR	Christian Scholar's Review
CTHPT	Cambridge Texts in the History of Political Thought
EB	Earth Bible
EBC	Earth Bible Commentary
ECL	Early Christianity & Its Literature
EBot	Economic Botany
EJPCA	European Journal of Post-Classical Archaeologies
EJSP	European Journal of Social Psychology
EPPET	Explorations in Practical, Pastoral, and Empirical Theology
ETL	Ephemerides Theologicae Lovanienses
F&F	Foundations & Facets
FBS	Fellowship for Biblical Studies
FRP	Fortress Resources for Preaching
FT	Feminist Theology
G&R	Greece and Rome
HTCNT	Herder's Theological Commentary on the New Testament
HCS	Hellenistic Culture and Society
Hermen	Hermeneia
HNT	Hebrew New Testament
HSCP	Harvard Studies in Classical Philology
HSNS	Historical Studies in the Natural Sciences
IATDC	Inter-Anglican Theological and Doctrinal Commission
IICM	Intercultural Institute for Contextual Ministry

Int	Interpretation
IVBS	International Voices in Biblical Studies
IVP	Inter-Varsity Press
JBCE	Joint Board of Christian Education
JBL	Journal of Biblical Literature
JRA	Journal of Roman Archaeology
JRMA	Journal of the Royal Musical Association
JSP	Journal for the Study of the Pseudepigrapha
JSNT	Journal for the Study of the New Testament
JSNTSup	Supplements to the Journal for the Study of the New Testament
JSJ	Journal for the Study of Judaism
JSJPHRP	Journal for the Study of Judaism in the Persian, Hellenistic and Roman Period
JSJSup	Supplements to the Journal for the Study of Judaism
JTI	Journal of Theological Interpretation
JTSA	Journal of Theology for Southern Africa
KJV	King James Version of Bible
KRS	Kirchanblatt für die reformierte Schweiz
LCL	Loeb Classical Library
LQ	Lutheran Quarterly
LNTS	Library of New Testament Studies
MCD	Melbourne College of Divinity
MCL	Martin Classical Lectures
MOW	Movement for the Ordination of Women
NB	New Blackfriars
NBC	New Bible Commentary: 21st Century Edition
NIB	New Interpreter's Bible in 12 volumes
NIV	New International Version of Bible
NRSV	New Revised Standard Version of Bible

NTTS&D	New Testament Tools, Studies and Documents	
NTS	New Testament Studies	
OECS	Oxford Early Christian Studies	
OTL	Old Testament Library	
OTR	Old Testament Readings	
Pac	Pacifica	
Paideia	Paideia Commentaries on the New Testament	
PCA	Post-Classical Archaeologies	
PEQ	Palestine Exploration Quarterly	
Phil	Philosophia	
PNTC	The Pillar New Testament Commentaries	
PPS	Perspective on Political Science	
RBPH	Revue Belge de Philologie et d'Histoire	
RCL	Revised Common Lectionary	
RM	Review of Metaphysics	
RUSCH	Rutgers University Studies in the Classical Humanities	
SBL	Society of Biblical Literature	
SBLDS	Society of Biblical Literature Dissertation Series	
SGRR	Studies in Greek and Roman Religion	
SHCT	Studies in the History of Christian Traditions	
SJT	Scottish Journal of Theology	
SNTS	Studiorum Novi Testamenti Societas	
SNTSMS	Society for New Testament Studies Monograph Series	
SVTQ	St Vladimir's Theological Quarterly	
TCPS	Transactions of the Cambridge Philological Society	
TNTC	Tyndale New Testament Commentaries	
T&S	Theory and Society	
TS	Theological Studies	
UBS	United Bible Society	
UBSHS	United Bible Society Handbook Series	

UD	University of Divinity
WBC	World Biblical Commentary
WC	Wisdom Commentary
WUNT	Wissenschaftliche Untersuchungen zum Neuen Testament
ZS	Zaccheus Studies

Introduction

IN OUR SMALL BUT diverse group of scholars associated with Trinity College Theological School and the University of Divinity, Melbourne, we share a common interest in the Gospel of John: as either Johannine scholars, researchers in areas adjacent to Johannine studies, or academics in other fields who find the Fourth Gospel significant and fruitful for their own disciplines. On this basis, we decided to work together to offer what we believe is an innovative as well as multi-disciplinary collection of reflections on John's Gospel. We have aimed it at a wide range of readers and not just at professional scholars and theologians.

But first, something about our faculty. Trinity College Theological School exists in relation to three institutions. Trinity College, the School's base, is historically connected to the University of Melbourne. The College was established in 1872, with a student body that included those training as Anglican clergy and formal theological study has been part of Trinity's identity since 1877. The University of Melbourne, from its founding in 1853, would not permit theology to be taught as one of its disciplines (a position it has maintained). For this reason, the Melbourne College of Divinity—now the University of Divinity—was established in 1910 by Act of the Parliament of Victoria as an ecumenical consortium for the academic study of theology. The Theological School is a member college of the University of Divinity. It is also the theological seminary for the Anglican Province of Victoria and particularly for the Diocese of Melbourne, training students in theology, including for lay and ordained ministries, with a broad, ecumenical focus.

In proposing this book, we recognized that New Testament studies can become too easily divorced from other kinds of theological research and from other disciplines. It seemed important to augment our understanding of this most eloquent and enduring Gospel with the perspective of those who, while not claiming to be Johannine scholars, nevertheless have insights to bring from their own fields of study and their own experience.

These insights include other areas within the New Testament, such as the Synoptic Gospels, as well as the Hebrew Scriptures and the archaeology of antiquity. But this volume goes further to embrace a wider range of Johannine devotees, including those engaged in history and theology, and in the study of the arts, particularly literature and music. It also encompasses working clergy in their liturgical use of Scripture in the lectionary, in their preparation and delivery of homilies, and in their pastoral care.

Now more than ever, with the widening division between disciplines, and even areas within the one discipline, it is imperative to find ways to cross widening boundaries and engage in critical and considerate dialogue. Otherwise a point will come (if it has not already) where we can no longer communicate across dispersed fields. The more isolated the discipline of New Testament is, the more impoverished it becomes, and the less able to translate to the lives of ordinary people.

This collection of essays offers the work of a varied array of New Testament scholars, scholars of antiquity, historians, philosophers and theologians, musicologists, and practical and pastoral theologians. For convenience, and despite the overlap, we have divided the essays into three sections: firstly, studies of the Johannine text itself; secondly, historical reflections on the Fourth Gospel; and thirdly, contemporary interpretations of the Gospel, whether contextual, theological, or practical.

The first five essays examine the Johannine text, either directly or through closely adjacent studies. The essay by Bob Derrenbacker—a scholar of the Synoptic Gospels—leads the way, exploring the current issue of John's relationship to the Synoptics, and especially the Gospel of Luke. Here he finds clear signs of the fourth evangelist's awareness of, and influence by, the Third Gospel, an awareness and influence that is consistent with Greco-Roman literary culture and the ways in which ancient authors were impacted by written source material.

The following three essays, written by Johannine scholars and lecturers within the faculty, make explicit links with other, related disciplines. Fergus King's essay, in dialogue with philosophy, investigates the relationship between John and ancient philosophy, giving in the process an outline of the core philosophical movements of the day. He argues that each tradition needs to be seen in its own light and that, while there are points of contact, there are also significant differences between the philosophical schools and the Fourth Gospel.

Dorothy Lee's essay works in dialogue with literary studies, and in particular ancient literary criticism—from Aristotle onwards—arguing that John's Gospel in its own day would have been received by its audience, whether consciously or unconsciously, as a distinct literary artefice,even if at a more popular level. The essay reveals three of the core literary devices employed in antiquity that can still offer insights into John's narrative craft for us today.

Christopher Porter's essay works in concert with social identity theory in the field of psychology, and explores the complex meaning of those called Ἰουδαῖοι (literally, "Jews") in the narrative of the Fourth Gospel. He demonstrates a broad comprehension of the terminology and its role within the Gospel narrative in relation to Jesus, the disciples, and Judaism—a sociological understanding that moves away from antisemitic readings of the text.

Finally, within this section, and from an archaeological perspective, Tamara Lewit uses the Gospel references to wine and vines as a springboard for understanding the ancient growing of vines, along with the art and science of viticulture as it was practiced in the first century CE. She focusses particularly on the wedding at Cana (Jn 2:1–9), the metaphor of the vine (Jn 15:1–6), and the drink on a sponge offered to Jesus on the cross (Jn 19:25–16). Her essay helps us to grasp the contextual background and the significance of both vines and wine imagery in John's Gospel for its first readers.

The second section of the book, loosely based on history, begins with Mark Lindsay's exploration of three key moments in church history where texts from the Fourth Gospel have lain at the heart of contention: Origen and the early church, the Protestant Reformation, and twentieth century Europe under Nazism. John's Gospel, he argues, has been effective over the generations in identifying heresy, understanding the Eucharist aright, and confirming Jewish-Christian solidarity in the light of antisemitism.

Writing as a musicologist and historian, Peter Campbell offers a general, historical survey of the use of various Johannine texts in musical expression in the Western tradition, particularly in concert works and liturgical compositions, from the Renaissance to the present day. This survey demonstrates the potent and enduring influence that the Gospel of John has, even in a medium as different as music, as demonstrated across many generations and different musical genres.

Katherine Firth and Andreas Loewe together investigate, from a musicological and theological viewpoint, the relationship between the Johannine Passion narrative (Jn 18–19) and Bach's magnificent St John Passion. This is the second essay focussing on music and musicology, and it hones in on a specific musical work and the theology which emerges from an intertextual "reading" of Bach's lyrics and music in relation to the Fourth Gospel.

Scott Kirkland's essay employs a literary, philosophical and theological perspective to consider Dostoyevsky's *Crime and Punishment*, which was published in 1866. The essay focusses on the central scene of the novel, which acts as a turning-point in the plot on the path towards redemption, where the main characters, Raskolnikov and Sonya (the murderer and the prostitute) read together the story of the Raising of Lazarus from John 11.

Finally in this section, Muriel Porter writes both as an historian and an active participant in synodical debates and elsewhere in the story of women's ordination in the Anglican Church of Australia: a battle that has not yet been won across the continent and that reflects similar struggles in and beyond the international Anglican Communion. She connects this experience to the influence of women as prominent disciples and leaders within the narrative world of the Fourth Gospel.

The third section of the book has as its focus the contemporary context. It begins with Brian Kolia's essay which presents a challenging example of contextual exegesis across the two Testaments, via the Walking on the Water in John 6:16–21. Kolia, a Hebrew Bible scholar, reads the scene in relation to Old Testament narratives and connects it to the situation of Pacifica peoples today, facing the devastations caused by climate change and the indifference of Western powers to their plight.

Alexander Ross offers a theological discussion of the significance of the church within the Anglican Communion, arguing for a re-capture of core Johannine concepts such as symbolism. He offers insights from the Fourth Gospel as a way to understand, in a refreshed way, the theological role of Anglicanism today. He argues that such an ecclesiology enables the church to mediate its place in the world as a participation in God's creation and the instrument by which the new creation is to be both heralded and sustained.

The next three essays of this section are concerned more explicitly with practical theology. In the first of these, Colleen O'Reilly surveys the way in which the Gospel of John is configured within the three-year Revised Common Lectionary. She argues that, though John appears at first glance to be of secondary import (having no separate "year" on its own but interwoven with readings from the other Gospels), the Fourth Gospel in fact holds the lectionary together.

This essay is complemented, appropriately enough, by a homiletical essay by Raewynne Whitely that speaks of the centrality of the incarnation (Jn 1:14) as the model for interpretation of the biblical text and for the event itself of preaching. The essay points to the significance of the incarnation at the beginning of the Gospel (Jn 1:1–18) and the call to discipleship and following Jesus at the end (Jn 21:15–19). It concludes with a sample sermon of her own from John 14:23–29.

The penultimate essay in this section is by Gary Heard, who writes as a practical theologian with considerable pastoral experience, offering a pastoral reading of the Fourth Gospel. He shows that the Gospel itself connects to the discipline of pastoral theology (a discipline whose parameters he outlines) at a number of significant points. In this analysis, he indicates not only the beauty of the text in its theology but also its power and effectiveness as a pastoral document for specific pastoral contexts.

Finally, we include a significant Address delivered by Garry Worete Deverell on the occasion of the Week of Prayer for Reconciliation/Christian Unity, a week to listen to Indigenous peoples and to take steps to redress decades, if not centuries, of injustice. This sermon presents an Indigenous reading of John 17 in light of the last two centuries and more of Western occupation of Australia on land never ceded by the Indigenous inhabitants. Such a tragic narrative is far from being unique to Australia. The sermon calls for a radical re-commitment to justice in order to achieve reconciliation on the basis of John's understanding of glory as self-sacrificing love.

This collection of essays, though varied, does not claim to be comprehensive. There are gaps in the range of disciplines and choice of subject matter that are self-evident. Many (though no means all) of us are Anglicans of one kind or another, and most of us are of migrant ancestry, which inevitably limits the breadth of our perspective. But our hope is that this collection will play a modest but exemplary role in demonstrating how disciplines can interact and speak to each other across the ever-expanding interpretative universe, particularly in a perennial Gospel such as that of John. Although exegesis, through the historical critical method, has developed considerably from the models employed in Patristic exegesis—both in outlining how text and context are intertwined and also in making explicit the political, ecological, and cultural dimensions of the text—we also need to recover something lost from that ancient past: the sense held by early Patristic writers that the biblical text has a range of interpretative methods which can and should be held together.

And from an even older past, we need to listen to compelling Indigenous voices and their call to justice. We need to learn from the way they connect the biblical text in their present experience of colonization and dispossession, and to their past experience of sensitively inhabiting and conserving the earth.

From this viewpoint, the book attempts to reclaim the Johannine text as possessing a generous range of meanings and to demonstrate its enduring impact across the generations. These meanings move in broader ways than the simple technicalities of exegesis, and do so in creative dialogue with other disciplines—whether they be spiritual, pastoral, political, theological, postcolonial, or artistic—with far-reaching consequences for the transformation of culture and people's lives. The Fourth Gospel is indeed a text in which, as the early church divined, an infant can safely paddle and an elephant can unreservedly swim.

We thank those who have assisted in the production of this book: Trinity College and its Warden, Professor Ken Hinchcliff, for continual support and encouragement; our students in the Theological School who inspire us and make our research worthwhile; Professor Frank Moloney SDB, an eminent Johannine scholar and good friend of Trinity, for agreeing to write the Foreword; Hugh McGinlay for his excellent and timely copy-editing; our Wipf & Stock editors, George and Emily Calihan, for their gracious attentiveness; the Australian Research Theology Foundation for it generous grant towards publication; and our families and close friends for sustaining us in this project, as in all our endeavors.

The Editors: Bob Derrenbacker, Dorothy Lee, Muriel Porter
Day of Pentecost, 5 June 2022

Part I

The Johannine Text

1

Echoes of Luke in John 20–21
ROBERT A. DERRENBACKER JR

Introduction

IT HAS LONG BEEN recognized that the agreements in wording and content shared by the Synoptic Gospels—Matthew, Mark, and Luke—are indicative of some sort of literary relationship between them; sorting out this literary relationship is described by Gospel scholars as the "Synoptic Problem," a problem that still remains "unsolved" despite some general scholarly consensus.[1] However, Johannine scholarship remains divided on the question of whether the author of the Fourth Gospel had a literary relationship with one or more of the Synoptic Gospels. The Synoptics and John do share some common material, which this particular question attempts to account for, with Johannine scholarship generally falling into one of two camps. On the one hand, there are those who argue that John is independent of the Synoptics, with any parallels between John and the Synoptics explained as a result of pre-literary common oral traditions or the existence of the putative "Signs Gospel" that was influenced by some Synoptic tradition.[2] On the other

---

1. The dominant "solution" to the Synoptic Problem remains the Two-Document Hypothesis (2DH), which posits that Matthew and Luke both independently accessed the Gospel of Mark (Markan priority) and a hypothetical written sayings source referred to as "Q" (short for *Quelle*, "source"). For a helpful introduction to the Synoptic Problem, see Stein, *The Synoptic Problem*.

2. E.g., Borgen, "John and the Synoptics," 408–37; Smith, *John among the Gospels*; Fortna, *The Fourth Gospel and its Predecessor*; and Brown, *Introduction to the Gospel*

hand, there is an increasing number of Gospel scholars who believe that John knew and utilized as sources at least the Gospel of Mark, if not the other Synoptics as well.[3]

In general, it seems that there is an "either-or" approach to the question of John and the Synoptics—either the Fourth Evangelist knew and therefore "used"[4] one or more Synoptics in the writing of his Gospel, or the Fourth Evangelist was not familiar with the written Synoptic Gospels, and therefore did not utilize them at all. Such a binary choice is somewhat anachronistic and does not allow for some sort of middle ground, nor does it account for a *spectrum* of literary dependence (see below). Thus, this essay will offer a sort of *via media* to the debate on the Fourth Gospel's relationship to the Synoptics. Specifically, this essay will look at parallels between John 20–21 and the Gospel of Luke, exploring whether there are "echoes" of Luke in the concluding two chapters of the Fourth Gospel.

Luke and John: Trends in Scholarship in the Twentieth and Twenty-First Centuries

The prospect of the Fourth Evangelist's knowledge of the Gospel of Luke is particularly intriguing within the larger question of John's use of the Synoptics. In his classic defense of the "Four-Document Hypothesis" (an early variation on the 2DH), B. H. Streeter argued that it was very "difficult to deny some literary connection between Luke and John,"[5] a view that was quite unpopular at the time. For Streeter, evidence for this literary connection included the sudden naming of Lazarus, Mary and Martha "of Bethany" in 11:1 "as if they were well-known characters";[6] the notion that the anointing story in John 12:1–8 may have been derived from Luke 7;[7] and, "[t]hree of the most remarkable points of contact" in the Passion Narrative: 1) Peter's visit to the empty tomb (Luke 24:12//

---

of John, esp. 90–114.

3. E.g., Barrett, *Gospel according to John*; Neirynck, "John and the Synoptics," 438–50; Lincoln, *Gospel according to Saint John*; and more recently, the contributors to Becker et al., eds., *John's Transformation of Mark*.

4. We will discuss the choices of verbs employed to describe relationships between texts below.

5. Streeter, *Four Gospels*, 405.

6. Streeter, *Four Gospels*, 402.

7. Streeter, *Four Gospels*, 402.

John 20:3–10); 2) Jesus' words "Peace be with you" at a post-resurrection appearance to his disciples (Luke 24:36//John 20:19, 21); and, 3) Jesus' demonstration of his resurrected state by showing his wounded hands to his disciples (Luke 24:39–40//John 20:20). Streeter continues: "To prove literary dependence [by John on Luke], we must find examples of the use of language more or less identical, where the resemblance is of a kind not readily explicable by coincidence; or we must be able to detect in some story additions or modifications of quite minor details of a kind not likely to have been preserved apart from the context in which they are embodied."[8] Listing a number of examples as evidence,[9] Streeter concluded that "it [is] difficult to deny some literary connection between Luke and John."[10]

Several decades later — despite arguing against John's knowledge of the Synoptics—Raymond E. Brown put the question this way: "In many ways, the possibility of cross-influence on John from *Luke* is the most interesting. In scenes shared by John and several Synoptics, the parallels between John and Luke are usually not impressive. Rather, it is with the peculiarly Lucan material that John has the important parallels."[11] Brown lists the following parallels:

- "One multiplication of loaves and fish

- "Mention of figures like Lazarus; Martha and Mary; one of the Twelve named Jude or Judas (not Iscariot); the high priest Annas

- "No night trial before Caiaphas

- "Double question put to Jesus concerning his messiahship and divinity (Luke 22:67, 70; John 10:24–25, 33)

- "Three 'not guilty' statements by Pilate during the trial of Jesus

---

8. Streeter, *Four Gospels*, 404.

9. Streeter's examples include: 1) the "Devil" motivating Judas (Luke 22:3//John 13:2); 2) Pilate's three-fold "I find no fault in him" (Luke 23:4, 14, 22//John 18:38; 19:4, 6); 3) the severed *right* ear of the high priest's slave (Luke 22:50//John 18:10); 4) Jesus buried in a tomb "in which no one had ever been laid"; 5) two angels at the empty tomb (cf. one messenger/angel in Mark and Matthew) seen by the female disciples; and 6) the fact that the language in Jesus' prediction of Peter's denial is similar in Luke and John (vs. Mark and Matthew) – see Luke 22:34//John 13:38 (Streeter, *Four Gospels*, 404–5).

10. Streeter, *Four Gospels*, 405.

11. Brown, *Introduction*, 102.

- "Post-resurrectional appearances of Jesus in Jerusalem; the similarity here is very strong if verses like Luke 24:12 and 40 are original
- "A miraculous catch of fish (Luke 5:4–9; John 21:5–11)"[12]

In the end, Brown is not convinced that the Fourth Evangelist knew and utilized the Gospel of Luke as a source, accounting for these parallels by postulating that "in the relations between Luke and John cross-influence is possible in both directions. Since such cross-influence does not express itself in identical wording, it may well have taken place at an oral stage in the history of Gospel composition without either evangelist reading the other's gospel."[13]

Streeter and Brown are two (competing) examples of major twentieth century Gospel scholars who sought to explain the curious parallels that the Gospels of Luke and John share. With renewed and fresh scholarly arguments in favor of the more general possibility of the Fourth Evangelist's knowledge of the Synoptics, it is worth revisiting the more specific question of whether the Fourth Gospel has a literary relationship with the Gospel of Luke.[14]

What do we Mean by "Literary Dependence" between the Synoptics and the Fourth Gospel?

Until recently, the question of the Synoptics and John has been largely framed within a binary choice: Either the Fourth Evangelist knew and utilized (at least) some of the Synoptic Gospels, or the Fourth Gospel and the Synoptics are literarily independent, with their common features explained without an appeal to direct literary dependence. I maintain that a more nuanced view is warranted, particularly as such a view can be seen more realistically within the methods and techniques of ancient writing practices.[15]

To begin to address this question, we first need to understand what we mean by "literary dependence" in antiquity. In my 2016 contribution

12. Brown, *Introduction*, 103.
13. Brown, *Introduction*, 103–4.
14. It should be noted that there are a few scholars who have argued that *Luke* knew *John*. See, for example, Shellard, *New Light on Luke*.
15. I believe that we see a more nuanced position in, for example, the work of Williams, especially in her contribution to Becker et al., *John's Transformation of Mark* ("John's 'Rewriting' of Mark," 51–66).

to the John S. Kloppenborg *Festschrift*,[16] I argue that literary dependence is much more than verbatim quotation. Instead, one needs to imagine a more nuanced *spectrum of literary dependence*, which ranges from subconscious allusion, conscious allusion, paraphrase, imitation, verbatim quotation, and scribal reproduction.[17] On to this spectrum, one can then map increasing degrees of verbatim verbal agreements.

Those who object to John's use of the Synoptics perhaps do not see strong enough verbal agreements between John and one or more of the Synoptic Gospels. For we see verbal agreements in the Triple Tradition (where all three Synoptics parallel each other at the level of pericope) in the range of 41–49% between Matthew and Mark, and Luke and Mark, data that lead scholars to (rightly) conclude that there is a literary relationship of some sort between the Synoptic Gospels.[18] These data are, however, indicative of a relatively (and abnormally) high rate of verbal parallel agreements compared to other ancient literature where source texts are identifiable.[19] Likewise, John S. Kloppenborg notes that the "very high degree of verbatim agreement"[20] in the Double Tradition is an "anomaly" when compared to other ancient texts.[21] Thus, we need to first recognize that while high rates of verbatim agreement between two ancient texts is, in all likelihood, indicative of a literary relationship, low degrees of verbatim agreement can constitute evidence for a literary relationship as well.

In addition, we need to recognize that a non-binary spectrum of literary relationships existed in antiquity (see above), a spectrum that needs to be realistically applied to the question of John and the Synoptics. Lincoln puts it thus:

> when it comes to exploring John's relationship to the Synoptics, it should not necessarily be assumed that the only form of

---

16. Derrenbacker, "Ancient Literacy," 81–95.
17. Derrenbacker, "Ancient Literacy," 85.
18. See Derrenbacker, "Ancient Literacy," 90–91.
19. Derrenbacker, "Ancient Literacy," 91–92.
20. Kloppenborg, "Variation?" 53 n 38.
21. Kloppenborg, "Variation," 63. Kloppenborg writes: "The practices of the Synoptic writers suggests that, if they can be classed as scribes, they were scribes of relatively modest accomplishment and status, though of course not without some degree of sophistication. They did on occasion rise to the level of rhetorical paraphrase of sources, and were capable of other elegant touches, even if on the whole their copying technique was rather wooden" (79).

> dependence is the sort of strictly literary one in which a writer has the written sources before him as he writes or that, if this kind of close copying of material cannot be proved throughout the bulk of the narrative, then the only alternative is to view the Fourth Gospel as working with independent traditions about the life of Jesus.[22]

After listing examples of John's reliance on the Synoptics,[23] Lincoln concludes the following:

> What should be clear from the preceding discussion is that the fourth evangelist handles his source material from the Synoptics with a creative and imaginative freedom in order to promote his own theological and persuasive ends. He is so thoroughly familiar with these earlier versions of the story of Jesus that, in reflecting on them in his own setting and in the light of the issues with which it confronts him, he is able to weave parts of them into his fresh attempt to set the story in a cosmic context and to penetrate the implications of its protagonist's unique relationship with God. In many ways to adopt this perspective is to return to what ancient interpreters meant by calling John a "spiritual Gospel" in relation to the Synoptics. The evangelist supplements the other Gospels not so much by providing additional historical information about Jesus but by enhancing their portrayal of him through a further narrative that makes more explicit the significance of his oneness with God.[24]

Thus, assuming a more nuanced understanding of literary dependence in antiquity should not rule out the Fourth Evangelist's familiarity with at least one of the Synoptic Gospels, if not more. We need to be able to imagine an ancient author's "knowledge" of (or "familiarity" with) ancient texts that were not necessarily source-texts for that ancient author. It is my contention that in addition to evidence of John's use of Mark,[25] there is also evidence for the Fourth Evangelist's familiarity with the Gospel of Luke, seen in various "echoes" of the Gospel of Luke in the Gospel of John. Richard B. Hays has utilized the noun "echoes" to describe the intertextuality that exists between the Jewish scriptures and the New

---

22. Lincoln, *John*, 31.
23. Lincoln, *John*, 33–38.
24. Lincoln, *John*, 38.
25. Again, see Becker et al., *John's Transformation of Mark*.

Testament.²⁶ Hays defines an "echo" as distinct from a "quotation" and an "allusion," a phenomenon that "may involve the inclusion of only a word or phrase that evokes, for the alert reader, a reminiscence of an earlier text."²⁷ And it is with this understanding of the noun "echoes" in mind that I proceed with the understanding of John's familiarity with Luke, at least in the last two chapters of the Fourth Gospel.

Echoes of Luke in John 20–21

The remainder of this essay will focus on three parallel passages in the empty tomb/post-resurrection sections of John 20-21, for in the post-burial of Jesus sections of all four Gospels one finds distinctive and unique material, some of which is (at least superficially) unparalleled. The empty tomb and post-resurrection appearance stories in the Fourth Gospel are worth comparing to Luke 24 (and Luke 5:1–11, as we will see below), for they provide one the opportunity to view distinctly "Lukan" sections of the Gospel according to Luke alongside some distinctly Johannine sections in the Fourth Gospel.

Peter and the Empty Tomb

Luke 24:12	John 20:3–10
12 But Peter got up and ran [ἔδραμεν from τρέχω] to the tomb [τὸ μνημεῖον];	3 Then Peter and the other disciple set out and went toward the tomb [εἰς τὸ μνημεῖον]. 4 The two were running [ἔτρεχον from τρέχω] together, but the other disciple outran Peter and reached the tomb first.

---

26. See Hays, *Echoes of Scripture in the Gospels*; Hays, *Echoes of Scripture in the Letters of Paul*.
27. Hays, *Echoes of Scripture in the Gospels*, 10.

Luke 24:12	John 20:3–10
stooping and looking in [καὶ παρακύψας βλέπει] he saw the linen cloths [τὰ ὀθόνια] by themselves;	5 He bent down to look in [καὶ παρακύψας βλέπει] and saw the linen wrappings [τὰ ὀθόνια] lying there, but he did not go in. 6 Then Simon Peter came, following him, and went into the tomb. He saw the linen wrappings lying there, 7 and the cloth that had been on Jesus' head, not lying with the linen wrappings but rolled up in a place by itself. 8 Then the other disciple, who reached the tomb first, also went in, and he saw and believed; 9 for as yet they did not understand the scripture, that he must rise from the dead. 10 Then the disciples returned to their homes [ἀπῆλθον οὖν πάλιν πρὸς αὐτούς].
then he went home [καὶ ἀπῆλθεν πρὸς ἑαυτόν], amazed at what had happened.	

Our first pericope—Peter's visit to the empty tomb (Luke 24:1–12// John 20:1–13)—provides an opportunity to observe potential echoes of Luke in the Fourth Gospel. In both Gospels, Mary Magdalene and (Simon) Peter play prominent roles in each account. In addition, there are a number of common elements (see table above) in Peter's visit to the empty tomb (Luke 24:12//John 20:3–10).[28] For example, we see Peter

---

28. Luke 24:12 has traditionally been seen as part of the so-called "Western Non-Interpolations" (or, more helpfully, the "Non-Western Interpolations"—see Ehrman, *The Orthodox Corruption of Scripture,* 223–7)—that is, "interpolated" verses added by later scribes into the (non-Western) manuscript tradition who were influenced by Johannine parallels. However, the United Bible Societies editorial committee includes this verse with some confidence at a rating of "B" in both the fourth and fifth editions of the Greek New Testament, published by the UBS. Metzger writes: "Although v. 12 is sometimes thought to be an interpolation . . . derived from Jn 20.3, 5, 6, 10, a majority of the Committee regarded the passage as a natural antecedent to v. 24 [in Luke 24], and was inclined to explain the similarity with the verses in John as due to the likelihood that both evangelists had drawn upon a common tradition" (*Textual Commentary,* 157–8). Fitzmyer agrees with this assessment (that Luke 24:12 is original), arguing that the relatively late publication of P^{75} (Bodmer Papyrus XIV–XV, published in 1961), which includes v. 12, was unknown at the time that Hort coined the term "Western Non-Interpolations" (*Gospel according to Luke,* 131, 1547). While Marshall is less convinced, arguing that explaining the verse's omission (i.e, the "non-interpolation") in some manuscripts remains difficult, nevertheless, the "external evidence for omission is not decisive" (*Gospel of Luke,* 888). For the purposes of this essay, I will be concurring with editors of UBS5 and assuming that 24:12 (as well as 24:36 and 40) was original to Luke. For a contrary view, see for example Carroll, *Luke,* 479–80. One

"running" to the tomb in both Gospels, Peter "stooping down and looking in the tomb," Peter seeing the linen burial cloths (τὰ ὀθόνια), and Peter (along with the "other disciple" in John) returning to "his own" place or home after visiting the empty tomb. In addition, we see Mary Magdalene reporting the news of the empty tomb to the apostles/disciples (Luke 24:10//John 20:18).

The table above demonstrates some of the interesting verbal parallels between Luke and John. Particularly relevant are Peter's actions of "running" (τρέχω) and "stooping down" (παρακύπτω) to take a look. The act of running in the ancient world, particularly for a male, is surprising; in the New Testament, we only see it in this scene and, as Bruce J. Malina and Richard L. Rohrbaugh note, males (especially older males) "in the Middle East do not run except in an emergency. Hiking up flowing robes in order to run not only lack dignity, it inappropriately exposes legs to public view and hence causes dishonor."[29] Yet both Luke and John describe Peter's (potentially embarrassing) action of "running" to the tomb in response to the news of the empty tomb he hears from Mary Magdalene. A curious detail shared by both that may indicate the Fourth Evangelist was familiar with the Gospel of Luke.[30]

In addition, the action of "stooping down" to "take a look" (καὶ παρακύψας βλέπει) in both Luke and John is notable, and is further evidence of echoes of Luke in the Fourth Gospel. The verb παρακύπτω is rare in the New Testament (5x), three instances of which occur here in the context of the empty tomb (Luke 24:12; John 20:5, 11). Barrett notes that while normally the verb "is often used of one looking down from a height," here it "signifies a glance . . . for which an inclination of the head is required."[31] Not only is the verb rare in the New Testament, but its use to denote a "stooping" or a "bending" down is atypical as well, which again indicates an echo of Luke in the Fourth Gospel.

---

wonders, however, if advocacy for the so-called "Non-Western Interpolations" is being kept alive by the putative independence of John from the Synoptics.

29. Malina and Rohrbaugh, *Social-Science Commentary on the Synoptic Gospels*, 372.

30. It should be noted that in Matthew's account of the empty tomb, Matthew portrays the women at the tomb "running" (ἔδραμεν from τρέχω) to tell the news to the disciples of Jesus (28:8), which is less surprising as it is females (who have less dignity to maintain) who are involved in the action of running and not males.

31. Barrett, *John*, 563.

As well, both Luke and John describe Peter finding the "linen wrappings" (τὰ ὀθόνια)[32] in the empty tomb. The noun ὀθόνιον is the diminutive form of ὀθόνη, and only occurs in the New Testament in John's account of the burial of Jesus (19:40) and here in Luke's and John's accounts of the empty tomb. Again, then, we have a unique Lukan expression (ὀθόνιον) that is echoed in the Fourth Evangelist's description of the empty tomb.

As well, it may be that the phrase "for as yet they did not understand the scripture, that he must rise from the dead" (John 20:19) is an echo of Luke's Road to Emmaus pericope (Luke 24:13–35). There, we see Jesus chastise Cleopas and the other disciple for being "slow of heart to believe all that the prophets have declared" (Luke 24:25), with Jesus then interpreting "to them the things about himself in the scriptures" (Luke 24:27).[33] As such, Lincoln notes that the two disciples at the empty tomb in John 20:1–10 parallels the two Emmaus Road disciples in Luke 24:13–35.[34]

Finally, the scene concludes in both Luke and John with Peter (Luke) and Peter and the Beloved Disciple (John) returning to his/their own home (both using the aorist active of ἀπέρχομαι, followed by πρός with a pronoun).

If echoes of Luke are found in the Fourth Gospel, it is then apparent that John's version of this scene is an expansion of Luke 24:12; Luke's single verse is expanded into eight in the Fourth Gospel. Lincoln argues that this expansion is largely due to the introduction of the Beloved Disciple in this scene alongside Peter, and the natural parallels and contrasts that the Fourth Evangelist is drawing between the two. Both disciples run to the empty tomb, but the Beloved Disciple runs faster (John 20:4), with the "early arrival of the Beloved Disciple [at the tomb] reinforces his status as the ideal disciple and is a sign of his greater love for Jesus. . . . [T]he reader is meant to assume that the Beloved Disciple is the first to believe that Jesus has been raised and that he demonstrates immediate and exemplary faith in contrast to Peter."[35]

---

32. Cf. the description of the burial of Jesus in a "linen shroud" (σινδών) by Joseph of Arimathea in Matt 27:59//Mark 15:46//Luke 23:53).

33. Cf. also Luke 24:44–45: "Then he said to them, 'These are my words that I spoke to you while I was still with you—that everything written about me in the law of Moses, the prophets, and the psalms must be fulfilled.' Then he opened their minds to understand the scriptures . . . .'"

34. Lincoln, *John*, 491.

35. Lincoln, *John*, 489, 491. Lincoln remarks that the Beloved Disciple "will also demonstrate his superior insight by believing on the basis of what he sees in contrast to Peter. The delay in entering the tomb is in order to make his response the climax of

In addition, John does more with the "linen [burial] wrappings" (τὰ ὀθόνια) that is an echo of Luke. In the Fourth Gospel, the linen cloths are supplemented with a "face-cloth" (σουδάριον), which was "rolled up in a place by itself" apart from the linen wrappings (20:7). This expansion of Luke serves at least two possible functions, according to Lincoln. First, the expanded description of the cloths demonstrates "Jesus' own sovereignty over death" when compared to Lazarus' experience of having to be extracted by his burial cloths upon his resurrection (John 11:44).[36] Second, the expansion had an "apologetic significance" for John, with the folded cloth indicating that the "tomb had not been robbed and the body stolen."[37]

Thus, Luke 24:12 is an echo that is amplified and repeated in John 20:3–10, serving specific purposes for the Fourth Evangelist, who takes his inspiration from Luke and though a knowledge of his Gospel.

The Resurrected Jesus Appears to his Disciples

Luke 24:36–40	John 20:19–22
36 While they were talking about this, Jesus himself stood among them and said to them, "Peace be with you." [αὐτὸς ἔστη ἐν μέσῳ αὐτῶν καὶ λέγει αὐτοῖς εἰρήνη ὑμῖν] 37 They were startled and terrified, and thought that they were seeing a ghost. 38 He said to them, "Why are you frightened, and why do doubts arise in your hearts? 39 Look at my hands and my feet; see that it is I myself. Touch me and see; for a ghost does not have flesh and bones as you see that I have."	19 When it was evening on that day, the first day of the week, and the doors of the house where the disciples had met were locked for fear of the Jews, Jesus came and stood among them and said, "Peace be with you." [ἦλθεν ὁ Ἰησοῦς καὶ ἔστη εἰς τὸ μέσον καὶ λέγει αὐτοῖς εἰρήνη ὑμῖν]

---

the episode" (489).

36. Lincoln, *John*, 490.

37. Lincoln, *John*, 490.

Luke 24:36-40	John 20:19-22
40 And when he had said this, he showed them his hands [καὶ τοῦτο εἰπὼν ἔδειξεν αὐτοῖς τὰς χεῖρας] and his feet.	20 After he said this, he showed them his hands [καὶ τοῦτο εἰπὼν ἔδειξεν τὰς χεῖρας . . . αὐτοῖς] and his side. Then the disciples rejoiced when they saw the Lord. 21 Jesus said to them again, "Peace be with you. As the Father has sent me, so I send you." 22 When he had said this, he breathed on them and said to them, "Receive the Holy Spirit."

The parallels between Luke and John continue in this next pericope, where the resurrected Jesus appears in the midst of his disciples (Luke 24:36-40//John 20:19-22). The common elements between the two include:

1. Jesus appearing dramatically (if not miraculously) in the midst of his disciples;

2. Jesus "standing among them" and saying "Peace be with you"; and,

3. The concluding narration of "After he said this," Jesus "showed them his hands."

While there are not the same sorts of verbal parallels in this scene, the echoes of Luke in the Fourth Gospel are apparent nonetheless.[38]

On these echoes of Luke in this Johannine pericope, Lincoln remarks:

> Jesus' appearance to the disciples on the evening of the first day of the week has its parallel in the longer, and most probably original, text of Luke 24.36-43. There also Jesus is said

---

38. As in the pericope above, two of the verbal parallels here are two of the so-called "Non-Western Interpolations" (Luke 24:36 and 40; see footnote 28). But again, the UBS include both the phrase "and he said to them, 'Peace be with you'" (v. 36) and v. 40 with relative certainty of a rating of "B" in both the fourth and fifth editions of the Greek New Testament, published by the UBS. Metzger remarks: "A majority of the Committee, impressed by the presence of numerous points of contact between Luke and John in their Passion and Easter accounts, preferred to follow the preponderance of external attestation and to retain the words in the text" (Metzger, *Textual Commentary*, 160). On including 24:40, Metzger notes that while a "minority of the Committee preferred to omit the verse as an interpolation . . . the majority, however, was of the opinion that, had the passage been interpolated from the Johannine account, copyists would probably have left some trace of its origin by retaining τὴν πλευρὰν ['side'] in place of τοὺς πόδας ['feet'] (either here only, or in ver. 39 also)" (Metzger, *Textual Commentary*, 160-61).

to have 'stood among them and said to them, "Peace be with you!"' (Luke 24.36). Luke also has Jesus showing the disciples his hands and feet (Luke 24.39-40). The fourth evangelist has taken up these traditions and elaborated on them, changing the showing of hands and feet to that of hands and side in order to reflect the distinctive interest of his crucifixion narrative in the spear thrust into Jesus side [19:34].[39]

It is worth noting that the motif of "peace" is distinctly Lukan, with Luke using the term εἰρήνη in most places redactionally or uniquely.[40] As in the Empty Tomb pericope (see above), John seems to amplify this Lukan motif, using the term εἰρήνη in three places in these post-resurrection appearances of Jesus (i.e., John 20:19, 21, 26).

In both Luke and John, Jesus "stood in the midst" of his disciples. In Luke, this appearance may have the sense of the miraculous, as the disciples "were startled and terrified, and thought they were seeing a ghost" (Luke 24:37). However, in John, the appearance of Jesus is made more explicitly miraculous as "the doors were locked" (John 20:19).

In Luke, the demonstration of the physical wounds of crucifixion (Luke 24:39-40) still does not convince the disciples that Jesus had indeed risen from the dead ("they were disbelieving and still wondering" [24:41]); it is only through the act of eating broiled fish (24:42-43) and "opening their minds to understand the scriptures" that seems to convince them. However, in the Fourth Gospel, the disciples respond immediately by "rejoicing" at the physical evidence of crucifixion (John 20:20), with this scene being bracketed by the saying of Jesus "Peace be with you" (vv. 19 and 21). In John's earlier Farewell Discourse (John 13-17), peace is promised to the disciples in conjunction with the promised Holy Spirit as Paraclete (see 14:25-31; cf. also 16:33). As in John 14, peace and the Holy Spirit are linked here as well.

This scene has been called the "Johannine Pentecost," for, as Lincoln puts it, "Luke spreads out the events chronologically and distinguishes between the episodes of resurrection, ascension, and giving of the Spirit, John brings them all together on one day."[41] Assuming (as we have)

39. Lincoln, *John*, 500.

40. See, for example, Luke 1:79, 2:14, 2:29, 7:50, 14:32, 19:38, 19:42, and 24:36. Luke uses the term 14 times in his Gospel and 7 times in Acts (compare once in Mark, four times in Matthew, and six times in John [John 14:27 (2x), 16:33, 20:19, 20:21, and 20:26]).

41. Lincoln, *John*, 500.

that the Fourth Evangelist is familiar with the Gospel of Luke, a logical question becomes: Is John familiar with Acts, especially Luke's account of Pentecost in Acts 2? Finding verbal parallels between the Fourth Gospel and Acts is more difficult, particularly as there is no overlap of subject material (as there is between Luke and John). But what can be said for sure is that the Fourth Evangelist would have been familiar with Luke 24:49 ("I am sending upon you what my Father promised; so stay here in the city until you have been clothed with power from on high"), which John advances into his story of the resurrected Jesus' appearance to his disciples, creating the "Johannine Pentecost."

Simon Peter and the Miraculous Catch of Fish

Luke 5:1–11	John 21:1–14
1 Once while Jesus was standing beside the lake of Gennesaret, and the crowd was pressing in on him to hear the word of God, 2 he saw two boats there at the shore of the lake; the fishermen had gone out of them and were washing their nets. 3 He got into one of the boats, the one belonging to Simon, and asked him to put out a little way from the shore. Then he sat down and taught the crowds from the boat. 4 When he had finished speaking, he said to Simon, "Put out into the deep water and let down your nets for a catch." 5 Simon answered, "Master, we have worked all night long but have caught nothing. Yet if you say so, I will let down the nets." 6 When they had done this, they caught so many fish that their nets were beginning to break.	1 After these things Jesus showed himself again to the disciples by the Sea of Tiberias; and he showed himself in this way. 2 Gathered there together were Simon Peter, Thomas called the Twin, Nathanael of Cana in Galilee, the sons of Zebedee, and two others of his disciples. 3 Simon Peter said to them, "I am going fishing." They said to him, "We will go with you." They went out and got into the boat, but that night they caught nothing. 4 Just after daybreak, Jesus stood on the beach; but the disciples did not know that it was Jesus. 5 Jesus said to them, "Children, you have no fish, have you?" They answered him, "No." 6 He said to them, "Cast the net to the right side of the boat, and you will find some." So they cast it, and now they were not able to haul it in because there were so many fish.

Luke 5:1–11	John 21:1–14
7 So they signaled their partners in the other boat to come and help them. And they came and filled both boats, so that they began to sink. 8 But when Simon Peter saw it, he fell down at Jesus' knees, saying, "Go away from me, Lord, for I am a sinful man!" 9 For he and all who were with him were amazed at the catch of fish that they had taken; 10 and so also were James and John, sons of Zebedee, who were partners with Simon. Then Jesus said to Simon, "Do not be afraid; from now on you will be catching people." 11 When they had brought their boats to shore, they left everything and followed him.	7 That disciple whom Jesus loved said to Peter, "It is the Lord!" When Simon Peter heard that it was the Lord, he put on some clothes, for he was naked, and jumped into the sea. 8 But the other disciples came in the boat, dragging the net full of fish, for they were not far from the land, only about a hundred yards off. 9 When they had gone ashore, they saw a charcoal fire there, with fish on it, and bread. 10 Jesus said to them, "Bring some of the fish that you have just caught." 11 So Simon Peter went aboard and hauled the net ashore, full of large fish, a hundred fifty-three of them; and though there were so many, the net was not torn. 12 Jesus said to them, "Come and have breakfast." Now none of the disciples dared to ask him, "Who are you?" because they knew it was the Lord. 13 Jesus came and took the bread and gave it to them, and did the same with the fish. 14 This was now the third time that Jesus appeared to the disciples after he was raised from the dead.

If there are echoes of Luke 5:1–11 in John 21:1–14, the echoes are more faint and more distant than the echoes we observed in the first two pericopes, with very little in the way of verbal parallels. However, Lincoln lists the following common elements between the two:[42]

1. The disciples fish all night with no success (Luke 5:5//John 21:3)

2. Jesus commands that they let their nets down and try again (Luke 5:4//John 21:6)

3. The disciples take in a huge catch of fish (Luke 5:6–7, 9//John 21:6, 8, 11)

4. Simon Peter is highlighted in both accounts (Luke 5:3–5, 8–10// John 21:2–3, 7, 11)

5. The sons of Zebedee also feature in the stories (Luke 5:10//John 21:2)

42. Lincoln, *John*, 514.

Lincoln notes that "the verbal agreements within these parallels are minimal (boat, net, night, nothing, great number of fish), and the framework (post-resurrection in John and initial call narrative in Luke) and the rest of the details are significantly different. It is noteworthy that, while Luke's account reports that the nets were tearing apart (5.6), John explicitly states that the net was not torn (v. 11)."[43] Nevertheless, Lincoln argues that the Fourth Evangelist is familiar with Luke 5:1–11—"the fourth evangelist knew of Luke's account and this provided the starting point for his own reworking of the story."[44]

Lincoln also remarks that the breakfast of bread and fish in John 21:12–14 is an example of "recognition scene at a meal with Jesus,"[45] which echoes the Road to Emmaus meal in Luke 24:28–35, as both meals "reveal" Jesus as resurrected.

It is worth noting that while Mark (and Matthew) include the call stories of the fishers Simon (Peter), Andrew, James and John (Matt 4:18–22//Mark 1:16–20), Luke does not, with 5:1–11 serving as the story of the call of Peter (and implicitly James and John as well [Luke 5:10]) to "fish for people" (Luke 5:10; cf. Matt 4:19//Mark 1:17). While it could be argued that Simon, Andrew, James and John "leave everything" to follow Jesus (nets, boat, father) in Matthew and Mark, it is only in Luke where it is said explicitly that Simon, James and John "leave everything" to follow Jesus (5:11; cf. Levi's "leaving everything" to follow Jesus in Luke 5:28). Perhaps this motif of costly discipleship "leaving everything" is something that the Fourth Evangelist also picks up from Luke and expands in John 21:15–19, especially in vv. 18–19 where Jesus predicts that Peter's hands will be bound as he is taken away to be executed at some point in the future, which concludes with Jesus' simple words to Simon Peter, perhaps words inspired by similar words related to calling in Luke 5:11 (and 5:27): "Follow me" (Jn 21:19).

Thus, while the echo of Luke in John's account of Simon Peter and the miraculous catch of fish is faint and subtle, it is, nonetheless, familiar, recognizable, and audible.

---

43. Lincoln, *John*, 514.
44. Lincoln, *John*, 514.
45. Lincoln, *John*, 515.

Conclusion

Matthew and Luke "knew" Mark—a less polished and less favored Gospel in the early Church. Why, then, would not John have known Luke, a more influential (and more thoroughly transcribed) Gospel in the early Christian scribal tradition? If we assume Markan priority and imagine that Matthew and Luke independently had access to the Gospel of Mark (at least on the 2DH and the Farrer Hypothesis which argues that Luke makes use of Matthew as well as Mark without the need for Q), it is also reasonable to assume that the Fourth Evangelist had knowledge of (and access to) at least one of the Synoptic Gospels. The level of parallel agreements between John and the Synoptics reflects what one would expect in ancient literature where there is knowledge and utilization of source material.

This essay has argued that the Fourth Evangelist did, in fact, "know" the Gospel of Luke, which can be particularly seen in three distinctly "Johannine" pericopes in John 20–21 that parallel three distinctly "Lukan" passages in the Gospel of Luke. Not only were the parallels between Luke and John highlighted in each analysis, but descriptions for how the Fourth Evangelist amplified and resonated the Lukan parallels were offered. This sort of "use" of Luke by the Fourth Evangelist makes sense in light of the "spectrum" of literary dependence and literary practices more largely in antiquity. The "echoes" of Luke in John are consistent with other known ancient examples of literary dependence, where verbal parallels are weak, but where the echoes of an earlier text in a later text are still audible.

The scholar Robert T. Fortna, who advocates that a hypothetical "Signs Gospel" was the chief source for the Fourth Evangelist and the means by which he accounts for the common material between the Synoptics and John, states the following: "I do not rule out the possibility that [the Fourth Evangelist] . . . was acquainted with one or more of the Synoptics. This could account, probably more by unconscious imitation than direct borrowing, for the very loose parallels, often only structural, that occasionally appear."[46] Fortna also describes the Synoptics as a "resource" "but not a source" for the Fourth Evangelist.[47] Perhaps Fortna's description of the Synoptics as a "resource" for John has some merit. If so, this essay has demonstrated that the Gospel of Luke likely served as

46. Fortna, *The Fourth Gospel*, 218.
47. Fortna, *The Fourth Gospel*, 218.

a "resource" for John, one that echoes and reverberates within the narratives of the Fourth Gospel, especially in its concluding chapters.

Bibliography

Barrett, C. K. *The Gospel according to John*. 2nd ed. London: SPCK, 1978.
Becker, Eve-Marie, Helen Bond and Catrin H. Williams, eds. *John's Transformation of Mark*. London: T&T Clark, 2021.
Borgen, Peder. "John and the Synoptics." In *The Interrelations of the Gospels*, edited by David L. Dungan, 408–37. BETL 95; Leuven: Peeters, 1990.
Brown, Raymond E. *An Introduction to the Gospel of John*. New York: Doubleday, 2003.
Carroll, John T. *Luke: A Commentary*. NTL; Louisville: Westminster John Knox, 2012.
Derrenbacker, Robert A., Jr. "Ancient Literacy, Ancient Literary Dependence, Ancient Media, and the Triple Tradition." In *Scribal Practices and Social Structures among Jesus Adherents*, edited by William Arnal et al., 81–95. BETL 285; Leuven: Peeters, 2016.
Ehrman, Bart D. *The Orthodox Corruption of Scripture. The Effect of Early Christological Controversies on the Text of the New Testament*. Oxford: Oxford University Press, 1996.
Fitzmyer, Joseph A. *The Gospel according to Luke*. AB 28; New York: Doubleday, 1981.
Fortna, Robert T. *The Fourth Gospel and its Predecessor*. Philadelphia: Fortress, 1988.
Hays, Richard B. *Echoes of Scripture in the Letters of Paul*. New Haven, CT: Yale University Press, 1993.
———. *Echoes of Scripture in the Gospels*. Waco, TX: Baylor University Press, 2016.
Kloppenborg, John S. "Variation in the Reproduction of the Double Tradition and an Oral Q?" *ETL* 83 (2007) 49–79.
Lincoln, Andrew T. *The Gospel according to Saint John*. BNT 4; London: Continuum, 2005.
Malina, Bruce J., and Richard L. Rohrbaugh. *Social-Science Commentary on the Synoptic Gospels*. Minneapolis: Fortress, 1992.
Marshall, I. Howard. *The Gospel of Luke*. Exeter, UK: Paternoster, 1978.
Metzger, Bruce M. *A Textual Commentary on the Greek New Testament*, 2nd ed. Stuttgart: United Bible Societies, 1994.
Neirynck, Frans. "John and the Synoptics: Response to P. Borgen." In *The Interrelations of the Gospels*, edited by David L. Dungan, pp. 438–50. BETL 95; Leuven: Peeters, 1990.
Shellard, Barbara. *New Light on Luke: Its Purpose, Sources and Literary Context*. JSNTSup 215; Sheffield: Sheffield Academic, 2002.
Smith, D. Moody. *John among the Gospels: The Relationship in Twentieth-Century Research*. Minneapolis: Fortress, 1992.
Stein, Robert H. *The Synoptic Problem: An Introduction*. Grand Rapids: Baker, 1994.
Streeter, B. H. *The Four Gospels*. London: Macmillan, 1924.
Williams, Catrin H. "John's 'Rewriting' of Mark: Some Insights from Ancient Jewish Analogues." In *John's Transformation of Mark*, edited by Eve-Marie Becker et al., pp. 51–66. London: T&T Clark, 2021.

2

Friends, Foes, or Rivals?
John Among the Philosophers

FERGUS J. KING

Introduction

IN MODERN SOCIETY, GREAT efforts are made to separate religion and theology from philosophy. However, any such divide in the ancient world would be anachronistic. Philosophical schools and religious sects shared common characteristics in antiquity. The Jewish historian, Josephus, compared the sects of Judaism with the schools of Greco-Roman philosophy.[1] They shared a purpose which embraced individual choice, personal commitment, an ordered and disciplined quest for perfection, and a rigor, seemingly impossible to attain, even if presented as an option for all which only a few might achieve: "religious virtuosity."[2]

Modern scholarship has pursued these commonalities. Thus R. Alan Culpepper adopted a primarily sociological approach,[3] and Troels Engberg-Pedersen noted common procedural concerns, since both Paul and John share with the schools "a manner which is distinctly philosophical."[4] Thus, the traditions are "friends" to the extent that their enterprises seem

---

1. Mason, "Philosophiai," 47–48.
2. Capper, "John," 96.
3. 3 Culpepper, *Johannine School*. For an overview of scholarship about the community, see Lamb, *Text*, 6–28.
4. Engberg-Pedersen, "Stoicism," 40; *John and Philosophy*, 29.

to have characteristics in common. But is this an illusion? Might they be foes or rivals?

Comparative Methodology

Studies like this are identified as comparative. Scholars have long recognized that comparisons can be complicated. Ludwig Wittgenstein castigated James Frazer for judging religious practice by his own standards.[5] Jonathan Z. Smith noted that Christian scholars often used comparative studies to score theological points off each other,[6] and that many comparisons lie in the mind of their maker.[7]

Recently, C. Kavin Rowe questioned the two main types of comparative studies: the "encyclopaedic" (which claim to identify common terms, ideas or practices) and the "genealogical" (which stress difference).[8] In place of these, Rowe articulated a "traditions" approach,[9] drawing on the work of Thomas Kuhn, who coined the term "paradigm shift." David Bosch offered a succinct description of this:

> In a nutshell, Kuhn's suggestion is that science does not really grow cumulatively (as if more and more knowledge and research bring us ever closer to final solutions of problems), but rather by way of "revolutions." A few individuals begin to perceive reality in ways *qualitatively* different from their predecessors and contemporaries, who are practising "normal science."[10]

Thus, in biology, a paradigm shift would occur, when, for example, Herbert Spencer (1820-1903) adopted Darwin's theory of evolution in place of Lamarck's early theory.[11]

Rowe used Kuhnian paradigm shifts to call the ancient schools and religious sects *incommensurable* "rival traditions."[12] For Kuhn, "incom-

---

5. Wittgenstein, "Frazer's *Golden Bough*," 125.

6. Smith, *Drudgery Divine*, 13-35, 83, 95-96. See also Martin, "Judaism/Hellenism Dichotomy," 58-59.

7. Smith, *Drudgery Divine*, 51, 53, 115.

8. Rowe, *One True Life*, 172-99. See Barclay and White, *New Testament* for critical responses to Rowe's proposals, not least his description of "encyclopaedic."

9. Rowe, *One True Life*, 182-4.

10. Bosch, *Transforming Mission*, 188.

11. Morvillo, *Science and Religion*, 254.

12. Rowe, *One True Life*, 7.

mensurable" meant that "there was no neutral measure that could be used to compare one paradigm with another, no paradigm-independent place in which to stand when considering competing paradigms."[13] Not everyone agreed. Philosophers were concerned that this implied a "breakdown of communication" because of "mutually untranslatable languages."[14] They saw no need to conclude with unintelligibility, or untranslatability.[15]

Furthermore, commensurability (that is, that some degree of communication is possible) persists.[16] The fact that different social, religious and intellectual traditions have points of convergence suggests that commensurability "emerge[s] ... from the partial overlaps of the multiple secular and religious traditions than mark all civilizational states."[17] The "porous boundaries" which exist between traditions and cultures allow for it.[18]

Movement between the different perspectives is also recognized: Kuhn himself seemed aware of this, given his description of the shift from one paradigm as a "conversion."[19] The question which persists, and this may be particularly true of religious conversion, is whether such breaks are clean. In scientific disciplines, the perspectives may be mutually exclusive, but this is not always the case in philosophical or religious matters: "Syncretism, or the phenomenon of one religion borrowing elements from another religion, has long been recognized as a nearly universal phenomenon."[20]

Others have questioned the accuracy of Rowe's term, "rival traditions." Thus A. G. Long considers terms like "rival traditions" unhelpful:

> When trying to understand the relations in this area [psychology] between Posidonius and Chrysippus, and Posidonius and Plato, it does not help to view the context as a battle between Stoics and Platonists.[21]

---

13. Garber, "Incommensurabilities," 504.

14. Garber, "Incommensurabilities," 505.

15. Respectively, Engberg-Pedersen, "Past is a Foreign Country," 46–47, 52; Martin, "Possibility of Comparison," 69.

16. Phillips, "Paradigms,"

17. Katzenstein, "Civilizational States," 156.

18. Ivanovic, *Cultural Tourism*, 26.

19. Bosch, *Transforming Mission*, 189.

20. Maroney, *Religious Syncretism*, xi–xii.

21. Long, "Plato," 29, 46.

Such hybrids might be dubbed any of "harmonization," "syncretism," "pooling of resources," or "eclecticism."[22] They suggest that the clean break of the paradigm shift may not actually be accurate to describe the ancient phenomena.

Lastly, the paradigm shift was used of modern intellectual traditions, not ancient schools. But, are modern "concrete models shared by scientific researchers in their scientific practice" comparable with ancient traditions?[23] Kuhn himself recognized the limits of the paradigm shift, restricting his discussion to natural sciences and excluding social sciences.[24] The difference between ancient and modern may be even greater. Ancient schools were primarily concerned with living well.[25] "Lived behavior" is absent from the modern phenomena: ancient oranges compared with modern apples.

If such factors are admitted, a comparison, albeit a scholarly construct, may proceed, following three steps: selection (identifying phenomena for comparison within their environments or traditions), generalization (the use of categories and constructs for comparison), and redescription (a supplementary re-evaluation from an alien perspective).[26]

Linguistics offers some space for this, not least because of its resistance to (in)commensurability.

The term "god" (θεός) is found in the philosophical schools and the Fourth Gospel. Yet, in each, it carries a very different load, because any given lexical field —that is, its place within a sentence (sentence semantics) and the broader narrative of the tradition (discourse semantics), as much as the word itself (lexical semantics)—provides meaning, shape and substance: a lexical meaning, "related to the outside world" as opposed to a grammatical one from the sentence alone.[27] Both etymologies and dictionary definitions must be put aside:[28] the meaning of θεός in any given passage is to be determined by its content, field, or domain rather

---

22. Engberg-Pedersen, "Introduction," 6.
23. Merquior, *Foucault*, 37.
24. Bosch, *Transforming Mission*, 188.
25. Hadot, *Ancient Philosophy?* 2–4.
26. Barclay, "'O wad some Power,'" 13–16.
27. For the terms used here, see Britton, *Structure*, 11.
28. Barr, *Semantics*, 107–160, 206–262, quotation from 216.

than overarching concepts, or an alien framework.[29] Such data is handled with the awareness that this is a scholarly construct.

One last point needs to be made. Comparative studies may be of two kinds: parallel or heuristic. In parallel comparisons,

> the purpose is fundamentally analogical: to see the two or more worldviews as deeply parallel to one another with all their similarities and differences, no matter how each worldview has come into being.[30]

Heuristic comparisons, on the other hand, attempt to use one tradition to explain the other: a concept from one comparandum is used to explicate the other. They risk overstating the potential influence of one on the other. Without caution, parallelomania ensues.[31]

What follows is a work of parallel, not heuristic, comparison. Modest conclusions about degrees of "resonance" and "dissonance," may, however, be made. Such resonances/dissonances may be extrapolated from "kindred atmospheres" and "key figures" shared by traditions.[32] They do not demand any direct linkage, but re-iterate the potential for "*analogous processes*, responding to parallel kinds of religious situations rather than continuing to construct genealogical relations between them."[33]

Thus, given the possibility of comparing the Gospel of John with the schools, brief vignettes of their understandings of "god" illustrate the comparative methodology advocated above.

God in the Gospel of John

The Gospel of John reveals a deity who is engaged in four significant activities. Firstly, the deity is revealed as creating all that is not divine (Jn 1:3). The presence of darkness provokes a conundrum: is it created by God, and thus indicative of a metaphysical dualism? Miroslav Volf suggests not: "No, because all things were created by God and therefore darkness can only be a 'no-thing', a negation of an original and originally

29. Rowe, "Making Friends," 27–30.
30. Engberg-Pedersen, "Foreign Country," 57.
31. Sandmel, "Parallelomania," 3.
32. African Christian hermeneutics are useful in this regard: King, "Vapid Sound," 84–89; Mwombeki, "Hermeneutic of Resonance," 8–9; Pope-Levison & Levison, *Jesus*, 95, 337–8.
33. Smith, *Drudgery Divine*, 112–13.

good creation."[34] However, "oppositional dualities" persist and the work of God to save or redeem the world involves their being overcome.[35] This redemptive work, which aims to reconcile an estranged cosmos (Jn 12:31), identifies God with love: an all-pervasive theme (e.g., 3:16; 13:1–38; 15:12–17; 17:1–26; 18:1–19:42; 20:1–31; 21:1–25).[36] It further involves sending (3:17) in two movements: first, of the Word (1:14), and then of the Spirit (14:26; 15:26; 16:13–14; 19:30; 20:22–23). These four actions (creating, redeeming/sanctifying, loving, sending) outline the God of the Fourth Gospel.

God in Middle Platonism

A revival of interest in the philosophy of Plato which began with Antiochus of Ascalon (130–68 BCE) marks the beginning of Middle Platonism: it is not "classic Platonism." Middle Platonism was sympathetic to both Aristotelian and Stoic thinking, and incorporated elements from both.[37] It persisted "throughout the entire Mediterranean cultural area," including Ascalon (Palestine), Southern Anatolia, and Syria.[38] The activity of Philo Judeus (c. 30 BCE–45 CE) attests to its importance both at Alexandria, and within Second Temple Judaism, as do other Jewish texts.[39] Plutarch of Chaeronea (45 CE–125 CE) reveals it in Boeotia (mainland Greece). Albinus of Smyrna (fl. 150 CE) reveals its presence within Asia Minor, if not explicitly at Ephesus. As Middle Platonism grew in popularity in this period,[40] the earlier the date attributed to the Fourth Gospel, the less may be the chance of engagement with it, and more with Stoicism and Epicureanism. It ends with Plotinus (204–270 CE), who marks the start of Neoplatonism.

Plato's *Timaeus* famously described the cosmos as the work of the Demiurge,[41] "who, imitating an unchanging and eternal model, imposes mathematical order on a pre-existent chaos to generate the ordered

---

34. Volf, "Johannine Dualism," 23.
35. Volf, "Johannine Dualism," 24.
36. Moloney, *Love*.
37. Engberg-Pedersen, "Introduction," 15–26.
38. Boyarin, *A Radical Jew*, 28.
39. Engberg-Pedersen, "Introduction," 19–22.
40. Witt, *Albinus*, 114.
41. Plato, *Timaeus* 28a6.

universe (κόσμος)."⁴² Creation was more an artistic process, a pattern also seen in Aristotle and Stoicism, than an act of love.⁴³

P. A. Meijer considers this a departure from Judaic and Christian cosmology: "The creator of this world is a Craftsman (Demiurge), not an engineer. The example of the cosmos precedes him: the ideas and even the 'matter' (ἐκμαγεῖον) come first. This is a clearly defined difference from the Jewish-Christian Creator."⁴⁴ So, the ideas exist first and shape the activity of god, who effectively copies them: an "ontic prius."⁴⁵

Later interpreters of Plato queried this, debating how many Principles (i.e. primary elements which have no predecessors) his schema demanded: two (matter and a cause of movement identified as the good or god [Theophrastus, 371–287 BCE]) or three ("the matter, the maker and the paradigm" [Alexander of Aphrodisias, late second–early third century CE]).⁴⁶ It is even possible to talk of two and a half principles if the paradigms are reckoned to be ideas of god, and therefore, not wholly independent.⁴⁷ None make the ideas, or paradigms, an "ontic prius." Moreover, the priority of god appears in thinkers like Varro (116–27 BCE) which would make the ideas "inferior to, and dependent on, the divine intellect."⁴⁸

The cosmos serves an ethical purpose, a model to be emulated through the cultivation of rationality: "it is through realigning the motions of our souls with those of the universe at large that we achieve our goal of living virtuously and happily."⁴⁹ Religious behavior like prayer is retained ("we can really only pray for what is beautiful and righteous"⁵⁰) only because it reflects philosophic ideals.⁵¹ Religious language and activity function as ciphers and aids for the philosophical quest.

---

42. Zeyl and Sattler, "Plato's Timaeus."
43. Watson, "Discovering the Imagination," 224.
44. Meijer, "Philosophers," 224.
45. Meijer, "Philosophers," 244.
46. Sharples, "Counting Plato's Principles," 69. I am grateful to Prof. David T. Runia for advice in negotiating this summary of Middle Platonism. See also Sedley, "Origins," 60–66.
47. Sharples, "Counting Plato's Principles," 74.
48. Sharples, "Counting Plato's Principles," 79.
49. Zeyl and Sattler, "Plato's *Timaeus*," np.
50. Plato, *Laws* 687 D– E.
51. Meijer, "Philosophers," 242.

The focus on rationality allowed λόγος (reason) to emerge in describing the principles and forces which shape the world: god may be called "reason."[52] This, or its Aristotelian or Stoic variants, was a likely precursor of λόγος in the Fourth Gospel (1:1, 14). Yet proving a derivation from any of these schools as opposed to a resonance, or "analogous process," is more fraught. The divine λόγος yielded a further consequence: the philosophical quest was identified as "becoming like god" (ὁμοίωσις θεῷ).[53] For the philosophers, this meant the cultivation of right thinking.[54] Yet Middle Platonism did not develop a theology which was as confident as that of the Gospel:[55] their tone is very different. Nor did the Gospel simply adopt terms in circulation: John 1:14, which introduces the novelty of the λόγος becoming flesh, makes this clear. It *re–accentuated* them for its own purposes.[56]

God in Aristotelianism

Pierre Hadot has noted the persistence of Aristotelian thinking in major cities in the imperial period.[57] Andronicus of Rhodes (fl. first century BCE) and Boethius of Sidon (mid-first century BCE) represented a critical engagement with Aristotelianism sometimes identified as the Peripatetic school.[58]

Aristotle's theology modified Platonism: god, the "first principle," is often identified as the "unmoved mover."[59] However, Aristotle's preferred terms, given that neither θεός nor θεῖος ("divine") are invested with detail, are "reason" or "intelligence" which are better translations in relation to god than "mind" (νοῦς)[60] and the good (ἀγαθόν): this differs from Plato's

---

52. Watson, "Discovering the Imagination," 224–5.

53. cf. Plato, *Theaetetus*, 176b.

54. Mazur, *Platonizing*, 29, fn. 9; Reydams-Schils, "'Becoming like God,'" 142.

55. Runia, "Beginnings of the End," 308.

56. Coined by Bakhtin, "re-accentuation" may be described as follows: "In the re-accentuation of terms . . . and in the new utterance that is created out of those traditional elements, it is possible to create the sense that one is only now understanding the true meaning of words that had long been familiar and important" (Newsom, "Apocalyptic Subjects," 7).

57. Hadot, *What is Philosophy?* 147.

58. See further Griffin, *Aristotle's Categories*; Sharples, *Peripatetic Philosophy*.

59. Menn, "Aristotle," 544–5.

60. Menn, "Aristotle," 555.

separation of the ideas and god.⁶¹ Effectively, "*nous* is king of heaven and earth, directly ruling the heavens, which in turn govern sublunar things."⁶² It is a "separately existing substance which is the ultimate cause of motion, order and goodness to the physical world ... *Nous* exists itself-by-itself, which means above all that it is separate from things which merely have *nous*."⁶³

It would be difficult, if not impossible, in this schema, to contemplate such a νοῦς as manifesting itself in a sensible form. This epistemology develops a chain of causes and recognitions incompatible with the Gospel,⁶⁴ in which god is identifiable best in a material form (Jn 1:14).

God is involved with the world, compared to a general and army,⁶⁵ potentially concerned for humanity,⁶⁶ and, perhaps, for the "sublunary region," the cosmic area from the earth to the moon.⁶⁷ However, while stressing the transcendence of god, later Aristotelians recognized human limitations in theologizing.⁶⁸ They would continue to speculate on the relationship between the Unmoved Mover and the different regions of the cosmos,⁶⁹ including the view that god was not interested in the sublunary regions.⁷⁰ The contrary, that God loves the cosmos (Jn 3:16-18) is, of course, a given in the Fourth Gospel.

As with Middle Platonism, this school addresses epistemology rather than a schema of sin and forgiveness as the means to salvation or transformation. The Aristotelian god models a self-sufficiency (αὐτάρκεια) which becomes the basis for the sage being autonomous and detached from the world,⁷¹ rather than indicating a relationship between god and disciple (Jn 1:38-39; 6:56; 14:10, 17).

---

61. Menn, "Aristotle," 546-7.
62. Menn, "Aristotle," 558.
63. Menn, "Aristotle," 561.
64. Menn, "Aristotle," 562-72.
65. Aristotle, *Metaphysics* Λ 1075a13-15.
66. Aristotle, *Eudemian Ethics* VIII 2, 1248a16-33.
67. Sharples, "Aristotelian Theology," 10-12.
68. Aristotle, *Eudemian Ethics* VIII 2, 1248a16-33. Runia, "Beginnings of the End," 305.
69. Sharples, "Aristotelian Theology," 13-22.
70. Sharples, "Aristotelian Theology," 22-36.
71. Desmond, *Cynics*, 176.

God in Cynicism

Cynicism has two discernible stages: early (fourth century BCE – mid-third century BCE), and later (mid-third century BCE – fifth century CE). The two are respectively identified as strong and weak, as later Cynics became "indistinguishable from other philosophers, or concentrated on perpetuating merely the external aspects of cynicism, without maintaining the intellectual basis of its tradition."[72] This tradition emphasized living according to nature, thus viewed positively, rather than by the conventions of society. They did not adopt an atheist position, but challenged conventional views, especially when these veered to the superstitious.[73] They agreed that god should be self-sufficient, and thus cultivated this practice.[74] They were critical of anthropomorphic depictions of gods, as they considered animals to have a higher degree of self-sufficiency than humanity.[75]

However, Cynic theory allowed for some variation. Thus, Antisthenes (c. 445 BCE–360 BCE) distinguished between "the single god at the level of unity, nature and truth, and the many gods of popular religion at the level of multiplicity, tradition and received opinion."[76] Elsewhere, Cynic theology is harder to identify beyond the use of god as a cipher for self-sufficiency and the critique of popular religion. Marie Odile Goulet-Cazé thus comments: "At the end of the day we discover that the gods are insignificant in Cynicism and that in Diogenes' philosophy there is no place for religious preoccupations."[77]

The gods effectively are identified with nature but are not objects of reverence.[78] Lucian of Samosata's (c. 125 CE–180 CE) depictions of Menippus of Gadara (c. third century BCE) describe his theology thus: the gods are powerless, philosophers cannot resolve the matter, and one does better "not attempting to penetrate the secrets of what lies beyond man."[79]

---

72. Navia, *Classical Cynicism*, 13.
73. Desmond, *Cynics*, 116–20.
74. Desmond, *Cynics*, 121, 176.
75. Desmond, *Cynics*, 121; Goulet-Cazé, "Religion and the Early Cynics," 61–64, 77.
76. Goulet-Cazé, "Early Cynics," 68.
77. Goulet-Cazé, "Early Cynics," 73.
78. Goulet-Cazé, "Early Cynics," 73–74.
79. Goulet-Cazé, "Early Cynics," 76.

These views would be difficult to reconcile with the Fourth Gospel. The insignificance of the gods in Cynicism indicates a very disposition from the God-centered theology and revelation of the Gospel, as does their view that such questions are really beyond the scope of human wisdom. Their low view of humanity would most likely struggle to see what was true or real revealed in a human life (Jn 1:14). Their tendency to identify god with nature would also indicate a difference from the Gospel's views on God and the estranged cosmos.

God in Epicureanism

Epicureanism, founded by Epicurus (341–270 BCE), spread across the Mediterranean, and continued into the early imperial period. It was found in all three of Ephesus, Alexandria, and Syria.[80] Although the Epicureans were identified as atheists (ἄθεοι) by their opponents, this is as much of a misnomer as its application to the early Christians.[81] Epicurean understandings of god may be gleaned from the extant writings of the school and its critics. They reveal two kinds of deity.

The first are the "intramundial" or "heavenly" gods, described as living in the spaces between worlds (*intramundia*). Theirs is the perfect life, free from the two things which Epicureans strived to avoid through right thinking which minimized mental stress (ἀταραξία) and physical pain (ἀπονία),[82] described anthropomorphically.[83] They are not creators: Epicurean metaphysics considered creation to be the product of the random collision of atoms.[84] They have absolutely no involvement with the world, or with humanity.[85] Whether they truly existed (a realist understanding), or were images apprehended through the mind (πρόληψις) remains moot, but essentially makes no difference to the consequences of their theology.[86] Completely removed from this realm, they should be feared neither as a source of stress, nor of pain. Such gods could never

---

80. King, *Epicureanism*, 13–16.
81. Tomlin, "Christians and Epicureans," 65.
82. King, *Epicureanism*, 21–23.
83. Essler, "Cicero's Use," 139–42; Sedley, "Epicurus' Theological Innatism," 49.
84. Lucretius, *On the Nature of Things*, 2.167–83, 1090–94; 5.156–194. Colman, "Lucretius on Religion," 233a; Mecci, "Ethical Implications," 198.
85. Lucretius, *On the Nature of Things* 1.45–6, 455–8; King, *Epicureanism*, 66, 72.
86. King, *Epicureanism*, 67–70.

be equated with the God of the Fourth Gospel, who creates, loves, and redeems the world by becoming human. All these would be simply impossible from an Epicurean perspective.[87]

Epicurean sages were a second kind of deity: *Deus ille fuit deus*— "He was a god ... a god he was!"—as Lucretius described Epicurus.[88] The Latin perfect tense is significant: Epicurus was a god, but only for the span of his life, and in later memory;[89] Epicureans had no place for post-mortem existence or eternal life.[90] Epicurus' right thinking and exemplary life, not love, accorded him divine status.

The same holds true for claims to be the Savior (σωτήρ). Epicurus "saves" by revealing how to live the good life, via right knowledge; Jesus, by being obedient to the point of death.[91] While Epicurean sages, as friends, might give their life for others (Diogenes Laertius, *Vitae* 10.120), such actions were predicated solely on the high value given to friendship,[92] and not concepts like redemption or the forgiveness of sin as understood in the Fourth Gospel. While sin has sometimes been associated with readings of Epicureanism, it is defined by behaviors which cause the loss of ἀταραξία or ἀπονία.[93] Johannine ἀταραξία (e.g., Jn 14:1, 27), if the vocabulary allows us to speak of such a thing, would be rooted in the faith that Jesus will deliver the promises he made to his disciples (Jn 14), and doing the will of God.

Epicureanism and the Fourth Gospel may both talk of god and Savior, but what they entail is very different.

God in Stoicism

Stoicism originated with Zeno of Citium (344–262 BCE), Cleanthes (d. 232 BCE) and Chrysippus (d. c. 206 BCE): the Old Stoa. It embraced a degree of diversity and continued to evolve in dialogue with other traditions, as Posidonius' writing reveals: Stoicism of this period is called the Middle Stoa. Well established in the early Imperial period across

---

87. King, *Epicureanism*, 72–73.
88. Lucretius, *On the Nature of Things*, 5.8.
89. Clay, "Cults," 27–28.
90. Segal, "Poetic Immortality," 199–202.
91. King, *Epicureanism*, 124–5.
92. Hibler, *Happiness*, 45; King, *Epicureanism*, 147.
93. King, "Failure," 62–63.

the Empire, with Lucius Annaeus Seneca (d. 65 CE), Epictetus (c. 50–c.135 CE), and Gaius Musonius Rufus (c. 30– c. 101 CE) amongst its adherents,[94] the Roman Stoa (a third stage) declined after the death of Marcus Aurelius (180 CE).[95]

Stoicism developed proofs for the existence of god which served as alternatives to contemporary myths and cults, correctives to popular theological views, and offered a right theology.[96] Stoics could still participate in cultic activities, but from an enlightened philosophical view,[97] potentially indicative of a "two-tier theory" (elite vs. popular).[98] Anthropomorphism was mostly considered a source of error, though it could occasionally represent "an important and true aspect of god."[99]

Stoicism was monotheistic, even if their god might be identified with Zeus, other traditional names from the pantheon,[100] or fate/providence.[101] It recognized a divine principle, often the λόγος or πνεῦμα (spirit), which gave shape and order to the world and to right living. Thus, the goals of the sage may be described as ὁμοίωσις θεῷ,[102] or being in harmony with the λόγος.[103] However, this λόγος was not viewed as a distinct entity, but as intimately connected with the cosmos.[104] For the Stoics, "god is directly present and active in absolutely everything that exists and happens in the world, from the most exalted beings or events to the lowliest ones."[105] This separates Stoicism from other traditions.

Stoic descriptions of god and the cosmos are often considered materialist or monist, suggesting that the two are one. This is not strictly accurate: dualistic features appear.[106] However, its "ontological monism" gives creation a more positive value than Platonic dualism.[107] Whilst both

---

94. Thornsteinsson, *Roman Christianity*, 13.
95. Thornsteinsson, *Roman Christianity*, 15.
96. Algra, "Stoic Philosophical Theology," 226; Meijer, *Stoic Theology*, 1.
97. Algra, "Stoic Theology," 177.
98. Algra, "Stoic Philosophical Theology," 231.
99. Algra, "Stoic Philosophical Theology," 243; "Stoic Theology," 177.
100. Algra, "Stoic Philosophical Theology," 225; Meijer, *Stoic Theology*, xi.
101. Algra, "Stoic Theology," 170.
102. Inwood, *Stoicism*, 69.
103. Long, *Stoic Studies*, 50.
104. Diogenes Laertius, *Lives*, 7.137. Sellars, *Stoicism*, 91.
105. Bétanouïl, "How Industrious," 23.
106. Algra, "Stoic Theology,"169; Engberg-Pedersen, *John*, 33.
107. Engberg-Pedersen, *John*, 33.

god and substance, two principles, are viewed as matter, they never exist independently, and are always mixed. These principles (ἀρχαί) may be described as active (ποιοῦν – creative) and passive (πάσχον –created).[108] God appears to be an active and seminal principle (σπερματικός λόγος—seminal/seeding/formative reason).[109] Thus, Gourinat concludes: "By introducing an active principle, which is identical with a seed, the Stoics depart from materialism, and tend towards vitalism, even if this seminal principle is always blended with matter and inherent in it."[110] This vitalism led some Stoics to claim that the cosmos was a conscious entity.[111] However, the creation was recognizably not perfect: despite their high view of creation, Stoics still had to contend with the problem of evil, which they did by severely constraining it to the realm of morality.

The Fourth Gospel does not share any such vitalism, preferring a bifurcation of god and creation. The close correlation of god and cosmos within Stoicism has no space for redemptive work (as the cosmos is not estranged from its god), nor may the deity "come into" the cosmos as both are already inextricably linked.

Stoicism focused on right thinking and moral rigor rather than an emotion like love which was viewed as unreliable and unstable, lying beyond the control of reason.[112] The difficulties in transposing Greco-Roman concepts into thinking informed by Judaism must also be reckoned: just as Philo's reading does not conform to Platonic or Stoic constructs, neither might the Gospel's.[113]

While the λόγος is significant in the early sections of the Johannine prologue, this interest is not sustained. Attention soon turns to the Son (1:18). Affiliation is more significant in the theology of the Gospel than any λόγος Christology.[114] Even the few mentions of the λόγος vary from Stoicism. The identification of the λόγος with God belies a simple equivalence. A modified, rather than a strict, monotheism may be at play.[115]

---

108. Algra, "Stoic Theology," 168; Sellars, *Stoicism*, 86.

109. Diogenes Laertius, *Lives*, 7.136. Watson, "Discovering the Imagination," 224.

110. Gourinat, "Stoics," 68.

111. Diogenes Laertius, *Lives* 7.142–3. Sellars, *Stoicism*, 94.

112. Nussbaum, *Therapy of Desire*, 442; Rowe, *One True Life*, 54.

113. Runia, "Beginnings of the End," 295–6.

114. Lee, "Creation," 109–11.

115. Thus, potentially unitarian, binary, binitarian, triadic, proto-trinitarian, or trinitarian versions of monotheism have been debated within emerging Christianity, see King, "*Lex orandi*," 34–35, 44–48.

Then, in John 1:14, the claim that the λόγος becomes flesh is without a Stoic parallel, and jars with Stoic views of anthropomorphism.

Stoicism further offers the potential for a λόγος theology to morph into a πνεῦμα theology (e.g., Jn 3:5–8; 4:23–24; 6:63; 11:33; 13:21; 14:16–17, 25; 15:26; 16:13; 19:30).[116] Stoicism identifies the cosmos with both λόγος and πνεῦμα, also used of the divine. While the Stoic πνεῦμα may be described as a "creative fire," synonymous with god and involved in the formation of the cosmos,[117] the Stoic god is neither immortal or imperishable,[118] as the world is divine and subject to a regenerative conflagration (ἐκπύρωσις).[119] However, the Fourth Gospel would not sit easily with that Stoic cosmology because it distinguishes the cosmos from both λόγος (Jn 1:10) and πνεῦμα (Jn 15:26; 16:13): the common issue of "coming into."[120]

Their concepts of right living also fragment. In Stoicism, right thinking about the cosmos (also identified with the λόγος) is fundamental. The Gospel of John focuses on relating to (μένειν [abide in], e.g., Jn 15:4–7) the λόγος made flesh (Jesus; Jn 1:14), but not the cosmos. The linkage of "abiding" with "love" (Jn 15:9–10) divides even more.

There is a degree of resonance between the Fourth Gospel and Stoicism in naming god as creator, but not in the relationship between the deity and the creation. Stoicism's ontological monism and epistemology do not tally with the "oppositional dualities" of the Fourth Gospel. The Gospel's terminology (salvation, abiding, loving, and sending) is alien to Stoic rationalism. While terms like λόγος and πνεῦμα offer possible points of resonance, their substance and juxtaposition within the two traditions is markedly different.

---

116. Buch-Hansen, *Spirit that Gives Life*; Engberg-Pedersen, *John* explores such a thesis. Stoic understanding of πνεῦμα offers an overlap between what is sometimes viewed as human spirit (John 11:33; 13:21) and the divine, see Buch-Hansen, *It is the Spirit*, 160.

117. Algra, "Stoic Theology," 166–167; Sellars, *Stoicism*, 91.

118. Long, *Epicurus to Epictetus*, 121.

119. Long, *Epicurus to Epictetus*, 123.

120. See also Rowe, *One True Life*, 226–8.

God in Skepticism

Skepticism persisted into the Roman imperial era in two forms: Academic and Pyrrhonian.[121] It was more a method than a dogmatic system. Like other schools, it cultivated right living through proper thinking. It challenged dogmatic assertions, and so freed its adherents from dubious ideologies. The Skeptic recognized diverse theological beliefs, used them as evidence that there was no certainty, and thus reduced the stress or fear they might induce. This did not lead to atheism, but rather to their saying "undogmatically that the gods exist, and we reverence them, and say that they have foreknowledge,"[122] or "they neither affirm or deny the existence of the gods."[123] They agree that the gods are both imperishable and blessed but debate the finer points.[124] Their principal target was not "the traditional features of the gods that the doctrinaire schools retain, but the rational innovations—the attempt to justify theological doctrines by appeal to experience, conceptual analysis, and argument."[125]

Sextus Empiricus' (late second century CE – early third CE) theological comments reveal an *aporia* about the existence and/or nature of the gods: the sheer variety of speculation expressed precludes this.[126] He does not so much criticize "disengaged divinities" like those of Aristotelianism or Epicureanism, as the problem of evil (theodicy), and a deity concerned for creatures and creation.[127] Whilst most likely aimed at Stoicism,[128] it would equally sit uneasily with the Gospel's God. Sextus rejected claims that god is wise, and knows of pain and pleasure. This raises questions about a classic attribute of god: wisdom.[129] Again, he aims at the Stoics.[130] For Sextus, the philosopher:

> abides by local traditions in saying that gods exist and in worshipping them. His refusal to commit himself is a philosophical

---

121. Thorsrud, *Ancient Scepticism*, 1.
122. Sextus Empiricus, *Pyrrhonism* 3.2. Translation from Hankinson, *Sceptics*, 214.
123. Long, *Epicurus to Epictetus*, 116.
124. Hankinson, *Sceptics*, 214.
125. Long, *Epicurus to Epictetus*, 116.
126. Runia, "Beginnings of the End," 281.
127. Hankinson, *Sceptics*, 214.
128. Hankinson, *Sceptics*, 216-9, see also Long, *Epicurus to Epictetus*, 116-7.
129. Warren, "What God Didn't Know," 66.
130. Warren, "What God Didn't Know," 43.

attitude (*Adversus mathematicos* ... 9.49), albeit one that enables him to conduct his life equably and uncontroversially."[131]

Given that the Fourth Gospel arguably enjoins a commitment to God through injunctions to stay or abide in Christ (e.g., 1:38–39; 6:56; 14:10, 17), there is a fundamental difference in intention and attitude between it and skepticism, let alone about claims regarding the nature of god, which are barely visible within the latter's rejection of philosophical and theological dogma.

Conclusion

The comparison of ancient philosophical and religious traditions remains complex: "a hermeneutical *Lehrstück* [lesson] in how any position on the matter reflects the intellectual background and interests of the speaker."[132] Those drawing comparisons risk importing anachronisms, alien constructs, and even value judgments rather than simply recognizing differences. Nor are the results uniform: function, method, process, and structure, not just substance and content, may vary.

The study of "god," for example, needs to explore each tradition in its own terms. Some concepts like "creator" are disparate; shared vocabulary, like λόγος, πνεῦμα, or σωτήρ, does not guarantee compatibility. Relating to god reveals that the schools focus on right thinking, but the Fourth Gospel concentrates on "abiding with Jesus." Detailed studies reveal potential points of resonance or dissonance, and a lack of uniformity.

The Fourth Gospel and the philosophical schools share common concerns: they aspire to correct falsehoods and delineate the good life. They may be "rival traditions," possibly incommensurable, depending on the definition, but not unintelligible. Borrowings, conversations, conversions, and re-accentuations remain possible. To that extent, they may relate to each other as any or all of friends, foes, or rivals.

Bibliography

Algra, Keimpe. "Stoic Philosophical Theology and Graeco-Roman Religion." In *God and Cosmos in Stoicism*, edited by Ricardo Salles, 224–51. Oxford: Oxford University Press, 2009.

131. Long, *Epicurus to Epictetus*, 116.
132. Engberg-Pedersen, "Stoicism in Early Christianity," 29.

———. "Stoic Theology." In *The Cambridge Companion to the Stoics*, edited by Brad Inwood, 153–78. Cambridge: Cambridge University Press, 2003.
Aristotle, *Athenian Constitution. Eudemian Ethics. Virtues and Vices*. Translated by H. Rackham. LCL 285. Cambridge, MS: Harvard University Press, 1935.
———. *Metaphysics*. Translated by Hugh Tredennick. LCL 271, 287, 2 vols. Cambridge, MS: Harvard University Press, 1933.
Barclay, John M. G. "'O wad some Power the giftie gie us, to see oursels as others see us!': Method and Purpose in Comparing the New Testament." In *The New Testament in Comparison: Validity, Method, and Purpose in Comparing Traditions*, edited by John M. G. Barclay and B. G. White, 9–22. LNTS 600. London: T&T Clark, 2020.
Barclay, John M. G. and B. G. White, eds. *The New Testament in Comparison: Validity, Method, and Purpose in Comparing Traditions*. LNTS 600. London: T&T Clark, 2020.
Barr, James. *The Semantics of Biblical Language*. London: Oxford University Press, 1961.
Bétanouïl, Thomas. "How Industrious Can Zeus Be? The Extent and Objects of Divine Activity in Stoicism." In *God and Cosmos in Stoicism*, edited by Ricardo Salles, 23–45. Oxford: Oxford University Press, 2009.
Bosch, David J. *Transforming Mission: Paradigm Shifts in Theology of Mission*. 20th Anniversary Edition. ASMS 16. Maryknoll, NY: Orbis, 2011.
Boyarin, Daniel. *A Radical Jew: Paul and the Politics of Identity*. Berkeley, CA: University of California Press, 1994.
Britton, Laurel J. *The Structure of Modern English: A Linguistic Introduction*. Amsterdam: John Benjamins, 2000.
Buch-Hansen, Gitte. *It is the Spirit that Gives Life: A Stoic Understanding of the Pneuma in John's Gospel*. BZNW 173. Berlin/New York, NY: De Gruyter, 2010.
Capper, Brian J. "John, Qumran and the Dead Sea Scrolls." In *John, Qumran, and the Dead Sea Scrolls: Sixty Years of Discovery and Debate*, edited by Mary L. Coloe and Tom Thatcher, 94–116. Atlanta, GA: SBL, 2011.
Clay, Diskin. "The Cults of Epicurus." *CE* 16 (1987) 11–28.
Colman, John. "Lucretius on Religion." *Perspective on Political Science* 38 (2009) 228–39.
Culpepper, R. Alan. *The Johannine School: An Evaluation of the Johannine School Hypothesis Based on an Investigation of the Nature of Ancient Schools*. SBLDS 26. Missoula, MT: Scholars, 1975.
Desmond, William. *The Cynics*. AP. Stocksfield: Acumen, 2008.
Diogenes Laertius. *Lives of Eminent Philosophers*. Translated by R. D. Hicks. LCL 184, 185, 2 vols. Cambridge, MS: Harvard University Press, 1925.
Engberg-Pedersen, Troels. "The Past is a Foreign Country." In *The New Testament in Comparison: Validity, Method, and Purpose in Comparing Traditions*, edited by John M. G. Barclay and B. G. White, 40–61. LNTS 600. London: T&T Clark, 2020.
———. "Introduction: A Historiographical Essay." In *From Stoicism to Platonism: The Development of Philosophy, 100 BCE to 100 CE*, edited by Troels Engberg-Pedersen, 40–61. Cambridge: Cambridge University Press, 2017.
———. *John and Philosophy: A New Reading of the Fourth Gospel*. Oxford: Oxford University Press, 2017.
———. "Stoicism in Early Christianity: The Apostle Paul and the Evangelist John as Stoics." In *The Routledge Handbook of the Stoic Tradition*, edited by John Sellars, 40–61. Abingdon: Routledge, 2016.

Essler, Holger. "Cicero's Use and Abuse of Epicurean Theology." In *Epicurus and the Epicurean Tradition*, edited by Jeffrey Fish and Kirk R. Sanders, 40–61. Cambridge: Cambridge University Press, 2011.

Garber, Daniel. "Incommensurabilities." *HSNS* 42 (2012) 504–509.

Goulet-Cazé, Marie-Odile. "Religion and the Early Cynics." In *The Cynics*, edited by R. Bracht Branham and M.-O. Goulet-Cazé, 40–61. Berkeley and Los Angeles, CA: University of California Press, 1996.

Gourinat, Jean-Baptiste. "The Stoics on Matter and Prime Matter: 'Corporealism' and the Imprint of Plato's Timaeus." In *God and Cosmos in Stoicism*, edited by Ricardo Salles, 40–61. Oxford: Oxford University Press, 2009.

Griffin, Michael J. *Aristotle's Categories in the Early Roman Empire*. Oxford: Oxford University Press, 2015.

Hadot, Pierre. *What is Ancient Philosophy?* Translated by Michael Chase. Cambridge MA: Harvard University Press, 2002.

Hankinson, R. J. *The Sceptics*. ArgPhil. London: Routledge, 1995.

Hibler, Richard W. *Happiness through Tranquillity: The School of Epicurus*. Lanham, MD: University Press of America, 1984.

Inwood, Brad. *Stoicism: A Very Short Introduction*. Oxford: Oxford University Press, 2018.

Ivanovic, Milena. *Cultural Tourism*. Cape Town: Juta, 2008.

Katzenstein, Peter J. "Civilizational States, Secularisms, and Religions." In *Rethinking Secularism*, edited by Craig Calhoun et al., 145–165. New York, NY: Oxford University Press, 2011.

King, Fergus J. "A Failure to Launch? Paul and the Philosophers of Athens (Acts 17: 16–34)." *ABR* (2021) 53–70.

———. *Epicureanism and the Gospel of John: A Study of their Compatibility*. WUNT 2/537. Tübingen: Mohr Siebeck, 2020.

———. "*Lex orandi, lex credendi*: Worship and Doctrine in Revelation 4–5." *SJT* 67 (2014) 33–49.

———. "More Than a Vapid Sound: The Case for a Hermeneutic of Resonance." *JTSA* 148 (2014) 83–98.

Lamb, David A. *Text, Context, and the Johannine Community*. LNTS 447. London: Bloomsbury, 2014.

Lee, Dorothy A. "Creation, Matter, and the Image of God in the Gospel of John." *SVTQ* 62 (2018) 101–17.

Long, A. A. *From Epicurus to Epictetus: Studies in Hellenistic and Roman Philosophy*. Oxford: Oxford University Press, 2006.

———. *Stoic Studies*. Berkeley, CA: University of California Press, 1996.

Long, A. G. "Plato, Chrysippus and Posidonius' Theory of Affective Movements." In *From Stoicism to Platonism: The Development of Philosophy, 100 BCE to 100 CE*, edited by Troels Engberg-Pedersen, 27–46. Cambridge: Cambridge University Press, 2017.

Lucretius. *On the Nature of Things*. Translated by W. H. D. Rouse. Revised by Martin F. Smith. LCL 181. Cambridge, MS: Harvard University Press, 1924.

Maroney, Eric. *Religious Syncretism*. London: SCM, 2006.

Martin, Dale B. "The Possibility of Comparison, the Necessity of Anachronism, and the Dangers of Purity." In *The New Testament in Comparison: Validity, Method, and*

Purpose in Comparing Traditions, edited by John M. G. Barclay and Benjamin G. White. LNTS 600, 63–77. London: T&T Clark, 2020.

———. "Paul and the Judaism/Hellenism Dichotomy." In *Paul Beyond the Judaism/Hellenism Divide*, edited by Troels Engberg-Pedersen, 29–61. Louisville, KY: Westminster John Knox.

Mason, Steve "Philosophiai: Graeco-Roman, Judaean and Christian." In *Voluntary Associations in the Graeco-Roman World*, edited by John S. Kloppenborg and Stephen G. Wilson, 31–58. London: Routledge, 2017.

Mazur, Alexander J. *The Platonizing Sethian Background of Plotinus's Mysticism*. Leiden: Brill, 2021.

Mecci, Stefano. "The Ethical Implications of Epicurus' Theology." *Phil* 48 (2018) 195–204.

Meijer, P. A. *Stoic Theology: Proofs for the Existence of the Cosmic God and of the Traditional Gods*. Delft: Eburon, 2007.

———. "Philosophers, Intellectuals and Religion in Hellas." In *Faith, Hope and Worship: Aspects of Religious Mentality in the Ancient World*, edited by H. S. Versnel. SGRR 2.216–62. Leiden: Brill, 1981.

Menn, Stephen "Aristotle and Plato on God as *Nous* and as the Good." *RM* 45 (1992) 543–573.

Merquior, J. G. *Foucault*. 2nd ed. London: Fontana, 1991.

Moloney, Francis J. *Love in the Gospel of John: An Exegetical, Theological, and Literary Study*. Grand Rapids, MI: Baker Academic, 2013.

Morvillo, Nancy, *Science and Religion: Understanding the Issues*. Chichester: John Wiley, 2010.

Mwombeki, Fidon R. "The Hermeneutic of Resonance: Making Biblical Theology Relevant Today." Paper presented at TLC Augsburg Convention, 2009. http://www.lutheranworld.org/What_We_Do/DTS/TLC_Augsburg/Papers/Mwombeki.pdf.

Navia, Luis E. *Classical Cynicism*. Westport, CT: Greenwood, 1996.

Newsom, Carol A. "Apocalyptic Subjects: Social Construction of the Self in the Qumran Hodayot." *JSP* 12 (2001) 3–35.

Nussbaum, Martha C. *The Therapy of Desire: Theory and Practice in Hellenistic Ethics*. MCL 2. Princeton, NJ: Princeton University Press, 1994.

Phillips, Derek L. "Paradigms and Incommensurability." *T&S* 2 (1975) 37–61.

Plato, *Theaetetus. Sophist*. Translated by Harold North Fowler. LCL 123. Cambridge, MS: Harvard University Press, 1921.

Plato, *Laws*. Translated by R. G. Bury, 2 vols. LCL 187, 192. Cambridge, MS: Harvard University Press, 1926.

Pope-Levison, Priscilla and John Levison. *Jesus in Global Contexts*. Louisville, KY: Westminster John Knox, 1992.

Reydams-Schils, G. "'Becoming like God' in Platonism and Stoicism." In *From Stoicism to Platonism: The Development of Philosophy, 100 BCE–100 CE*, edited by Troels Engberg-Pedersen, 142–58. Cambridge: Cambridge University Press, 2007.

Rowe, C. Kavin. "Making Friends and Comparing Lives." In *The New Testament in Comparison: Validity, Method, and Purpose in Comparing Traditions*, edited by John M. G. Barclay and B. G. White; LNTS 600, 23–40. London: T&T Clark, 2020.

———. *One True Life: The Stoics and Early Christians as Rival Traditions*. New Haven, CT/London: Yale University Press, 2016.

Runia, David T. "The Beginnings of the End: Philo of Alexandria and Hellenistic Theology." In *Traditions of Theology: Studies in Hellenistic Theology, Its Background and Aftermath*, edited by Dorothea Frede and André Laks, 281–316. Leiden: Brill, 2001.

Sandmel, Samuel. "Parallelomania." *JBL* 81 (1962) 1–13.

Sedley, David. "Epicurus' Theological Innatism." In *Epicurus and the Epicurean Tradition*, edited by Jeffrey Fish and Kirk R. Sanders, 29–52. Cambridge: Cambridge University Press, 2011.

———. "The Origins of the Stoic God." In *Traditions of Theology: Studies in Hellenistic Theology, Its Background and Aftermath*, edited by Dorothea Frede and André Laks, 41–83. Leiden: Brill, 2001.

Segal, Charles. "Poetic Immortality and the Fear of Death: The Second Proem of the De Rerum Natura." *HSCP* 92 (1989) 193–212.

Sellars, John. *Stoicism*. Durham: Acumen, 2006.

Sextus Empiricus. *Outlines of Pyrrhonism*. Translated by R. G. Bury. LCL 273. Cambridge, MS: Harvard University Press, 1933.

Sharples, Robert W. *Peripatetic Philosophy 200BC to AD 200: An Introduction and Collection of Sources in Translations*. Cambridge: Cambridge University Press, 2010.

———. "Aristotelian Theology after Aristotle." In *Traditions of Theology: Studies in Hellenistic Theology, Its Background and Aftermath*, edited by Dorothea Frede and André Laks, 1–40. Leiden: Brill, 2001.

———. "Counting Plato's Principles." In *The Passionate Intellect: Essays on the Transformation of Classical Traditions Presented to Professor I. G. Kidd*, edited by L. Ayres, RUSCH 7, 67–82. New Brunswick, NJ: Transaction, 1995.

Smith, Jonathan Z. *Drudgery Divine: On the Comparison of Early Christianities and the Religions of Late Antiquity*. Chicago, IL: University of Chicago Press, 1990.

Thornsteinsson, Runar M. *Roman Christianity and Roman Stoicism: A Comparative Study of Ancient Morality*. Oxford: Oxford University Press, 2010.

Thorsrud, Harald. *Ancient Scepticism*. Abingdon: Routledge, 2014.

Tomlin, Graham. "Christians and Epicureans." *JSNT* 68 (1997) 51–72.

Volf, Miroslav. "Johannine Dualism and Contemporary Pluralism." In *The Gospel of John and Christian Theology*, edited by Richard Bauckham and Carl Mosser, 19–50. Grand Rapids, MI: Eerdmans, 2008.

Warren, James. "What God Didn't Know (Sextus Empiricus AM IX 162–166)." In *New Essays on Ancient Pyrrhonism*, edited by Diego E. Machuca, 41–68. Leiden: Brill, 2011.

Watson, G. "Discovering the Imagination: Platonists and Stoics on Phantasia." In *The Question of "Eclecticism": Studies in Later Greek Philosophy*, edited by John M. Dillon and A A. Long. HCS III, 208–233. Berkeley/ Los Angeles, CA: University of California Press, 1988.

Witt, Reginald E. *Albinus and the History of Middle Platonism*. TCPS, vol 7. Cambridge: Cambridge University Press, 1937.

Wittgenstein, Ludwig. "Remarks on Frazer's *Golden Bough*." In *Ludwig Wittgenstein, Philosophical Occasions 1912–1951*, edited by James Klagge and Alfred Nordmann, 118–59. Indianapolis, IN: Hackett, 1993.

Zeyl, Donald and Barbara Sattler. "Plato's *Timaeus*." In *The Stanford Encyclopedia of Philosophy*, edited by Edward N. Zalta. Summer 2019. https://plato.stanford.edu/archives/sum2019/entries/plato-timaeus/.

3

The Fourth Gospel as Ancient Literary Artefact
Dorothy A. Lee

Introduction

SENSITIVITY TO THE LITERARY devices employed in the Fourth Gospel clarifies its artistry, revealing not only what the text communicates but also how it does so. The literary features make possible the reader's engagement with the text, since form and meaning belong inextricably together.[1] Modern perspectives on literary criticism reflect and shape contemporary readings, but ancient audiences had their own perceptions, based on different cultural understandings—though with the same implicit awareness of the coherence of form and content.[2] Such influence operated alongside the compelling literary stimulus of the Old Testament in its poetry, prophecy, and narrative.[3] This essay explores the Fourth Gospel as a literary artefact of the Greco-Roman world,[4] one that uses the artistic conventions of antiquity in three areas: style, visualization, and plot.

---

1. Lee, *Symbolic Narratives*, 23–28.

2. Culpepper's *Anatomy* is considered the inspiration for contemporary literary approaches to the Fourth Gospel.

3. "The primary literary feature of the [Fourth] Gospel is its continual drawing upon the Scriptures of Israel . . . , Jewish festivals, symbols, and theology" (Coloe, *John 1–10*, lxxvii).

4. On Gospel manuscripts as "material artefacts" that possess identity-forming significance in the ancient world alongside its oral culture, see Keith, *Gospel as Manuscript*, esp. 1–69.

Greek and Roman writings have a good deal to say about the artistic and linguistic skills needed for composition. This awareness includes rhetoric, a core element of education in the Greco-Roman curriculum.[5] The two areas—the literary and the rhetorical—overlap and formed the basis of Greco-Roman practice in which Judaism by the first century CE was immersed.[6] Both forms were grounded in reading aloud and performance,[7] the main means of communication for the illiterate in the world of antiquity. The oral nature of rhetoric is obvious, but it is also true of literary works that were communicated orally, even within the book culture of antiquity:[8] Greek drama, for instance, or the public recitations of Homer's *Iliad* and *Odyssey*.[9]

Aristotle stands at the head of ancient views of both literature and rhetoric. His *Poetics* offers a framework for the composition and comprehension of Greek poetry in which are included epic and drama, with a particular focus on tragedy.[10] The classic discussion of rhetoric is found in Aristotle's *Art of Rhetoric* which is concerned with the kind of persuasive speech designed to win over an audience to the orator's viewpoint.[11]

It could be argued that the author of a text written in popular language to a small, counter-cultural religious group within the wider Greco-Roman world is hardly likely to have consulted literary critics or to have encountered the literature on which their analysis is based. This is particularly so of the *Iliad* and the *Odyssey*, Homer being the guiding star for ancient literature and the source as well as embodiment of its genius. Yet these works need not have been read or heard for their

---

5. See Myers, "Rhetoric," 187–93.

6. On the porous boundaries between Judaism and Hellenism, and the extensive Hellenization of Judaism (without sacrifice to religious identity), see Gruen, *Hellenistic Judaism*, 21–75.

7. Witherington, *New Testament Rhetoric*, 1–5, 11–13. For a history of rhetoric in the classical periods of Greece and Rome, see Kennedy, *Classical Rhetoric*, 30–200.

8. As Keith rightly points out, "oral" and "literate" are not in opposition in antiquity: "[i]lliterate individuals had multiple avenues for participating in literature culture . . . the Jesus tradition emerged in a culture that was not oral *rather than* textual, but oral *and* textual" ("Performance of the Text," 59–60).

9. The two long epic poems of Homer, *The Iliad* and *The Odyssey*, were initially oral in composition and transmission. For the history and implications of their orality, see esp. Foley, "'Reading' Homer," 1–28.

10. Aristotle, *Poet.* (c. 335 BCE).

11. Aristotle's *Rhet.* was written c. 350 BCE.

methods and devices to be employed within the culture of the day.¹² Jo-Ann Brant makes the point in her study of the influence of Greek tragedy on the Fourth Gospel: "Writing is not a natural, spontaneous gesture but one reliant upon conventions or the artful disregard or inversion of conventions."¹³ Literary convention floats in the air and in whatever elements of education people have imbibed, consciously or not.¹⁴

Style

The first of these literary and rhetorical devices is that of style (λέξις)—"diction," as it is often called (note again the concern with orality). Aristotle speaks of three contexts that determine style in rhetoric: the deliberative, concerned to encourage or dissuade particularly in large political assemblies; the forensic, focused on accusation or vindication in the law-courts; and the epideictic, which offers praise or blame in order to lead the audience to virtue.¹⁵ Subsequent writers consider this a useful categorization but also sometimes too narrow to encompass the wide range of rhetorical practice.¹⁶

Under the influence of Aristotle, Demetrius identifies four literary styles: the grand, suitable for epic (such as the *Iliad* and *Odyssey*); the elegant, communicating charm; the plain, aiming at clarity and lucidity; and the forceful, associated with compactness and vigor.¹⁷ There is also the possibility of mixed styles within the same composition.¹⁸ In the Roman world, Cicero identifies three basic rhetorical styles: the plain, the

---

12. See MacDonald, *Homeric Epics*, who seeks to demonstrate that Mark's Gospel is a conscious imitation of the Odyssey and parts of the Iliad; and that Homer and the Greek Old Testament were Mark's main influences.

13. Brant, *Dialogue and Drama*, 256.

14. While literary composition and rhetorical activity belonged largely in the male domain, women could also be active as writers and orators; see Kennedy, *Classical Rhetoric*, 15–19. Women possessing power and education were a reality, if exceptional, in the Greco-Roman and Jewish worlds, including the early church, see Brooten, *Women Leaders*, 5–99, Cohick, *Ancient Ways of Life*, 225–56, Hylen, *Thekla*, 7–42, and Lee, *Ministry of Women*, 5–7, 153–70.

15. Aristotle, *Rhet.* 1.3.

16. Hesk, "Types of Oratory," 145–7 (145–61).

17. Demetrius, *Style* 307–521. The dating, like the authorship, is contentious, ranging from the second century BCE to the first century CE.

18. Demetrius, *Style* 36.

middle and the grand.¹⁹ These are further elaborated in Quintilian more than a century later, where the grand style, particularly appropriate for "matters pertaining to divinity,"²⁰ engages most powerfully the hearer.²¹ This style is apparent in the use of amplification, balanced constructions, repetition, and other rhetorical figures such as comparison and hidden meanings.²²

Unity and simplicity are important features of literary style.²³ The Roman poet Horace acclaims these qualities, the overarching wholeness of a literary text supported by its details.²⁴ There is an ideal balance between charm and usefulness for instruction (*dulce, utile*), articulated with brevity and succinctness.²⁵ The beauty of the language needs to captivate the readers so that they too experience the emotions,²⁶ and the style should be familiar to the hearer and apposite to its contents. Above all, the author needs to pursue wisdom: *scribendi recte sapere est et principium et fons* ("the beginning and fount of writing is rightly to be wise"),²⁷ composing from high ideals while possessing natural talent and gifts in communication.²⁸ This moral focus is a distinctive feature of ancient literary composition.

Ancient Greco-Roman literary critics are also sensitive to the way in which style or diction contributes to emotion. Elevated language has the capacity to express something of the "sublime" (τὸ ὕψος): those great literary moments which raise the spirits to a sense of ecstasy and awe. For the writer known as "Longinus," the two basic elements are grand conceptions and strong emotion.²⁹ Other elements are more requiring

---

19. Cicero, *Orat.* 28.97 (46 BCE). See Black, "Grandeur," 222.

20. Black, "Grandeur," 223.

21. Quintilian, *Or. Ed.* 12.10, 58–80. See Black, "Grandeur," 220.

22. Black identifies these elements in the Farewell Discourse (Jn 14–17), which he sees as representing the grand style of rhetoric ("Grandeur," 223-9).

23. See esp. the collected of essays in Stibbe, *John as Literature*, which presupposes the narrative unity of the Gospel.

24. Horace, *Poet.* 1–23. The text, also entitled "Epistle to the Pisos" (a father and his two sons), was written some time in the late first century BCE.

25. Horace, *Poet.* 333–46.

26. Horace, *Poet.* 99–118.

27. Horace, *Poet.* 309.

28. Horace, *Poet.* 408–18.

29. Longinus, *Subl.*. Details of this text (author, dating, venue) are unknown: most likely somewhere in the first century CE.

of artistry (τέχνη): the creation of figures of thought and speech, "noble language" (γενναία φράσις), and appropriate word-arrangement.[30] These features include emphasis, use of the historic present tense, and word choice. Longinus even includes in his examples of elevated language the opening cadences of Genesis.[31]

The style of the Fourth Gospel is not that of the great literature of ancient Greece, from the poetry of Homer and the tragedians to the Roman epic writers and poets. John's writing style is popular and its word range limited—the smallest in the New Testament; the sentence structure is modest and unpretentious. For all that, there is a dignity and at times grandeur to the language and on occasions a winsome beauty and charm to the prose, even in the relative austerity of sentence formation and vocabulary.[32] The Gospel is far from being without literary and rhetorical artifice. These are apparent in the prologue which acts as the "theological prolegomenon" of the Gospel,[33] its unusual movement aptly compared to the waves of the sea coming ever closer on the incoming tide.[34] Take, for example, the "wave" that comprises the second cycle of the prologue, a cycle that begins and ends with the motif of "believing" (1:6–13). While the language at first conforms to the plain and lucid (1:6–8), the second part moves in a different and loftier direction (1:9–13):[35]

> [9] He [λόγος/φῶς, "word/light"] was the genuine light,
> which enlightens every person,
> coming into the world.
> [10] He was in the world
> and the world through him became
> and the world knew him not.
> [11] To his own things he came,
> and his own people did not welcome him.
> [12] But as many as did accept him,
> he gave to them authority to become God's children,

---

30. Longinus, *Subl.* VII.1 2. Word order is more easily activated in an inflected language such as Greek than in English.

31. Longinus, *Subl.* IX.9; he would have encountered Genesis from the Septuagint (LXX), the Greek translation of the Old Testament, which emerged from Diaspora Judaism in the third and second centuries BCE.

32. Black, "Grandeur," 220-3 (220-39).

33. Culpepper, "Prologue," 3-26.

34. So Moloney, *John*, 34.

35. On this structure for the prologue (a much-disputed area), see Zumstein, *Saint Jean*, 55-68; also Lee, *Hallowed*, 32.

to those believing in his name
¹³ who, not of blood nor of the will of flesh nor of the will of a man (ἀνήρ),
but of God were born.

In addition to the Hebrew parallelism of 1:10–11 (where "his own" parallels "the world")[36] there are also features familiar to a Greco-Roman literary reader. The vocabulary is simple but stylized, and the composition an example of the grand style which possesses something of the dignity and solemnity of epic, both in its divine content and articulation. There is a note of portentous tragedy in that the world has, astoundingly, failed to recognize its own Creator.[37] Rhetorically, the intention is to beguile the audience from one camp to the other: from ignorant blindness to enlightened insight leading to transformation—the restoration of an original status with God. The passage thus corresponds to the epideictic style of rhetoric with its suggestions of blame (on those rejecting) and praise (on those accepting) who embark on a life of virtue and goodness, figuratively imaged as new birth.

That the language is elevated is confirmed by repetition and word order. The term κόσμος ("world," referring here to the created realm) is repeated three times after its initial usage (1:10–11), expressing the origins of the world, the entry of the λόγος–φῶς, its habitation in the same domain and its rejection: "this light is not one of the phenomena of the physical world; it is not intrinsic to the world ... Indeed, the world was made through this Logos–Light."[38] The ownership of the κόσμος by right of creation is emphasized in the parallel notion of "his own" which underlines the connection of the λόγος–φῶς to the κόσμος and its tragic impercipience.[39] The word order of the last two verses is particularly significant. Believers gain a new authority (ἐξουσία)—a freedom—to become children of God yet without human contrivance. The three synonymous phrases eliminate all human sources, building up tension

---

36. Parallelism is a technique familiar from the Old Testament where two statements correspond to each other in similar but not identical wording to bring emphasis and variety to a specific point.

37. Behr argues that the Passion lies at the heart of the prologue, as it does of the Fourth Gospel in general (*John the Theologian*, esp. 245–70).

38. Thompson, "'Light' (φῶς)," 279.

39. According to Byrne, "his own" refers to Israel (its leadership) and is extended later in the Gospel to Johannine believers (*Life Abounding*, 28–29).

that is not released till the phrase "but of God,"⁴⁰ the whole construction concluding with the main verb "were born." English translations place the verb early in the sentence (e.g., "who were born not of blood ... but of God" [NRSV]) but lose the emphasis of the original which brings the sentence to its culmination in the final clause, "*but of God were born.*"

With such subject matter and language, Longinus might well discern the presence of the "sublime." At this point, the role is not so much to persuade as to enflame, inspire, transfigure. By working on the emotions, the passage entices its hearers into identifying with the children of God, provoking a yearning for a new identity and congruence with the Creator. It creates an upheaval, a sense of turmoil, working on complex sentiments: dismay at the rejection, longing to be included in the elevated community,⁴¹ and perplexity as to its mechanics. The audience is primed for further revelation into what that nativity means and how it is attained. The diction is potent enough to entice its readers into the dramatic flow.

Visualization

"Visualization" is included among several other devices that serve to communicate lofty concepts. It refers to the art of description which formulates immediate images (φαντασίαι) in the mind of the hearer. Connected to the five senses and not just to "seeing,"⁴² these images give rise to an imaginative experience of amazement (ἔκπληξις), conveying the listeners onto another plane of reality.⁴³ This phenomenon signifies the capacity of the text to fire up the imagination—an integral dimension of which is emotion, as we have already seen, which plays a substantial role in its actualization.⁴⁴ In this process, metaphor in particular plays a key role.

Metaphor is a widely recognized feature of ancient composition, one of the multiple ways in which language can be used to great effect.⁴⁵ For Aristotle, metaphor (μεταφορά, literally, "a bearing across") is about the

---

40. On the meaning of the synonymous phrases, see Lee, *Flesh and Glory*, 33.

41. On the problems of speaking of an insular Johannine "community" in the Fourth Gospel, see Porter, *Johannine Social Identity*, 228–35.

42. Lee, "Five Senses," 115–27.

43. Longinus, *Subl.* XV.1–2.

44. Unfortunately, Longinus' manuscript breaks off before his discussion of emotions.

45. As Ricoeur points out, Aristotle sees metaphor as belonging to both rhetoric and poetics (*Rule*, 12–13).

transference (ἐπιφορά, literally "a bearing upon") of a name or experience that belongs to something else by analogy.[46] It is perhaps a writer's greatest gift to "be metaphorical" (τὸ μεταφορικὸν εἶναι) because "to employ metaphor well [lit. 'to metaphorize well'] is to perceive likeness," thus requiring sensitivity to envisage the connections.[47] Metaphor also conveys the sublime in a way that combines beauty with vigor.[48] Literary figures such as metaphor play a critical role in delivering exalted meaning and conveying life-changing emotion.[49]

The poetic features of the Fourth Gospel are most apparent in its use of imagery,[50] interwoven into the narrative, so that meaning emerges from the narrative through symbols, while the narrative serves in turn to draws out their significance.[51] A distinctive type of metaphor in the Fourth Gospel is located in the "I am" sayings, most of which involve the kind of transference of which Aristotle speaks, yet which also communicate new meaning. They include bread (6:35), light (8:12; 9:5), door (10:7–9), shepherd (10:11–16), road (14:6), and vine (15:1–7). In each case, something concrete and familiar is visualized in the mind of the hearer, common to everyday life in the Greco-Roman world:[52]

Bread

Bread was the staple food of the ancient world,[53] varying in quality from rich to poor and made either from wheat (most commonly) or barley (for the very poor): "Most of the nutritional needs of most inhabitants of the ancient Roman world seem to have been met by cereal grains, usually

---

46. Aristotle, *Poet.* XXI. Ricoeur argues that metaphor is not simply about labels and substitution but the creation of new semantic meaning (Ricoeur, *Rule*, 13–26; Lee, *Symbolic Narratives*, 30–32).

47. Aristotle, *Poet.* XXII.

48. For Longinus, the use of metaphor can tempt the writer to extravagance; although he adds that temperate and sober writing is generally inferior to a lively style that might occasionally go to excess (*Subl.* XXXII.7–8)!

49. Longinus, *Subl.* VIII.

50. See Zimmermann, "Imagery in John," 1–43, and Lee, "Imagery," 151–70.

51. Lee, *Symbolic Narratives*, 11–22.

52. These sayings are also rooted in the traditions of the Old Testament (Ball, "*I Am*," 204–48).

53. McGowan, *Ascetic Eucharists*, 35–39.

in the form of bread."[54] It is supplemented with olives and olive oil, salt, fish, and some vegetables and legumes (meat being a rarity except for the rich). The baking of bread was mostly the work of women as a daily task, the family's survival and well-being dependent on it.

Light

Apart from the sun, moon, and stars (which the ancients studied carefully[55]), lighting in the ancient world was scanty, supplied by wax candles or bronze and terracotta lamps and torches with olive or fish oil. None of it provided anything like a bright and consistent light. Most ancient homes had at best a dim and murky luminosity and cities were unlit. All this stands in stark contrast to modern experience in cities and homes. Reading at night was difficult if not impossible in most households, walking abroad on dark urban streets was perilous, and the notion of a source of light that would fully illuminate the road ahead in the darkness was inconceivable.

Sheepfold

Sheep-farming was one of the commoner forms of animal husbandry in the ancient world, alongside the fishing industry, the animals tended for their wool, milk, and meat.[56] The doorway to the sheepfold gave access to pasture by day and safety by night for the flock: protection against cold weather and predatory animals. The picture of a responsible shepherd who did everything within reason to protect his flock was commended in a Greco-Roman context where animal husbandry was sophisticated and animals generally well nurtured and cared for.[57]

---

54. McGowan, *Ascetic Eucharists*, 38.

55. Note the discovery in 1908 of the Antikythera mechanism, an analogue computer, which could accurately predict the movements of the planets and eclipses, dating to some time in the second or first centuries BCE ("Wisdom Land").

56. Kron, "Animal Husbandry," 289–351.

57. Howe, "Domestication," 265–82.

Way/Road

Main thoroughfares (*viae publicae*) constructed and developed under imperial Rome were well-built, straight, and smooth, making transit relatively easy for the ancient traveler (many of these roads still surviving today), even if their chief purpose was to consolidate the Roman *imperium* and the movement of its armies. These were "both foundation and means of power" and considered in the ancient world "a characteristic feature of this world empire . . . listed ... among Rome's greatest achievements."[58] They were considered a symbol of "order and culture," implying Roman belief in their self-assigned colonizing role as "bringers of salvation and civilizing order;"[59] they also played a significant role in the economy. The road could also be used as a philosophical metaphor, expressing the search for wisdom and the happy life. Philosophy itself, as the pursuit of wisdom, was considered a *way* of life and not simply discourse based on reason and logic.[60] The image of seeking the path to authentic life was a familiar aspiration.

Vine

Viticulture was a major industry of the ancient world, wine being the preferred drink across the economic spectrum (though it varied in quality from rich to poor).[61] A fertile vine on which branches grew and grapes clustered was a common sight in the rural context.[62] Wine was not simply a staple of ancient diet, however, but also associated with joy and celebration. The symposium in ancient Greece and its Roman equivalent, the *convivium*, in which (mainly) men of high standing participated, involved the consumption of wine at a banquet, where edifying discourse was the main attraction, along with entertainment such as music and dancing.[63] Wine was both a staple for the everyday and a source of sociality and joy.

---

58. Kolb, "*Via ducta*," 8–9 (3–21).

59. Kolb, "*Via ducta*," 9.

60. Hadot, *Philosophy as a Way of Life*, 264–76. For more on ancient philosophical schools in John's day, see also King, "Friends, Foes, or Rivals?"

61. McGowan, *Ascetic Eucharists*, 43–45.

62. Further on vines and viticulture in the Johannine world, see Lewit, "Vine and Wines."

63. McGowan, *Ascetic Eucharists*, 47–52.

Figurative Meaning

Through the wider narrative in which they are embedded, these images gain metaphorical meaning, often through misunderstanding on the part of the interlocutors. At least two function as Johannine parables: the sheepfold and the vine.[64] In these instances the figurative language creates a sense of familiarity and aspiration, while shaping an affective association of joy, safety, and plenitude; it might also extend or even overturn familiar expectations. In each case, there is a critical theological transference that takes place within the Fourth Gospel to create metaphor from the image.[65]

First and foremost, each image is transferred to Jesus himself. He is the bread which "abides to eternal life" (6:27); the light which blazes out in the darkness of ignorance, fear, danger, and evil; the guarded door keeping safe the people of God while giving them access to "life in abundance" (10:10); the dying and rising Savior who possesses divine authority over life and death; the authentic pathway to truth; and the life-giving association that brings joy and quenches the thirst for life. The commonplace and everyday take on sublime meaning in this equation, embraced by the Creator who has entered mortal "flesh:" the very stuff of the created order. Eternity is fused with time, place, and mortality in this metaphorical transference. The images become major symbols in the Christology of the Fourth Gospel,[66] binding the Johannine Jesus as the Image of God to the features of common life and the deepest human longings, which are gathered into his own eternal yet contingent identity.[67]

The "I am" saying absent from this discussion, "I am the resurrection and the life" (11:25–26), is not strictly a metaphor but a revelation that gives theological substance to the others. What lies at the root of the "I am" sayings is the gift of life itself: not simply the ongoing life of creation, although the connection is palpable enough, but enabling the hearer to envisage a life that transcends death overcoming the privations of mortality. This utterance turns the raised body of Lazarus into a form

---

64. For a definition of parable that embraces all four Gospels, see Zimmermann, *Puzzling the Parables*, 137–50.

65. On the literary place of the "I am" sayings in their narrative contexts, see Ball, "*I Am*," 60–145.

66. Further on symbol, see Lee, "Symbolism and Signs," 55–73.

67. On the relationship between image and matter in Johannine Christology, see Lee, "Creation," 101–17.

of metaphor—a symbol—for Jesus' own body which, unlike that of Lazarus, will attain a radical new life untouched by creaturely limitation.[68]

Secondly, the hearer of the Gospel is drawn into relationship through the metaphor.[69] In most cases, the "I am" sayings spell out the horizontal implications for believers: those who are hungry will be satisfied, those who walk in darkness will be illuminated, those who seek the path to God will find it. The two parables—the sheepfold and the vine—function as ecclesial symbols for the people of God, the company of faith,[70] who are offered life in relationship with one another and summoned to fruit-bearing mission.[71] Discipleship and kinship are as much outcomes of the metaphors as their Christology, serving a vital function in visualizing believing existence.

Plot

For Aristotle, who is deeply concerned with the shape of drama, poetry is a form of "mimesis"—that is, the representation of characters with whom the hearer can identify. The most important of these in tragedy is action (πρᾶξις) as it is unfolded in the plot (μῦθος), evoking emotive rejoinder in the reader, especially pity and awe (ἔλεος, φόβος).[72] Aristotle defines plot as having a beginning without causative precedent, a middle flowing causally from the beginning and having its own consequences, and an ending, in which the consequences are in some way resolved.[73] The plot does its work particularly through "reversals and recognitions" (περιπετείαι, ἀναγνωρίσεις),[74] which also include suffering (πάθος). The focus is not so much on the tragic hero (a more modern conception) but

---

68. Lee, *Symbolic Narratives*, 223–4. Byrne makes the point succinctly: "the raising of Lazarus functions as both anticipation and foil for the resurrection of Jesus" (*Life Abounding*, 199).

69. On the twofold structure of the predicated (metaphorical) "I am" sayings in the Fourth Gospel, see Ball, "*I Am*," 162–6.

70. For the relationship between Christology and the Gospel's understanding of church (particularly around the temple imagery), see esp. Coloe, *God Dwells with Us*.

71. On the connection between discipleship and mission, see esp. Gorman, *Abide and Go*.

72. For a discussion of plot in John from a modern perspective that is nonetheless influenced by Aristotle, see Larsen, "Plot," 97–113.

73. Aristotle, *Poet.* VI.25–34.

74. Aristotle, *Poet.* VI, XI.

the action itself: the change of circumstance which the drama depicts.[75] While no plot should reveal good characters whose story ends in misfortune, or bad characters finding happiness, the main focus is on the tragic alteration of situation that arouses pity and awe.[76]

Although it does not belong in the genre of ancient drama,[77] the Fourth Gospel has a number of parallel elements in the plot,[78] such as the presence of a prologue, dramatic dialogue between characters and Jesus, sequences of episodes, and transitions that unite them.[79] Such a comparison illustrates that, most likely unconsciously, the evangelist "uses the craft of the Greek tragedians to represent these plot elements when they occur."[80] There are also significant differences. Aristotle is indifferent to how the tragic movement should occur, upward or downward;[81] it is the mutability of fate that is of chief concern: "what matters is that the action shall have room to display life's bottomless instability."[82] This is a far cry from the driving narrative voice and salvific focus of the Fourth Gospel.[83]

Nevertheless, the two main elements of Aristotle's definition are present in John. Reversal spells out the plot of the Gospel, indicated already in the prologue: darkness seeking to overpower (lit. "grasp") the light (1:5) and creation failing to recognize its Creator (1:10-11).[84] For all that, the light banishes the darkness enabling people to rediscover their true identity as children of God. The motif of reversal drives the plot with the increasing ferocity of Jesus' enemies seen in spontaneous attempts on his life (8:59; 10:31) and the final conspiracy against him by the Jerusalem authorities (11:47-53). Yet it is a double reversal. At each point

75. See Jones, *On Aristotle and Greek Tragedy*, 12-29.

76. Aristotle, *Poet.*, XIII.

77. Jewish writers did turn their hand to drama, epic poetry, and romance narrative in Greek from the second centuries BCE to CE, using Greek genres, some though not all of which survive; their sources and setting are in each case biblical (Gruen, *Hellenistic Judaism*, 24-33).

78. Brant, *Dialogue and Drama*,

79. A good example is the story of the Raising of Lazarus which holds together a sequence of seven episodes in chiastic arrangement; Lee, *Symbolic Narratives*, 191-7.

80. Brant, *Dialogue and Drama*, 43.

81. Jones, *On Aristotle and Greek Tragedy*, 18-20.

82. Jones, *On Aristotle and Greek Tragedy*, 47.

83. Brant, *Dialogue and Drama*, 257.

84. Brant draws a comparison between the reversal motif in John and that of Sophocles' *Oedipus Tyrannos* (c. 429 BCE), particularly in the imagery of blindness and sight (*Dialogue and Drama*, 43-50).

of hostility and suffering, something occurs to unleash an explosion of light and love which is the last word on Jesus' life.[85] This reversal trumps anything in Greek tragedy, turning the plot into a triumphant victory of life over death, and love over enmity and hatred. The Johannine Jesus does not have his life taken from him but surrenders it of his own accord (19:30b) and, with the same divine authority, reclaims it (10:17–18).

The second element of Greek tragedy is that of "recognition," often linked to revelation. For Aristotle, recognition scenes are a core element of the plot more than a manifestation of character.[86] They represent the movement from ignorance to knowledge, whatever effect that knowledge may have, and are generally personal, "a fateful moment determining the fortune of the recognizer,"[87] involving the presence of tokens, authorial intervention, memory, and reasoning.[88] The recognition may be accepted or resisted. Thus in Aeschylus' play, *The Libation Bearers* (c. 458 BCE), at the tomb of Agamemnon (who has been murdered by his wife, Clytemnestra), their daughter Electra, overwhelmed with grief, slowly recognizes the signs of her banished brother Orestes' presence: a lock of his hair, his footprints in the sand, an old piece of clothing she once wove for him.[89] With restrained joy she attains recognition,[90] and together brother and sister, in company with the chorus, plot stealthy revenge on their mother. The same scene in different format is played out in other tragedies with the same characters.[91]

Much of John's Gospel is concerned with revelation through which characters in the Gospel come to recognize (or reject) the identity of Jesus. Many scenes follow a similar pattern as something of Jesus' divine identity is grasped, usually through motifs of misunderstanding and metaphor.[92] The story of the man born blind is perhaps the best example (9:1–41), since at each step the man comes to a fuller recognition of his

85. On the theme of love as it develops across the plot, see Moloney, *Love in the Gospel of John*.

86. Brant, *Dialogue and Drama*, 57.

87. Larsen, *Recognizing the Stranger*, 27.

88. Larsen, *Recognizing the Stranger*, 29–31.

89. Aeschylus, *Libation*, written c. 458 BCE.

90. Aeschylus, *Libation* 165–240.

91. Sophocles, *Electra* (c. 410 BCE) and Euripides, *Electra* (c. 420 BCE). For a comparison, see Perrin, "Recognition Scenes," 371–404.

92. See e.g. Nathanael (1:49), the Samaritan woman (4:29), Simon Peter (6:68), and Martha of Bethany (11:21–27).

healer whom he does not literally *see* until the final episode, when he gains both sight and insight (9:35–38). The token of recognition is his physical healing but also, ironically, his persecution by the authorities which pushes him towards recognition. The consequences are his transferal of allegiance from those who have rejected him to Jesus whom he now worships.[93]

The two prominent recognition scenes in the Easter narratives follow a similar pattern to the Electra stories: the meeting of familiar characters separated by death, the tokens of recognition, the movement towards it, and the implications which flow from it.[94] In the first case, Mary Magdalene comes to recognition of Jesus' new identity, beginning with grief and incomprehension and moving, through misunderstanding, to a full recognition and a new status as the "apostle" of the resurrection.[95] The main token of recognition is the calling of her name: Μαριάμ (20:16). The beloved disciple also has his moment of recognition. It may be that the folded head cloth in the tomb is the token which provokes recognition,[96] but it is more likely, given the ambiguity of 20:8–10, that the real recognition occurs at the Sea of Galilee. There, in company with six other disciples, the beloved disciple recognizes the Risen Jesus through the token of the miraculous catch of fish (21:4–7). He then is given a future role as the composer of the Gospel and source of its message (21:24).[97]

Johannine readers are gathered affectively into these recognition scenes, experiencing through identification with the characters the surprise and joy of the recognition, along with a sense of awe at Jesus' identity. Pity is more likely to be provoked by those potential recognition scenes that fail: where characters are unable to attain recognition and reject Jesus. This is the pattern of John 6 where the crowds, despite the token of the miraculous feeding, finally reject the revelation of Jesus as the Bread of Life (6:66).[98] It is perhaps most poignant at the Last Sup-

---

93. See Lee, *Symbolic Narratives*, 161–87.

94. Larsen sees four recognition scenes in John 20: the beloved disciple, Mary Magdalene, the disciples, and Thomas (*Recognizing the Stranger*, 186–211).

95. See Lee, *Flesh and Glory*, 220–229. For an analysis of Sophocles' play *Electra* in relation to Mary Magdalene, see Brant, *Dialogue and Drama*, 52–57.

96. E.g. Byrne, "Faith of the Beloved Disciple," 83–97.

97. For John 21 as a (sympathetic) addition to the Gospel, see Moloney, "John 21," 237–51. For the view that John 21 is integral to the Gospel, cf. Schneiders, "John 21:1–14," 70–75, Brant, *John*, 263–90, and Keith, *Gospel as Manuscript*, 132–4.

98. Lee, *Symbolic Narratives*, 126–60.

per where, from within the circle of love and intimacy and following the footwashing (in which he has participated), Judas Iscariot receives the morsel from Jesus' hand and fades into the darkness of betrayal (13:30).[99] Whether negative or positive, recognition and reversal are key features of the plot of the Fourth Gospel.

Conclusion

The characteristic features of ancient literature, with its complex mix of textuality and orality, give access to the mindset of another time and place. The familiar forms of antiquity connect its ancient readers to their own experience of storytelling and rhetoric, enabling them to make meaning and form identity within their own cultural framework. These points of connection need not be overt for their effects to be felt. The audience has the capacity, both literate and illiterate, to feel at home in the diction of the Fourth Gospel with its simplicity and grandeur, to visualize the power of its metaphors, and to follow the plot imaginatively through reversals and moments of recognition that heighten the beauty and dynamism of the text with its gracious invitation and challenge. The radical message of life and love is couched in the habitual contours of ancient narrative, rhetoric, and poetic discourse, in much the same way the Johannine narrator places the Word within the habitat of mortal flesh. For the ancient hearer, the Fourth Gospel communicates itself as a recognizable and effective literary artefact.

Bibliography

Aeschylus. *Oresteia: Agamemnon. Libation-Bearers. Eumenides.* Translated by Alan H. Sommerstein. LCL 146. Cambridge, MS and London: Harvard University Press, 2009.

Aristotle. *Art of Rhetoric.* Translated by J. H. Freese and Gisela Striker. LCL 193. Cambridge, MS: Harvard University Press, 2020.

———. *Poetics.* Translated by Stephen Halliwell. LCL 199. Cambridge, MS: Harvard University Press, 1995

Ball, David Mark. *"I Am" in John's Gospel: Literary Function, Background and Theological Implications.* LNTS 124. Sheffield: Sheffield Academic, 1996.

Behr, John. *John the Theologian and his Paschal Gospel: A Prologue to Theology.* Oxford: Oxford University Press, 2019.

---

99. Moloney, *John*, 381–5.

Black, C. Clifton. "'The Words That You Gave to Me I Have Given to Them:' The Grandeur of Johannine Rhetoric." In *Exploring the Gospel of John: In Honor of D. Moody Smith*, edited by R. Alan Culpepper and C. Clifton Black, 220–39. Louisville: Westminster John Knox, 1996.

Brant, Jo-Ann A. *Dialogue and Drama: Elements of Greek Tragedy in the Fourth Gospel*. Peabody: Hendrickson, 2004.

———. *John*. Paideia. Grand Rapids, Baker Academic, 2011.

Brooten, Bernadette. *Women Leaders in the Ancient Synagogue: Inscriptional Evidence and Background Issues*. Chico, CA: Scholars, 1982.

Byrne, Brendan. "The Faith of the Beloved Disciple and the Community in John 20." *JSNT* 23 (1985) 83–97.

———. *Life Abounding: A Reading of John's Gospel*. Collegeville: Liturgical Press, 2014.

Cicero. *Brutus. Orator*. Translated by G. I. Hendrickson and H. M. Hubbell. LCL 342. Cambridge, MS: Harvard University Press, 1939.

Cohick, Lynn. *Women in the World of the Earliest Christians: Illuminating Ancient Ways of Life*. Grand Rapids: Baker Academic, 2009.

Coloe, Mary L. *God Dwells With Us: Temple Symbolism in the Fourth Gospel*. Collegeville: Liturgical 2001.

———. *John 1–10*. WC. Collegeville: Liturgical 2021.

Culpepper, R. Alan. *Anatomy of the Fourth Gospel: A Study in Literary Design*. Philadelphia: Fortress, 1983.

———. "The Prologue as Theological Prolegomenon to the Gospel of John." In *The Prologue of the Gospel of John. Its Literary, Theological and Philosophical Contexts*, edited by J. van der Watt et al., 3–26. WUNT. Tübingen: Mohr Siebeck, 2016.

Demetrius. *On Style*. Translated by Doreen C. Innes and W. Rhys Roberts. LCL. Cambridge, MS: Harvard University Press, 1995.

Foley, John Miles. "'Reading' Homer Through Oral Tradition." *College Literature* 34 (2007) 1–28.

Gorman, Michael. *Abide and Go: Missional Theosis in the Gospel of John*. Didsbury Lectures. Eugene, OR: Cascade Books, 2018.

Gruen, Erich S. *Constructs of Identity in Hellenistic Judaism*. Berlin: de Gruyter, 2016.

Hadot, Pierre. *Philosophy as a Way of Life: Spiritual Exercises from Socrates to Foucault*. Translated by Michael Chase. Oxford: Blackwell, 1995.

Hesk, Jon. "Types of Oratory." In *The Cambridge Companion to Ancient Rhetoric*, edited by Erik Gunderson, 145–61. Cambridge: Cambridge University Press, 2009.

Homer. *The Iliad*. Translated by A. T. Murray. Revised by William F. Wyatt. LCL 170, 2 vols. Cambridge, MA: Harvard University Press, 1924, 1999.

———. *The Odyssey*. Translated by A. T. Murray. Revised by George E. Dimock. LCL 104, 2 vols. Cambridge, MA: Harvard University Press, 1919, 1995.

Horace. *Satires, Epistles, Art of Poetry*. Translated by H.R. Fairclough. LCL. 2nd ed. Cambridge, MS: Harvard University Press, 1929.

Howe, Timothy. "Domestication and Breeding of Livestock: Horses, Mules, Cattle, Sheep, Goats, and Swine." In *The Oxford Handbook of Animals in Classical Thought and Life*, edited by G. L. Campbell, 265–82. Oxford: Oxford University Press, 2014.

Hylen, Susan. *A Modest Apostle: Thecla and the History of Women in the Early Church*. Oxford: Oxford University Press, 2015.

Jones, John. *On Aristotle and Greek Tragedy*. London: Chatto & Windus, 1962.

Keith, Chris. *The Gospel as Manuscript. An Early History of the Jesus Tradition as Material Artefact.* Oxford: Oxford University Press, 2020.

———. "A Performance of the Text: The Adulteress's Entrance into John's Gospel." In *The Fourth Gospel in First-Century Media Culture*, edited by Anthony Le Donne and Tom Thatcher. LNTS 426, 49–69. London: Bloomsbury, 2011.

Kennedy, George A. *Classical Rhetoric and its Christian and Secular Tradition from Ancient to Modern Times.* 2nd ed. Chapel Hill and London: University of North Carolina Press, 1999.

———. *A New History of Classical Rhetoric.* Princeton: Princeton University Press, 1994.

King, Fergus J. "Friends, Foes, or Rivals? John among the Philosophers." In *The Enduring Impact of the Gospel of John: Interdisciplinary Readings*, edited by Robert A. Derrenbacker, Jr. et al., Eugene, OR: Wipf & Stock, 2022.

Kolb, Anne. "*Via ducta*—Roman Road Building: An Introduction to Its Significance, the Sources and the State of Research." In *Roman Roads: New Evidence—New Perspectives*, edited by Anne Kolb, 3–21. Berlin and Boston: de Gruyter, 2019.

Kron, Geoffrey. "Animal Husbandry." In *The Oxford Handbook of Animals in Classical Thought and Life*, edited by G. L. Campbell, 289–351. Oxford: Oxford University Press, 2014.

Larsen, Kaspar Bro. "Plot." In *How John Works: Storytelling in the Fourth Gospel*, edited by Douglas Estes and Ruth Sheridan, 97–113. Atlanta: SBL Press, 2016.

———. *Recognizing the Stranger: Recognition Scenes in the Gospel of John.* BIS. Leiden and Boston: Brill, 2008.

Lee, Dorothy A. *Flesh and Glory: Symbolism, Gender and Theology in the Gospel of John.* New York: Crossroad, 2002.

———. "The Gospel of John and the Five Senses." JBL 129 (2010) 115–27.

———. *Hallowed in Truth and Love: Spirituality in the Johannine Literature.* Eugene, OR: Wipf & Stock, 2012.

———. "Imagery." In *How John Works: Storytelling in the Fourth Gospel*, edited by Douglas Estes and Ruth Sheridan, 151–70. Atlanta: SBL, 2016.

———. *The Ministry of Women in the New Testament: Reclaiming the Biblical Vision of Church Leadership.* Grand Rapids, MI: Baker Academic, 2021.

———. *The Symbolic Narratives of the Fourth Gospel: The Interplay of Form and Meaning.* LNTS. Sheffield: Sheffield Academic, 1994.

———. "Symbolism and 'Signs' in the Fourth Gospel." In *Handbook of Johannine Studies*, edited by Judith Lieu and Martinus de Boer, 259–73. Oxford: Oxford University Press, 2018.

———. "Creation, Matter and the Image of God in the Gospel of John." SVTQ 62 (2018) 101–17.

Lewit, Tamara. "Vines and Wines in First Century Galilee." In *The Enduring Impact of the Gospel of John: Interdisciplinary Readings*, edited by Robert A. Derrenbacker, Jr. et al. Eugene, OR: Wipf & Stock, 2023.

Longinus. *On the Sublime [Περὶ ὕψους].* Translated by W. H. Fyfe and Donald Russell. LCL 199. Cambridge, MS: Harvard University Press, 1995.

MacDonald, Dennis R. *The Homeric Epics and the Gospel of Mark.* New Haven: Yale University Press, 2000.

McGowan, Andrew B. *Ascetic Eucharists: Food and Drink in Early Christian Ritual Meals.* OECS. Oxford: Clarendon, 1999.

Moloney, Francis J. *The Gospel of John*. Sacra Pagina 4. Collegeville: Liturgical, 1998.

———. "John 21 and the Johannine Story." In *Anatomies of Narrative Criticism. The Past, Present, and Futures of the Fourth Gospel as Literature*, edited by Tom Thatcher Stephen D. Moore, 237–51. Atlanta: SBL, 2008.

———. *Love in the Gospel of John: An Exegetical, Theological, and Literary Study*. Grand Rapids: Baker Academic, 2013.

Myers, Alicia D. "Rhetoric." In *How John Works: Storytelling in the Fourth Gospel*, edited by Douglas Estes and Ruth Sheridan, 187–203. Atlanta: SBL, 2016.

Perrin, B. "Recognition Scenes in Greek Literature." *AJP* 30 (1909) 371–404.

Porter, Christopher A. *Johannine Social Identity Formation after the Fall of the Jerusalem Temple: Negotiating Identity in Crisis*. BIS 194. Leiden: Brill, 2022.

Quintilian. *The Orator's Education: Books 11–12*. Translated by Donald A. Russell. LCL 494. Cambridge, MS: Harvard University Press, 2002.

Ricoeur, Paul. *The Rule of Metaphor. The Creation of Meaning in Language*. Translated by Robert Czerny et al. London and New York: Routledge, 1977.

Schneiders, Sandra M. "John 21:1–14." *Int* 43 (1989) 70–75.

Stibbe, Mark W. G. *The Gospel of John as Literature. An Anthology of Twentieth-Century Perspectives*. NTTS&D 17. Leiden: Brill, 1993.

Thompson, Marianne Meye. "'Light' (φῶς): The Philosophical Content of the Term and the Gospel of John." In *The Prologue of the Gospel of John. Its Literary, Theological and Philosophical Contexts*, edited by J. van der Watt et al., 273–83. WUNT. Tübingen: Mohr Siebeck, 2016.

Wisdom Land. "2,000 Year Old Computer—Decoding the Antikythera Mechanism." https://www.youtube.com/watch?v=Eq8ocE3Kopw.

Witherington III, Ben. *New Testament Rhetoric: An Introductory Guide to the Art of Persuasion in and of the New Testament*. Eugene, OR: Cascade Books, 2009.

Zimmermann, Ruben. "Imagery in John: Opening Up Paths into the Tangled Thicket of John's Figurative World." In *Imagery in the Gospel of John: Terms, Forms, Themes, and Theology of Johannine Figurative Language*, edited by Jörg Frey et al., 1–43. WUNT. Tübingen: Mohr Siebeck, 2006.

———. *Puzzling the Parables of Jesus: Methods and Interpretation*. Minneapolis: Fortress, 2015.Zumstein, Jean. *L'Évangile selon Saint Jean (1–12)*. CNT2. Genève: Labor et Fides, 2014.

4

Will the Real Ἰουδαῖοι Please Stand Up?
CHRISTOPHER A. PORTER

Introduction

THE IDENTIFICATION, TRANSLATION, AND interpretation of the Greek term Ἰουδαῖοι in the Fourth Gospel causes significant consternation in biblical scholarship. While a basic translation of Ἰουδαῖοι can be rendered simply as "Jews," this is often misleading within the text. Instead, some have proposed that it should be translated as "Judeans," reflecting the geopolitical landscape of the first century, rather than a notional religious context. Others have suggested that the Ἰουδαῖοι are not representative of the entire group, but rather a subset, such as the "Jewish-leaders," or as a metonym representing the "Pharisees" or "Chief-priests." Many of these interpretations have much to commend them, and yet the vast majority of scholars opt for a variegated interpretation. However, this variegated interpretation is often less than satisfactory overall. Therefore, in line with such luminaries as Marcus Licinius Crassus and Eminem, we will ask "Will the real Ἰουδαῖοι please stand up?" In this vein, we must begin with the context of the Fourth Gospel, and then examine way that the author or authors of the Fourth Gospel construe the Ἰουδαῖοι through the lens of Social Identity Theory—a socio-cognitive approach to group identity—before returning to the broader geopolitical environment.

Background to Social Identity

First, however, some broader context is required. The topic of this essay is one that I approach with some trepidation: not just because such luminaries of Fourth Gospel scholarship as J. L. Martyn, Martin Hengel, Adele Reinhartz and a host of others have offered their significant assessment and opinion, and I will disagree with them at various points. The subject itself, however, does not just reveal something of the history, "religion," or culture at hand but something about us, as an audience of the text. Therefore, because this essay is not simply anchored within the biblical text or the historical background of the time but rather in a socio-cognitive approach to human interaction and group formation, it is necessary to give somewhat of a broader introduction than would normally be given for an essay of this ilk.

For this author, the story of social-identity construction does not begin in the first century BCE, but rather must start in 1996 with a then little-known fish and chip shop owner from Ipswich, Queensland: Pauline Hanson. In 1996, the Member for Oxley was elected to the Australian Federal Parliament on the back of a campaign that construed her as "Just an Ordinary Australian."[1] This theme she carried through into her maiden speech to Parliament on the 10th of September of that year. Listening to that speech as a high-schooler, I could not analyze the speech through the socio-scientific lenses and cognitive frameworks that I engaged with a decade later. But even then, at a basal level, I understood the identity construction that Hanson was engaging in to construct the identity of "Australian." And perhaps even more critically than understanding the social identity construction that she was building, I could grasp who were being excluded from this social identity construction: Asian Australians, like me!

This is predominantly because the patterns of argument that Hanson used in her maiden speech to Parliament, and throughout her campaign, are neither novel, nor rhetorically sophisticated. This enterprise of social identity construction and contrast is practised in the school yard by young children, honed in sporting rivalries, and deployed throughout our societal discourse; and has been done so for millennia. Therefore, it is in this context that we must approach the question of the Ἰουδαῖοι like a tessellated mural, looking broadly from afar before diving into the

---

1. See the extended analysis in Rapley, "'Just an Ordinary Australian.'"

details—beginning with a broader brush than the Fourth Gospel before we start looking at the contours of Johannine identity formation.

Making Distinctive Social Groups: Retelling and Contextualization of Shared Social Narratives

Social Identity Theory (SIT) is a socio-cognitive approach, originally developed by Henri Tajfel and his student John Turner, at the University of Bristol, that seeks to describe the process of group development and dynamics from an observational perspective. To quote Stephen Reicher et al.:

> Rather than using psychology to supercede [sic] other levels of explanation of human action, the aim is to account for when and how social structures and belief systems impact on what people do.[2]

To this end, Tajfel and Turner specifically define social identity as that which

> will be understood as that part of the individuals' self-concept which derives from their knowledge of their membership of a social group (or groups) together with the value and emotional significance attached to that membership.[3]

From this basis, the nature of social identities as an integrated part of community and individual identity is hardly challenged.[4] Indeed, as SIT moves from externally observable group processes towards internal cognitive processes it naturally lends itself to historical investigations.[5]

Investigating social identity works through three interweaved processes. Firstly, there is a pattern of intrinsically understanding internal group norms, which is what matters to the group: *normative fit*. Second is the practice of construing externally based group differences in relation to one's social group, namely why these items are different from other groups: *comparative fit*. Third, and finally, there is the cognitive mechanism of sorting the perceived world into categories for mental mapping:

---

2. Reicher, Spears, and Haslam, "The Social-Identity Approach in Social Psychology."

3. Tajfel, *Social Identity and Intergroup Relations*, 2.

4. Haslam, *Psychology in Organizations*, 27.

5. Reicher et al., "Saving Bulgaria's Jews."

categorization. Or more generally put, it concerns knowing who is in your group, who is out of the group, and on what basis these groups are constructed. The socio-cognitive understanding of social identity has been effectively used as an exploratory tool for understanding topics as broad as Protestant and Catholic division in Ireland, Bulgarian Jewish ethnic identity in the holocaust, university riots in London, and positions for and against women's ordination in the Church of England, to name but a few.[6]

To investigate how these inter- and intra-group comparisons are engaged with, social identity theorists Stephen Reicher and Fabio Sani analyzed how social groups leveraged group dynamics to argue for their identity construction, within the contexts of group schism. From this analysis a framework termed Structured Analysis of Group Arguments (SAGA) "sought to demonstrate that the rhetorical debates over self-categories are important because of their social-cognitive consequences."[7] That is, rhetorical debates allow for the construction of distinctive social groups through arguments regarding shared social narratives.

Within the SAGA model, Reicher and Sani enumerated four primary types of group arguments, of which two are directly pertinent to our analysis here. The first, Type A, involves an appeal to a positive view of the parent (superordinate) group, along with a consonantly positive in-group argument, and a dissonantly negative out-group argument. The second, Type B, consists of a negative superordinate group argument, with a dissonantly positive in-group argument, and a consonantly negative out-group argument. The other two argumentative patterns, Type C and D, present a hypothetical empty set counterpoint. Reicher and Sani observed that Type A and B forms of the group arguments combined to argue that "the in-group faction perpetuates the true identity of the parent group and negates negations of that identity, whereas the out-group faction subverts the true identity of the parent group and perpetuates negations of that identity."[8]

We can see this clearly at hand in the Member for Oxley's maiden speech where she sought to categorize herself as a prototypical "ordinary Australian" (line 4) and her entitlement to membership in, and

---

6. Reicher, "The St. Paul's Riot"; Reicher and Sani, "Introducing SAGA"; Reicher et al., "Saving Bulgaria's Jews."

7. Reicher and Sani, "Introducing SAGA," 270.

8. Reicher and Sani, 279.

representation of, that constructed category.⁹ But simultaneously she also sought to create stereotypes of "polished politicians" (line 3), Aboriginals (line 9 etc), multiculturalists (line 13), and her favorite target the "swamping by Asians" (line 122) as distinctively not within this created group of "Australian."¹⁰ Therefore she constructed herself as a prototypical Australian, embedding the identity within her own brand of politics, and construing others as distinctly "un-Australian."

Ancient Identity Formation

Given this pattern of identity construction is so prevalent in modern discourse, does the same hold for the ancient world? Therefore, we will briefly examine some broadly contemporary ancient texts to the Fourth Gospel.

Daniel: the New Joseph

Pertinent to our discussion is the prevalence of this pattern within Second Temple Jewish groups. Although, even before this period, we gain inklings of this—as Mark Brett has highlighted in his work on the *Procreation and the Politics of Identity*—the received compilation of the Joseph narrative functions as a type of counter-Persian group argument situated in the Diaspora.¹¹ Indeed, within our time-period, the canonical Book of Daniel picks up this pattern as a Joseph retelling, to encourage the creation of a new social identity based on a broader engagement of narrative reconstruction. Daniel functions as a new and better Joseph, fulfilling many of the requirements of Torah that Joseph evidently neglected, despite the revisionist attempts within the *Joseph and Aseneth* novella.¹² At the least, Daniel refuses foreign food (Dan 1:8–16), remains distinct within the palace (Dan 2:25), and prays regularly (Dan 6:10). Simply put, Daniel is presented as a superior Joseph, one who, although well acculturated, does not accommodate or assimilate to the surrounding culture, and presents a point of strong comparative fit for an audience tempted to

---

9. Following speech quotations from Australia, Parliamentary Debates, 10 September 1996, 3859 (Pauline Hanson, Member for Oxley).
10. Rapley, "'Just an Ordinary Australian.'"
11. Brett, *Genesis*.
12. Ahearne-Kroll, "Joseph and Aseneth and Jewish Identity."

integrate with a Diaspora culture. Furthermore, this pattern is continued throughout the apocryphal addition, Bel and the Dragon, which continues the attempt to draw a Diaspora Jewish in-group closer to the claims of the super-ordinate group while simultaneously distancing them from the surrounding culture.[13]

Qumran: Social Identity Formation in the Desert

A similar pattern may be seen from the communities in the desert, as the scrolls at Qumran show the same degree of social differentiation and claim of continuity as other forms of social category engagement. Indeed, the Damascus Document (CD) and the Rule of the Community (QS) display this feature as they function as constitutive documents for these social groups.

In its formation of group identity, CD draws upon the shared schematic narrative stemming from the "boundary shifters" of Deuteronomy 27:17 // CD 1.16 and the "growing of Israel and Aaron" in Ezekiel 47 // CD 1.7–8.[14] Here these references function as memory keys to unlock the shared narrative of Israelite history.[15] CD draws on this shared social discourse to build its own narrative that parallels, but does not contradict, the discourse found in Torah. From this the author seeks to transform the shared group narrative through the lens of the in-group and uses it to facilitate their exegetical argument to present a series of group distinctions to the audience. Here the author leans upon the schematic narrative to support a transformed exegesis of Numbers 21:18 to link the positive assessment of "diggers of the well"[16] to this community who "went out ... to dwell in the land of Damascus."[17] In contrast, the out-group is denigrated as "those who despise him"[18] and "shoddy wall-builders."[19] This transformed exegesis further reinforces the schematic narrative by providing

---

13. Porter, "Hic Sunt Dracones."

14. Porter, *Johannine Social Identity Formation*, 44–45; Wacholder, *New Damascus Document*, 146.

15. Campbell, *Use of Scripture*, 206.

16. CD 6.4.

17. CD 6.5.

18. CD 1.2.

19. CD 4.19.

justification for the in-group having the authoritative interpretation of the wider Jewish social memory.

These differences in use of shared discourse to create a schematic narrative also impact upon the presentation of group structures to reinforce and build the argument at hand. Throughout the broad narrative presented in the Damascus Document, the author builds a robust in-group through appeals to the shared narrative. This in-group is presented in contrast to a similar out-group that the author also defines from the same shared narrative. The keying of these two groups also highlights the presence of the super-ordinate group "Israel" through the shared frame. Taken together, the in-group becomes linked to the super-ordinate group and reinforces the place of the in-group within the sphere of corporate Israel. Within this sphere, the author anchors both in-group and out-group identities within the Israelite identity but construes them as inextricable, binary opposites. Therefore, this anchorage constructs a claim to be the rightful inheritors of the Israelite social narrative and identity, and highlights the fit of the in-group, and the associated rejection of the out-group. Together, it builds the case for the community being the new representation of the super-ordinate group.

Philo: *Life of Moses*

That sectarian groups use this pattern of argument should not surprise us. But what of non-sectarian groups? We can see examples of the same pattern of identity formation in the works of Philo and Josephus. Philo engages in several works of scriptural retelling which serve to re-inscribe an identity for his audience; here we will briefly examine *The Life of Moses*.

The Life of Moses presents a "competitive history" by re-narrating Moses' life in the form of a *bios* (that is, an ancient biography) of the "the greatest and most perfect of men."[20] While Philo draws the structure of his biography from Torah narratives, he construes Moses as a prototypical Greek. In the opening of the work, Philo frames Moses' Hebrew heritage in an Egyptian setting, like his own.[21] Therefore Philo retells elements of shared narrative, such as Moses's education, in typical elite Greek style.[22] However, Philo does not seek to remove Moses from his Jewish context,

---

20. Philo, *Mos. 1.*, I.1.
21. Philo, *Mos. 1.*, I.5. Dawson, *Allegorical Readers*, 118.
22. Philo, *Mos. 1.*, I.21–24. Schenck, *Brief Guide to Philo*, 101.

but rather to contextualise the narrative within a Greek Stoic frame.[23] Therefore Philo's competitive history does double duty, correcting what he sees as problematic representations for a Diaspora context, and setting up Moses as the type of a Greek philosopher *par excellence*. For example, Philo's Moses is never presented as tending sheep in the wilderness (Exod 3:1), but rather as "devoting himself . . . to the most virtuous pursuits of life . . . and to the continual study of the doctrines of philosophy, which he easily and thoroughly comprehended."[24]

Philo's competitive histories—both here in *The Life of Moses* and in his other narratives—serve two purposes. First, they function apologetically for a Greek audience, construing Moses within their frame of reference. Second, they also build a Greek apologetic for a Jewish audience, showing how the Greek philosophical tradition may cohere with the constitutive narrative in Exodus. Overall Philo reflects on positive or negative aspects of Jewish identity and compares these as consonant or dissonant with a Grecophile Moses. These social group arguments both legitimate a Grecophile Jewish Diaspora in-group within broader Israel, and positively engender the same group within the broader Greek Diaspora community.

Josephus: *Antiquities* and Passover

Moving forward to after the Roman general Titus' razing of Jerusalem in 70 CE, Josephus employs similar social group arguments in his *Antiquities* and *Jewish War*.[25] A brief example can be seen in his description of the Passover. Here the Passover memorial is separated from its temple location, instead emphasizing its origins in Egypt during slavery.[26] This serves as a competitive history to contend that the feast can be appropriately conducted without the Temple apparatus. But Josephus does not restrict his reconstruction of Passover to a Jewish context but demonstrates its regularity within a Roman calendrical system. Colautti observes the social dimensions of this as strengthening "the bonds of brotherhood among those that identified themselves openly with the *politea/politeuma*

---

23. Philo, *Mos.* 1., I.44.
24. Philo, *Mos.* 1., I.47–48.
25. Josephus, *Ant* 2.14.6 and *J. W.* 6.5.3.
26. Colautti, *Passover*, 238.

of the Jews."²⁷ Through these social arguments, Josephus argued for a post-temple construct to "build around himself a form of Judaism capable of surviving the destruction of A.D. 70."²⁸

Through the social group arguments in these communities, we find an approach to the question of Israelite identity construction within a "broadly exilic" context, be that through a Diaspora location such as Alexandria, a self-imposed exilic condition in Qumran, or the cataclysmic destruction of Jerusalem—and the Temple—in 70 CE.²⁹ In these environments, we find communities seeking to reclaim or build a new Israel from the old constructions that are no longer tenable. They are seeking to claim the super-ordinate group identity of "Israel" for their own group. It is through this lens of temple-removed identity formation, and specifically the cultic cataclysm of 70 CE, that I propose we should interpret the construal of the Ἰουδαῖοι and read the animus of the Fourth Gospel. Therefore, we will now turn to a brief analysis of the narrative constructions in the Fourth Gospel where we find instances of structured group arguments found in almost every scene of Jesus' public ministry.³⁰

John 2: The Clearing of the Temple

In the clearing of the temple recorded in John 2:13–22 we see a narrative anchored within the location of cultic identity construction. For an audience of cultically observant Jews in the post-70 CE environment, this frame would have been especially relevant with the loss of the annually repeated ritual temple observance and associated identity construction.³¹ In this context we find a robust structured group argument deployed against the destroyed cultic apparatus. Despite the destruction of the temple, the narrative of John 2 positively frames the intent of cultic worship, and therefore the super-ordinate group identity structure associated with it.³² Jesus' actions of clearing the temple consonantly align the Christ-following in-group with the ideals of cultic worship, effectively

---

27. Colautti, *Passover*, 240.
28. Colautti, *Passover*, 5.
29. See discussion in Keener, *John*, 140–2.
30. For more, see the extended argumentation in Porter, *Johannine Social Identity Formation*.
31. Coloe, *God Dwells with Us*, 69.
32. Kerr, *Temple of Jesus' Body*, 79.

giving an option for continuing the identity structure of the super-ordinate group "Israel."³³ However, in contrast to the positive assessment of the Christ-following group, the clearing narrative also presents a negative depiction of the buying and selling going on within the temple (2:14), as a subversion of the identity of the super-ordinate group "Israel."

These social-group assessments culminate in a challenge from the Ἰουδαῖοι about who authorised clearing the temple (2:18). Narratively, this portrays the Ἰουδαῖοι as the stereotype of the out-group who are involved in converting the temple into a marketplace (2:14) and thereby construing them as a negation of the super-ordinate identity.³⁴ However, Jesus' response highlights the confusion of the out-group (2:19–20) and reinforces the differences between the groups. In turn, the conflation of Jesus' body with the temple building links the in-group with the super-ordinate group, and the positive construal of each.³⁵ Furthermore, linking the in-group with the temple highlights the loss of cultic observance for the out-group via destruction of the temple by Titus, along with the potential for continued observance through Jesus as the in-group prototype.

Together the structured group argument positively presents the cultic actions in the temple, while contrasting this with the negative activities in the temple courts. Jesus' clearing of the temple, and the memorial justification for the actions, all construe the in-group positively in relation to the cultic activity of the super-ordinate group. All of this is set within the politically contested frame of the temple destruction, for an audience wrestling with the lack of a significant identity construct.³⁶

John 6: The Manna and Bread of Life

Turning to the Johannine recounting of the feeding of the five thousand in John 6 we find a strong narrative anchor unlocked within the Exodus memory, keyed by the temporal marker in 6:4 regarding the Passover, and again in 6:31 which invokes the Mosaic feeding of manna. Against this narrative frame the Evangelist juxtaposes Jesus as the "bread of life"

33. This restoration of cultic purity coheres with the Day of the Lord description from Zechariah 14, which highlights the removal of 'traders' from the temple; Chanikuzhy, *Eschatological Temple*, 261, 266.
34. Moloney, "From Cana to Cana," 831.
35. Chanikuzhy, *Eschatological Temple*, 315–6.
36. Porter, *Johannine Social Identity Formation*, 95.

in 6:35 which drives a dissonance between the social-category of those expecting physical sustenance—akin to that of Moses in the wilderness—and the broader construct of the spiritual sustenance that is on offer.[37] This culminates in the confrontation of 6:49–51:

> Your ancestors ate the manna in the wilderness, yet they died. But here is the bread that comes down from heaven, which anyone may eat and not die. I am the living bread that came down from heaven. Whoever eats this bread will live forever. This bread is my flesh, which I will give for the life of the world [38]

The positive perspective on desiring spiritual sustenance is already relevant for the Johannine audience as a desire of the super-ordinate group and is reused as an anchor for the social group argument. Subsequently, Jesus' declaration of himself as the "bread of life" positively coheres the in-group and super-ordinate group arguments. But as the crowd begins to grumble (6:41) and argue (6:52), just as their forebears did in the desert (Exod 16:2–3), a negative corollary emerges, eventually leading to the rejection of the spiritual nourishment as described in John 6:66.[39]

Through this brief episode, the Evangelist has presented the positive interpretation of the manna in the wilderness as an historical schematic narrative—the positive super-ordinate group argument—along with the positive in-group interpretation of the confrontation of Jesus' spiritual nourishment, and the negative out-group response from the crowd; cumulatively forming a SAGA Type A argument structure.[40] Simply put, super-ordinate Israel should be seeking spiritual nourishment, and so therefore we "Johannine Christ-followers" are seeking spiritual nourishment with Jesus as the Bread.

John 7: Meribah and Sukkoth (Tabernacles)

The following episode recorded in John 7 builds on that in John 6, shifting from the Passover (6:4) to the congruent schematic history of "the Jewish Festival of Tabernacles" (ἡ ἑορτὴ τῶν Ἰουδαίων ἡ σκηνοπηγία; 7:2).[41]

---

37. Borgen, *Bread from Heaven*, 172.
38. Translations from the New Testament are my own.
39. Hakola, *Reconsidering Johannine Christianity*, 122.
40. Porter, *Johannine Social Identity Formation*, 115.
41. See Lev 23:42–43 and Zech 14; Wheaton, *Jewish Feasts*, 128–9.

This key is further clarified in 7:37 with the second temporal referent of the "last and greatest day of the festival."

Against this background of the Festival of Tabernacles and the Meribah sustenance, the Evangelist places the confrontation of Jesus providing the desired spiritual water in the unlocked Tabernacles memory.[42] Similar to the episode in John 6, this festival provides a positive super-ordinate group interpretation, demonstrating the desire for water and purity as a desirable quality. Here the evangelist presents Jesus as the fulfilment of this desire; rather than Moses' provision of water, Jesus becomes the "rock that must be struck" for provision.[43] This confrontation emphasises the in-group desire and adherence to this interpretation, thereby showcasing their identity as "true members" of the super-ordinate group. Conversely, the negative out-group response (7:41) is characterized by those who reject the desire for water and purity, and implicitly reject the Christological challenge; overall presenting another SAGA Type A argument.

John 19: The Trial of an In-Group Prototype

Finally, we will turn briefly to the trial scene of John 19. While this trial scene represents a complex narratively embedded social group argument, we may pick out some key pivots for analysis.[44] First, we see the Evangelist positively assessing the super-ordinate group: the desire for a king is an appropriate frame of reference (Exod 15:18, Jdg 8:23, 1 Sam 8:7), along with the framework of Messianic deliverance.[45] Second, the linking of Jesus with the kingly rule over Israel—and his subsequent death with the slaughter of Passover lambs—displays the in-group in a positive light.[46] But, the assessment of the out-group is strongly negative—contrasting with the super-ordinate group—finding its crescendo in "we have no king but Caesar" (19:15). Thus, the Ἰουδαῖοι in this scene self-exclude from the super-ordinate group, especially based on YHWH's regency.[47]

---

42. Kerr, *Temple of Jesus' Body*, 226.
43. Yee, *Jewish Feasts*, 82.
44. See further in Porter, *Johannine Social Identity Formation*, 136.
45. Kierspel, *The Jews and the World*, 70.
46. Keener, *John*, 1131.
47. Barrett, *Gospel According to St. John*, 546.

In this scene, the evangelist plays off the dual out-groups of Ἰουδαῖοι and Rome to coalesce the in-group with the super-ordinate group. Functionally, this aligns the Ἰουδαῖοι with Pilate and the Romans, portraying the out-group as not only dissonant with the super-ordinate group, but implicitly responsible for the events of 70 CE. This represents the strongest SAGA Type A argument in the Gospel and inscribes a clear separation of the out-group from the super-ordinate group. The Evangelist's series of social group arguments has built to its climax. By their declaration of Caesar's kingship, the out-group have removed themselves from membership of the super-ordinate group "Israel." In contrast, the super-ordinate group aspirations find their fulfilment in the in-group prototype—Jesus—and align the desires of the super-ordinate group "Israel" with the Christ-following in-group.

Can the Real Ἰουδαῖοι Please Stand up?

How then would a Johannine audience interpret these varied presentations of the Ἰουδαῖοι? If we ask "Can the real Ἰουδαῖοι please stand up?" we get a scene like that of *Spartacus*, as almost every group in the Gospel is identified with the Ἰουδαῖοι at some point.

However, through a Social Identity lens, the usage of the moniker Ἰουδαῖοι gains clarity in this variegation. The various contextual embedding of these groups emphasizes the difference in identification between the targets of the descriptor, to effect a considered social argument. To this end, the author utilizes the label in three primary constructions. We will describe these separately and then look at their interactions with the authors' social construal.

First, and most simply, Ἰουδαῖοι is used as a label for members of the super-ordinate group "Israel"; *pace* Philip Esler and Steve Mason.[48] We may further specify this as *the super-ordinate group consisting of those ascribing to the social memory of corporate Israel*.[49] Although this is a broad social group, it may be more precisely defined by considering the relevant fit characteristics. Super-ordinate groups will take the aspirations and identity of Israel—including memories of its traditions—as normative for their membership within the group. In the Fourth Gospel, we can easily

---

48. Mason, "Jews, Judaeans, Judaizing, Judaism"; Esler and Piper, *Lazarus, Mary and Martha*, 163; Esler, *Conflict and Identity*, 68.

49. Porter, *Johannine Social Identity Formation*, 141.

find these in the positive representations of cultic practices (Jn 2:6), the Temple (2:13), the festivals—as seen in many of the scene introductions, such as the "festival of the Jews" (5:1, 6:4 or 7:2)—and Mosaic patterned narratives.[50] Comparatively, the Evangelist often presents the Ἰουδαῖοι in contrast with other characters. We see a brief example with the ascription of the ethnic identity "Samaritan" to Jesus in John 8:48, and the earlier interaction with the Samaritan woman (4:7–9). These brief examples represent a broader comparative pattern of Ἰουδαῖοι through consistent comparison with an out-group.

Second, the most common usage of Ἰουδαῖοι is for describing an out-group of equal social hierarchy to the Evangelist's group (2:18, 5:10, 11:8). This usage of Ἰουδαῖοι as the out-group describes a logical subset of the broader super-ordinate group that uses the same name, as described above. Often this out-group is distinguished from the super-ordinate group via a social group argument portraying the out-group as distinct from the super-ordinate group "Israel."[51] The most blatant example of this comes with the ascription of Caesar as Lord in John 19, as the out-group (19:12,14) ascribe the title "King" to Caesar (19:15).

The final, and perhaps most interesting, use of the label Ἰουδαῖοι is the description of those who are re-categorizing from the super-ordinate group to the "Christ follower" in-group. Those in this category find themselves fitting both within the super-ordinate group, and the in-group, but in comparison with the out-group—all using the same label. We see this with the on-the-fence Ἰουδαῖοι of John 8:31–33 who later stop following Jesus to return to the super-ordinate group, the mixed report of those at Lazarus's tomb (11:45–46), or Nicodemus who moves from a liminal space to perhaps part of the in-group (19:39–40). Although infrequent, this is the most important category in the Fourth Gospel, as it highlights the social-category struggle and transference within the super-ordinate group. Simply put, this category highlights the intra-mural nature of the Ἰουδαῖοι disputes in the Fourth Gospel.

Conceiving of the "Real" Ἰουδαῖοι?

Given these variegated descriptions of the Ἰουδαῖοι how should we understand the social-group interactions in the Fourth Gospel? I suggest that

50. Sahlin, *Zur Typologie*.
51. Porter, *Johannine Social Identity Formation*, 142, esp. Fig 4.11.

this description of the social-identity considerations behind the description of the Ἰουδαῖοι has four primary outcomes for our reading of the social dynamics of the Fourth Gospel.

First, with relation to the polemic and animosity foregrounded in the Fourth Gospel: as noted above, these depictions often serve to distance the out-group Ἰουδαῖοι from both the Christ-following in-group and the super-ordinate group Ἰουδαῖοι. This is not to minimize the strong vitriol inherent in the polemics regarding the Ἰουδαῖοι, including their portrayal as murderers and children of the devil (8:44). However, the self-identification and social-group interaction in the text should inform our interpretation. Here the vitriol is mediated through near-social group dynamics, specifically intra-mural interactions between close sub-groups of a super-ordinate group.[52] Indeed, in this social context, the Fourth Gospel's vituperative polemic should be expected, as social groups need to define themselves in relation to their close neighbors, due to sharing significant similarities. We can see Pierre Bourdieu's observation on "symbolic violence" being played out, directed "against what is closest, which represents the greatest threat."[53] Within this context, the structured group arguments of the Fourth Gospel are powered by the intra-mural polemic. Furthermore, this would suggest that—similar to our other comparative literature—the Gospel itself is intended as a "reform movement" within the super-ordinate group.[54]

Second, what is the relationship between the Ἰουδαῖοι and the author's in-group? Through the lens of social identity theory, the out-group Ἰουδαῖοι is another group with equal social hierarchical status.[55] This is evident in the social group arguments, where they are often described as an out-group that fails to embody the super-ordinate group—as seen above. Portraying them as a dissonant sub-group of the super-ordinate group provides two comparisons, one with the in-group and one with the super-ordinate group. This culminates in John 19 where the authorial in-group is loyal to the presented "king of the Jews" while the out-group Ἰουδαῖοι, by their acclamation of Caesar as Lord (19:15), are presented as dissonant to not just the in-group prototype, but also to the key super-ordinate group belief of having no king but YHWH (Exod 15:18 / Ps

---

52. Williamson, *House of Israel*, 145.
53. Bourdieu, *Distinction*.
54. Porter, *Johannine Social Identity Formation*, 144.
55. Haslam, *Psychology in Organizations*, 25.

102:12). In this case, the Ἰουδαῖοι are described as a sub-group of the super-ordinate group Ἰουδαῖοι. However, they consistently do not display the positive attributes of the super-ordinate group but instead enact dissonant attributes (SAGA Type A); or, inversely, embody negative attributes of the super-ordinate group and reject positive constructs (SAGA Type B). This usage of the Ἰουδαῖοι constructs a competitive out-group to the authorial group: two groups competing for the "proper" inheritance of the super-ordinate group "Israel."[56] Titus' cataclysmic destruction of Jerusalem in 70 CE is likely the watershed for this intra-mural contest; as it is in other contemporary presentations.

Third, the Ἰουδαῖοι is not only an out-group to the Evangelist's "Christ-follower" in-group. Throughout the Gospel, we find descriptions of Ἰουδαῖοι passing through permeable boundaries between the groups; from the out-group or super-ordinate group to the in-group. Furthermore, even Jesus is described as one of the Ἰουδαῖοι (4:9, 22, 18:35). The Evangelist uses this permeability to emphasize the social stability of the in-group and the rightful continuance of the super-ordinate group—as groups with porous boundaries are internally socially stable groups.[57] Nicodemus provides a quintessential example, moving from enquiring at night in John 3 and muted advocacy in John 7, culminating in secret association in John 19. However, some examples highlight the temporary nature of these porous boundaries such as the change in membership in John 6 or 8. This recognizes the social reality that, while the in-group may be socially stable internally, there is a socially unstable relationship with the out-group.[58] Overall, this highlights the fragile interactions between the two groups both described as Ἰουδαῖοι.

However, the final—and probably most surprising—portrayal of the Ἰουδαῖοι involves, not just the description of the out-group or the super-ordinate group, but of the Christ-following in-group standing up as well. Through the Johannine use of super-ordinate group social schematic narratives and structured group arguments with the out-group over their *proper* interpretation, the Evangelist constructs their group as a possible future social identity fulfillment of the super-ordinate group.[59] Throughout the Gospel, the in-group is described as embodying the

---

56. Porter, *Johannine Social Identity Formation*, 145.
57. Haslam, *Psychology in Organizations*, 25.
58. Haslam, 24.
59. Porter, *Johannine Social Identity Formation*, 145.

positive characteristics of the super-ordinate group in contrast to the out-group—such as the disciples remaining with Jesus in John 6 as a re-presentation of the manna provision in Exodus 16. The repeated nature of these constructions builds a cumulative picture of the in-group as the proper representation of the super-ordinate group, concluding in the ascription of the title "King of the Jews" to Jesus (19:19). This construal makes the in-group the rightful inheritors and interpreters of the social memory of the super-ordinate group.

Conclusion

Thus—shockingly—in the Evangelist's construction of the social-group interaction in the Fourth Gospel, the authorial in-group is construed as the proper inheritors of the Ἰουδαῖοι; or, conversely. the in-group ultimately claims to be the Ἰουδαῖοι.[60] Some may object that this is nonsensical, given the conflation of the moniker Ἰουδαῖοι with the out-group. However, the social group arguments and presented possible future identity of the Ἰουδαῖοι in the Fourth Gospel, indicates that this is a desired outcome. This future projection leads to the Jewish in-group "Christ-follower" embodying the proper representation of the super-ordinate group, to the exclusion of other challengers.[61]

While this may be surprising from a modern historical position, especially post-Shoah, it appears congruent with the social reality of the Fourth Gospel as a piece of post-Temple intra-mural political rhetoric, one where we have a host of Ἰουδαῖοι "standing up."

Bibliography

Ahearne-Kroll, Patricia D. "Joseph and Aseneth and Jewish Identity in Greco-Roman Egypt." University of Chicago, Divinity School, 2005.

Australia. Parliamentary Debates, § House of Representatives (2017). http://parlinfo.aph.gov.au/parlInfo/download/chamber/hansards/a2ed5e4b-78d1-48d8-8c31-324bfa714c4e/toc_pdf/Senate_2017_11_13_5728_Official.pdf;fileType=application%2Fpdf.

Barrett, C. K. *The Gospel According to St. John.* 2nd ed. Philadelphia: Westminster John Knox, 1978.

Borgen, Peder. *Bread from Heaven: An Exegetical Study of the Concept of Manna in the Gospel of John and the Writings of Philo.* Leiden: Brill, 1965.

60. Porter, 146.

61. In part, *pace* Reinhartz, *Cast Out of the Covenant.*

Bourdieu, Pierre. *Distinction: A Social Critique of the Judgement of Taste.* Translated by Richard Nice. Cambridge, MA: Harvard University Press, 1979.

Brett, Mark G. *Genesis: Procreation and the Politics of Identity.* OTR. London; New York: Routledge, 2000.

Campbell, Jonathan Goodson. *The Use of Scripture in the Damascus Document 1-8, 19-20.* New York: Walter de Gruyter, 1995.

Chanikuzhy, Jacob. *Jesus, the Eschatological Temple: An Exegetical Study of Jn 2,13-22 in the Light of the Pre-70 C.E. Eschatological Temple Hopes and the Synoptic Temple Action.* Leuven: Peeters, 2012.

Colautti, Federico M. *Passover in the Works of Josephus.* JSJSup 75. Leiden: Brill, 2002.

Coloe, Mary L. *God Dwells with Us: Temple Symbolism in the Fourth Gospel.* Collegeville, MN: Liturgical, 2001.

Dawson, David. *Allegorical Readers and Cultural Revision in Ancient Alexandria.* Berkeley: University of California Press, 1991.

Esler, Philip F. *Conflict and Identity in Romans.* Minneapolis: Augsburg Books, 2003.

Esler, Philip F., and Ronald Piper. *Lazarus, Mary and Martha: Social-Scientific Approaches to the Gospel of John.* Minneapolis, MN: Fortress, 2006.

Hakola, Raimo. *Reconsidering Johannine Christianity: A Social Identity Approach.* Florence: Taylor and Francis, 2015.

Haslam, S. Alexander. *Psychology in Organizations.* Thousand Oaks, CA: SAGE, 2004.

Josephus. *Jewish Antiquities, Vol II.* Translated by H. St. J. Thackeray and Ralph Marcus. LCL 490. Cambridge, MA: Harvard University Press, 1930.

———. *The Jewish War, Vol III.* Translated by H. St. J. Thackeray. LCL 210. Cambridge, MA: Harvard University Press, 1928.

Keener, Craig S. *The Gospel of John: A Commentary.* Grand Rapids, MI: Baker Academic, 2003.

Kerr, Alan. *The Temple of Jesus' Body: The Temple Theme in the Gospel of John.* JSNTSup 220. London: Sheffield Academic, 2002.

Kierspel, Lars. *The Jews and the World in the Fourth Gospel: Parallelism, Function, and Context.* Tübingen: Mohr Siebeck, 2006.

Mason, Steve. "Jews, Judaeans, Judaizing, Judaism: Problems of Categorization in Ancient History." *JSJPHRP* 38 (2007) 457–512.

Moloney, Francis J. "From Cana to Cana (Jn. 2:1–4:54) and the Fourth Evangelist's Concept of Correct (and Incorrect) Faith." *Salesianum* 40 (1978): 817–43.

Philo. *On Abraham. On Joseph. On Moses.* Translated by F. H. Colson. LCL 289. Cambridge, MA: Harvard University Press, 1935.

Porter, Christopher A. "'Hic Sunt Dracones:' Mapping the Rebellious Social Dynamics of Bel and the Snake from the Daniel and Joseph Competitive Court-Tales." *BTB* 51 (2021) 78–87. https://doi.org/10.1177/0146107921997107.

———. *Johannine Social Identity Formation after the Fall of the Jerusalem Temple: Negotiating Identity in Crisis.* BINS 194. Leiden: Brill, 2021. https://doi.org/10.1163/9789004469822.

Rapley, Mark. "'Just an Ordinary Australian': Self-Categorization and the Discursive Construction of Facticity in 'New Racist' Political Rhetoric." *BJSP* 37 (1998) 325–44. https://doi.org/10.1111/j.2044-8309.1998.tb01175.x.

Reicher, S. D. "The St. Paul's Riot: An Explanation of the Limits of Crowd Action in Terms of a Social Identity Model." *EJSP* 14 (1984) 1–21. https://doi.org/10.1002/ejsp.2420140102.

Reicher, Stephen, et al."Saving Bulgaria's Jews: An Analysis of Social Identity and the Mobilisation of Social Solidarity." *EJSP* 36 (2006) 49–72.

Reicher, Stephen D., et. "The Social-Identity Approach in Social Psychology." In *The SAGE Handbook of Identities*, edited by Margaret Wetherell and Chandra Talpade Mohanty. Thousand Oaks, CA: SAGE, 2010.

Reicher, Stephen, and Fabio Sani. "Introducing SAGA: Structural Analysis of Group Arguments." *Group Dynamics: Theory, Research, and Practice*, Research Methods, 2, no. 4 (December 1998) 267–84. https://doi.org/10.1037/1089-2699.2.4.267.

Reinhartz, Adele. *Cast Out of the Covenant: Jews and Anti-Judaism in the Gospel of John*. Lanham, MD: Lexington Books/Fortress Academic, 2018.

Sahlin, Harald Axel. *Zur Typologie Des Johannesevangeliums*. Uppsala Universitets Årsskrift. Uppsala, 1950.

Schenck, Kenneth. *A Brief Guide to Philo*. Louisville, KY: Westminster John Knox, 2005.

Tajfel, Henri. *Social Identity and Intergroup Relations*. Cambridge: Cambridge University Press, 1982.

Wacholder, Ben Zion. *Studies on the Texts of the Desert of Judah, Volume 56: New Damascus Document : The Midrash on the Eschatological Torah of the Dead Sea Scrolls: Reconstruction, Translation and Commentary*. Boston, MA: Brill Academic, 2007.

Wheaton, Gerry. *The Role of Jewish Feasts in John's Gospel*. Cambridge: Cambridge University Press, 2015.

Williamson, Clark M. *A Guest in the House of Israel: Post-Holocaust Church Theology*. Louisville, KY: Westminster John Knox, 1993.

Yee, Gale A. *Jewish Feasts and the Gospel of John*. Zaccheus Studies. Wilmington, DE: Michael Glazier, 1989.

5

Vines and Wines in First-Century Galilee
TAMARA LEWIT

Introduction

VINES AND WINE APPEAR prominently in several sections of the Gospel of John, but to twenty-first-century readers these topics do not have the same resonance which they would have had for his contemporary audience. During the first century CE in the Levant, and in succeeding centuries at least up to the Islamic conquests, tending grape vines and the processes of producing and drinking wine would have been a fundamental part of the daily lives of the entire population. At least 80 percent of the population lived in rural farms and villages where vine cultivation and wine production were major activities. Production was also often carried out in towns, where the population was involved in the transport, sale and mass consumption of wine. These factors form the essential background of John 2:1–10, 15:1–6, and 19:28–29. This essay will explain the practices and context which would have been obvious and a familiar part of daily life to John and to his first-century audience.

Vines

> I am the true vine, and my Father is the vinegrower [γεωργός]. ² He removes [αἴρει] every branch in me that bears no fruit. Every branch that bears fruit he prunes [καθαίρει] to make it bear

more fruit. . . . ⁶Whoever does not abide in me is thrown away like a branch and withers; such branches are gathered, thrown into the fire, and burned [καίεται] (Jn 15:1–6, NRSV).

The "vine" referred to in this metaphor is the grape vine, *vitis vinifera*. Originating from a wild plant native to Anatolia, it was cultivated in the Levant for millennia.[1] In ancient times, grapes were rarely eaten as table fruit, but rather were usually processed and their nutrients consumed as wine. The expansion and unified trade and communication network of the Roman Empire had stimulated large scale vine planting, commercial production and trade in wine around the Mediterranean by the first century CE. Written accounts, archaeological excavation of wine production sites, pottery kilns for the firing of clay wine-transport vessels (known as amphorae), and finds of such vessels distributed throughout the Empire, all attest the widespread and dominant nature of vine cultivation and wine production in the Mediterranean provinces.[2]

Evidence for wine production in the Syro-Palestine region in particular is extensive.[3] Vines were cultivated throughout the region, from Syria in the North to the Negev in the South, and from the fertile coastal area of Tyre to semi-arid inland and highland regions around Palmyra and Mount Carmel.[4] The first-century CE Jewish historian Josephus singles out the Lake Galilee region as rich in grapevines, claiming that "for ten months without intermission it supplies those kings of fruits, the grape and the fig," but also tells us that vines grew even in "part desert" regions.[5] In the Talmud, wines of Carmel, Sharon, Samaria, Tiberias and the area East of Jericho are named.[6] Some Syro-Palestinian wines were

---

1. Zohary et al., *Domestication of Plants*, 124–6.

2. See, for example, Kingsley, "The Economic Impact of the Palestinian Wine Trade," 50–51.

3. The geographic term "Syro-Palestine" is used by scholars of the ancient world to refer to the ancient region now encompassed by modern Israel and the Palestinian Territories, Lebanon, Jordan, Syria, and part of southern Turkey. In the first century the Roman province in which Galilee and Jerusalem were located was called *Iudaea*, but it was incorporated into a newly-named Roman province of *Syria Palaestina* from the second century.

4. Decker, *Tilling the Hateful Earth*, 139.

5. Josephus, *J. W.* 3.10.8.519; 3.3.3.45.

6. Frankel, *Wine and Oil*, 201–2.

considered high quality, listed among the best wines by the first-century CE Italian writer Pliny, and their fame endured up to the fifth century.[7]

While the physical remains of vineyards are rarely preserved in the archaeological record, the remains of wine processing equipment are, by contrast, durable and clearly evident in archaeological investigations. Processing equipment included stone or waterproofed treading floors, large fermentation vats, machinery with stone parts, and specially constructed rooms with identifiable spaces for processing—all of which survive well within the archaeological record and have been the subject of intensive study.[8] The presence of such installations serves as proxy evidence for the vineyards which provided the grapes for processing, and the size and capacity of vats can be used to calculate approximate quantities of grapes processed, and therefore the probable size of vineyards.[9]

Such wine-making equipment appears with great frequency at Roman period rural sites in Syro-Palestine, where it has been estimated that tens of thousands of installations existed.[10] In certain areas, including Galilee and the Jerusalem region, particularly large concentrations of wine-processing remains have been found. Many had a capacity for processing thousands of liters of wine per year.[11] An example is the agricultural settlement of Sumaqa, in the Carmel hills. Consisting of around twenty dwelling complexes, a synagogue, and workshops for processing agricultural products, the settlement of around 1000 people developed in the second century on a site previously occupied in the first century.[12] At least five wine-making areas were identified in the initial excavations, but twelve additional workshops with thirty large stone rollers have since been identified as specialized production sites for sweet raisin wine. The community must have produced hundreds of thousands of liters of wine annually, and a large proportion of the surrounding terraced land must have been dedicated to vineyards.[13] Wine was also produced in towns:

---

7. Pliny the Elder *Nat.* 14.9.7 lists wine from the region of around Tyre as among the most esteemed. Their quality is still noted by Sidonius in fifth-century Gaul (*Carm.* 17.15–16).

8. Major works on this region include, for example, Frankel, *Wine and Oil*; Brun, *Archéologie du vin*; Ayalon et al., *Oil and Wine Presses*.

9. For example, Van Limbergen, "Figuring Out the Balance," 169–90.

10. Frankel, *Wine and Oil*, 51.

11. Kingsley, "The Economic Impact," 49; See also Brun *Archéologie du vin*, 124–5.

12. Dar, *Sumaqa*, 16, 139–43.

13. Dar, *Sumaqa*, 77, 100, 107; Van Limbergen, "Changing Perspectives," 309, 314;

for example, fourteen wine-processing installations existed in the small town of H. Castra near the western flank of Mt. Carmel.[14] Many other sites in Syro-Palestine also produced wine without recourse to such complex workshops, simply through treading grapes on a sloping surface which drained into a fermentation vat, a method capable of extracting the majority of juice from the grapes.[15] Vineyards and wine-making were thus a dominant and pervasive feature of Syro-Palestinian life under the Roman Empire.

Care of vineyards was one of most intensive elements of farming work, demanding careful planning, concentrated labor, and skill, with nothing left to chance. "[L]et us plant our vineyards with great resolve and tend them with greater zeal," writes Columella in his first-century CE agricultural manual.[16] With these words, he encapsulates the dominance of vine cultivation within Mediterranean farming and the intensive care which vines demand of their cultivators. Grape vines require year-round and intensive labor, including trenching, pruning, protection from frost, shaping, digging, clearing, and maintenance of support structures. Work on vines appears in every month of the farm calendar in the *Geoponika*, a summary of Greco-Roman agricultural knowledge based on both western and eastern Mediterranean sources,[17] and is also frequently referred to in the Talmud.[18] Thus John's metaphor of vine care would have had profound resonance for his contemporary audience.

Pruning is an essential part of vine-growing, ensuring both the quality and quantity of the grapes borne by the vines. The natural habit of *vitis vinifera* is to produce luxuriant leaf-growth and a proliferation of fruit which is consumed by birds and animals before it fully ripens. The excessive fruit production also results in years of poor fruiting. In order to produce a consistent annual crop of high quality, fully-ripened grapes

Kingsley "Economic Impact," 72. Note that Dar's and Kingsley's calculations of the quantity of wine production do not include the 12 "workshops."

14. Yeivin and Finkielsztejn, "Wine and Oil Presses at H. Castra," 105–18.

15. Frankel, *Wine and Oil*, 49–56.

16. Columella, *Agr.*. 4.4.1.

17. Books 4, 5, 6, 7 and 8 (of 20) are dedicated to vines and wine production. The same is true of Palladius' fourth-century agricultural calendar, with the sole exception of June: Palladius *Op. agr.* 2.1, 10–13, 3. 9–16, 29–30, 4.1, 7, 5.2, 6.2, 4, 8.1, 9.1–3, 10.1, 11, 17–18, 11.4–7, 9, 12.2–4, 9–10, 13.2. Columella devotes most of book 3 (11–21) and the whole of book 4 to vine care.

18. Goor, "The History of the Grape-Vine," 55. See also White, *Roman Farming*, 231–66.

that contain enough sugars to ferment for making wine, two distinct procedures of pruning and thinning are required, both of which are referred to in John 15:1–2.

During the dormant season, shoots that will not produce fruit must be severely cut away. This process is referred to in John 15:2 as the removal of unfruitful branches, using the verb αἴρει ('cleanse'). Even some fruiting canes must also be cut off, in order to train the vine and prevent the over-fruiting which results in a poorer long-term crop.[19] Columella dedicates innumerable pages to the details of such vine pruning, summarizing its importance thus: "the luxuriant vine... is wasted with too much wood and leaves. A weak vine, when it is burdened with too much fruit, is weakened... Guardianship of vines must be constant."[20] Pruning is a highly skilled task, requiring knowledge and careful judgement, although perhaps not everyone followed the advice reported in the *Geoponika* that "The vine will bear well if the vine-pruner wears an ivy wreath"![21] John 15:1 refers to this skilled worker simply as γεωργός, a word which encompasses any kind of farmer or worker on the land.[22] Columella uses both the equivalent Latin term *rusticus*, and the more precise *vinitor*, designating an expert vine-worker.[23]

A separate process of thinning must be carried out as grapes begin to grow. Excess foliage needs to be removed, and a judgement must be made as to how much fruit can be carried by the vine. Some fruiting shoots must be removed to ensure full ripening and the quality of the crop.[24] This process is referred to in John 15:2 as pruning every branch to make it bear more fruit, using the verb καθαίρει ("purify"). The process is again set out in detail by Columella:

> Therefore it is the part of an intelligent vine-dresser, and one especially expert, to take stock and consider in what places he should allow the growth of firm wood for the year, and to remove not only the branches that are destitute of buds, but fruitful branches as well, if their number has gone beyond proper

---

19. Thurmond, *From Vines to Wines*, 129–35.

20. Columella, *Agr.* 4.21.2–3; author's translation.

21. *Geoponika*, 5.24.

22. The translation "gardener," which appears in some translations, is most misleading. The Vulgate translation as "*agricola*" also means any kind of farmer or worker on the land.

23. Columella, *Agr.* 4.27.4–6.

24. Thurmond, *From Vines to Wines*, 127–9.

> bounds. ... For it is the business of a wise husbandman to consider whether the vine has bedecked itself with a greater quantity of fruit than it can carry to maturity. Accordingly, he will wish, not only to pick off superfluous foliage, which should always be done, but sometimes to shake off a part of the fruit so as to lighten a vine that is overburdened by its own productiveness.[25]

In his agricultural poem, the first-century Virgil vividly expresses the labor expended on these tasks: "Twice the shade thickens on the vines, twice weeds cover the vineyard with thronging briars. Heavy is either toil."[26]

The pruned wood must be carefully removed from the vineyard so as not to harbor disease or pests. Columella instructs: "When our vineyards are so put in order, we will hurry to clean them out, and to free them from prunings and deadwood."[27] Traditionally, these prunings have been used for fuel, and evidence indicates that they were put to the same good use in the ancient world. In wine-growing regions, large amounts of fuel were needed to fire kilns for the production of wine-transport vessels. Wood was an expensive item, and difficult to transport. An analysis of the fuel used in such kilns in Roman Egypt indicates the use of vine cuttings when available during the annual farming cycle.[28] Virgil (*Georg.* 2.408) refers to the vine prunings being "carried away [and] burned" (*devecta cremato sarmenta*).[29] This is the burning referred to in John 15:6 with the verb καίεται.

Wines

> On the third day there was a wedding in Cana of Galilee, and the mother of Jesus was there. [2] Jesus and his disciples had also been invited to the wedding. [3] When the wine gave out, the mother of Jesus said to him, "They have no wine." [4] And Jesus said to her, "Woman, what concern is that to you and to me? My hour has not yet come." [5] His mother said to the servants, "Do whatever

---

25. Columella, *Agr.* 4.27.4–5.
26. Virgil, *Georg.* 2.410–12.
27. Columella, *Agr.* 4.27.1; author's translation.
28. Möller and Rieger, "Necessity is the mother of invention," 71–86; Vine cuttings have also been found in fuel used for the bakery ovens at Pompeii: Coubray et al., "Of olives and wood," 121–34.
29. Virgil, *Georg.* 2.408; author's translation.

he tells you." ⁶ Now standing there were six stone water jars for the Jewish rites of purification, each holding twenty or thirty gallons. ⁷ Jesus said to them, "Fill the jars with water." And they filled them up to the brim. ⁸ He said to them, "Now draw some out, and take it to the chief steward [ἀρχιτρίκλινος]." So they took it. ⁹ When the steward tasted the water that had become wine, and did not know where it came from (though the servants who had drawn the water knew), the steward called the bridegroom" (Jn 2:1–9, NRSV).

The dominance of vine cultivation in Mediterranean farming reflects the vital importance of wine and other grape-based drinks within the Roman diet.[30] Wine was "the universal beverage for the ancient world,"[31] not only a luxury or festive product, but—in various forms—an integral part of the diet throughout society. Wine was also drunk by children and even infants were weaned onto wine.[32] When monasteries were founded in late antique Syro-Palestine, they typically produced their own wine for consumption within their community.[33] In the Roman Empire, wine was always heavily diluted with water, except when used for rituals. Approximately one part of wine was mixed with two or three parts of water, although preferences and recommendations for dilution vary.[34] This practice and the ratio of one part wine to three parts water is attested for the Jewish population in the Talmud.[35] Either heated or cold water chilled with ice could be used, according to personal taste and availability.[36] Since water could be contaminated and cause parasitic and bacterial infections,[37] there were important health benefits to adding any form of

---

30. In some provinces such as Britain, north-east Gaul and Egypt beer continued to be an important beverage: Van Limbergen, "What Romans ate," 16.

31. Decker, *Tilling the Hateful Earth*, 121.

32. Celsus, *Med.* 1.3.32; Soranus *Gyn.* 2.46 recommends that a six-month-old baby be weaned using sweet wine or raisin wine.

33. For example, at the monastery of Deir Ghazali just outside Jerusalem, which had two wine making rooms with crosses depicted in the plaster coating on the walls, on the sides of the wine vat, and in the mosaic of the floor on which the grapes were trodden: Avner, "Deir Ghazali," 160. Monks drank wine diluted, when sick, and during the liturgy: Taxel, *Khirbet Es-Suyyagh*, 213.

34. See, for example, Athenaeus *Deipn.* 10 (third century CE).

35. Frankel, *Wine and Oil*, 203.

36. Dunbabin, "Wine and Water," 116–41.

37. Pliny the Elder acknowledges the dangers of "unhealthy water" (*aquae insalubres*): *Nat.* 20.54.152; 31.29. For evidence for the presence in the Roman period of

wine to the drink. The acidic pH, tannic acid, and alcohol content of wine kill pathogens.[38] In the ancient world, fresh fruits and vegetables were unavailable for periods of the year, and wine (especially young wine) represented a storable fruit product.[39] Fermentation acts as a preservative by destroying bacteria, so wine provided a means for the nutritional and calorific value of grape products to be preserved and safely transported. In contrast, milk could not be preserved in liquid form, and even beer, made without hops, could easily spoil.[40]

Wine consumption per person has been estimated at an average of 140–180 liters per annum for males and perhaps half of that quantity for females, although the wealthier population could afford more (and better) wine, and the poor would drink less.[41] Based on this widely-used estimate, the Syro-Palestinian provinces would have consumed more than seventy million liters of wine per annum.[42] The description in John 2:6 of six jars each with a capacity of "twenty or thirty gallons" (ἀνὰ μετρητὰς δύο ἢ τρεῖς, equivalent to 78–117 liters each[43]), making a total of 600–700 liters which would be mixed with around 2000 liters of water, implies an abundant and generous quantity for consumption during the last part of a wedding feast, enough to supply hundreds of guests.

More than 200 varieties of both white and red grapes were known in the Roman Empire.[44] Wines were described by Pliny as "white, deep yellow, blood-red, and black" (*albus, fulvus, sanguineus, niger*).[45] Talmudic sources also refer to "red," "black," "dark" and "white" wines.[46] However, none of our textual sources mention the process of leaving grape skins in the juice for a period that gives the color to red wine,[47] suggesting that

parasites caused by drinking contaminated water, see Mitchell, "Human Parasites," 52.

38. Singleton, "An Enologist's Commentary," 75.

39. Singleton, "An Enologist's Commentary," 73 and discussion in Thurmond, *A Handbook*, 114–5. The nutrients contained in wine include iron and Vitamin C: Kingsley, "The Economic Impact," 46; Evers et al., "Vitamins in wine."

40. Broekaert, "Wine and other beverages," 142.

41. Tchernia, *Le vin*, 26; Broekaert, "Wine and other beverages," 145.

42. Kingsley "The Economic Impact," 49.

43. The liquid measure of a μετρητής was the largest measure of quantity, equivalent to approximately 39 liters.

44. Thurmond, *From Vines to Wines*, 57.

45. Pliny, *HN* 14.80; author's translation.

46. Frankel, *Wine and Oil*, 200.

47. White wine can be made from either red or green grapes, since the color of the

most Roman wine would have been what we call "white wine" today. The variety of colors mentioned in the sources could rather have been the result of aging or of spontaneous infiltration of color during treading.[48]

> Everyone serves the good (καλὸν οἶνον) wine first, and then the inferior (ἐλάσσω) wine after the guests have become drunk. But you have kept the good wine until now (Jn 2:10)

Wine and grape-based drinks encompassed a wide range of production methods and qualities. Fine and vintage wines, particularly those from specific regions, were prized—including some from Syro-Palestine, known for its sweet wine.[49] A *sextarius* (approximately half a liter) of high-quality wine is priced at around half a day's wages for a skilled laborer in Diocletian's *Edict on Maximum Prices*. However, the cheapest wine is approximately one quarter of this price, equivalent to the cost of eight eggs.[50] Very cheap wine sold for one small coin is listed for sale in a Pompeian bar.[51] Even slaves or farm laborers drank wine-like drinks made from the skins and pips of grapes soaked in water (called δευτέριος in Greek or *lora* in Latin), referred to in the Talmud, or a drink of water and goat's milk mixed with wine.[52]

The serving by a host of different quality wines was a stock point of reference in Roman literature, comedy, and social commentary. One cliché of such commentary was the rich man —or his servant, such as the ἀρχιτρίκλινος (literally, "chief of the dining room") in John—who served better quality wine to higher rank or favored guests, and inferior wine to others.[53] The first-century CE poet Martial refers to a miserly host serv-

wine is determined by this process, not the color of the grapes used.

48. See discussions in Tchernia, *Le vin de l'Italie*, 343–4; Thurmond, *From Vines to Wines*, 153–5; Harutyunyan and Malfeito-Ferreira, "Historical and Heritage Sustainability."

49. The wines of Tyre, Gaza and the Ashkelon region became popular and were very widely traded, especially from the fourth century: Kingsley "The Economic Impact"; Lantos et al., "Wine from the Desert."

50. *Edict Diocl.* II.1–9, VI.43, VII.2–7 (301 CE).

51. *CIL* IV 1679, which lists the cheapest at 1 *as*, or fraction of a *denarius*. Due to extensive inflation and changes in the coinage, however, it is difficult to compare this first-century evidence with that from the fourth century CE.

52. Varro, *Agr.* 1.54.3; Palladius, *Farming*. 14.1.2; Frankel, *Wine and Oil*, 202 for discussion of Talmud. Skins and pips of grapes soaked in water, then distilled, is used to make modern grappa.

53. E. g. Martial, *Epigrams* 13.121: "Don't drink it yourself, but let your freedman do so." Pliny the Younger, *Letters* 2. 6 describes a host serving three qualities of wine

ing fine wine mixed with "the worst," presumably to make it go further.[54] In a series of epigrams known as the *Xenia*, Martial also presents the components of a feast in the order in which they are served, beginning with the usual hors d'oeuvres (such as eggs and mushrooms). He then proceeds to the wines for the after-dinner drinking party, starting with the finest wines, followed by a humorous description of cheaper wines (13.106–125).[55] This seems to imply a practice referred to in John 2:1–10 of serving inferior wine to all the guests once they had become tipsy enough on a good one to blur their tastes!

> After this, when Jesus knew that all was now finished, he said (in order to fulfill the scripture), "I am thirsty." A jar full of sour wine [ὄξους] was standing there. So they put a sponge full of the wine on a branch of hyssop and held it to his mouth (Jn 19:28–29, NRSV)

A cheap grade of sour wine was called ὄξους in Greek and *acetum* in Latin, the same word as used for vinegar. The Roman terminology did not make a strict distinction between the two substances, which both consist of fermented grape juice affected by acetic acid bacteria, and are today defined by the percentage of acid present.[56] This ὄξους/*acetum* is listed in a bilingual Latin and Greek text originating in the first century as one of the varied qualities of wine which could be served at lunch.[57] Such sour wine, much diluted with water, was drunk by farm workers and was distributed as rations to Roman soldiers. This was the drink described as offered to Jesus on the cross.[58]

The very wide variation in the quality of Roman wines expressed by John in the phrases "good wine," "inferior," and "sour wine" (καλὸν οἶνον, ἐλάσσω, and ὄξους) resulted from the processes of production used in the ancient world, which differed in many respects from modern wine

to guests of different ranks; see discussion in Dunbabin, "Wine and Water." Lucian's description of a reversal of social norms during the Saturnalia festival includes the exclamation that the attendants (διάκονοι) will not favor anyone, but "all shall drink the same wine, and neither stomach trouble nor headache shall give the rich man an excuse for being the only one to drink the better quality" (Sat. 3.17).

54. Martial, *Epigrams* 1.18; author's translation.

55. See discussion in Leary, "Martial's Christmas Winelist," 34–41.

56. Tchernia, *Le vin de l'Italie*, 11–19, with Greek and Latin classical references. See also for example Vilela-Moura et al. "The impact of acetate metabolism," 271–80.

57. *Colloquia Monacensia-Einsidlensia* 8d-e.

58. John 19:29, Tchernia, *Le vin de l'Italie*, 14. The Vulgate uses the Latin *acetum*.

production. While modern wines are produced in sanitized and controlled conditions, and are treated with sulfur dioxide to kill undesirable microorganisms and then with cultured yeast to enhance fermentation, these methods were not available in the ancient world.[59] In these uncontrolled conditions, ancient wine making could easily go awry due to factors such as either too high or too low temperatures, or insufficient or excessive concentration of sugars. For this reason, Roman wine was far more liable to turn either sour or moldy, as revealed by rulings in Roman and Talmudic law.[60] The problem is summarized by Pliny: "It is a peculiarity of wine among liquids to go moldy or else to turn into vinegar; and whole volumes of instructions how to remedy this have been published."[61]

Grapes were picked when very ripe, in order to have sufficient sugars for fermentation, and thus contained less acid than is considered desirable in modern harvesting to prevent spoiling and stabilizing the taste. The timing of the harvest and its speed had a significant impact on the quality and quantity of wine, and Roman agricultural writers carefully advise readers to prepare equipment weeks beforehand, so that no time will be wasted, and how to decide when grapes are ready to harvest.[62]

Sixth-century CE mosaic from the pilgrim Church of Saints Lot and Procopius, Mount Nebo, Khirbet al-Mukhayyat, Jordan. Photo Jean Housen https://commons.wikimedia.org/wiki/Category:Church_of_SS._Lot_and_Procopius_(Khirbet_al-Mukhayyat)#/media/File:20100924_st_lot09a.jpg

59. Singleton, "An Enologist's Commentary," 76; Thurmond, *A Handbook*, 117; Harutyunyan and Malfeito-Ferreira, "Historical and Heritage Sustainability."

60. Frankel, *Wine and Oil*, 43.

61. Pliny, *HN* 14. 26.131. Cato (*Agr.* 148.1) also refers to saleable wine as "neither soured nor moldy" (author's translation) See discussion in Thurmond, *From Vines to Wines*, 178–82.

62. For example, Columella, *Agr.* 11.2.67–71.

Grapes were cut with a small, very sharp, curved knife or sickle almost identical to that still used up to the twentieth century. Such a knife can be seen in the hand of the figure near the base on the right side of the mosaic from the Church of Saints Lot and Procopius, Mount Nebo (figure 1).[63] The harvested grapes were placed in baskets to be transported by human workers or by donkey for processing, as seen in the same mosaic.[64] Grapes could be processed in any well-ventilated or open-air space, preferably shaded to prevent too-rapid fermentation—due to the ripeness of the grapes, the juice would have begun to ferment almost immediately.[65] The juice which flowed naturally from these just-picked grapes could be kept separately to be made into a very sweet wine.[66]

The next step in the ancient wine-making process was to tread the grapes, a process carried out on a treading floor. This could be simply a flat rock surface, or it could be a well-constructed raised, walled and sloped shallow trough, often sealed with lime mortar.[67] This floor or trough was known as a ληνός in Greek, *forus* or *calcatorium* in Latin, and is referred to as 'גת' (gt) in the Hebrew Bible and Talmud.[68] Roman images show this process being carried out by two or three adult men, stripped to loincloths and holding hands, sticks or ropes to prevent slipping. The men stamp with their feet on the grapes, sometimes to the rhythm set by a pipe-player, as shown in the mosaics from the Church of Saints Lot and Procopius, Mount Nebo, and from the town of Mérida (figures 1 and 2). The juice produced from only lightly trodden grapes could be used to make high quality sweet wine.[69] Vigorous treading over a number of hours would extract the majority of the juice, which is termed "must."[70]

63. White, *Agricultural Implements*, 96–97.

64. Described in *Geoponika* 11.

65. Dodd, *Roman and Late Antique Wine*, 35; Walsh and Zorn, "New Insights"; Thurmond, *From Vines to Wines*, 178. Good ventilation is essential due to the large amount of carbon dioxide released during fermentation.

66. "[T]he juice that flows down of its own accord before the grapes are trodden ... as soon as it flows is put into special flagons and allowed to ferment": Pliny the Elder *Nat.* 14.12.85; see also *Geoponika* 6.16.

67. Walsh and Zorn, "New Insights"; Frankel, *Wine and Oil*, 41–42; Dodd, *Roman and Late Antique Wine*, 32.

68. White, *Farm Equipment*, 130–31; Frankel, *Wine and Oil*, 185–86; Amouretti and Brun, *La production du vin*, 587.

69. *Geoponika* 6.16; Columella, *Agr.*. 12.27, 12.41.

70. While ancient sources do not tell us how long treading lasted, twentieth-century comparisons suggest a period of several hours: Frankel, *Wine and Oil*, 41.

The must flowed from the treading floor into large vats for several days of rapid initial fermentation, before its longer secondary fermentation in terracotta pots or vats. It should be noted that the ληνός referred to in Revelation 14:19–20 is not a "wine press," as it is invariably translated (for example in the NRSV). A wine press was a specialized machine termed πιεστήρ, used for processing trodden grape pulp enclosed in baskets, as explained below. The ληνός in Revelation is a treading floor, onto which—as the New Testament text describes—the newly-harvested grapes would be thrown to be trodden (ἐπατήθη).[71]

Figure 2: Third-century CE mosaic from
the House of the Amphitheatre, Mérida, Spain. Photo doalex
https://commons.wikimedia.org/wiki/File:Mosaico_en_la_Casa_del_Anfiteatro_
de_Merida.jpg]

71. This is also the case for the reference to wine making in Isaiah 63.2–3, as is abundantly clear from its similar reference to treading and its use of the term "gt." The Vulgate translation of Revelation 14:20 uses the term "trodden" (*calcatus est*) but translates ληνός equally incorrectly as *lacus*, a term which means not the treading floor but the deep vat into which the grape must flows as a result of treading: White, *Farm Equipment*, 158; Amouretti and Brun, *La production du vin*, 593. The Vulgate is faithfully translated into the English "wynefat" by Tyndale, but in the Wycliffe translation the Vulgate *lacus* becomes "lake," an alternative meaning of the Latin word but incorrect in the context of winemaking. Both the Latin translation *lacus* and the English translation "wine press" make nonsense of the phrase ἐπατήθη ἡ ληνός, since neither a vat nor a press can in any way be trodden, a process carried out on the treading floor. The mosaic from Mérida (figure 2) shows how the must (or blood, in Revelation) would flow from the treading floor into a container such as a vat.

Many ancient wine-making installations produced wine from treading alone.[72] However to maximize production and produce cheaper, lower quality wines, the trodden grape pulp could be collected, placed into flat baskets, and compressed further to extract more juice in a large specialized machine termed a "press" (πιεστήρ in ancient Greek and *prelum* or *torcular* in Latin terminology).[73] These machines first appeared in the Syro-Palestine region from around the late second to early first millennium BCE. They consisted of a massive wooden beam several meters in length, held in place by robust stone pillars or a wall-built niche, and weighted with large stone weights. In the first century CE, such machines were in wide use in this region, usually employing multiple cylindrical or bell-shaped weights approximately one meter in height, and each weighing around 600–800 kg, which were raised by rope winches attached to the beam (see figures 3 and 4).[74]

72. For which there is abundant archaeological evidence, and as described, for example, in Palladius' fourth-century agricultural manual (*Op. agr.* 1.18) which gives a detailed description of a winery with a treading floor and fermentation equipment.

73. Amouretti and Brun, *La production du vin*, 587; White, *Farm Equipment*, 113.

74. Frankel, *Wine and Oil*, 62–67, 99–101; Lewit and Burton, "Wine and Oil Presses," 97–99. Note that exact the same types of press were used for both wine and oil making.

Figure 3: A reconstructed oil press of a type used from the Hellenistic to late antique period, at Maresha, near Jerusalem, Israel. Photo chai https://ceb.wikipedia.org/wiki/Tel_Maresha#/media/Payl:Beit_Guvrin_4.JPG

While the wooden beams have not survived in the archaeological record, the stone parts attest the widespread presence of such presses. These very large machines, used only for a short season during the wine harvest, represented a considerable investment in space, materials, and resources, and further indicate the importance of wine production. After the first pressing, the compressed grape solids would be cut apart and again placed in baskets to be pressed a second time. After pressing, the grape residue of skins and flesh was then added to water to produce the poorest quality weak wine for slaves, as described above, or used as animal fodder.[75] The must produced from a second pressing was kept separate from the better quality must from treading and first pressing, and fermented separately to make inferior wine.[76]

---

75. See above, and *Geoponika* 6.13.
76. Varro, *Agr.* 1.54; Columella, *Agr.* 12.36.

Figure 4: Limestone press weight stone of a type used from the Hellenistic to late antique period, probably from the Galilee. Photo courtesy of Eretz Israel Museum, Tel Aviv, Israel.

A specific process was used in the Syro-Palestine region to produce a particular sort of sweet raisin wine: the grapes were first semi-dried in the sun for several days to increase the sugar to water ratio, and resulting alcohol content. This is recorded in both Roman sources and in the Talmud.[77] Stone rollers seem to have been used for crushing the harder-skinned semi-dried grapes, which would have resisted simple treading. These rollers are found at wineries in regions noted for the production of raisin wine, including the Mount Carmel in Galilee, Samaria, and Jerusalem regions, as well as northern Syria.[78] Such raisin wine was a highly regarded product. Due to its higher sugar and alcohol content, it was less likely to spoil, and aged well.[79] It was prized by local Jewish communities in Levant, and used in ancient Passover celebrations.[80] This may possibly be the "good wine" referred to in John 2. Even today, sweet "Kosher Carmel" wine from the same region is still selected by Jews worldwide for festive occasions such as the sabbath and Passover.

The grape harvest was the focus of the agricultural year and a time of intense and rapid work, lasting several weeks and drawing on every available source of labor including the entire community and/or hired laborers.[81] It was also an occasion for great festivity.[82] The second-century CE novel *Daphnis and Chloe* (set on the island of Lesbos) describes the busy preparations, the eponymous teenaged shepherd and goatherd leaving their animals to join the harvest, and the festive (and bawdy) atmosphere:

> With the fruit season now at its peak and vintage-time drawing near, everyone was busy on the farms. Some repaired wine treading troughs, some scrubbed jars, some plaited baskets; someone saw to a small sickle for cutting clusters of grapes, someone else to a stone fit for crushing the juice from the clusters, another to a

---

77. Van Limbergen "Changing Perspectives on Roller Presses," 318.

78. Van Limbergen "Changing Perspectives on Roller Presses," 309.

79. Van Limbergen "Changing Perspectives on Roller Presses," 316.

80. Dodd, *Roman and Late Antique Wine*, 62.

81. Cato (*Agr.* 11) recommends 40 grape-harvesting knives for a vineyard normally farmed by 10 men; while Columella (*Agr.* 1.17.1–4) specifies that additional hired men are needed for the wine harvest.

82. Brun *Le vin et l'huile*, 45–46.

dry willow twig, pounded into shreds, by whose light the must[83] could be drawn after dark. So Daphnis and Chloe stopped tending their goats and sheep and lent the others a helping hand: he hoisted bunches of grapes in baskets, dumped them into the treading troughs and trod them, and collected the wine into the jars, while she made meals for the vintners, poured them a drink of more mature wine, and harvested the fruit from the vines nearer the ground ... the women who had been called in from the nearby farms to lend a hand cast glances at Daphnis and praised him ... one of the more forward ones even kissed him ... Meanwhile the men in the treading troughs flung manifold compliments at Chloe and pranced madly about her.[84]

In this passage, we see that every person in the community has a role: while the men tread the grapes, Chloe, as a young female, harvests only the vines closest to the ground and prepares food for the harvesters.[85] A nineteenth-century account describes the town of Hebron as deserted when all its inhabitants flock to the vineyards to harvest the grapes.[86] Even the elite were involved: the first-century CE aristocrat Pliny the Younger describes visiting his country estate for the grape harvest, to "pick a grape, look over the press, taste the grape juice in the vat,"[87] as does the second-century Emperor Marcus Aurelius: "We put ourselves to work picking grapes, and we sweated and we celebrated".[88]

During the fermentation process which followed this harvesting, treading and pressing of the grapes, innumerable additives were used to flavor the wine to counteract the uncontrolled conditions which could affect quality, turning the wine sour or moldy. These included sugary boiled grape-juice, salt, marble dust, gypsum, pine resin, shellfish shells, olive oil, and—less alarmingly—herbs or spices.[89] Temperature fluctuations or other mishaps during fermentation, traces of lees remaining in

83. "Must" is the grape juice produced by treading (see above).

84. Longus, *Daphn.* 2.1-2. Translated by J. Henderson, with my own correction of the translation of "ληνοῖς" to "treading troughs" throughout.

85. See discussion of roles in Lewit, "Young children."

86. Robinson and Smith, *Biblical researches*, vol. I, 314.

87. Pliny, *Letters.* 9.20.2.

88. Fronto, *Correspondence* Vat. 185; author's translations.

89. Bouvier, "Recherches sur les goûts"; Thurmond, *From Vines to Wines*, 176-88; discussion of the chemical effects of additives in Komar, *Eastern Wines*, 83-86. Extensive and detailed recipes for such additives appear in every Roman farm manual – for example, Columella, *Agr.*. 12.19-20; summarized in *Geoponika* 7. 12-17.

the liquid, and storage and transport in poorly-sealed pitched terracotta containers (see figure 5) all caused further wide variations in quality. This is brought home by Columella's advice to the wine maker watching over his fermenting must: "If any creature has fallen into the must and died there, such as a snake or a mouse or a shrew-mouse, in order that it may not give the wine an evil odor, let the body . . . be burnt and its ashes when cool be poured into the vessel into which it had fallen and stirred in with a wooden ladle; this will cure the trouble"![90] It is probable that most Roman wines were drunk within the year, and only the very best could be aged, due to their tendency to spoil.[91]

Figure 5: Wine being transported in amphorae. Late antique church mosaic, Samuel and Saidye Bronfman Archaeology Wing in the Israel Museum in Jerusalem. Photo Yoav Dothan
https://en.wikipedia.org/wiki/Gaza_Jar#/media/File:Samuel_and_Saidye_Bronfman_Archaeology_WingDSCN4921.JPG

Each of the processes described, and the varied options which could be selected, would affect the quality of wines or grape-based drinks produced. The ancient audience of John 2:10 and 19:28–29 would have been acutely aware of the different types of wine referred to, and their respective significance within the structures of civilian and military life.

---

90. Columella, *Agr.* 12.31.
91. Thurmond, *From Vines to Wines*, 189.

Conclusion

Wine and the care of grapevines were fundamental elements of life for people in the first century CE, in all Mediterranean regions and particularly in Syro-Palestine. The cultivation and harvesting of the vine consumed a large proportion of time and effort for people of all ages and many levels of society in the countryside, and sometimes even in towns, and the livelihoods of many depended on its successful conduct. Pruning a vine was an activity which all John's audience would instantly have recognized as fundamental to life. Wine of many different qualities was the dominant and essential drink within the diet of all ages and ranks, added to water to prevent illness and provide nutrients. Its variations in quality—sweet or sour, fine or inferior—played a clear social role in distinguishing soldier from civilian, rich from poor, the generous from the stingy. These practices and context would have been a prominent part of daily life to John and to his first-century CE audience.

Bibliography

Amouretti, Marie-Claire, and Jean-Pierre Brun, eds., *La production du vin et de l'huile en Méditerranée. Oil and Wine Production in the Mediterranean Area.* Paris: Boccard, 1993.

Athenaeus. *The Learned Banqueters.* Translated by S. Douglas Olson. LCL 274. Cambridge, MS: Harvard University Press, 2006–2008.

Avner, Rina. "Deir Ghazali: A Byzantine Monastery Northeast of Jerusalem." *'Atiqot* 40 (2000) 25–52 (Hebrew), 160–61 (English summary).

Ayalon, Etan, Rafael Frankel, and Amos Kloner, eds. *Oil and Wine Presses in Israel from the Hellenistic, Roman and Byzantine Periods.* Oxford: Archaeopress, 2009.

Bouvier, Michel. "Recherches sur les goûts des vins antiques." *Pallas* 53 (2000) 115–33.

Broekaert, Wim "Wine and other beverages." In *The Routledge Handbook of Diet and Nutrition in the Roman World*, edited by Paul Erdkamp and Claire Holleran, 140–149. London: Routledge, 2018.

Brun, Jean-Pierre. *Archéologie du vin et de l'huile dans l'Empire romain.* Paris: Errance, 2004.

———. *Le vin et l'huile dans la Méditerranée antique.* Paris: Errance, 2003.

Cato. *On Agr.* Translated by William Davis Hooper, revised by Harrison Boyd Ash. LCL. Cambridge, MS: Harvard University Press, 1934.

Columella. *On Agriculture.* Translated by Harrison Boyd Ash. LCL. Cambridge, MS: Harvard University Press, 1941.

The Colloquia of the Hermeneumata Pseudodositheana. Edited with introduction, translation and commentary by Eleanor Dickey. Cambridge: Cambridge University Press, 2012–2015.

Coubray, Sylvie et al. "Of Olives and Wood: Baking Bread in Pompeii." In *Fuel and Fire in the Ancient Roman World*, edited by Robyn Veal and Victoria Leitch, 121–34. Cambridge: McDonald Institute for Archaeological Research, 2019.

Dar, Shimon. *Sumaqa. A Roman and Byzantine Jewish Village on Mount Carmel, Israel*. Oxford: Archaeopress, 1999.

Decker, Michael. *Tilling the Hateful Earth*. Oxford: Oxford University Press, 2009.

Dodd, Emlyn. *Roman and Late Antique Wine Production in the Eastern Mediterranean: A Comparative Archaeological Study at Antiochia ad Cragum (Turkey) and Delos (Greece)*. Oxford: Archaeopress, 2020.

Dunbabin, Katherine M. D. "Wine and Water at the Roman Convivium." *JRA* 6 (1993) 116–141.

Evers, Marie Sarah et al. "Vitamins in Wine: Which, What For, and How Much?" *CRFSFS* 20 (2021) 2991– 3035. https://doi.org/10.1111/1541-4337.12743

Frankel, Rafael. *Wine and Oil Production in Antiquity in Israel and Other Mediterranean Countries*. Sheffield: Sheffield Academic, 1999.

Fronto. *Correspondence*. Translated by C. R. Haines. LCL. Cambridge, MS: Harvard University Press, 1919.

Geoponika. Farm Work. Translated by Andrew Dalby. London: Prospect Books, 2011.

Josephus. *Jewish War*. Translated by H. St. J. Thackeray. LCL. Cambridge, MS: Harvard University Press, 1927–1928.

Goor, Asaph. "The History of the Grape-Vine in the Holy Land." *EBot* 20 (1966) 46–64.

Graser, Elsa, R. "The Edict of Diocletian on Maximum Prices." In *An Economic Survey of Ancient Rome*, edited by Tenney Frank, vol. V. Baltimore: The Johns Hopkins Press, 1940.

Harutyunyan, Mkrtich and Manuel Malfeito-Ferreira. "Historical and Heritage Sustainability for the Revival of Ancient Wine-Making Techniques and Wine Styles." *Beverages* 8 (2022) https://doi.org/10.3390/beverages8010010.

Kingsley, Sean. "The Economic Impact of the Palestinian Wine Trade in Late Antiquity." In *Economy and Exchange in the East Mediterranean during Late Antiquity*, edited by Sean Kingsley and Michael Decker, 44–68. Oxford: Oxbow Books, 2001.

Komar, Paulina. *Eastern Wines on Western Tables*. Leiden: Brill, 2020.

Lantos, Sara et al. "Wine from the Desert: Late-Antique Negev Viniculture and the Famous Gaza Wine." *NEA* 83 (2020) 56–64.

Leary, T. J. "Martial's Christmas Winelist." *G&R* 46 (1999) 34–41.

Lewit, Tamara. "Young Children in the Roman Farming Economy (Western Mediterranean): Evidence, Problems and Possibilities." In *Divergent Economies in the Roman World. Holistic Views on Habitual and Aberrant Practices (300 BC-AD 300)*, edited by Dimitri Van Limbergen et al.. London: Palgrave Macmillan, forthcoming.

Lewit, Tamara and Paul Burton. "Wine and Oil Presses in the Roman to Late Antique Near East and Mediterranean: Balancing Textual and Archaeological Evidence." In *Stone Tools in the Ancient Near East and Egypt. Ground Stone Tools, Rock-cut Installations and Stone Vessels from Prehistory to Late Antiquity*, edited by Andrea Squitieri and David Eitam, 97–110. Oxford: Archaeopress, 2018.

Longus. *Daphnis and Chloe*. Translated by Jeffrey Henderson. LCL. Cambridge, MS.: Harvard University Press, 2009.

Lucian. *Saturnalia*. Translated by K. Kilburn. LCL 430. Cambridge, MA.: Harvard University Press, 1959.

Martial. *Epigrams*. Translated by D. R. Shackleton Bailey. LCL. Cambridge, MS: Harvard University Press, 1993.
Mitchell, Piers D. "Human Parasites in the Roman World: Health Consequences of Conquering an Empire." *Parasitology* 144 (2017) 48–58.
Möller Heike and Anna-Katharina Rieger. "Necessity is the Mother of Invention: The Fuel of Graeco-Roman Pottery Kilns in the Semi-arid Eastern Marmarica." In *Fuel and Fire in the Ancient Roman World*, edited by Robyn Veal and Victoria Leitch, 71–86. Cambridge: McDonald Institute for Archaeological Research, 2019.
Palladius *The Work of Farming*. Translated by John. G. Fitch. Totnes: Prospect Books, 2013.
Pliny the Elder. *Natural History*. Translated by H. Rackham. LCL. Cambridge, MS: Harvard University Press, 1938–1962.
Pliny the Younger. *Letters*. Translated by B. Radice. LCL. Cambridge, MS: Harvard University Press, 1969.
Robinson, Edward and Eli Smith. *Biblical Researches in Palestine, Mount Sinai, and Arabia Petraea*. Boston: Crocker & Brewster, 1841.
Sidonius. Poems. Letters. Translated by W. B. Anderson. LCL. Cambridge, MS: Harvard University Press, 1936.
Singleton, Vernon L. "An Enologist's Commentary on Ancient Wines." In *The Origins and Ancient History of Wine*, edited by Patrick E. McGovern et al., 67–78. Amsterdam: Gordon and Breach, 1996.
Taxel, Itamar. *Khirbet Es-Suyyagh. A Byzantine Monastery in the Judaean Shephelah*. Tel Aviv: Tel Aviv University, 2009.
Tchernia, Andrea. *Le vin de l'Italie romaine*. Paris: De Boccard, 1986.
Thurmond, David L. *From Vines to Wines in Classical Rome*. Leiden: Brill, 2017.
———.. *A Handbook of Food Processing in Classical Rome: For Her Bounty No Winter*. Leiden: Brill, 2006.
Van Limbergen, Dimitri. "Changing Perspectives on Roller Presses in Late Antique Northern Syria." *Syria* 94 (2017) 307–23.
———. "Figuring Out the Balance Between Intra-Regional Consumption and Extra-Regional Export of Wine and Olive Oil in Late Antique Northern Syria." In *Olive Oil and Wine Production in Eastern Mediterranean during Antiquity*, edited by Adnan Diler et al., 169–90. İzmir: Ege Üniversitesi Yayınları, 2015.
———. "What Romans Ate and How Much They Ate of It. Old and New Research on Eating Habits and Dietary Proportions in Classical Antiquity." *RBPH* 96 (2018) 1–44.
Varro. *On Agriculture*. Translated by William Davis Hooper, revised by Harrison Boyd Ash. LCL. Cambridge, MS: Harvard University Press, 1934.
Vilela-Moura, Alice et al. "The Impact of Acetate Metabolism on Yeast Fermentative Performance and Wine Quality: Reduction of Volatile Acidity of Grape Musts and Wines." *AM&B* 89 (2011) 271–80.
Virgil. *Eclogues. Georgics. Aeneid I-VI*. Translated by H. Rushton Fairclough. LCL. Cambridge, MS: Harvard University Press, 1978.
Walsh, Carey and Jeffrey R. Zorn. "New Insights from Old Wine Presses." *PEQ* 130 (1998) 154–61.
White, Kenneth D. *Agricultural Implements of the Roman World*. Cambridge: Cambridge University Press, 1967.

———. *Farm Equipment of the Roman World.* Cambridge: Cambridge University Press, 1975.

———. *Roman Farming.* Ithaca: Cornell University Press, 1970.

Yeivin, Ze'ev and Gerald Finkielsztejn. "Wine and Oil Presses at H. Castra." In *Oil and Wine Presses in Israel from the Hellenistic, Roman and Byzantine Periods*, edited by Etan Ayalon et al., 105–18. Oxford: Archaeopress, 2009.

Zohary, Daniel et al., *Domestication of Plants in the Old World. The Origin and Spread of Domesticated Plants in Southwest Asia, Europe, and the Mediterranean Basin.* 4th ed. Oxford: Oxford University Press, 2012.

Part II

Historical Interpretations

6

The Interpretation of John through Key Moments of Church History

Mark R. Lindsay

Introduction

In his magisterial study of the presbyter-heretic, Arius, Rowan Williams argues that those trinitarian debates that culminated in the Council of Nicaea in 325 CE were primarily exegetical, rather than dogmatic, in nature.[1] He is, no doubt, correct. However, his point should be extended through much of the rest of church history as well. Even today, the controversies around sexuality that threaten the unity of the Anglican Communion are essentially arguments over the legitimacy of competing biblical interpretations, and interpretive methods, rather than being debates about contrasting moral visions of the world. When the church has been riven by such exegetical controversies, the ground on which the battles have been fought has not infrequently been the Gospel of John. In this essay, I will consider three moments of church contestation, in which the demarcation of Christian orthodoxy was debated by reference to competing exegeses of small sections of John's Gospel. First, I will consider Origen's deployment of the Johannine prologue in his *Commentary on John*, as his way of articulating Christianity over against Gnosticism[2] and its "half-brother" Marcionism. Second,

---

1. Williams, *Arius*, 108.

2. It is widely accepted that "Gnosticism" is an unhelpful term that gathers within the one undifferentiated category a diverse range of religious and philosophical

I will explore the ultimately irreconcilable hermeneutics of Huldrych Zwingli and Martin Luther, in their 1529 disputation over John 6, and its utility for eucharistic theology. Finally, I will turn to a 1941 debate between Karl Barth and Emil Brunner, that centered upon the theological tense (past or present?) of John 4:22, and the implications of their respective arguments for church action on behalf of the persecuted Jews of Hitler's Europe.

Origen on the Johannine Prologue

Origen's reputation is undeniably tarnished. "The most learned and one of the profoundest thinkers of the early Church," he was nonetheless prone to idiosyncratic speculation.[3] Indeed, Origen was condemned as a heretic by the Second Council of Constantinople in 553 CE for his "impious writings."[4] And yet, it would be a mistake to side-line him too quickly. As Behr has observed, Origen was "the greatest theological luminary of his age," whose expertise was routinely called upon by episcopal conferences throughout the Mediterranean, at which he was asked both to "expound the faith and to examine the faith of others."[5]

Of particular interest is Origen's use of the Scriptures. Too frequently dismissed as an allegorist, as though that was his only hermeneutical method,[6] in fact Origen's methodology was intricately nuanced. In *First Principles*, Origen proposes a three-layered strata of meanings within the Scriptures. First, they instruct humanity as to ourselves and our context; second, the Scriptures occlude those meanings to those

---

worldviews. Part of the difficulty with the label is that "there is no true consensus on a definition of the category 'gnosticism' . . . " Insofar as it is an umbrella-term, the label seeks to do too much – and thus does too little. See Williams, *Rethinking "Gnosticism,"* 3–4. With this caveat, I will nevertheless speak of Gnosticism, simply because my argument is not about the appropriateness or otherwise of the term, but about Origen's debates with those who have been labelled "Gnostics."

3. See Berkhof, *Christian Doctrines*, 71; Bromiley, *Historical Theology*, 48–49.

4. See anathema XI of that Council, in which Origen is specifically named along with 'all other heretics.' Traditionally, a list of fifteen anathemas specifically directed against Origen has been attributed to this Council, in addition to the more general 11th anathema. See Percival, *Seven Ecumenical Councils*, 456, 458–9; Price, *Council of Constantinople*, 270–99.

5. Behr, "Introduction." In Origen, *First Principles I*, 1.xv–xvi.

6. See for example, McGrath, *Christian Theology*, 115–16; Boyarin, "Origen as Theorist," 39.

unwilling to search them deeply, and yet—even to the unwilling—they contain the benefit of moral instruction; and third, the Scriptures contain so many obvious "stumbling blocks" that all but the most willfully obtuse must recognize that deeper truths lie hidden within.[7] For our purposes, though, Origen's most important insistence is that the determining Subject of the whole of Scripture is Christ, whose words "are not only those which he spoke when he became . . . dwelt in the flesh" but also those words spoken through Moses and the prophets, in whom Christ equally dwelt.[8] As we will see, this christological imperative, which finds its most sustained account in his exegesis of the Johannine prologue, was critical to Origen's refutation of Marcionite and Valentinian Gnosticism.

According to Eusebius, Origen first encountered a form of gnostic heresy while completing his education under the patronage of an Alexandrian benefactress, who was also supporting a certain "Paul" from Antioch. Suspecting him of heresy, Origen sought to distance himself from Paul, "loathing" his teachings, and associating with him only "of necessity." Origen, however, could not avoid the Antiochene entirely.[9] Their enforced proximity, occasioned by having the same patron, meant that Origen became intimately acquainted with the form of Gnosticism that Paul was teaching. Soon, his own writings began to convey a profound understanding—and repudiation—of gnostic thought, with Marcion and Valentinus being especially anathema. Origen was particularly opposed to their denials that the God and Father of Jesus Christ was also the God of Israel and the creator of the world.[10] Determined to refute such errors, Origen turned to the prologue of John's Gospel.

Origen held the Fourth Gospel in particular esteem. While the entirety of the New Testament is, he said, "gospel"—in contrast to the Hebrew Scriptures—and the Synoptics are the "first-fruits" of all Scripture, the Gospel of John stands above them all as the "first-fruits of the Gospels," because it contains "the greater and more perfect expressions concerning Christ."[11] None of the Synoptic Gospels "revealed [Jesus']

---

7. Origen, *First Principles*, li.
8. Origen, *First Principles*, 11.
9. Eusebius, *History*, 6.2, 7–8.
10. Trigg, *Origen*, 7–8.
11. This priority given to John was not reflected in Origen's best-known work, *First Principles*. Completed the year before he began work on his John commentary, Origen refutes both Marcion, and Valentinus, as well as 'certain [other] heretics . . . ' Origen, *First Principles. Volume II*, 217. John 1:1–3 is cited against Marcion's theology of the

divinity as straightforwardly as John did."¹² Famously, Origen's determination of John's preeminence is not (only) because, as the last of the Gospels to be written, it completed and perfected what the other three lacked, but more particularly because of the Evangelist's privileged place alongside Jesus. Origen makes much of John's intimacy with Christ, as evidenced by his "leaning on Jesus' breast" (Jn 13:25)—a reference, argues Origen, to John's proximity to "the ground of Jesus' heart and . . . the inward meanings of his teaching."[13]

The opening section of the commentary is presented in a manner similar to the prefaces of contemporaneous philosophical commentaries.[14] It is not, however, "merely" a set of prefatory remarks. On the contrary, even in the introduction, Origen takes aim at heterodoxy. His objective in these first 89 paragraphs is to establish what he means by the term "gospel," discuss the extent to which the Old and New Testaments constitute that "gospel," and prove the preeminence of John as the exemplary gospel. Precisely here, he targets Marcionism. Marcion's infamy, of course, derives from his radical distinction between the Hebrew Bible and the Christian Scriptures; between the God of Israel and the God revealed through Jesus. He did not deny that the Hebrew God was divine. He did, however, insist that the angry God of Israel could not be identified with the God of grace personified in Jesus. That is, Marcion's worldview was inherently dualistic, in which an evil God—who created the world which was, thereby, itself evil—existed alongside a good God, who was the Father of Jesus Christ. Christ, as the manifestation of that good God, was therefore also logically docetic, without any physicality, in order that he not be tainted by the evil that was intrinsic to created matter.[15]

Part of Origen's response to Marcionism, which he prosecutes here in the opening part of his John commentary, was to christologically

---

created order. Origen, *First Principles II*, 243. But nowhere does Origen reference the prologue in any great detail. Matthew's Gospel, and St. Paul's letters to the Roman and Corinthian churches, are cited significantly more frequently. When Origen does reference the Johannine prologue, it is to emphasise the role of Christ in creation, his place as a mediator between God and humanity, and as a proof-text for the Son's co-eternality. See Origen, *First Principles II*, §§ 2.6.1, 2.9.4, 4.4.1 and 4.4.3.

12. Trigg, *Origen*, 109.

13. Origen, *Commentarius in Canticum*, 1.2.4). Cited in DeCock, *Gospel of John*, 48.

14. Trigg, *Origen*, 103.

15. See Kaatz, *Early Controversies*, 52.

re-unify the Scriptures. True, the Hebrew Bible cannot be self-evidently understood as "gospel," apart from a knowledge of Christ. "[T]he law of Moses is the *firstlings*," rather than the first-fruits. The "old Scripture is not gospel since it does not disclose but [only] heralds in advance."[16] Yet this is not the whole story. Whereas Marcion refused to allow any Christian appropriation of the Hebrew Bible, Origen insists that "there was a presence of Christ before his fleshly presence," and that the Patriarchs, Moses and Israel's prophets were recipients of it.[17] Of course, Origen does not thereby claim that such forerunners were in any sense Christian. Nevertheless, he does grant that, after Christ's incarnation, that mysterious presence of his within Hebrew history and Scripture is "clarified." Thus, "before Christ's presence, the law and the prophets did not possess the promise implied by the . . . gospel," because Christ had not yet appeared to clarify their mysteries. "Nonetheless, when the Savior became present, acting so as to embody the gospel, he made them all into gospel by the gospel."[18] In the light of the incarnation, therefore, the Hebrew Scriptures become more than simply non-promissory heralds, but true gospel, in which Christian truth can be apprehended.[19] Such a conclusion would have been impossible for Marcion, with his *Antitheses* having been written precisely to show the irreconcilability of the Hebrew and Christian Scriptures.[20]

Having established the christological unity of the two Testaments in the preface, Origen turns in the next section to a somewhat convoluted discussion of the term "beginning," from John 1:1. Here we see Origen's denunciation of another form of gnostic heresy. The Father, he insists, is the "beginning" of the Son. By this Origen contends, not that the Father had a temporal start-point, but that he is the "principle'" of the Son. He is that in accordance with which the Son is.[21] "It is not absurd to say that the God of the Universe is evidently a beginning . . . on the grounds that because the Father is the beginning of the Son . . . God is also, in an absolute sense, the beginning of existing things." This is proved by "in the

---

16. Origen, "Commentary," 107–8. Emphasis added.
17. Origen, "Commentary," 112.
18. Origen, "Commentary," 111.
19. This is consistent with his contention in section 4 of *First Principles*.
20. Kaatz, *Early Controversies*, 47–51.
21. By "principle," Origen means that reality in accordance with which something exists, or according to the form of which something corresponds. So, as Christ is the "image," or in the form of, "the invisible God" (Col 1:15), God is Christ's "principle."

beginning was the Word," understanding the Word as the Son, so that as a result of his being in the Father, he is said to be "in the beginning."[22] By the same token, the Son, as the "artisan" of all "fashioned" things, is in turn the "beginning" of all things, in that he is the principle according to which creation has come to be. That is to say, the Father is the originating principle of the Son, and the Son is the originating principle of creation, with both Son and creation taking their form in accordance with their respective principle.

This is not simply pedantry. Origen's argument demolishes any suggestion that there is a distinction between the Son of God, who is identified with Jesus Christ, and the God who stands at the head of all creation. This, it will be recalled, was understood by Origen to be one of the basic errors of Gnostic thought, in particular in its Valentinian form. Ismo Dunderberg has demonstrated that there was at least one stream of Valentinian Gnosticism in which the Creator-God is not only distinct from, and inferior to, his mother, Achemoth, but is also ontologically other than the "Savior"-figure, by whom this Creator-God needs to be converted from his spiritual and moral ignorance.[23] For Origen to insist, on the basis of John 1, on the necessary unity between an unbegotten creator and a Savior-Son, whose "beginning" is that same creator, was thus to proclaim a fundamental irreconcilability between Christianity and Valentinianism.

In two relatively short, albeit dense, sections of text, Origen thus expounds the opening verses of the Johannine prologue in a way that undermines the logical integrity of two influential heresies, Valentinian Gnosticism and Marcionism. Macauley's claim, that Origen's John commentary is "one of the most serious attempts at a systematic construction of a christological position in the history of Christian thought," is excessive.[24] Nevertheless, Origen does present a significant contribution to Patristic Christology, affirming christological orthodoxy in the face of already-anathematized alternatives. If he was determined to counter those heterodox claims that already lay outside the boundaries of the church, some of the later Reformation debates occurred *inter*-confessionally, and for more sacramental rather than doctrinal purposes. It is to one of those contests that we now turn.

22. Origen, "Commentary," 122.
23. Dunderberg, *Beyond Gnosticism*, 121–4.
24. Macauley, "Nature of Christ," 176.

Zwingli and Luther on John 6

Traditional historiographies of the European Reformation have typically foregrounded the breach between Rome and the magisterial reformers, precipitated in 1517 by Martin Luther's 95 Theses. However, despite the often fiery rhetoric, this ecclesial rupture was not the site of the most vitriolic arguments of the Reformation. Arguably the more brutal antagonisms were between the reformers themselves, not least Luther and his Swiss contemporary Huldrych Zwingli. In 1529, their mutual animosity became so entrenched that Philip of Hesse's last hopes of a united Protestant front against both Rome and the Emperor Charles V were destroyed. While the political occasion for this breach between Luther and Zwingli was the Marburg Colloquy of October 1529, and the theological cause their failure to agree on a definition of the eucharistic real presence, the exegetical distinction between them—on which their respective theologies were grounded—centered largely upon John 6:35–65.

The theological-philosophical background to this controversy was the nature of the Mass, and the legitimacy of the dogma of transubstantiation that had been dogmatized in 1215 at the Fourth Lateran Council.[25] In a treatise on the subject in 1518,[26] Luther had articulated a thoroughly Roman opinion. There, he affirmed that transubstantiation of the eucharistic elements was effected, and that that this was done through the ordained capacity of the priest. Through the dogmatic principle of *ex opere operato*, the sacrament was deemed to be effective simply by virtue of it having been administered validly, without any requirement that either the priest or the communicant be participating in faith. Over the next few years, Luther's position changed to better reflect his new understanding of justification. That justification not be understood as a meritorious act, the Mass had to become for him no longer something that is done (for example, by the priest), but something that is given (as a gift, by God).

---

25. The Fourth Lateran Council was convoked by Pope Innocent III in April 1215. Canon 1, *Caput firmiter*, expounded the Roman faith, including the following: "§3. There is one Universal Church of the faithful, outside of which there is absolutely no salvation. In which there is the same priest and sacrifice, Jesus Christ, whose body and blood are truly contained in the sacrament of the altar under the forms of bread and wine; the bread being changed *(transsubstantiatio)* by divine power into the body, and the wine into the blood, so that to realize the mystery of unity we may receive of Him what He has received of us."

26. Luther, "Sermo," 325–4.

Luther's first major assault upon the Roman sacramental system appeared in the second of his three major treatises of 1520, "The Babylonian Captivity of the Church."[27] In this "most influential and hated"[28] of Luther's tractates from that year, the reformer distinguished between the obtaining of forgiveness, which happens uniquely at the Cross, and the distribution of it, which takes place recurrently through the Eucharist.[29] Again, this shift of emphasis was to de-centralize the role of the priest, and re-centralize the gracious actions of God.

Not once in his critique of the Roman Mass, however, did Luther deny the corporeal presence of Christ in the eucharistic elements. He rejected the Aristotelian-Thomist dogma of transubstantiation, because it rested upon an overly-complex philosophical commitment, rather than upon the Word of God. As Herrmann says, "it [was] precisely the perceived lack of attention to Scripture ... that dr[ove] Luther's ire and polemic."[30] For Luther, the words of the scriptural narrative were plain, simple, and sufficient. Insofar as Jesus had said "This is my body, etc. ...," so must the elements *really be* Jesus' body and blood—not by virtue of Aristotelian metaphysical gymnastics, nor because the Fourth Lateran had dogmatized it, but because the living Word of God itself makes them so. Thus, "it is real bread and real wine, in which Christ's real flesh and real blood are present in no other way and to no less a degree than the [Thomists] assert ... [but who do so] without support of Scripture or reason ... "[31] This was the conviction that Luther took with him to Marburg in 1529.

---

27. Over four months in the second half of 1520, Luther wrote three explosive essays. "To the Christian Nobility of the German Nation" (June 1520); "The Babylonian Captivity of the Church" (October 1520); and "The Freedom of a Christian" (November 1520). It was the second of Luther's treatises that prompted Henry VIII to write *Assertio Septem Sacramentorum* ("In Defence of the Seven Sacraments") in 1521, and which in turn won him the title *Fidei Defensor* ("Defender of the Faith") from Pope Leo X.

28. Marius, *Luther*, 125.

29. Regarding the Mass as a sacrifice was, said Luther, "by far the most wicked abuse of all ... " Later in the treatise, he explained that: "The Mass is the promise or testament of Christ ... [Just] as distributing a testament or accepting a promise differs diametrically from offering a sacrifice, so it is a contradiction in terms to call the Mass a sacrifice, for the former is something that we receive and the latter is something that we give." Luther, "Babylonian Captivity," 38, 54.

30. Herrmann, Introduction to Luther, in "Babylonian Captivity, 1520," 10.

31. Luther, "Babylonian Captivity, 1520," 31.

Luther's Swiss contemporary, Huldrych Zwingli, however, had come to a different view. In 1524, Luther's former colleague at Wittenberg, Andreas Karlstadt, published three pamphlets in which he rejected any notion of Christ's real presence in the Mass. This was consistent with Karlstadt's increasingly mystical theology, according to which "body and spirit were antagonistic to each other."[32] Zwingli was persuaded by Karlstadt's reasoning and began to argue in his own sermons and writings that the words of institution ("This is my body, this is my blood …") must be understood figuratively, not literally. Both Zwingli and Karlstadt were also impressed by the humanist reasoning of the Dutch jurist Cornelius Hoen (1460–1524) who, in his treatise of 1525—*Epistola christiana admodum*—had argued that "is" must mean "signify."[33] According to Bart Spruyt, Zwingli had seized upon this hermeneutical discovery as "a great pearl."[34]

The liturgical consequence was that Zwingli became ever more convinced that the communion meal—he much preferred the term *Abendmahl* (Last Supper) to either Eucharist or Mass—is a simple act of remembrance, and not a vehicle of grace or a vessel of the divine body. "The Lord's Supper is a commemoration of Christ's death, not a remitting of sins."[35] This does not mean that he thereby thought the meal to be an "'empty' ritual, devoid of emotional or spiritual impact."[36] Nevertheless, if the bread and wine were signifiers of Christ's body and blood, rather than *being* those in any real sense, then their power was in pointing to Christ's atoning work and not in effecting its grace. As he argued in his 1525 *Commentary on True and False Religion*, just as the baptismal water symbolized the Holy Spirit's cleansing of a person's sins but did not effect it, neither did the eucharistic bread carry the salvation enacted by Christ's cruciform sacrifice, but only signified it.[37]

It was with these sharply divergent theologies of the eucharistic elements as their respective presuppositions that Luther and Zwingli traded

---

32. Marius, *Luther*, 166.

33. See Spruyt, "Wessel Gansfort," 22.

34. Spruyt, *Cornelius Henrici Hoen*, xii.

35. Zwingli, *True and False Religion*, 228. It is "a joyful commemoration . . . and thanksgiving" (200).

36. Euler, "Zwingli," 58.

37. Zwingli, *True and False Religion*, 181. Note that the 1525 commentary was to be understood as "outweighing" everything he had offered earlier on this theme. *True and False Religion*, 198.

rhetorical blows over the proper interpretation of John 6, with the key verse in the whole passage being, for both of them, John 6:63: "The Spirit gives life, the flesh counts for nothing." Again, the two approached the text with contrasting hermeneutics. For Zwingli, so critical was this passage as the interpretive key to the words of institution that he commenced his chapter on the Eucharist in *Commentary on True and False Religion* with a symbolic interpretation of this Johannine text. Referencing John 6:29, he insisted that the "food" to which Christ refers can only be the spiritual food of faith. Thus, "they are utterly wrong who think that Christ in this whole chapter is saying something about sacramental food."[38] Zwingli was not arguing that Christ's flesh *as such* "counts for nothing;" rather, its profit for us is in its having been slain on our behalf, not in its being eaten.[39] For Zwingli, any who argue that in this passage Christ is speaking of a sacramental eating of his flesh and blood are no better than "the Jews" who had originally so misunderstood Christ's words.[40]

Zwingli turns next to the institution narrative itself. In contrast to others whose interpretive emphasis was on the word "this," Zwingli centers his own argument on the verbal "is." Citing other Scriptural examples of where "is" must mean "signify" (Gen.41:26–27; Ex.12:11; Matt.13:38; Lk.8:11 etc. . . .), Zwingli argues that the same holds true for the words of institution. "Testimony enough has now been adduced to prove that 'is' and its cognate forms can be used to mean 'signify.'"[41] Indeed, not only *can* it mean "signify" but, in respect of the institution narrative, *must* mean "signify." "This is not my judgment, but that of eternal God."[42] Time and again, Zwingli returns, in justification of his interpretation, to John 6:63: "the flesh counts for nothing."[43] There were, of course, other elements to Zwingli's argument, not least his denial of the *communicatio idiomatum* and thus his repudiation of Christ's bodily ubiquity, and his insistence on the community-forming character of the Supper ritual. Nevertheless, it was Zwingli's dogged determination that a necessarily spiritual interpretation of the "flesh-food" discourse in John 6 logically

38. Zwingli, *True and False Religion*, 201.
39. Zwingli, *True and False Religion*, 209.
40. Zwingli, *True and False Religion*, 209.
41. Zwingli, *True and False Religion*, 225.
42. Zwingli, *True and False Religion*, 227.
43. Zwingli cites this verse 24 times throughout this one chapter, at least twelve of which are in direct support of his position.

entailed a significationist rendering of the institution narrative that kept him forever at odds with Luther.

Luther, conversely, argued that John 6 had nothing specifically to do with the Eucharist, and so could not be used as the hermeneutical key to the words of institution. In his lengthiest treatise on the subject—*That These Words of Christ, 'This is my body,' etc, Still Stand Firm Against the Fanatics*, from 1527—Luther commenced his argument with a passionate defense of the literality of the institution narrative. "Now, here stands the text, stating clearly and lucidly that Christ gives his body to eat when he distributes the bread. [Thus] . . . we eat and take to ourselves Christ's body truly and physically. But how this takes place or how he is in the bread, we do not know and are not meant to know. We should believe God's Word without setting bounds or measure to it."[44] Then, taking aim at Zwingli's significationist reading, Luther expounded his own view of the John 6 passage. In the first instance, Luther denied, against the certainty of "the fanatics," that the "flesh" of John 6:63 was a reference to Christ's own flesh.[45] If the reference in this verse was to Christ's flesh being of no avail, and that on this basis Christ could not possibly be present corporeally in the Eucharist, then it would follow that Christ could not have been present corporeally in Mary's womb, or the manger of Bethlehem. If such was the case, argued Luther, "there would immediately come swarming in droves all the ancient heresies."[46]

How, then, did Luther believe John 6 should be understood? The flesh of v. 63 refers, not to Christ's flesh, but to the "old flesh" of sinful humanity (Jn 3:6). This, he claimed, is always the case when Scripture places "flesh" and "spirit" in opposition.[47] The flesh that profits nothing cannot be the body of Christ—which, Luther is at pains to point out, is both physical and spiritual[48]—but the corrupted humanity of the old

---

44. Luther, "These Words of Christ," 183.

45. According to Luther, on every occasion when Jesus speaks of his own flesh, he uses the phrase "my flesh" and never simply "flesh." That he does not employ the pronoun in John 6:63 thus means that he is referring to flesh generally, and not to his own particular flesh. Luther, "These Words of Christ . . . ," 222–3.

46. Luther, "These Words of Christ," 224–5. He has in mind the various gnostic and docetic traditions of the first and second centuries.

47. Luther, "These Words of Christ," 236.

48. "Christ's flesh is distinguished from all flesh and is solely a spiritual flesh for all, born not of the flesh but of Spirit, [thus] it is also spiritual food." Luther, "These Words of Christ," 240. Zwingli, for his part, never accepted the concept of "spiritual flesh."

Adam.⁴⁹ Thus, the verse cannot be used as the key to interpreting the words of institution. On the contrary, the words, "This is my body . . . " are "completely certain, lucid and clear . . . ," regardless of how "the fanatics" might try to twist them.⁵⁰ As with Zwingli, there were other aspects to Luther's arguments. His Cyrillian Christology, according to which Christ's two natures were far more inextricably connected than Zwingli's semi-Nestorianism would allow, enabled him to conceive without difficulty Christ's corporeal ubiquity—at God's right hand, and in the consecrated elements. Similarly, Luther's ontology of relationship—that is, that the reality of a thing is determined by that from which it arises—allowed him to argue that something (such as Christ's flesh) might be "spiritual" if it derived from the Spirit, no matter how substantially it might still be flesh—a logic that permitted him to insist that Christ's real flesh could nonetheless still be spiritually eaten.⁵¹

Certainly, the argument between Luther and Zwingli was rhetorically hostile, to the point that Luther greeted Zwingli's death on the battlefield at Kappel with applause. The "fanatic" had received what he deserved. Nevertheless, their disagreements over Johannine exegesis did not carry quite the same life-and-death consequences as was the case in the third of our case studies, to which we now attend.

Barth and Brunner on John 4

In mid-November 1941, the Swiss Evangelical Aid Society (SEAS) convened for its fourth annual conference in the Zurich suburb of Wipkingen. Founded in 1938, the aid agency sought to provide material assistance, encouragement and advocacy for the German Confessing Church. During the war years, it became one of the most prominent refugee support services, taking a particular interest in sheltering Jewish escapees from Nazi occupied territories. From the outset, SEAS had directly addressed the so-called "Jewish question." In October 1938, it issued a memorandum declaring that "The persecution of the Jews . . . is becoming more horrible day by day . . . Rise up in the power of the Holy Spirit and refrain from letting Christendom be contaminated by anti-Semitism."⁵² A month later,

---

49. Luther, "These Words of Christ . . . ," 236–7.
50. Luther, "That These Words of Christ . . . ," 238.
51. See Leppin, "Luther," 51–52.
52. *Das Heil kommt von den Juden: Memorandum zur Judenfrage*, Die theologische

following *Kristallnacht*, SEAS issued another declaration which spoke of "the smoking ruins of the synagogues, the wrecked homes and businesses ...," and warned ominously of "the frightful impending fate of the Jews .... if they are not saved in this final hour ..."[53] In December 1938, Karl Barth—who had largely authored SEAS's earlier memoranda—issued his own, theologically incisive, and even more politically provocative, anathema. Diagnosing National Socialism not simply as a political aberration but as an institutionally embodied violation of the First Commandment, Barth proclaimed his verdict: "the really decisive, biblical-theological" reason why the Church must say No! to Nazism was to be found in its inherent antisemitism which "precisely in these last weeks has so especially moved us." "Antisemitism," insisted Barth, "is a sin against the Holy Spirit," and thus—at least according to St Matthew—unforgiveable.[54]

Even before the war began, then, both Barth and the Swiss Aid Society had made their opposition to the Nazis' persecution of the Jews widely known. Not surprisingly, therefore, the denunciations continued at the 1941 Wipkingen conference. It should be remembered that the preceding year had seen a sharp escalation in the programmatic destruction of Europe's Jewish population. Twelve months before the 1941 conference, the Warsaw ghetto had been sealed, in preparation for the deportation of its inhabitants to "the east."[55] In June 1941, Germany had invaded Russia, a battlefront that enabled the *Einsatzgruppen*—mobile killing units, consisting largely of highly-trained SS soldiers—to roam the countryside behind the front and massacre any Jews they found. The most infamous of such atrocities was the murder of nearly 34,000 Jews in the ravine at Babi Yar on just two days between 29–30 September. Then, in October 1941, construction of the extermination camp at Auschwitz II (Birkenau) commenced. Over the next four years, Birkenau was the "killing factory" for more than 1,100,000 Jews.

Kommission des schweizerischen evangelischen Hilfswerkes für die Bekennende Kirche in Deutschland, October 1938. In the Karl Barth-Archiv.

53. "Aufruf an die dem schweizerischen evanglischen Hilfswerk für die bekennende Kirche angeschlossenen reformierten Pfarrämter und Gemeinden zur Hilfeleistung für die bedrängten Glaubensbrüder jüdischer Abstammung," 1. In the Karl Barth-Archiv.

54. Barth, "Die Kirche," 89–90.

55. "The east" was a euphemistic reference to the Nazi death camps in places like Bełżec, Sobibor, Chełmno, Treblinka, and Auschwitz.

All this was the immediate context in which the fourth Wipkingen conference took place, and at which Barth and Emil Brunner publicly, and vociferously, argued. At the heart of their debate was a shared desire once again to denounce the Nazis' war against the Jews. In itself, this was non-controversial territory for the Aid Society. Leading ecumenist Willem Visser't Hooft opened the conference with a speech that drew heavily upon Barth's views, insisting that the unity of the present Church was under threat of destruction by the demand that Christians belong to a certain people (*Volk*) and race. Citing a declaration from the Dutch Reformed Church, he asserted that "anyone who takes a position against Israel is opposed to the God of Israel ... [W]e consider anti-Semitism to be something that is far more dangerous than any inhumane ideology of race. We consider it to be the most stubborn and deadly form of resistance against the holy and merciful God, whose name we profess."[56] To this point, there was general consensus among the Wipkingen delegates. Brunner, spurred on by Visser't Hooft's charge, proposed a motion to compel the Swiss Confederation of Churches to take a public stance in opposition to the Nazis' persecution of the Jews. The wording of the motion was unanimously endorsed. It declared that

> 1. the Church, entrusted with the gospel of divine mercy, invites her members to pray for the suffering Jewish communities and to do everything possible to alleviate these sufferings. 2. the Church, entrusted with the message of the creation of humankind in the image of God, condemns the desecration of that image of God, in the despising and persecution of a race, as an outrage against the will of God as creator. 3. the Church, to which the message of the revelation of God in the people of Israel and in the Son of God, born of the seed of David, is entrusted, as the community of Jesus Christ, knows that it is connected to the fate of the Jewish people in a special way. Because, as it is written, salvation comes from the Jews, anti-Semitism is incompatible with membership of the Christian community.[57]

In other words, the Wipkingen delegates—determined to ground their opposition to the Nazis' *Judenkrieg* in Scripture—proposed a statement that a) committed the Church to a repudiation of all antisemitism, b) did so on the basis that the Jewishness of Jesus binds the Christian community

---

56. Busch, *Unter dem Bogen*, 374.
57. Wieser, "Die vierte Wipkinger Tagung," 374–6.

in solidarity with the Jewish people, and c) that affirmed this solidarity to be because "Salvation comes from the Jews" (Jn 4:22).

Notwithstanding a shared commitment to unified Christian action on behalf of Europe's Jews, it was the third clause of this statement that provoked intense disagreement, with the Wipkingen delegates dividing roughly into two factions: the Baslers, who followed Barth, and Zurichers, who sided with Brunner. What was already a fractious relationship between Barth and Brunner deteriorated even further, with the two men coming, once again, to theological blows.[58] In this case, the issue at hand was the proper rendering of John 4. For Barth, the verse—and thus the soteriological consequence—must be parsed in the continuing present tense. The salvation of the world, including the Church, is not merely *historically* dependent upon "biblical Israel" as the ancient medium of God's merciful revelation, but *continues* to be dependent upon God's continuing election of the Jewish people. As Barth himself put it shortly after the war, "[I]n order to be elect ourselves . . . we must either be Jews or belong to this Jew."[59] "We Christians," Barth insisted, "have [the promises of God] . . . only as those chosen with [the Jews], as guests in their house."[60] There is no hint of supersessionary logic here: the Church has replaced neither biblical nor post-biblical Israel as the elect of God, but participates in that election only alongside the kinfolk of Jesus, in all their generations. Thus, the Basler camp at Wipkingen insisted that the Church's covenantal bond with the Jews was not merely "special," as Brunner wished to say, but "indissoluble."

Conversely, the Zurichers, following Brunner's lead, understood Israel's role in God's salvific economy to be historically contingent. In Brunner's own copy of the motion proposed to the conference, he had underlined the third thesis heavily, phrasing it in the past tense: "Because its [the Church's] salvation *came* from the Jews . . . " (*Weil ihr Heil von den Judem kam* . . .).[61] John 4:22 was thus parsed to imply a superses-

---

58. Barth and Brunner first met in 1916 and, together with Eduard Thurneysen, Friedrich Gogarten and (on the fringes) Rudolf Bultmann, established what would become known as "dialectical theology." By 1921, Barth and Brunner were beginning to quarrel, with the decisive rupture between the two coming in 1934 over the legitimacy (or not) of natural theology. Brunner's *Natur und Gnade*, and Barth's retort, *Nein! Antwort am Emil Brunner,* entrenched them in their opposition to one another.

59. Barth, *Christian Dogmatics* III/3, 225.

60. Barth, "Jewish Problem," 200.

61. Busch, *Unter dem Bogen*, 376n.40.

sionary substitution of Israel by the Church. Five years later, Brunner "doubled-down" on this interpretation. In marked contrast to Barth's vision of God's gracious election, Brunner spoke of Israel as "presently rejected," with its future salvation dependent on the Jewish people choosing not to remain in their disobedience.[62] This was not a matter simply for the biblical people of Israel, but for "the empirical contemporary Jewish people."[63] For Brunner, the "vessels of wrath," to which Paul refers in Romans 9, are "the Jews . . . the whole people of Israel . . . ," in both their biblical and post-biblical form. He does not mean by this that Jewish people as such are, therefore, the "*reprobi*"—the eternally reprobated ones of whom a Calvinistic doctrine of double predestination speaks. "[The] point is not that the 'People' as a whole will be lost eternally . . . " Nevertheless, the Jews' salvation is dependent upon their Christian conversion. "[Only] after they have been converted, will [the Jews' part in salvation history] become a positive one."[64] With such supersessionary logic at play, Brunner was simply unable to accept that non-converted Jewish contemporaries could play a presently positive role in God's salvific economy. Salvation may historically have come from the Jews, insofar as it came through the Jew Jesus—but it can do so no longer. According to Busch, Barth was so incensed by Brunner's view, and by the fact that a majority of the conference delegates seemed inclined to agree with him, that he nearly broke with SEAS entirely, believing that he "could not talk theology with anyone who had this understanding of the Jews."[65]

Of course, Brunner's perspective was hardly controversial. Most Christians of his day—and many still in our own—would have agreed that salvation for the Jews is possible only through their conversion to Christ. It was, on the contrary, Karl Barth who was going out on a theological limb, by insisting on the continuing election of the Jewish people. Not by any action of its own, insisted Barth in 1942—at the very moment at which the Nazis' genocidal machinery was kicking into top-gear—can Israel "annul the covenant of mercy . . . [or] alter the fact that the promise is given and applies to itself, that in and with the election of Jesus Christ *it and no other* is God's elected people."[66] Neither biblical nor post-biblical

---

62. Brunner, *Doctrine of God*, 327–8.
63. Brunner, *Doctrine of God*, 328.
64. Brunner, *Doctrine of God*, 330.
65. Busch, *Barth*, 313.
66. Barth, *Christian Dogmatics* II/2, 237.

Israel—nor indeed Nazi Germany, nor even the Church—can "create any fact that finally turns the scale against [the Jews'] own election."[67] Irrespective of their faith or unbelief, "the fundamental blessing, the election, is still confirmed . . . [The] final word is one of testimony to the divine yes to Israel."[68] These last sentiments were articulated by Barth in his mature doctrine of election, that he published at Pentecost 1942, and which had been uppermost in his mind five months earlier at Wipkingen. Just as Brunner's supersessionary grammar compelled him to parse John 4:22 in the past tense, Barth's doctrine of election—and the place within it that he accorded the Jewish people of both past and present—required him to insist that the verse be understood in the present tense. In the end, their respective parsings did not fundamentally alter their shared commitment to aiding—and where possible, rescuing—Jewish refugees from Nazism. But, it must be acknowledged that Brunner's past tense rendering—"salvation *came* from the Jews"—made the grounding of his aid work theologically unstable.

Conclusion

Through these three historical case studies—from the Patristic era, the Reformation, and twentieth century modernity—we have noted the use of John's Gospel as a site of contest and controversy. At issue was, respectively, the repudiation of heresy, a proper theology of the Eucharist, and an adequate ground for Christian-Jewish solidarity. In no case was the debate based on exegeting large swathes of the Fourth Gospel. On the contrary, the theologians whose works we have considered drew broad conclusions from short texts—sometimes, even just a word or two. And perhaps this is the key take-away: that John's Gospel is so rich, that even the shortest verse can be mined for the profoundest of insights.

Bibliography

Barth, Karl. *Church Dogmatics II/2: The Doctrine of God*. Edited and translated by Thomas F. Torrance and Geoffrey W. Bromiley. Edinburgh: T&T Clark, 1957.
Barth, Karl. *Church Dogmatics III/3: The Doctrine of Creation*. Edited and translated by Thomas F. Torrance and Geoffrey W. Bromiley. Edinburgh: T&T Clark, 1960.

67. Barth, *Christian Dogmatics* II/2, 209.
68. Barth, *Christian Dogmatics* II/2, 15.

Barth, Karl. "The Jewish Problem and the Christian Answer." In *Against the Stream: Shorter Post-War Writings*. Translated by E. M. Delacour and S. Godman. London: SCM Press, 1954.

Barth, Karl. "Die Kirche und die politische Frage von heute." In *Eine Schweizer Stimme, 1938–1945*. Leipzig: Evangelischer, 1945.

Berkhof, Louis. *The History of Christian Doctrines*, Grand Rapids: Baker, 1975.

Boyarin, Daniel. "Origen as Theorist of Allegory: Alexandrian Contexts." In *The Cambridge Companion to Allegory*, edited by Rita Copeland and P. T. Struck, 39–54. Cambridge: Cambridge University Press, 2010.

Bromiley, Geoffrey W. *Historical Theology: An Introduction*. Edinburgh: T&T Clark, 1978.

Brunner, Emil. *The Christian Doctrine of God. Dogmatics Vol I*. Translated by Olive Wyon. London: Lutterworth, 1949.

Busch, Eberhard. *Karl Barth: His Life from Letters and Autobiographical Texts*. Translated by John Bowden. Grand Rapids: Eerdmans, 1994.

Busch, Eberhard. *Unter dem Bogen des einen Bundes: Karl Barth und die Juden 1933–1945*. Neukirchen-Vluyn: Neukirchener, 1996.

DeCock, Miriam. *Interpreting the Gospel of John in Antioch and Alexandria*. Atlanta: SBL, 2020.

Dunderberg, Ismo. *Beyond Gnosticism: Myth, Lifestyle, and Society in the School of Valentinus*. New York: Columbia University Press, 2008.

Euler, Carrie. "Huldrych Zwingli and Heinrich Bullinger." In *A Companion to the Eucharist in the Reformation*, edited by Lee Palmer Wandel, 57–74. Leiden: Brill, 2013.

Eusebius of Caesarea, *Ecclesiastical History. Books 6–10*. The Fathers of the Church 29. Washington, DC: Catholic University of America Press, 1955.

Kaatz, Kevin W. *Early Controversies and the Growth of Christianity*. Santa Barbara, CA: Praeger, 2012.

Leppin, Volker. "Martin Luther." In *A Companion to the Eucharist in the Reformation*, edited by Lee Palmer Wandel, 39–56. Leiden: Brill, 2013.

Luther, Martin. "Sermo de digna praeparatione cordis pro suscipiendo sacramento eucharistiae." In *D. Martin Luthers Werke. Kritische Gesamtausabe. 1. Band*, edited by Joachim K. F. Knaake, 325–334. Weimar: Hermann Böhlau, 1883.

———. "The Babylonian Captivity of the Church, 1520." In *The Annotated Luther, Volume 3: Church and Sacraments*, edited by Paul Robinson et al., 9–130. Minneapolis, MN: Fortress, 2016.

———. "That These Words of Christ, 'This is my body,' etc, Still Stand Firm Against the Fanatics." In *The Annotated Luther, Vol 3: Church and Sacraments*, edited by Paul Robinson et al., 163–274. Minneapolis, MN: Fortress, 2016.

Marius, Richard. *Luther*. London: Quartet Books, 1974.

Macauley, Williamina M. "The Nature of Christ in Origen's *Commentary on John*." *SJT* 19 (1996) 176–87.

McGrath, Alister E. *Christian Theology: An Introduction*. Chichester, UK: Wiley Blackwell, 2017.

Origen, *On First Principles*. Volumes I–II, edited and translated by John Behr. Oxford: Oxford University Press, 2017.

Origen, "Commentary on John, Book One." In Joseph W. Trigg, *Origen*, 103–49. London and New York: Routledge, 1998.

Percival, Henry R. *The Seven Ecumenical Councils*. Oxford: Benediction Classic, 2011.
Price, Richard. *The Acts of the Council of Constantinople of 553 with Related Texts on the Three Chapters Controversy*. Liverpool: Liverpool University Press, 2009.
Spruyt, Bart Jan. "Wessel Gansfort and Cornelius Hoen's *Epistola Christiana*: 'The Ring as a Pledge of Love.'" In *Wessel Gansfort (1419-1489) and Northern Humanism*, edited by Fokke Akkermann et al., 122–41. Leiden: Brill, 1993.
Spruyt, Bart Jan. *Cornelius Henrici Hoen (Honius) and his Epistle on the Eucharist (1525)*. Leiden: Brill, 2006.
Trigg, Joseph W. *Origen*, 103–49. London and New York: Routledge, 1998.
Wieser, Gerhard. "Die vierte Wipkinger Tagung." *KRS* 97 (1941) 374–6.
Williams, Rowan. *Arius: Heresy and Tradition*. Grand Rapids, MN: Eerdmans 2002.
Williams, Michael Allen. *Rethinking "Gnosticism:" An Argument for Dismantling a Dubious Category*. Princeton: Princeton University Press, 1996.
Zwingli, Huldrych. *Commentary on True and False Religion*, edited and translated by Samuel Macauley Jackson. Durham, NC: Labyrinth, 1981.

7

"Come, Holy Ghost, our souls inspire:"
The Musical Inspiration of John's Gospel

Peter Campbell

Introduction

MUSIC MAKES FREQUENT APPEARANCE in the Bible, as joyful praise or sorrowful lament, and it is clear that the early Christians continued Jewish traditions of singing the Psalms and of composing hymns for worship. Much of the New Testament is, however, devoid of musical reference, especially once quotations from the Old Testament are removed. It is from Ephesians 5:18b–20 (see Col 3:16) that we take the exhortation to:

> be filled with the Spirit, as you sing psalms and hymns and spiritual songs among yourselves, singing and making melody to the Lord in your hearts, giving thanks to God the Father at all times and for everything in the name of our Lord Jesus Christ.[1]

James 5:13 advises those who are suffering to pray and those who are cheerful to sing songs of praise, while Acts 16:25 notes that in jail Paul and Silas were "praying and singing hymns to God"; and there will also be plenty of singing at the end of days (Rev. 4:8–10, 5:9–13, 7:12, 11:17, 14:3 and 15:3). Yet the Gospels are almost entirely silent in musical terms,

---

1. NRSV. English translations in this essay usually follow the KJV, the version most often set by composers.

apart from the "canticles" of Luke's birth narrative (1:46–55; 1:68–79; 2:14; 2:29–32). Luke 15:25 makes a passing reference to there being music at the party for the prodigal son, and all three Synoptic Gospels mention dancing, though not any music associated with it.

In talking of music and John's Gospel, it is thus not in regard to any specific music-related text. Instead, John can be examined as a source of inspiration for musicians through the ages.[2] This takes two forms. The first is using John as the source text of a new musical work, either directly, or in paraphrase. The second is inspiration in a broader sense. John 14:26 reads: "But the Comforter, *which is* the Holy Ghost, whom the Father will send in my name, he shall teach you all things, and bring all things to your remembrance." Unlike the Πνεῦμα Ἅγιον, the breath of God that fills the apostles in a rather violent wind and tongues of flame in Acts 2, the Holy Spirit in John 20:22 is "received" by them though the seemingly gentle breath of the risen Jesus (20:22), sent by the Father as advocate, helper, and comforter. This is the inspiration discussed here.

Before examining specific musical works, it is worth noting that John 1:29 is the origin of the text in the "Gloria" referring to the Lamb of God, and thus also of the later-formed "Agnus Dei." Both are ancient, the Gloria being a probably second-century hymn that was chanted at Matins and introduced into the Mass liturgy in the fifth century, while the Agnus Dei was added to the Roman Rite at the end of the seventh century.[3] Both date to well before written notation of music, but it is heartening to know that a small piece of Johannine text is with us at each Eucharist and in each musical setting of the Mass.

Extended Texts Using John as Source

It is impossible to know where or when sung daily offices in the monasteries first occurred, as this necessarily predates the earliest written evidence. From chants, perhaps on a single reciting tone, there began to emerge in the Middle Ages dramatizations created by assigning roles to different individuals in the sung liturgy (and also in spoken Passion plays). Christ's Passion was one Bible story treated in this manner, but the mystery or miracle plays that developed widespread popularity in

---

2. For a general overview, see Letellier *Bible in Music*.

3. See Duffy, *Saints and Sinners*, 78–79; Nedungatt, "Council in Trullo Revisited," 651–76.

Medieval Europe included the *Quem Quaertitis* ("Whom do you seek?") in which the angel speaks to the women at the empty tomb, and *The Woman Taken in Adultery* relating the story in John 8:1–11, although that is no longer considered part of the Johannine text.

Polyphonic Dramatizations of the Passion

For church use, during the fifteenth century, polyphonic (multi-voice) settings of the entire Passion text began to be written, essentially as extended Latin motets. The earliest known is that of Jacobus Obrecht (c. 1450–1505), for four voices throughout, employing the existing plainchant as the "cantus firmus" or underlying melody in one of the voices. Obrecht chose to set the Johannine Passion text. Extant versions of the John Passion from the Renaissance come from Spain, composed by Francisco Guerrero (1528–1599) and Tomás Luis de Victoria (1548–1611) and from Italy by Cypriano de Rore (c. 1515–1565) and Orlande de Lassus (c. 1532–1594), among others.

An alternative style, known as a "Responsorial Passion," where only the crowd scenes were set as polyphony, the narrative sections and words of Christ remaining in chant, also developed. This is the form of English composer William Byrd's setting of John, published in 1605 (see Ex. 1).

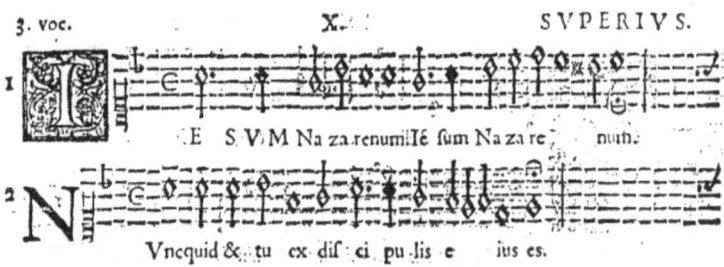

Example 1. The opening of the Superius (highest) part of Byrd's setting for three voices from the *Gradualia ac cantiones sacrae* (1605), showing the text "Jesum Nazarenum" (Jn 18:7b) and "Nunquid et tu ex discipulis eius es" (Jn 18:17b).

Latin Passion settings are found in Italy from this period, including settings of John by Vincenzo Amato in Palermo dating from the 1660s. Amato's nephew Alessandro Scarlatti wrote a John Passion, perhaps dating from around 1685, with a countertenor as Evangelist. His colleague Gaetano Venezio (1665–1716), organist at the Royal Chapel in Naples, also wrote a setting. In 1744, Francesco Feo was commissioned to write a new "Passio secundum Joannem" to replace the now out-of-fashion Scarlatti work for Naples. It is set, like Scarlatti, for countertenor (Evangelist), two tenors (Jesus and Pilate), choir, strings and continuo.[4] Though not a Passion oratorio, Antonio Caldara's *Maddalena ai piedi di Cristo* (Magdalene at the feet of Christ) from about 1700, sets part of the preceding story from John 11–12.

Another Bible-based Lenten musical form that developed during the 1500s was the *Seven Last Words*. Three of the seven are taken from John: "Woman, behold your son" (19:26–27); "I thirst" (19:28); and "It is finished" (19:30). The texts were set in Latin by Lassus and in German by composers including Schütz (1645), Christoph Graupner (1743) and Joseph Haydn (1787). A Latin setting from the 1730s has been attributed to Italian composer Giovanni Pergolesi. Later composers to take up the challenge of these evocative words include three significant figures from France in the nineteenth-century: Charles Gounod (1855), César Franck (1859), and Théodore Dubois (1867).[5] Closer to our time are settings for organ solo by Charles Tournemire (1935) and for choir by the American Daniel Pinkham, Norwegian Knut Nystedt (1960), Frenchman Patrick Burgan (1996) and Scottish composer James MacMillan (1993), and an instrumental work titled *Sieben Worte* (1982) by Sofia Gubaidulina. Both MacMillan and Gubaidulina later wrote Passions using John's Gospel.

The Passion in Protestant Germany

Following the Reformation, there was a significant tradition in northern Germany of performance of large-scale settings of the Passion in the vernacular during Holy Week. This can be traced back to Johann Walther (1496–1570) who worked closely with Luther during the 1520s on texts and music for reformed worship. Luther consulted Walther in 1524 on his own *Deutsche Messe*, and then Walther composed two complete Passions setting Luther's text of the Gospels of Matthew and John sometime between 1525 and 1530, possibly with Luther's assistance. His John Passion was in use in Zittau, in a Czech translation, certainly until at least

---

4. Murphy-Manley, CD review, 141–3.
5. See, for example, Roste, "Seven Last Words of Christ."

1816.[6] Walther was followed in setting John's Gospel by Thomas Selle in 1643,[7] Heinrich Schütz in 1666,[8] and Johann Sebastian Bach in 1724.

Bach wrote his *Passion According to St John* for Good Friday Vespers in Leipzig on 7 April 1724.[9] In such "oratorio passions," the strict biblical narrative is interspersed with other texts of two kinds, arias sung by solo singers, and chorales sung by the chorus, both of which comment on the action. The chorales, chiefly Luther's translations of Latin hymns, were all well known to the congregation, though it would not have joined in singing them during this part of the liturgy.[10] Today, Bach's Passions are most often heard as concert works, largely divorced from their liturgical origin, and familiarity with the chorales has essentially been lost outside Lutheran practice, though some tunes are in regular use.

Among the best known is the so-called Passion Chorale, "O Haupt voll Blut und Wunden" ("O Sacred Head, sore wounded"), which Bach harmonized for his *St Matthew Passion*. The ultimate origin of the text lies in John 19:2, "And the soldiers plaited a crown of thorns, and put it on his head," though there is also a parallel text at Matthew 27:27. At the same point in Bach's *St John Passion*, there is also a chorale, "Durch dein Gefängnis, Gottes Sohn" ("Through your prison, Son of God"). This text is based on an aria from an earlier *Johannes-Passion*, written about 1704, possibly by Christian Ritter or George Bohm—or even George Frederic Handel—with a text by Christian Heinrich Postel.[11] Bach uses a significant portion of Postel's libretto for his *St John Passion*, and it had also been used by Johan Mattheson for his John-based Passion titled *Das Lied des Lammes*.[12]

---

6. Buszin, "Johann Walther," [93].

7. Pöche, *Thomas Selles Musik für Hamburg*, 237.

8. Schütz, *Historia des Leidens und Sterbens unsers Herrn und Heilandes Jesus Christi nach dem Evangelisten St. Johannem*. His text concludes with a stanza of a hymn by Michael Weiße (ca. 1488–1534), "O hilf, Christe, Gottes Sohn" ("O help, Christus, Son of God"), which was also used by Bach in his *St John Passion*.

9. For a broader discussion of this area, see Shenton, "Musical Setting," 111–43. On Bach's theology and setting of biblical text, see Loewe, "God's Capellmeister," 141–71, and the essay by Firth and Loewe in this collection ("Johannine Glory in Bach's John Passion").

10. Wustmann, "Konnte Bachs Gemeinde bei Seinen Einfachen Choralsätzen Mitsingen?," 101–24.

11. For the attribution to Handel, see Kleinertz, "Handel's *St John Passion*," 59–80.

12. See Kleinertz, "Handel's St John Passion," 59–80.

Extant John Passion settings from the generations following include those by Georg Gebel around 1740,[13] eleven different setting by Georg Philipp Telemann between 1725 and 1765 for Hamburg,[14] and five by J. S. Bach's son Carl Philipp Emanuel Bach written between 1772 and 1788.[15] After that date, the true oratorio Passion fell out of favor, entirely replaced by the freer and more "tuneful" Passion oratorio that did away almost entirely with the recitative (narration) and substituted paraphrase for the remainder.[16]

Large-scale Oratorios after Bach

German-speaking composers continued a tradition of writing works on the life of Christ, but usually for concert presentation rather than liturgical use. Felix Mendelssohn famously revived performances of J. S. Bach's passions in 1829.[17] Mendelssohn himself wrote several large-scale biblical oratorios, notably *Paulus* [St Paul] (1836), *Elias* [Elijah] (1846) and an unfinished score for *Christus* [The Christ], with structural parallels to Handel's *Messiah*. The few surviving movements of *Christus* suggest Mendelssohn may have intended using Matthew as the key text. Jennens' libretto for *Messiah* used only one verse from John, the "Lamb of God" reference in 1:29, and *Paulus* is largely drawn from Acts, but Mendelssohn does set 1 John 3:1 ("See what love the Father has given us") as a reflective chorus at the very end of the oratorio.

Franz Liszt's *Christus* set Latin texts assembled by the composer himself. It was completed in 1866 and is not so much a narrative as a series of scenes. Movement eight, on the "Foundation of the Church," sets Matthew 16:18 ("Tu es Petrus") and then John 21:15-17, Jesus' commissioning of Peter to "feed my sheep." Movement 10, the entry to Jerusalem, uses verses from all four Gospels, including the "Hosanna" of John 12:13.[18] Franz Schubert wrote his *Lazarus, oder Die Feier der Auferstehung* (Lazarus, or the Celebration of the Resurrection) for a performance at Easter

13. See, for example, the extended review by Johan van Veen of a 2002 recording: http://www.musicweb-international.com/classrev/2003/sept03/LveenGebel_St-John_Passion.htm.
14. See Grant, *Rise of Lyricism*.
15. See Sanders, *Carl Philipp Emanuel Bach*.
16. See Braun, "Passion," 282-4.
17. Miz, "Revival of Bach," 201-21; Wolff, "Bach Cult," 26-31.
18. Smither, *History of the Oratorio*, 226-48.

1820. The libretto by August Hermann Niemeyer is based on John 11, though much of the music for Act 2 (burial) is incomplete and Act 3 (raising) was never begun.

There is also a strong tradition of biblical oratorios in Catholic France in the nineteenth century. Specific Johannine references appear in the *Oratorio de Noël*, opus 12, by Camille Saint-Saëns, written (in Latin) in 1858. While the narrative is based on Luke 2, there is one setting of John 11:27, "Domine, ego crediti" ("I believe thou art the Christ"). Jules Massenet's popular oratorio *Marie-Magdaleine*, premiered in 1873, is a setting of a libretto by Louis Gallet, written largely from John's Gospel.[19] The three acts are "Mary Magdalene at the Well," "Jesus at the House of Mary Magdalene," and "Golgotha, the Magdalene at the Cross, the Tomb of Jesus and the Resurrection." Massenet's 1880 *legend sacrée* titled *La Vierge*, to a French libretto by Charles Grandmougin, similarly depicts four scenes from the life of the Virgin Mary, including the Wedding at Cana that appears only in John's Gospel. Charles Gounod's *Mors et Vita* (Death and Life), dating from 1885, includes a baritone solo setting of John 11:25–26 ("I am the Resurrection and the Life"). A modern setting of the passion-oratorio in French is *Golgotha* by Swizz composer Frank Martin, completed in 1948. His John texts are from 12:12–13 and 27–32.

The English Oratorio

Following Handel and Mendelssohn, oratorio flourished in England in the nineteenth century, with several works remaining in the repertoire to the present day. One is John Stainer's *The Crucifixion* of 1887, a straightforward work with organ accompaniment that included five hymns acting exactly as did the German chorales, though here they were definitely meant for the congregation. The text, compiled by W. J. Sparrow Simpson, employs several verses from John: "God so loved the world" (3:14–17) and "When Jesus saw his mother" (19:26–27). Before the final hymn, the tenor sings the words of John 19:30, "And he bowed his head and gave up the ghost," without accompaniment.

One work that did not find a permanent place was Arthur Sullivan's 1873 oratorio *The Light of the World*. The text in the title, from John 8:12 and 9:5, does not actually appear in the libretto, which was "compiled

---

19. Renan's racial theories have largely been debunked. See Heschel, *The Aryan Jesus*, 34.

from the Holy Scriptures" by the composer and George Grove.[20] Part One is divided into scenes called "Bethlehem," "Nazareth," "Lazarus," and "The Way to Jerusalem." Part Two is set in Jerusalem and includes a scene titled "At the Sepulcher," though the Crucifixion is not portrayed directly. The first direct quote from John is 6:42, the chorus commenting on Jesus' appearance in the synagogue in Nazareth. An unnamed soloist responds with the words from 12:40 ("He hath blinded their eyes, and hardened their heart"). The story of Lazarus is based clearly on John 11. The journey to Jerusalem relies on Luke 13, though John 11:48–51, 12:13 and 12:19 are also referenced. In Part Two, the quotations from John are 16:33 ("Be of good cheer") and 20:15 ("Tell me where thou hast laid him").[21]

More straightforward in its biblical source is *The Light of Life* by Edward Elgar, first performed in 1896. Elgar intended this, his first oratorio, to be called "Lux Christi," but was dissuaded by his publisher from doing so. It is not exclusively a setting of the story of the blind beggar from John 9, but that is its central theme, and there are paraphrases from other parts of the Gospel, including "I am the Good Shepherd" (10:11–18) and "Light of the world" (8:12). After the lukewarm reception of his setting of John Henry Newman's *Dream of Gerontius* in 1900, Elgar returned to strictly biblical sources, apparently in the hope of being more "acceptable" to Anglican audiences or perhaps to "appease his Protestant countrymen."[22] The result was *The Apostles* of 1903. The text was assembled entirely from the Bible, intricately woven together in order to give his central characters of Mary Magdalene and Judas significant amounts of text, words that are not assigned to them in the Bible.[23] The KJV predominates, but there are instances of the use of the RSV where the composer preferred an alternative word or a different number of syllables.[24] There are a dozen Johannine texts, concentrated in the parts relating to the Passion (Jn 11:53; 18: 3–5, 8, 17, 26, 28) and the Ascension (Jn 10:15; 16:33; 17:4, 11).[25] Despite the work's name, there are no texts taken from Acts excepting a few on

---

20. For a discussion of the work within the composer's life, see Bradley, *Arthur Sullivan*, 96–103.

21. I am grateful to Robin Gordon-Powell for providing his detailed notes on the work and introduction to his new edition of *The Light of the World*.

22. Cowgill, "Elgar's War Requiem," 317–65.

23. Jaeger, *Apostles by Edward Elgar*; Gorton, *The Apostles*.

24. Powell, "Words of 'The Apostles,'" 201–4.

25. See Lloyd, "Edward Elgar's The Apostles," 27–45.

the Ascension, as Elgar's focus is on the "inner struggle to believe" of those closest to Jesus during his life, a struggle Elgar, too, perhaps faced.[26]

J. H. Maunder's (1858–1920) *Olivet to Calvary* of 1904 is described as a "sacred cantata recalling some of the incidents in the last days of the Savior's life on earth." The text, written and arranged by Shapcott Wensley, includes prose and versified Bible passages. Quotations from John appear first at the beginning of Part Two, "A New Commandment" (13:34–35), and in the scene "Before Pilate" (John 19), though the score also acknowledges the parallel passages in Matthew 27 and Luke 23.

Contemporary Passion Settings

While ostensibly a setting of Luke, the Passion setting written in 1966 by Polish composer Krzysztof Penderecki (b. 1933) includes three excerpts from John, rendered in Latin to provide it with a "universal, humanistic character."[27] Structured in twenty-seven sections divided into two parts, the work requires a narrator (spoken), soloists, large chorus and very large orchestra, and is essentially atonal, with the singers required to shout, hiss, whistle and even giggle.[28] The first of the Johannine texts is 19:17 ("So they took Jesus, and he went out, bearing his own cross"), used perhaps because it is the only Gospel to make specific mention of Jesus carrying his own cross. Similarly, John is the only one to describe Jesus talking to his mother at the foot of the cross (19:25–27), which Penderecki places immediately before the Stabat Mater. Lastly, Penderecki appends John 19:30 ("It is finished") to the final words from the cross in Luke 23:46.

Tim Rice's lyrics for Andrew Lloyd Webber's ground-breaking rock opera *Jesus Christ Superstar* (1970) were based largely on John's Gospel, with a specific reference in the title of the final number, "John Nineteen Forty One," an orchestral movement that accompanies the removal of Christ's body to the tomb. In 2006, Howard Blake wrote a dramatic oratorio called *The Passion of Mary*, enlarged from an earlier version titled "Stabat Mater," telling the passion story from the viewpoint of Jesus'

---

26. See, for example, McGuire, "Measure of a Man," 3–38; Taycher, "Redeeming the Betrayer."

27. The work premiered in Holy Week 1966, at a concert marking the 700th anniversary of Münster Cathedral, and was inspired by the 1000th anniversary of the adoption of Christianity in Poland.

28. See Robinson and Winold, *St Luke Passion*.

mother. Particularly Johannine movements concern the Crucifixion and Resurrection, though again the other Gospels are also used as sources.

Estonian Arvo Pärt (b. 1935) wrote his *Passio Domini Nostri Jesu Christi secundum Joannem* in 1982, using the Vulgate. It is through-composed, in a single 70-minutes movement, thought there are breaks at punctuation. The text of John 18 and 19 (stopping at verse 30) is introduced by an *Exordio* and ended with a *Conclusio* sung by the choir: "Qui passus es pro nobis, miserere nobis. Amen" ("You who have suffered for us, have mercy upon us. Amen"). While the roles of Jesus (baritone) and Pilate (tenor) are soloists, the Evangelist (narrator) is sung by a vocal quartet. The limited melodic material and lack of any true harmonic change removes any sense of dramatic movement through the story and creates instead a meditation. One reviewer of the first recording described the work as:

> what must surely be the bleakest, most ritualistic Passion to be composed since Heinrich Schütz's settings . . . Pärt has selected the most severe, detached and economical musical style . . . More a liturgical act than a concert piece, it makes no concessions whatever to modern conventions of Passion music. Stubbornly repetitive and monochrome, deliberately anti-dramatic and neutral, it achieves its extraordinary and noble effect through the simplest of means: measured recitative, piquant chanted choruses and the clear, bright timbres of a small instrumental ensemble.[29]

Sofia Gubaidulina (b. 1931) was one of four artists commissioned by the Internationale Bachakademie in Stuttgart to write settings of the Gospel passions in commemoration of the Bach 250 anniversary celebrations in 2000. Gubaidulina was assigned the Gospel of John. Her *Johannes-Passion*, with a Russian text, later translated into German, is scored for four vocal soloists, two choirs and large orchestra, clearly marking it as a concert work, though she described it as fulfilling her artistic "desire to realize my religious needs."[30] She "assimilated techniques and traditions from the history of Russian church music," but with an "interesting juxtaposition of both a flavor of and also a strong rebellion from Russian Orthodox tradition."[31] John's Gospel is interspersed with passages from

---

29. *Gramophone* magazine, https://www.gramophone.co.uk/review/p%C3%A4rt-passio.

30. Lukomsky, "The Eucharist in My Fantasy," 33.

31. Cheng, "A Conductor's Guide," 16.

Revelation as Gubaidulina "weaves textures of immense complexity ... or draws out tellingly simple, sparingly harmonized chants or recitatives."[32] These additional texts extend the narrative to include the consequence for the world that flow from Jesus' death and resurrection. As the composer explains:

> I feel that St. John's Gospel is what people need most nowadays and that it ought to be sung. The most important question brought up in St. John's Gospel is concern over the destinies of the world shared by God and humanity; concern over what the world needs and what Jesus Christ's sufferings mean to the world and to Creation.[33]

James MacMillan (b. 1959) wrote his *St John Passion* in 2007 for solo baritone, chorus and full orchestra. The baritone takes the role of Christus, with a four-part chamber choir acting as narrator. A large mixed choir takes the remaining roles. The work is divided into nine movements, each concluding with a Latin text, "which take[s] something of the general theme and development of the story, and allows time for a more objective and detached reflection," with a final instrumental postlude.[34] The texts added by MacMillan include the Stabat Mater, "Tu es Petrus," and the Improperia or Reproaches set for Good Friday, marking it as a particularly Roman Catholic work.

A Latin setting by Slovenian composer Damijan Mocnik (b. 1967) for similar voices, though requiring four soloists, including a soprano as "Historicus", was premiered in 2011. After an "In principio erat Verbum," there are five scenes relating to the Passover, Gethsemane, Peter, Pilate and a concluding "Amor in aeternum." The composer stated that he had "placed the passion in the context of the whole life of Christ, because in this story we find universal themes that are also characteristic of today: betrayal, repentance, forgiveness, love."[35]

Last in this overview of passion music is a recent *St John Passion* by English composer Bob Chilcott (b. 1955). Written for Palm Sunday 2013, the work consists of seventeen movements, seven of which set the Gospel text for tenor (Evangelist), two baritones (Jesus and Pilate) and soprano soloist, chorus and instrumental ensemble. Like the Passions of

---

32. Johnson, *BBC Music Magazine*.
33. "Sofia Gubaidulina."
34. MacMillan, "Composer's Notes."
35. "Umetnik v dialogu s poslušalci."

Bach, Chilcott's work includes meditative movements—here set for the soprano and/or chorus, to non-biblical English texts from the thirteenth to seventeenth centuries—and six "well-known Passiontide hymn[s] ... designed to be sung by the choir and audience/congregation together."[36]

The final large-scale composition deserving of mention lies outside any of the structural forms discussed to this point. John Tavener's *Veil of the Temple: All Night Vigil* was commissioned by the Temple Church for performances in July 2003. In its full form, the work lasts seven hours. The first seven of its eight "cycles" each follow the same structural pattern, with an opening soprano solo, a Kyrie, several anthem-like choral movements, a Psalm, a setting of part of John's Gospel for solo baritone, and an Alleluia being the most prominent. Each cycle builds on its predecessor, becoming more extended and complex and rising one step in pitch to form a "gigantic prayer wheel." The settings of John are: (i) 13:31–38; (ii) 14:1–9; (iii) 14:10–20; (iv) 14:21–15:12; (v) 15:13–16:4; (vi) 16:5–33; and (vii) 17:1–18.

Shorter Works with Johannine Texts

John 1

The opening of John's Gospel is set down for the Eucharist on Christmas Day, so it is a text set to music often, and the densely packed imagery has provided fertile ground for composers. The most used verse in the early section of the Gospel is 1:14 ("And the Word was made Flesh." At least thirty settings of the Vulgate text ("Verbum caro factum est") can be identified from the Renaissance alone, the most well known being by Lassus, Praetorius and Josquin, with later settings by Schütz and Telemann. There is also a direct reference to the "Word of the Father, now in flesh appearing" in the hymn "O come, all ye faithful," dating from the mid-eighteenth century. John 1:16 ("Of his fullness have all we received") is the inspiration for Horatius Bonar's famous Johannine hymn "I heard the voice of Jesus say."

Verses 19–23 ("This is the record of John") are famous today largely for a single English setting by Orlando Gibbons. The "Agnus Dei," based on John 1:29, has already been mentioned, though the most famous perhaps of standalone settings is that by Samuel Barber (1967). There

---

36. Chilcott, "St John Passion."

are also numerous settings of "Behold the Lamb of God," including in "Tomorrow" (1981) by rock band U2, and the associated imagery of the innocent lamb of William Blake's 1789 poem, set to music by Vaughan Williams in *Ten Blake Songs* (1957) and as an anthem by John Tavener in 1982. The characters of the fishermen-disciples, noted in John 1:38–40, are portrayed in the 2008 musical by Roger Jones, *Rock: The Story of Simon Peter*.

Cana to Cana (John 2:1–4:54)

Massenet's depiction of the Wedding at Cana has been mentioned, but another is the "chancel opera" *The Awaking* by Susan Hulsman Bingham (b. 1944), to a libretto by Neil Olson. It is one of eighteen liturgico-dramatic works she has produced since 1979. Premiered in Trinity Church, New Haven, in 1980, the work selects four passages dealing with the ministry of women, including John 20, after the Resurrection. One of the *Four Biblical Dances* for organ by Czech composer Petr Eben (1929–2007) depicts the celebrations at Cana. *Jesus and the Traders* (*Jezus es a Kufarok*) is an unaccompanied choral work by Hungarian Zoltán Kodály dating from 1927 and based on the cleansing of the Temple scene in John 2:15–22.

In contrast, there are dozens of settings of John 3:16, "God so loved the world," in Latin, German and English (including that by Stainer noted above), Gibbons, Schütz, Telemann, Hugo Distler—as number 16 of a set of 52 three-part motets forming a "Cycle of the Year" (*Jahrkreis*) that he published in 1933—and present-day English composers Bob Chilcott and Will Todd. There is a rap song titled "John 3:16" by DJ Muggs published on his 1997 album *Soul Assassins* that questions how the modern world filled with hate and sorrow could be loved by God.

In 1868, English composer William Sterndale Bennett published his oratorio *The Woman of Samaria*, opus 44, a setting of a large part of Chapter 4, with additions mostly from the Psalms. The movement setting verse 24 ("God is a Spirit"), is frequently excerpted as a separate anthem, and there is also a setting of that verse by the American Randall Thompson, while verses 13–14, the water of everlasting life, can also be found in several settings.

John 6–12

"Jesus walking on the water" is a rock song by the Violent Femmes from 1984 and based on the Gospel accounts, including John 6:16–21. John 6:35 (and 6:48–50) gives us "I am the bread of life," with its obvious suitability for the Eucharist, and there are settings by Palestrina and William Byrd, which are followed closely by 6:53–56 ("Verily, verily, I say unto you"), set by Thomas Tallis. The text "Caro mea vere est cibus" ("For my flesh is meat indeed"), a setting of John 6:55 and following verses, was commonly set as a Communion motet, including by Manchicourt (1535), de Rore (1559), Palestrina (1575), de Monte, Andrea Gabrieli (1576), Guerrero (1589), Bassano (1598), and Caldara (1715).

John 7:38, the "living water," again provides imagery ripe for musical commentary, especially from hymn writers, including Charles Wesley ("Jesus, lover of my soul," 1740) and Horatius Bonar ("I heard the voice of Jesus say," 1846). Similar inspiration is given by 8:12 ("I am the light of the world")—there is a motet by Lassus—though the parallel in Matthew 5:14 sometimes makes the exact source unclear. The ancient Greek hymn *Phos Hilaron* may derive its inspiration from John 8:12, well known in its English setting by Charles Wood: *Hail Gladdening Light*.

The healing of the blind man in John 9 has been set as a chancel opera titled *By the Pool of Siloam* for six soloists by Susan Hulsman Bingham. From chapters 10 and 11 of John's Gospel, we get three great "I am" statements: "I am the door" (10:7 and 9), "I am the good shepherd" (10:11 and 14) and "I am the resurrection and the life" (11:25). The metaphor of the shepherd was taken into the second responsory for Matins on Easter Monday, "Surrexit pastor bonus,"[37] with settings by Lassus, Palestrina, Schütz, Samuel Scheidt, Giovanni Gabrieli, and Mendelssohn. "I am the resurrection" inspired anthems by at least seventeen English composers in the sixteenth and early seventeenth centuries including Wilkinson, Tomkins, Batten, Gibbons, Morley, Milton, Croft and Goss,[38] motets on the continent by Lassus, Buxtehude, Hassler and Scheidt, from Healey Willan and Ray Repp in the twentieth century, and even a rock anthem released by The Stone Roses in 1989.[39] American composer Dan Lock-

---

37. "The Good Shepherd is risen, who laid down his life for his sheep, and vouchsafed to die for his flock"; cf John 10:14–15.

38. See Morehen, ed., *English Choral Practice*, 215.

39. It is the last track on the self-titled album and believed to have influenced their next album, titled *Second Coming* (1994).

lair set verses 25–26 as a solo movement in his 2015 *Requiem*, in which he also set 14:1–4 ("Let not your heart be troubled").[40]

The raising of Lazarus was the subject of a song by Rachmaninoff ("Voskresenije Lazarja," Op. 34, No. 6, to a text by Aleksei Khomiakov), a country song by Patty Loveless (2001), a Gospel song by Carman (2013), a rock song by British band Placebo (2006), and another titled "Dig, Lazarus, dig!!!" by Australian band Nick Cave and the Bad Seeds, released in 2008. Cave imagines the problems of modern-day "Larry," noting: "We are all, of course, in awe of the greatest of Christ's miracles—raising a man from the dead—but I couldn't help but wonder how Lazarus felt about it."[41] *The Lazarus Requiem* is a six-movement work by Patrick Hawes written in 2005.

John 12 begins with the story of Mary anointing Jesus, to Judas' disapproval. Songwriter Sydney Carter wrote "Judas and Mary" in 1964 and it has since had many cover versions and appeared in hymnbooks. The chapter then moves to Jesus' entry to Jerusalem, giving us the hymn "Ride on! Ride on in majesty." Chapter 13:34 gives us one of the most recognized texts from John's Gospel, "A new commandment," set in the sixteenth century by Sheppard, Mundy and Tallis, and in our time by Peter Nardone, Peter Aston, Richard Shephard, and Paul Carey, as well as influencing Bob Marley's "One Love" from his 1977 album *Exodus*.

Farewell Discourse (John 13:1–17:26)

Chapter 14 is dense with important texts. The opening, "Let not thy heart be troubled," is set by Sheppard, Jacquet de Mantua and Manchicourt (1539), and in many modern anthems or songs in English, including those by Daniel Read,[42] Mark Dickey, Henry A. Clarke, Gordon Young, Carl F. Mueller, and Oley Speaks. Jazz composer Dave Brubeck's 1968 oratorio *The Light in the Wilderness* includes settings of John 14:1 and 14:27. Verse 6 ("I am the way, the truth and the life"), has many settings, including one from Australian composer Alfred Wheeler ("Allan's Anthems," No. 25, c. 1935), and by Dan and Heidi Goeller, Gordon Young, and Philip Spaeth.

---

40. https://www.locklair.com/compositions/choral/requiem
41. "Nick Cave: I was traumatised by bible."
42. Kroeger, *Early American Anthems, Part 2*, 142–6.

John 14:15 ("If ye love me"), is today most frequently heard in the setting by Tallis from 1565. Continental Latin settings include that by Lassus from 1577, and there are more recent settings by the Canadian-based Healy Willan and Graham George, Englishman Caleb Simper and Americans Daniel Pinkham and George Nevin. Verse 16 ("And I will pray the Father") is also incorporated into a large Ascension anthem by Palestrina, *Ascendo ad Patrem* ("I ascend to the Father"), which sets John 20:17, 15:26, 16:22 and 14:16.[43] "I will not leave you comfortless" (14:18), a Magnificat antiphon for Vespers at Pentecost, was set by Byrd, Clemens non Papa, Ludwig Senfl and Ignazio Donati. Howard Goodall (b. 1958), composer of the theme music to *Mr. Bean* and *The Vicar of Dibley*, included a setting of John 14:18 in his 2009 reimagining of *The Beatitudes*. It is verse 27 to which modern composers have been drawn more often: "Peace I leave with you" has been set by Knud Nystedt, H. Elliot Button, Edwin A. Clare, David Eddleman, Dale Jergenson, Jean Middleswarth, Charles McHugh, J. Varley Roberts, Judith Snowdon, Ruth Turner, F. W. Waddeley, David York, and Gordon Young, among many others.

Arvo Pärt composed *I am the True Vine* (John 15:1) for Norwich Cathedral's 900th anniversary in 1996. Other settings are by Peter Aston and Americans Margaret Sandresy (b. 1921), Allen Pote, Philip Gehring, Kevin J. Sadawski, Michael Jothen, Carlton Young, and Paul D. Weber. John 15:12 is set as a Communion antiphon for Easter V, while verse 13 ("Greater love hath no man than this") has settings by Erik Routley and Carl F. Mueller, and is incorporated in John Ireland's famous anthem "Many Waters Cannot Quench Love" dating from 1912. The advent of World War I saw other settings commemorating casualties, including one by William Wolstenholme and a song by Rachmaninoff, "Iz evangeliya ot Iaonna" (From the Gospel of John), published in 1915.[44] Verses 9–13 were set as the anthem "As the Father" by Philip Moore for a collection of 44 works dedicated to Elisabeth II for her Diamond Jubilee in 2012 called *Choirbook for the Queen*.

In all of J. S. Bach's 200-odd extant cantatas, there are 17 setting texts directly from John's Gospel. Like the arias of the great passion settings, the texts of Bach's cantatas are made up largely of poetic reflections, so the proportion of direct biblical quotations is relatively small, but it is interesting to note the significant use of John during the Easter period,

---

43. *Motettorum liber secundus*, for 5, 6 and 8 voices, Venice, 1572.

44. An interesting use of John 15:13 occurs at the conclusion of Arthur Honegger's 1938 opera *Jeanne d'Arc au bûcher* (Joan of Ark at the Stake).

and particularly Bach's reliance on chapter 16, making up half of all his known use of the Gospel in direct quotation.

Other verses of Chapter 16 are also of note. Peter Philips and Melchior Vilpius set verse 20 ("Your sorrow shall be turned into joy") in Latin and verses 23–24 ("Whatever ye shall ask") was set in German by Andreas Hammerschmidt (1611/12–1675) and later in English by Healey Willan and Jan Bender. Johannes Brahms published his *Ein deutsches Requiem, nach Worten der heiligen Schrift* (A German Requiem, to Words of the Holy Scriptures), Op. 45, in 1868, taking his texts from the Luther Bible. John 16:22 ("And ye now therefore have sorrow") is set for soprano solo at the beginning of a movement Brahms added after the first performance. Hugo Distler set verse 33, ("In der Welt habt ihr Angst") as movement 7 of his opus 12 set of motets.

Passion and Resurrection (John 18:1–21:25)

Chapters 18 and 19 have largely been dealt with above in regard to passion music, though it is worth noting that the Holy Week responsory "Tenebrae factae sunt" is drawn from Matthew 27:45–46, John 19:30 ("and he bowed his head and gave up the ghost") and Luke 23:46. There are many settings, including those of Palestrina, Lassus, Victoria, Gesualdo, Croce, Charpentier, Zelenka, Michael Haydn, and Poulenc.

The empty tomb of John 20:2 and its parallel text in 20:13 is the basis for the Easter Day motets by Gombert (1554), Lassus (1566), Palestrina (1569), Philippe de Monte (1587), Morley (1597), Hieronymus Praetorius (1599), Michael Praetorius (1607), Scheidt (1620) and Schütz (before 1625). There are settings in English by Stainer and Pinkham (a movement from his 1979 Easter Cantata *When God Arose*). Verse 17 ("I ascend unto my Father") is the core text for a Vespers antiphon for Ascension and was set in Latin by Palestrina (1572) and German by Jacob Handl (1587) and Samuel Scheidt (1620), among others. "*Surgens Jesus*" is a text based on 20:19b and 20b, "The risen Jesus . . . said: peace be with you;" there are settings by Lassus, Monteverdi and Peter Philips. "Peace be unto you" is also the text for anthems by Knud Nystedt, Robert Wetzler, and Walter Samuel. Verse 29 ("Blessed are they that have not seen, and yet have believed") is set as the Magnificat antiphon for the Feast of St Thomas on 21 December. Latin settings include those by Lassus

(1563), Monteverdi (1582), Marenzio (1585), Palestrina (1587), Handl (1590), and Hassler (1591).

Conclusion

This survey of the textual sources from John's Gospel that composers have engaged with across the centuries has concentrated first on concert works and second on liturgical repertoire. The vast repertoire of hymns based on John is a work for another time. That the Fourth Gospel has been the inspiration for so many large-scale works—operas, oratorios and cantatas—for the concert hall, as well as for composers and musicians beyond the traditions of Christian worship, is testament to the enduring and continued fascination we as humans have with this Gospel, its stories, teachings and commentaries, applicable just as much now as in earlier generations. It shows clearly that the Holy Spirit continues to inspire our creative souls to praise and worship through the medium of John's Gospel.

Bibliography

Bradley, Ian. *Arthur Sullivan: A Life of Divine Emollient*. Oxford: Oxford University Press, 2021.

Braun, Werner. "Passion." In *The New Grove Dictionary of Music and Musicians*, vol 14, 282–84. London: Macmillan, 1980.

Buszin, Walter E. "Johann Walther: Composer, Pioneer, and Luther's Musical Consultant." In *The Musical Heritage of the Church*, vol. III. Valparaiso, IN: Valparaiso University Press, 1946 http://www.ctsfw.net/media/pdfs/MusicalHeritageoftheChurchIII.pdf.

Cheng, Wei. "A Conductor's Guide to Sofia Gubaidulina's St John Passion." DMA diss., University of Cincinnati, 2006.

Chilcott, Bob. "St John Passion," Oxford University Press, online, https://global.oup.com/academic/product/st-john-passion-9780193397590

Cowgill, Rachel. "Elgar's War Requiem." In *Edward Elgar and His World*, 317–65, edited by Byron Adams. Princeton: Princeton University Press, 2007.

Duffy, Eamon. *Saints and Sinners: A History of the Popes*. New Haven: Yale University Press, 2006.

Gordon-Powell, Robin. *The Light of the World*, 2nd ed. London: The Amber Ring, 2018.

Gorton, C. V. *The Apostles. A Sacred Oratorio by Edward Elgar: An Interpretation of the Libretto*. London: Novello, 1903.

Grant, Jason. *The Rise of Lyricism and the Decline of Biblical Narration in the Late Liturgical Passions of Georg Philipp Telemann*, PhD diss., University of Pittsburgh, 2005.

Heschel, Susannah. *The Aryan Jesus: Christian Theologians and the Bible in Nazi Germany*. Princeton, NJ: Princeton University Press, 2008.
Jaeger, A. J. *The Apostles by Edward Elgar, Op. 49, Book of Words with Analytical and Descriptive Notes*. London: Novello, 1903.
Johnson, Stephen. BBC *Music Magazine*, 20 Jan 2012. https://www.classical-music.com/reviews/gubaidulina-o/.
Kleinertz, Rainer. "Handel's *St John Passion*: A Fresh Look at the Evidence from Mattheson's *Critica Musica*," *The Consort* 61 (2005) 59–80.
Kroeger, Karl. ed. *Early American Anthems, Part 2: Anthems for Special Occasions*. Madison, WI: A-R Editions, 2000.
Letellier, Robert I. *The Bible in Music* Newcastle upon Tyne: Cambridge Scholars, 2017.
Lloyd, Thomas. "Edward Elgar's The Apostles: A Major Oratorio Standing Outside Tradition." *Choral Journal* 58 (2017) 27–45. https://www.buckschoral.org/edward-elgar-the-apostles-1.Loewe, Andreas. "'God's Capellmeister': The Proclamation of Scripture in the Music of J. S. Bach," *Pacifica* 24 (2011) 141–71.
Lukomsky, Vera. "'The Eucharist in My Fantasy': Interview with Sofia Gubaidulina." *Tempo: A Quarterly Review of Modern Music* 206 (1998) 33.
McGuire, Charles E. "Measure of a Man: Catechizing Elgar's Catholic Avatars." In *Edward Elgar and His World*, 3–38, edited by Byron Adams. Princeton: Princeton University Press, 2007.
MacMillan, James. "Composer's Notes," Boosey & Hawkes, website, https://www.boosey.com/cr/music/James-MacMillan-St-John-Passion/49500.
Mintz, Donald. "Some Aspects of the Revival of Bach." *The Musical Quarterly* 40 (1954) 201–21.
Morehen, John. "The English Anthem Text, 12549–1660," *JRMA* 117 (1992) 62–85.
———. ed., *English Choral Practice 1400–1650*. Cambridge: Cambridge University Press, 1995.
Murphy-Manley, Sheryl. CD review, *Eighteenth-Century Music*. 8 (2011) 141–3.
Nedungatt, George. "The Council in Trullo Revisited: Ecumenism and the Canon of the Councils," *TS* 71 (2010) 651–76.
"Nick Cave: I was traumatised by bible," https://www.nme.com/news/music/nick-cave-and-the-bad-seeds-43-1351551.
Pöche, Juliane, *Thomas Selles Musik für Hamburg: Komponieren in einer frühneuzeitlichen Metropole*, Musica poetica, vol. 2. Bern, 2019.
Powell, Richard. "The Words of 'The Apostles' and 'The Kingdom,'" *The Musical Times* 1265 (1948) 201–4.
———. "The Words of 'The Apostles' and 'The Kingdom'—Part II: Another Point of View." *The Musical Times* 1275 (1949) 149–52.Robinson, Ray and Allen Winold. *A Study of the Penderecki St Luke Passion*. Celle: Moeck, 1983.
Roste, Vaughn. "The Seven Last Words of Christ: A Comparison of Three French Romantic Musical Settings by Gounod, Franck, and Dubois," DMA thesis, Louisiana State University, 2013.
Sanders, Reginald. *Carl Philipp Emanuel Bach and Liturgical Music at the Hamburg Principal Churches from 1768 to 1788*. PhD diss., Yale University, 2001.
Shenton, Andrew. "Musical Setting of the Passions Texts," *Engaging the Passion: Perspectives on the Death of Jesus*, edited by Oliver L. Yarbrough, 111–43. Minneapolis: Fortress, 2015.

Smither, Howard E. *A History of the Oratorio*, vol. 4. Chapel Hill/London: University of North Carolina Press, 2000.

"Sofia Gubaidulina: The Harmony of the World." *Voice of Russia*, 13 Nov. 2001. http://www.vor.ru/culture/cultarch190_eng.html#1.

Taycher, Ryan. "Redeeming the Betrayer: Elgar's Portrayal of Judas in *The Apostles*." MA diss., University of North Texas, 2013."Umetnik v dialogu s poslušalci" ("An artist in dialogue with listeners"), https://www.dnevnik.si/1042510629

Wolff, Christoph. "A Bach Cult in Late-Eighteenth-Century Berlin: Sara Levy's Musical Salon." *AAA&S* 58 (2005) 26–31.

Wustmann, Rudolf. "Konnte Bachs Gemeinde bei Seinen Einfachen Choralsätzen Mitsingen?" ("Could Bach's Congregation Sing along with the Simpler Chorale Settings?"), *Bach-Jahrbuch* 4 (1909) 102–24.

8

Johannine Glory in Bach's John Passion: "In deepest lowliness made noble"

KATHERINE FIRTH AND ANDREAS LOEWE

Introduction

JOHANN SEBASTIAN BACH'S *John Passion* (BWV 245, 1724) sets to music chapters 18–19 of the Gospel of John, plus hymns and contemporary poetry which reflect on the Scriptures and story. The work's majestic opening chorus, *Herr, unser Herrscher* ("Lord, our Lord"), explores the Johannine theological concept of Christ's glory being revealed in suffering. This chapter provides an in-depth reading of the music and text of the opening movement, to demonstrate how Bach's highly-trained understanding of John's theology of glory impacted the composer's artistic choices to represent those ideas in words and music.

As we have demonstrated extensively elsewhere, Bach's profound theological understanding significantly influenced the libretto texts he selected and the music he composed, setting orthodox Lutheran theology as "sermons in sound."[1] Michael Marissen, in *Bach & God*, makes the case for scholarly translations of Bach's texts alongside Luther's Bible in order fully to understand the Biblical allusions and theological meaning, as well as analyzing the music.[2] In this chapter, we make use of our own

---

1. Loewe, "Sermons in Sound," 1–11, Loewe, "God's Capellmeister," 141–71, Loewe, *Theological Commentary*, 100–34. All translations of Bach's libretto are taken from Firth, "Study Translation," 100–34. Loewe, "Christology," 79–90.

2. Marissen, *Bach & God*, 31.

2014 scholarly translation and commentary, *Johann Sebastian Bach's St John Passion: A Theological Commentary*, to elucidate further a central concept in John's Gospel and in Bach's *Passion*.

John's Gospel explains how each of the events of the crucifixion fulfills the prophecies of the Old Testament by showing that Christ is the Messiah.[3] Jesus also speaks of power, ascension and glory in his farewell discourses (Jn 13–17), in which he sets out his paradoxical role as a servant king, who can be killed but also has eternal life, who is both God and man, and whose glory is attested through the most shameful and painful kind of execution. Eric Chafe has already extensively made the case for Bach's Johannine theology in both the *John Passion* and the cantatas composed in spring 1725.[4] In his monumental eponymous book, *J. S. Bach's Johannine Theology in the St John Passion and the cantatas for spring 1725*, he argues that Bach takes a Christus Victor-approach of the atonement in the *John Passion*, using the "classic" theory of Christus Victor as a "drama of stark oppositions: light versus darkness, good versus evil."[5] Chafe further claims that, "undoubtedly, the greatest manifestation of the idea of opposition in the *St John Passion* is that given right from the outset in the opening chorus," with the "juxtaposition" of *Herrlichkeit* ("lordliness") and *Niedrigkeit* ("lowliness.")[6] The theological concept of kenotic Christology—Christ's incarnation and crucifixion as self-giving, self-emptying—was only introduced into German Lutheran theology by Gottfried Thomasius (1802–75) in the nineteenth century and so we do not use that term in this chapter.[7] Rather, Luther translates ἐκένωσεν in Phil 2:7 as *erniedrigte*, "lowered," and contemporary German theologians

---

3. For example, in John 3, Jesus links his exaltation to heaven with the lifting up of the bronze snake by Moses in the desert, in the context of his salvific act (Jn 3:14–16; Num 21:6–9); and in John 19, he quotes Ps 22 in explaining why the soldiers gambled for Jesus' clothing. In John 19, the words are πληρωθῇ— "fulfilled," v. 24; τελειωθῇ— "completed," v. 28; the word for accomplished is τετέλεσται— "it has been made," "the preparations have led to the thing being built," "it has been wrought."

4. Chafe, *Bach's Johannine Theology*, 110–4.

5. Chafe, *Bach's Johannine Theology*, 113, draws on Gustav Aulén's classification of atonement theory of the same name, *Christus Victor*. See further Chafe, *Analyzing Bach Cantatas*, 23–41, and Pelikan, "Christus Victor," 106.

6. Chafe, *Bach's Johannine Theology*, 151.

7. For a more detailed history of Gottfried's *Christi Person und Werk*, see for example Law, "Kenotic Christology."

used contrasting tropes of high and low, what Luther called the "glory" and "majesty" versus the "humility" and "ignominy" of the cross.[8]

In the *John Passion*, the Luther Bible translation of chapters 18–19 of John's Gospel is set to music in a sparse recitative style, with solo voices chanting the story, and instruments providing simple continuo accompaniment, generally as one-or-two pitches per measure minim phrases. In contrast, the reflective hymns and poems, like the crowd scenes, are given highly ornamented and multi-part vocal and instrumental musical settings. The opening movement, *Herr, unser Herrscher* uses polyphonic and contrapuntal musical forms: it has complex four-part harmony sung by a full choir and Baroque orchestra, and many musical flourishes. Careful listening shows where the musical lines often contrast, even conflict, melodically, harmoniously, and rhythmically.

Such rich, complex and busy settings, contrasting with the stark simplicity of the recitative, was typical for the Baroque cantata-style music of Bach's time. His audience would expect to hear music of this level in the weekly cantata written and performed by Bach at St Thomas' and St Nikolai Leipzig, where church goers had significant appreciation and understanding of music. Bach provided libretto booklets to subscribers, and so many hearers would also have had access to the published cantata texts.[9] Finally, the congregation would be familiar with Luther's theology and Bible translation, and to these concepts being spelled out in hymns and cantatas, sermons, religious commentaries, and poetry collections.[10] Rather than present a radical reading of the text, therefore, this chapter attempts to make accessible to a modern, English-speaking audience some aspects of the *John Passion* that would have been obvious or implicit to the original audience.

---

8. The word ἐκένωσεν is a form only used in Phil 2:7. Cognate versions in Rom 4:14, 1 Cor 1:17, 9:15, 2 Cor 9:3, are about making a power or promise "empty" or "void," while the classical Greek form suggests something more like "purging" or "waning." The Lutheran theologian Johann Jakob Rambach, whose *Betrachtungen* Bach owned, interpreted Phil 2:7 in terms of Christ "exchang[ing] greatest glory for deepest lowliness, / utmost bliss for greatest sorrow / and highest pleasure for utmost pain" (*die höchste Ehre mit der tieffsten Schmach / die höchste Freude mit der grösten Traurigkeit / die höchste Vergnügung mit den äussersten Schmertzen/ zu verwechseln*). For Rambach's work in Bach's theological library, see Leaver, *Bachs theologische Bibliothek*, 121, 150.

9. Loewe, *Theological Commentary*, 66.

10. For more on Luther's approach to church music, see Loewe, Firth, "Mighty Fortress," 124–7, and Loewe, Firth, *Luther and the Arts*, Chap 2.

The Biblical and Theological Background

Bach's Lutheran understanding of the meaning of the Gospel of John and of Christ's crucifixion is central to his selection of words and compositional choices in his *John Passion*. Martin Luther emphasized the cross as a central moment of both "glory" and "majesty," and also "humility" and "ignominy," in his Heidelberg Disputation (1518), in which he postulated:

> It is never enough, nor does it profit anyone who regards God in glory and majesty, and does not recognize him in the humility and ignominy of the cross. In this way "I will destroy the wisdom of the wise etc." [1 Cor 1:19]. As Isaiah says: "Truly you are a hidden God" [Isa 45:15].[11]

In Luther's reading, the narrative retelling of the event of the crucifixion in the four Gospels is also buttressed by evidence from the Old and New Testaments. Thus it is consistent that the words to Bach's opening movement to his *John Passion* were primarily drawn from two Psalms and the creedal hymn from Philippians 2:5–8.

The opening lines of the movement are drawn from two Psalms (which make up the movement's A-section): "O Lord, our Sovereign, how majestic is your name in all the earth" (Ps 8:1, 9);[12] and "Your name, O God, like your glory, reaches to the ends of the earth" (Ps 48:11).[13] These statements of praise are part of celebratory psalms praising the power, greatness and rule of "the Lord God" (*der HERR*).[14] These Jewish hymns of praise are contrasted with the early Christian creedal hymn from Phil 2:5–8. Our literal translation from Luther's *Deutsche Bibel* highlights some of the language that would be integrated into the opening movement, and a number of the reflective poems set in the *Passion*:[15]

---

11. Luther, *Heidelberg Disputation*. WA 1: 362, 11–14: "Ita ut nulli iam satis sit ac prosit, qui cognoscit Deum in gloria et maiestate, nisi cognoscat eundem in humilitate et ignominia crucis. Sic perdit sapientiam sapientum &c sicut Isaias dicit: Vere absconditus tu es Deus."

12. In Luther's 1546, *Deutsche Bibel*, WA DB 10/1, 123: "HERR, vnser Herrscher, wie herrlich ist dein Name in allen Landen. Da man dir dancket im Himel."

13. Following the verse division in Luther's 1546 translation of the Bible, the *Deutsche Bibel*, Ps 48:10 in most English translations. Luther, WA DB 10/1, 255: "Gott, wie dein Name, so ist auch dein Rhum bis an der Welt ende, Deine Rechte ist vol Gerechtigkeit."

14. The "Lord" from Psalm 8:1,9 is הְוָ֣ה אֲדֹנֵ֗ינוּ —"*ădōnênū Yahweh*," while in Psalm 48:11 [48:10] the psalmist invokes אֱלֹהִ֑ים —"*ĕlōhîm*."

15. Luther, *Deutsche Bibel*. WA DB 7, 217.

Phil 2:5 EJn iglicher sey gesinnet, wie Jhesus Christus auch war:	⁵ Each one [of you] be of the mindset, how Jesus Christ also was,
⁶ welcher, ob er wohl in göttlicher gestalt war, hielt ers nicht fur einen raub, Gotte gleich sein.	⁶ who, while he doubtlessly was in divine form, held he it not as a robbery, to be equal with God.
⁷ Sondern eussert sich selbs und nam Knechts gestalt an, ward gleich wie ein ander Mensch vnd an geberden als ein Mensch erfunden,	⁷ Rather, alienated [sold] himself and took on slave's form, became equal as another human and in manner invented himself as a human;
⁸ Erniedriget sich selbs, vnd ward gehorsam bis zum tode, ja zum tode am Creutz.	⁸ Lowered himself and became obedient unto death, yes, unto death on a cross.

Luther's translation from the Greek identifies the "lowering" of Christ as spiritual and physical, but also social and economic. Christ is in the form of God and equal with God the Father, but he also becomes in the form of a human and equal with humans. The entitlement to equality is framed as "not as a robbery." Similarly, the means of lowering himself is through selling himself into slavery. Such a debasement is not only a contrast between heaven to earth, and "glory" to "humility" (*humilitate*), modesty about one's own importance, but also "majesty" (*maiestate*), dignity and prestige, to "ignominy" (*ignominia*), public shame or disgrace.[16] We are therefore encouraged to understand Christ's self-lowering through the lens of both theological eternity, and also contemporary social-economic power structures.

The central moment of the death on a cross as depicted in John's telling of the crucifixion is the pivotal moment where Christ exclaims, *Es ist vollbracht! und neigte das Haupt und verschied*—"it is accomplished [brought to fullness or completion]! and bowed his head and expired [breathed his last]." Hung from a cross, naked, having given away his last remaining family on earth, Jesus is presented as alone and humbled in his

---

16. Latin, *humilis*—"lowliness," "degradation" or "humiliation," or "submissiveness;" *ignominia*—"dishonor" or "disgrace;" *maiestate*—"majesty," "dignity," "prestige." *Majestät* ("Your Majesty") in German could also be used at the time to address the Holy Roman Emperor of the German Nation, and later as an address for other monarchs, but is most frequently used to speak of God's majesty.

moment of death. Yet the term *vollbracht* has a double meaning, intended by John, by Luther, and exploited by Bach's setting. He is "done:" his life is over, he has died in circumstances of total public disgrace and personal submissiveness. His work on earth is also "complete": the prophecies are fulfilled, he has successfully carried out his mission. At this moment, Christ has also won victory over death and sin, and enabled all people to enter into eternal life with God, as the Passion librettist writes in movement 30: *der Held aus Juda siegt mit Macht / und schließt den Kampf. / Es ist vollbracht!* ("the hero of Judah triumphs with power / And concludes the conflict. / It is accomplished!").

"Herr, unser Herrscher": Movement 1, BWV 245

Chorus (Flute I/II, Oboe I/II, Violin I/II, Viola, Continuo)

Herr, unser Herrscher,	Lord, our Lord,
dessen Ruhm in allen Landen herrlich ist,	whose fame in all lands is noble!
Zeig uns durch deine Passion,	Show us through your passion
daß du, der wahre Gottessohn,	that you, the true son of God,
zu aller Zeit,	for all time,
auch in der größten Niedrigkeit,	even in the deepest lowliness,
verherrlicht worden bist.	have been made noble.[17]

As the *John Passion*'s opening movement, *Herr unser Herrscher* uses the full powers of the assembled musicians: the choir, two flute parts, two oboe parts, two violin parts, a viola and a continuo part played usually on cello, bassoon, chamber organ, and string bass.[17] One of the longest movements of the Passion, the chorus has three main sections. The A-section includes a full minute of instrumental music alone before the choir enters and repeats three times: *Herr, unser Herrscher, / dessen Ruhm in allen Landen herrlich ist.* In the B-section, the latter five lines are sung twice: *Zeig uns durch deine Passion, / daß du, der wahre Gottessohn,/ zu aller Zeit, / auch in der größten Niedrigkeit, / verherrlicht worden bist.* The

---

17. The instrumentation in Bach's four versions of the *John Passion* varied; see Dürr, *St John Passion Genesis*, 20–27. We use the Bärenreiter Urtext Score, *Johannes-Passion BWV 245*, which includes oboes/transverse flutes, violins, viola, and a continuo of cello, bassoon, portatif organ and bass strings.

music then returns *da capo* ("to the beginning") and the instrumental and choral elements of the A-section are repeated.

There is no named author for the text. Previously we have suggested a single compiler who through-constructed the libretto as a whole, in close collaboration with Bach.[18] Line 1 quotes Psalm 8:1, line 2 quotes Psalm 48:11 [48:10], while lines 3–7 are free paraphrases drawing on Philippians 2:5–8 and John 3:14–16. The poem's lines range from 4–11 syllables in each line, but rhymes A B CC DD B with two couplets bracketed by an almost perfect rhyme on declensions of the verb 'to be'. The rhymes establish aural and theological connections between the words and lines:

Passion—Gottessohn	Passion—son of God
aller Zeit—Niedrigkeit	all time—lowliness
ist—bist	is—been

The initial line "Lord, our Lord" stands at the head of the poem, providing the internal repeated syllable *Herr* ("Lord").

The Words: "The Lord" as a Contrast of Glory and Humility

The contrast, or paradox, of glory and humility, is encapsulated in the opening chorus of the *John Passion* where we see a group of cognate words celebrating Jesus Christ's nobility.[19] *Herr, Herrscher, herrlich* and *verherrlicht* must be translated in English variously as "Lord" (a mode of address), "Lord" (a position), "noble" (or lordly), and "made noble" (or ennobled). Contemporary understanding of these terms as theologically significant has already been comprehensively demonstrated. For example, in the passion sermons of Pietist theologian August Hermann Franke (1663–1727), Jesus' *Herrlichkeit* means "his divinity, manifested in his foreknowledge of and voluntary undertaking of the events of the passion," as summarized by Chafe.[20] Christ's glorification *Verherrlichung*—his

---

18. Loewe, *Theological Commentary*, 85–86.

19. This whole section unpacks Firth's earlier arguments in "Study Translation," 104, footnotes 4–7. For more on the history and source texts, see Loewe, *Theological Commentary*, 141–6.

20. Chafe, *Bach's Johannine Theology*, 169.

ennoblement—is also his *Erhöhung*—his lifting up onto the physical structure of the cross (Jn 3:14).[21]

Yet this connected group of words also places Christ as powerful in the aristocratic political structure of Bach's time. As Ulrich Siegele has pointed out, Leipzig in Bach's time was impacted by the pan-European shift towards absolute power of the sovereign, away from the "Estates" (parliament or *Landschaft*).[22] Bach was elected to the role of Thomaskantor as "a candidate of the absolutist Court Party," and although he was commissioned court composer by the sovereign, whose court was at Dresden, he was employed by the city of Leipzig, leading to regular opposition from the Estates Party.[23] Siegele posits that Bach's *Matthew Passion* may have been particularly impacted by his "absolutist mandate;" but here we show that absolutist concepts are also strongly present in this opening movement of the *John Passion*.[24]

Nobility in Bach's Germany was inherited through a patrilinear line, and so it was relevant that in this movement the librettist makes Christ's legitimacy and maleness clear, as *der wahre Gottessohn* ("the true son of God").[25] Nobility in this libretto also evokes the medieval and Renaissance concepts of behavior befitting a noble person—nobility is a mode of good behavior to which all should aspire.[26] Thus it is important that his international glory, fame or praise, is noble (*Ruhm in allen Landen herrlich ist*).[27] In Bach's time, nobles had power because they had power

21. As Luther translates ὕψωσεν: "raising high," "exalting," "glorifying."

22. Siegele, "Domestic Politics," 17–34.

23. Siegele, "Domestic Politics," 25.

24. Chafe, *Bach's Johannine Theology*, 31. Another and interesting pathway for discussion here is opened by Janice B. Stockigt's "Liturgical Music for a New Elector," in which she highlights the confessional conflicts between Friedrich August's personal Catholic faith and role as head of the state Lutheran Church.

25. Germany was subject to Salic Law which included Agnatic succession—the total exclusion of women from inheritance of a throne or fief.

26. For more on Luther's thoughts about German nobility as defenders of evangelical doctrine and protectors of the *armen seelen heyl* ("poor souls' weal") residing in their lands, see Luther, *An den christlichen Adel deutscher Nation*. WA 6, 409, and 428: 23–25: "Thus the Christian nobility shall stand against the Pope as one, facing a common enemy and destroyer of Christianity, for the sake of the poor souls' weal, who must be protected from such tyranny" (*Szo sol hie der Christlich adel sich gegen yhm [den Papst] setzen als wider eynen gemeynen feynd und zustorer der Christenheit umb der armen seelen heyl willen, die durch solch tyranny vortrerben mussen*).

27. For more on Christ's name, see Loewe, *Theological Commentary*, 143, for his *Ruhm* ("renown"), see Firth, "Study Translation," 104; and Chafe, *Bach's Johannine*

over lands and, in movement 5, the Lord God is to be obeyed *zugleich / auf Erden wie im Himmelreich* ("equally / on earth as in the kingdom of heaven.").

Christ's nobility is *zu aller Zeit*: both "for all time" but also "of all time" and "from all time." *Zu* typically means "to" or "for" but in noble titles can mean "of." The German nobility included both those who inherited their nobility from ancient times, *Uradel*, and those who were granted nobility by the sovereign through letters patent. On the one hand, therefore, Christ's Father is from before the very foundation of the world—no nobility is more "Ur." Yet, even with this inherited nobility, Christ is granted even greater power and glory; he is ennobled even further due to his heroic actions on the cross. Thus Christ also earns his nobility, he is "made noble" (*verherrlicht worden bist*).

Nobility is contrasted in this opening movement with *der größten Niedrigkeit* ("the deepest lowliness"), with a suggestion of being "brought low" or "humiliated." This is not an unusual move for the *John Passion's* librettist: *Herr* is used in a further five movements across the libretto, each of which make similar comparisons, sometimes in relation to Jesus Christ, and sometimes to God the Father.

In movement 5, *Herr Gott* ("Lord God") is to be obeyed "equally / on earth as in the kingdom of heaven." The lowliness of earth in contrast to the elevation of heaven is a regular contrast in the Lutheran theology of Bach's time. In movement 13, the sin that causes the librettist pain in their heart is caused *weil der Knecht den Herrn verleugnet hat* ("because the slave has denied his Lord"), referring to Peter's denial of Jesus in the preceding recitative. In movement 26, the cross sparkles in the depths of the librettist's heart in consolation because Herr Christ, so full of mercy, has bled to death. In movement 32, the *lieber Herre* ("beloved Lord") bows or lowers his head (*neigest du das Haupt*) in submission to death and suffering. In movement 40, the *Passion's* concluding movement, the *Herr* is enjoined to carry (*tragen*) the body asleep in its tomb up into Abraham's bosom until Judgement Day. The pairing of nobility with lowliness (depth, humility, humiliation, or suffering), is a pairing of elevation with debasement whether social, locational, or allegorical.[28]

It may be useful to contrast these pairings using the word *Herr* with other words and symbols of rulership and power in the *Passion*, such

---

Theology, 151–4.

28. For a further exploration of "lowering" in movements 1, 26 and 40, see Loewe, "Christology," 79–90.

as "king," "kingdom," "crown," or "hero." In movement 16, Pilate asks, "Are you the King of the Jews?" and Jesus replies, "My kingdom is not of this world," to which the choir responds in the following movement, *Ach großer König, groß zu aller Zeiten, / Wie kann ich gnugsam diese Treu ausbreiten?* ("O great King, great for all time, How can I sufficiently broadcast this faithfulness?"). The phrasing parallels the language in movement 1, and yet the rest of the chorale does not focus on the contrast of elevation and debasement, but rather on the impossibility of repaying the great debt.

Similarly, in movements 29–30, Jesus says, *Es ist vollbracht* ("It is completed"), and the aria responds that *Der Held aus Juda siegt mit Macht / Und schließt den Kampf. / Es ist vollbracht!* ("the hero of Judah triumphs with power / and concludes the conflict. / It is accomplished!"). The pairing is of the dark night of mourning (*Trauernacht*), followed by the day of victory.[29] The arioso movement 19, on the crown of thorns, reflects on the paradox of the wounded healer. The recitative and chorus in 25–26, where Pilate directs the sign on the cross to say, "Jesus of Nazareth, the King of the Jews," is reflected on by a chorale with the weakest of the elevation and lowliness pairings in the lyrics: *in meines Herzens Grunde* ("in the depths of my heart") is not very low, nor very close in the text to *Herr Christ* ("Lord Christ").

When the *Passion* was re-performed and partially revised in 1725, a year after its first performance, the new introductory movement, *O Mensch, bewein' dein Sünde groß* ("O human, weep for your great sin") replaced the focus on the lordship of Christ with the narrative of Jesus' incarnation, healing ministry, and sacrifice. In the new movement, Christ is depicted as mediator and advocate (*der Mittler*), healer and sacrifice, with no mention of rulership or glory at all. From 1729, *O Mensch, bewein' dein Sünde groß* would instead become the concluding movement of Part I of the *Matthew Passion* (BWV 244). This would give credence to Chafe's argument that while Bach takes the "classic" *Christus Victor* theory with its "drama of stark opposites" in the *John Passion*, in the *Matthew Passion*, he instead tends towards the satisfaction theory of atonement, first formulated by Anselm of Canterbury, where "redemption ... is a work in which Jesus's humanity is the key."[30] *Herr unser Herrscher* was

29. For a theological reading of this aria, see Loewe, *Theological Commentary*, 267–74, Breyfogle, "Redemption and Human Freedom," 340, and Chafe, *Tonal Allegory*, 284.

30. Chafe, *Tonal Allegory*, 13.

returned to be the opening of the *John Passion* for all subsequent versions performed between 1728–50.

The "high/low paradox" is therefore only one of the sets of contrasts that the librettist sets up in the *Passion*. The pairing of lordship with submission and humiliation or debasement is most closely associated to *Herr* and its cognates. It is only when the text speaks of "the LORD" or "lordliness" that Luther's contrast between glory and majesty and humility and ignominy is highlighted. Other terms for rulership are linked to other contrasts—between God's greatness and our ability to proclaim it, or God's suffering and healing, or God's victory and the challenge of battle. As the greatest concentration of such terms, movement 1 of the *Passion* is a heightened focus on the specifically "high/low aspect" of Christ's glory through his suffering and death on the cross.

Bach's Music: a Contrast of "High" and "Low"

The music of the opening section famously makes use of a range of tropes understood to represent "high" and "low," including: high and low pitch, rising and falling melodic lines, loud and soft volume, fast or slow rhythm or pace, and contrasting Baroque music theories about the meaning of key signatures.[31] Bach patterns these sequentially and simultaneously, so that sometimes a high element will be followed by a low element, at other times a high element will be set over a low element. Together these multiple techniques richly set the theological and textual contrasts of "high" and "low," or glory and majesty and humility and ignominy.[32]

For example, the shift from singing together in block chords for the opening lines towards the greater complexity of counterpoint may map the theories of eighteenth-century music theorist Martin Heinrich Fuhrmann (1669–1745), who believed that earthly music is a "monophony" (*choraliter*) that prefigures the contrapuntal "polyphony" (*figuraliter*) of heaven.[33] The nineteenth-century musicologist Philipp Spitta (1841–

---

31. For a clear introduction to the relevant tonal theories, see Chafe, *Bach's Johannine Theology* 181–93, and his longer work *Tonal Allegory*.

32. Luther, *Heidelberg Disputation*, WA 1: 362, 11–14.

33. Fuhrmann, *Satans-Capelle*, 20: "in the same way in which musicians in the lower choir on earth make music in unison, there in the upper choir they will let the counterpoint resound even unto the ages of ages" (*so sie im untern Chor auf Erden nur choraliter musiciret, dort im obern Chor figuraliter in die Ewigkeit der Ewigkeiten warden erschallen lassen*); see also Butt, "Bach's metaphysics of music," 51.

94) notes the darkness of the instrumental parts, compared to the force and power of the vocal parts, which Spitta interpreted as Bach intending "to combine, in one image, the majesty and power of the son of God as well as his deep humiliation."[34]

Spitta uses the image of "giant waves" to describe the force and rise and fall of the vocal and instrumental lines.[35] Eric Chafe points out the contrast between the "almost inevitable sounding" line of rising circle-of-fifths sixteenth-notes, and the "chromatic writing in the oboes above the 'throbbing' pedal tones," which "brings out the theme of suffering."[36] Albert Dürr describes the "circling semiquaver figure" as "unusually agitated;" and where it is present in the vocal parts, the figure emphasizes *Herrscher* ("Lord"), *herrlich* ("noble,), *Landen* ("lands"), and *verherrlicht* ("made noble") which Dürr speculates may be "a kind of glorification of God in his abasement."[37]

Across the movement, the violins play these waves of sixteenth-notes almost ceaselessly, except for three striking inversions where the "high" violins swap with the "low" bass of the continuo. In these passages, the violins join the woodwind to take up the emphatic crotchet block chords of the opening *Herr, Herr, Herr* ("Lord, Lord, Lord,") and the sixteenth-notes waves are taken up instead by the cello, bassoon, bass strings, and portatif organ continuo. This inversion is used for the only staggered entry of the voices on *Herr, unser Herrscher* (measures 33–36), and the two staggered entries on *Zeig uns* (measures 58–66, 78–83): *Herr unser Herrscher . . . Zeig uns durch deine Passion, / daß du, der wahre Gottessohn* ("Lord, our Lord . . . Show us through your passion / that you, the true son of God.") The instrumental parts thus enact the drama of the Lord descending to earth from heaven and dying on the cross to show his true nature, shockingly swapping "high" and "low" instrumental parts.

The music takes the listener from the heights into the depths and then back again in the B-section, too. In measures 59–60, in the first two notes of each voice *Zeig uns durch deine Passion* ("show us through your passion"), the melody descends an octave and then returns in an

---

34. Spitta, *Bach*, 365: "Er wollte die Majestät und Gewalt des Gottessohnes und zugleich seine tiefe Erniedrigung . . . in ein Bild zusammenfassen."

35. Spitta, *Bach*, 36: "Meereswogen."

36. Loewe, *Theological Commentary*, 202–3.

37. Dürr, *St John Passion Genesis*, 75–78.

ascending scale motif.[38] Chafe has suggested that octave jumps in the vocal melody further contrast the high and low of heaven and earth.[39]

Herr, unser Herrscher uses the key of G minor, a balanced key, "moderate" and "tempered" according to eighteenth-century music theorist Johann Mattheson (1681–1764).[40] Such a setting evoked the political ideals of "decorum" or *politische Klugheit* ("Political Prudence"), the values of restrained, just, and acceptable behavior for the nobility, as espoused by contemporary thinkers such as the Enlightenment Leipzig jurist and philosopher Christian Thomasius (1655–1728), and Christian Weise (1642–1708), the poet whose work Bach adapted for movement 13 of the *John Passion*.[41] The melodic descent simultaneously takes the listener away from the tonic G minor, away from this noble balance. But as Christ's passion demonstrates that he is the true son of God, the tenors develop the theme to move us back to the tonic key, followed by a rising tonic arpeggio on *zu aller Zeit* ("for all times") in measure 66ff., which returns listeners to the strength, tempered joy, and melodic heights.[42]

A second descent is set through "the deepest lowliness" (measures 68–69, and 84–85). The line also goes quieter withdrawing from the *forte* ("loudness," "strength") to *piano* ("softness," "quiet") for the phrase *Auch in der größten Niedrigkeit* ("Even in the deepest lowliness"), and the woodwind takes more than a measure of silence. *Niedrigkeit* ("lowliness") is set with the lowest notes in the melody in all four voices, emphasized by block chords and punctuated by a rest in all voices, before launching into a *forte* entry on *verherrlicht worden bist* ("have been made noble"), the wind instruments enter, and the music moves into an echo of the opening *Herrscher*-theme from the opening measures. The section ends strongly, by concluding in the dominant, and "martial," key of D major.[43]

---

38. Loewe, *Theological Commentary*, 145.

39. Chafe, "Bach's St John Passion" in Frankin, *New Bach Studies*, 78.

40. See Loewe, *Theological Commentary*, 142.

41. Notably Thomasius, *Politische Klugheit*. Bach used an adaptation of the first verse of Christian Weise's poem *Der weinende Petrus* for the text of the aria *Ach, mein Sinn* (movement 13). See Whaley, *Holy Roman Empire*, 233. For an exploration of "decorum" as part of a "high/low" dichotomy in Christian Weise's work, see Solbach, "Transgression als Verletzung des Decorum," 33.

42. Loewe, *Theological Commentary*, 145.

43. Mattheson, *Orchestre*, 242: "kriegerisch;" Loewe, *Theological Commentary*, 146.

The A-section is repeated, returning to the plaintive and restless strings with contrasting melodic lines moving down and up, and then the first two lines are repeated, further emphasizing the importance of the concept of nobility, majesty, and glory.

Bach sets the word *Herr* in ways that emphasize its importance, and yet he uses a range of different techniques to achieve this aim: including singing a single syllable to a note on the onbeat, alternating sound with silence; or extending a single syllable across up to 32 sixteenth notes. The first word of the *Passion*—*Herr*—is repeated three times as a block chord, with a beat rest between each repetition, for emphasis and also likely to address the threefold person of God as Father, Son, and Holy Spirit.[44] The second half of the line has an extended two-measure melisma on *Herrscher* ("Lord"), expanding and emphasizing the first syllable. The choir repeats the first line, including the three statements of *Herr* and extended *Herrscher*, three times. Similarly, in the final repetition, the sopranos and tenors sing *herrlich* four times and the altos five times. The climactic and repeated melisma on the *"herr"* in *verherrlicht* in the B-section also can last up to two measures. While Bach often has the four vocal lines singing different words in staggered layers, he is most likely to bring the lines together to sing the same syllable on *Herr, Herr(scher), herrlich* and *(ver)herr(licht)*: "my Lord," "the Lord," "noble," and "been made noble."

For Bach, Christ's lordly glory is the most insistent musical meaning of the opening chorus, with the high concepts of heaven, nobility, power, might, and praise being contrasted with low concepts of earth, debasement, humility, softness, loss, and shame. The movement uses repetition, variation, ornamentation, pitch, volume, rhythm, instrumentation, and changing key signatures to explain the paradoxical theology in John's Gospel through music. In the final movement of the *Passion*, Bach returns to address *Ach Herr* ("O Lord") in a contrasting simple four-part lullaby hymn, with no repetitions, little ornamentation, and minimal instrumental accompaniment. This quiet, humble setting—literally without fanfare—however, accompanies words addressing Christ risen in glory at the end of time, *Mein Heiland und Genadenthron* ("My Savior and throne of mercy").[45] This contrast of high and low in the theology of Christ's glory as set out in the Gospel of John thus bookends the *John*

---

44. Loewe, *Theological Commentary*, 142.
45. Firth, "Study Translation," 133-4.

Passion: in its majestic opening and subdued ending movements, Christ's heavenly nobility comes down to earth, and through his deepest lowliness, humans are granted salvation and eternal life.

Conclusion

The *John Passion* opens with an extended reflection on the majesty and glory of Christ, drawing on the Psalms, Philippians, and the Gospel of John. The words and music demonstrate Bach's theological understanding of the Johannine theological concept of Christ's glory being revealed in suffering. This chapter provides an in-depth reading of the music and text of *Herr, unser Herrscher*, placed in its contemporary theological, musicological, and social context.

We attempt to make the multiple levels of meaning legible to audiences who may not have extensive technical understanding of these fields or languages. We further extend our interdisciplinary methodology drawing on cultural history, theory, translation, close textual analysis, and close musicological analysis.[46] Expanding from our earlier research, we elucidate here the lack of kenotic Christology in eighteenth-century German religious thought, instead highlighting Luther's focus on "lowering." While our previous work has focused more on the relationship of Bach to his civic setting, in this chapter we also highlight how his choices in representing Christ's nobility were influenced by the pan-European rise of absolutist sovereigns.

In the opening movement of the *John Passion*, we can see how Bach's understanding of heavenly and worldly glory are reflected in the words chosen and the musical setting. Luther's perception of the cross as a moment of both glory and majesty and humility and ignominy are here explored through text and music: not in contrast to one another, but part of the same concept. In this way, the opening movement of Bach's first Passion oratorio amplifies the message at the heart of John's Passion: that the Incarnate Christ who shared in the glory of God from before the world existed (Jn 17:5), is truly glorified in the events of the cross, and that his followers might likewise find their glory when they join with him in walking the way of the cross. That Christ, *der wahre Gottesohn, / zu aller Zeit, / auch in der größten Niedrigkeit, / verherrlicht worden ist* ("the

---

46. Firth, "The MacNeices and their Circles," 21–26.

true son of God, / for all time, / even in the deepest lowliness, / has been made noble").

Bibliography

Aulén, Gustav. *Christus Victor*. Translated by A. G. Herbert. New York, NY: Macmillan, 1969.
Bach, Johann Sebastian. *Johannes-Passion BWV 245*, edited by Arthur Mendel. Neue Bach-Ausgabe Serie II: Messen, Passionen, oratorische Werke, IV. Kassel: Bärenreiter, 1973.
Breyfogle, Todd. "Redemption and Human Freedom in the Bach 'Passions.'" *NB* 84 (2003) 335–45.
Butt, John. "Bach's Metaphysics of Music." In *The Cambridge Companion to Bach*, edited by John Butt, 46–59. Cambridge: Cambridge University Press, 1997.
Chafe, Eric T. *Tonal Allegory in the Vocal Music of Johann Sebastian Bach*. Berkeley, CA: University of California Press, 1991.
———. *Analyzing Bach Cantatas*. New York, NY: Oxford University Press, 2003.
———. *J. S. Bach's Johannine Theology: The St John Passion and the Cantatas for Spring 1725*. New York, NY: Oxford University Press, 2014.
———. "The Lutheran "Metaphysical" Tradition in Music and Music Theory." In Chafe, *Analyzing Bach's Cantatas*, 23–41.
———. "Bach's St John Passion: Theology and Musical Structure." In *New Bach Studies*, edited by Don O. Franklin, 75–122. Cambridge: Cambridge University Press, 1989.
Dürr, Alfred. *Johann Sebastian Bach's St John Passion: Genesis, Transmission and Meaning*. Oxford: Oxford University Press, 2000.
Firth, Katherine. "The MacNeices and their Circles: Poets and Composers in Collaboration on Art Song, 1939–54." PhD diss., Oxford Brookes University, 2008.
———. "Study Translation." In *Johann Sebastian Bach's St John Passion (BWV 245): A Theological Commentary with a New Study Translation by Katherine Firth and a Foreword by N. T. Wright*. SHCT 168. Leiden: Brill, 2014, 100–134.
"Frischmuth, Marco Hilario" [Fuhrmann, Martin Heinrich]. *Die an der Kirchen Gottes gebaute Satans-Capelle*. "Cölln am Rhein" [Alt-Kölln/Berlin]: Verlegt von der Heiligen Drei Könige Erben, 1729.
Franklin, Don O. (ed), *New Bach Studies*. Cambridge: Cambridge University Press, 1989.
Gottfried, Thomasius. *Christi Person und Werk. Darstellung der evangelisch lutherischen Dogmatik vom Mittelpunkte der Christologie aus*. Erlangen: Thomas Bläsing, 1851–1861.
Law, David R. "The Nature of Kenotic Christology." In *Kierkegaard's Kenotic Christology*, edited by David R. Law, 34–63. Oxford: Oxford University Press, 2010.
Leaver, Robin A. *Bachs theologische Bibliothek: Eine kritische Bibliographie*. Neuhausen-Stuttgart: Hänssler Verlag, 1985.
Loewe, Andreas. *Johann Sebastian Bach's St John Passion (BWV 245): A Theological Commentary: With a New Study Translation by Katherine Firth*. SHCT 168. Leiden: Brill, 2014.

———. "Sermons in Sound: The Theology of Johann Sebastian Bach's Passions." UD Repository (2010): 1–11. https://repository.divinity.edu.au/841/

———. "'God's Capellmeister:: The Proclamation of Scripture in the Music of J. S. Bach." *Pac* 24 (2011) 141–71.

———. "'Zeig uns durch deine Passion:' The Christology of Bach's St John Passion." *Paradosis* 3 (2016) 79–90.

———. and Firth, Katherine. "Luther's 'Mighty Fortress.'" *LQ* 32 (2018) 125–45.

———. and Firth, Katherine. *Martin Luther and the Arts: Music, Images and Drama to Promote the Reformation*. Leiden: Brill (forthcoming).

Luther, Martin. *D. Martin Luthers Werke: Kritische Gesamtausgabe* [WA], edited by Joachim Karl Friedrich Knaake et al. Weimar: Hermann Böhlau, 1883–1985.

———. *Werke: Die Deutsche Bibel* [WA DB], edited by Joachim Karl Friedrich Knaake et al. Weimar: Hermann Böhlau, 1906–1961.

Marissen, Michael. *Bach & God*. New York, NY: Oxford University Press, 2016.

———. Review of *Bach & God*, by Markus Rathey. *CSR* 46 (2017) 292.

Mattheson, Johann. *Das Neu-eröffnete Orchestre*. Hamburg: by the author, 1713.

Pelikan, Jaroslav. *Bach among the Theologians*. Philadelphia, PA: Fortress, 1986.

———. "Christus Victor in the Saint John Passion." In *Bach among the Theologians*, 102–29.

Rambach, Johann Jakob. *Betrachtungen über die Sieben letzten Worte des gecreutzigten Jesu*. Halle: Waisenhaus, 1732.

Rathey, Markus. "Memory, Morals, and Contemplation in Leipzig Passion Texts from the 1720s: A New Perspective on J. S. Bach's *St John Passion* from 1724." *Bach* 51 (2020) 44–69.

Siegele, Ulrich. "Bach and the Domestic Politics of Electoral Saxony." Translated by Kay LaRae Henschel. In *Cambridge Companion to Bach*, edited by John Butt, 17–34. Cambridge: Cambridge University Press, 1997.

Solbach, Andreas. "Transgression als Verletzung des Decorum bei Christian Weise, J. J. Chr. von Grimmelshausen und in Johann Beers 'Narrenspital.'" *Daphnis* 20 (1991) 33–60.

Spitta, Philipp. *Johann Sebastian Bach*. Leipzig: Breitkopf und Härtel, 1873–1880.

Stockigt, Janice B. "Liturgical Music for a New Elector: Origins of Bach's 1733 Missa Revisited." In *Bach and the Counterpoint of Religion*, edited by Robin A. Leaver, 6383. Urbana, IL: University of Illinois Press, 2018.

Thomasius, Christian. *Kurzer Entwurf der Politischen Klugheit*. Reprint Hildesheim: Olms, 2002.

Whaley, Joachim. *Germany and the Holy Roman Empire. Vol. II: The Peace of Westphalia to the Dissolution of the Reich, 1648–1806*. Oxford: Oxford University Press, 2012.

9

Dostoevsky's Use of the Gospel of John in *Crime and Punishment*

SCOTT A. KIRKLAND

Introduction

ONE OF DOSTOEVSKY'S GREAT polemics against what he considered to be Western nihilism, the novel *Crime and Punishment*, finds its high point in the fourth chapter of the fourth book. Reading the eleventh chapter of the Fourth Gospel, Sonya Marmadelov emphasizes that Lazarus has been dead four days (Jn 11:17). The repetition of the number four points to the structure of Dostoevsky's narrative. At the point at which the stench of death is at its height, after four days lying in the tomb (Jn 11:39)—one more than Christ himself—the prostitute, Sonya, and the murderer, Raskolnikov, "strangely encountered each other in the reading of the eternal book."[1] While contemporary Johannine scholars may think differently about the structure of the Fourth Gospel, the story of the raising of Lazarus was for Dostoevsky the turning point.[2] For it is here that Raskolnikov begins his motion toward repentance, reparation, and salvation, asking Sonya to join him.

This essay will proceed by way of three parts. First, I will outline some of the broad contours of Dostoevsky's critique of the west. Second,

---

1. Dostoevsky, *Crime and Punishment*, 391.

2. In Johannine scholarship, John 11:1–12:50 (of which the Raising of Lazarus is part) stands at the center of the Johannine plot: it represents the climax of Jesus' ministry and the turning towards his death (Moloney, *John*, 322–69).

I will turn to the particulars of the narrative of Raskolnikov and Sonya in *Crime and Punishment*, drawing particular attention to the questions of narrative form in both the novel and the Gospel. Finally, I will point to the gesture with which the narrative of Raskolnikov and Sonya's encounter concludes, that of swapping crosses, in order to reflect more broadly on the question of bearing the cross and the way the Gospel proceeds from chapter 12 onwards toward the cross.

Tale of Two Cities

Nineteenth century Russia lived in the wake of a century of contested Westernization inaugurated by Peter the Great (1672–1725). Peter had been enchanted by the great cities and cultures of Western Europe, and was intent on integrating Russia into this European sphere. This took place through cultural reform, but also though the conquest of ports in the Baltic Sea allowing for the development of the Imperial Russian Navy, and through the development of institutions such as the University of St Petersburg. Russia, of course, has often sat uneasily between Europe and Asia, as a threshold between the two. Indeed, one might suggest that precisely as this threshold of difference, Russia's relationship to Europe is constitutive of the latter term.

One of Peter the Great's projects was establishing a new capital, St Petersburg, not insignificantly the setting of Dostoevsky's *Crime and Punishment*. In contradistinction to Moscow and much of old Russia, St Petersburg is architecturally much more similar to Western European capitals. It was built on the site of a captured Swedish fort, and is constructed largely on swampy terrain which gives it the humid, breathless air that Dostoevsky narrates, as the murderer Raskolnikov stumbles through the streets:

> The heat in the street was terrible: with the humidity to make it worse; and the crowds of people, the slaked lime everywhere, the scaffolding, bricks and dust all about him, and that special Petersburg stench, so familiar to all who are unable to get out of town in summer—all worked painfully upon the young man's already jangled nerves.[3]

Crime and Punishment is set in the midst of this ongoing conflict over Russia's relationship to the West. From around 1830 onwards, a

---

3. Dostoevsky, *Crime and Punishment*, 6.

movement whose affiliates we now know as the Slavophiles were beginning to have an influence on Russian intellectual life, particularly in Moscow. These thinkers took recourse to Russia's pre-Petrine past in order to point to a form of life bound to Russian Orthodoxy and to the peasant community, in contrast to the decadence of Western Roman Catholic and Protestant traditions. These thinkers were particularly influential through the 1840–50s, *Crime and Punishment* being published in 1866.

During his formative years as a writer, Dostoevsky had been involved in a circle around the atheist literary critic, Vissarion Belinsky.[4] Belinsky was attracted to Western socialist ideals, and through him Dostoevsky too became acquainted with this world. Yet Dostoevsky's religious commitments meant that he retained a reluctance to fully integrate into this literary world. While in his early work this difference is noticeable, it becomes ever more exaggerated after Dostoevsky's return from exile and the major works that follow. Dostoevsky had been a member of the Petrashevksy circle, a socialist reformist movement, and a mock execution was held for his involvement, though he himself was spared with exile.

What should be clear in this brief biographical excursus is that conflict with Western ideas and ideals was central to Russian life in the middle of the nineteenth century. Between Slavophiles and westernizers, Russia's place in European modernity was in question. Dostoevsky had moved between both worlds by the time we arrive at *Crime and Punishment*, which is set in the symbolically and literally westernized capital, St Petersburg. In the novella immediately preceding the publication of *Crime and Punishment, Notes from Underground* (1864), the antihero protagonist, the Underground Man, speaks of "St Petersburg, the most abstract and intentional city on the entire globe (Cities can be intentional or unintentional.)"[5] The intentionality of St Petersburg might be read as its planned character, the way by sheer force of authoritarian will Peter the Great erects it on the swamp as a symbol of Russia's entrance into the air of modernity. This gives it the abstract character of a Promethean fever dream, a kind of unreality. Indeed, the Underground Man, the man living in a tomb, writes:

> I am told the Petersburg climate is bad for me, and that with my small means it is very expensive to live in Petersburg. I know all that better than all these sage and experienced counsellors and

---

4. For a discussion see Frank, *Dostoevsky*.
5. Dostoevsky, *Notes from Underground* and *The Double*, 26.

monitors.... But I am remaining in Petersburg: I am not going away from Petersburg! I am not going away because ... Oh, it does not matter after all whether I go away or I don't.[6]

Dostoevsky's critique of the West began at least as early as his *Winter Notes on Summer Impressions* (1863), a book which, in the guise of a travel diary, provides a litany of the ills of Western capital cities, London and Paris. London in particular is cast as a grim, alienated, cesspool of gin-palaces and brothels. The great accomplishment of modernity, the Crystal Palace, stands in the text like a great monstrosity of the alienation of the people from their land under the pressure of the great force of modernization and factory production. So it is here that we have a kind of Russian tale of two cities, between St Petersburg and Moscow, between Western modernity and Russian Orthodoxy and the Russian "way." The very city of St Petersburg takes on the character of a tomb, as we find ourselves suffering for breath in Raskolnikov's fever dream reality. The setting of the novel places Raskolnikov in the situation of Lazarus, the tomb at Bethany becoming the feverish nightmare of Raskolnikov's humid summer caught in a tiny apartment. We read in *Crime and Punishment* that "this is a city of half-crazy people ... there are few places where you'll find so many gloomy, harsh and strange influences on the soul of a man as in St Petersburg."[7] And as we eventually turn to the center of the drama of Dostoevsky's novel, the reading of John 11, we find ourselves deep in the bowels of Petersburg.

Reading Together

Figuration of the Gospel

As mentioned at the outset, the turning point of the novel takes place in the fourth chapter of the fourth book in a reading of the Fourth Gospel "after eleven," of course echoing the fact that the raising of Lazarus is the eleventh chapter of the Gospel. The scene is set as Raskolnikov arrives at Sonya's apartment. He enters having been "wandering about in darkness," and accidentally runs into an embarrassed Sonya who takes him into her rented room. The room is described as "low-ceilinged ... [resembling] a sort of barn, possessing the form of a highly irregular rectangle, and this

---

6. Dostoevsky, *Notes from Underground*, 25.
7. Dostoevsky, *Crime and Punishment*, 557.

gave it a misshapen appearance."[8] One might read this description and think of the shape of a coffin, the slightly obtuse angles of the rectangular wall accommodating the shoulders of the dead figure, the low ceilings giving way to the feeling of claustrophobia. Before we proceed to the details of their reading of John 11, it is important to notice several elements in the novel which foreshadow this encounter. Indeed, this encounter retroactively discloses many signs previously given, and illuminates to us the movement forward.

Raskolnikov is described throughout the earliest stages of the novel as

> remarkably handsome, with beautiful dark eyes and dark, chestnut coloured hair; he was taller than average slim, and well-built. But soon he appeared to fall into a deep brooding, which might more correctly have been described as a kind of oblivion.

The oblivion is shared by the city itself, as Dostoevsky then describes how Raskolnikov was so "poorly dressed . . . [that] even one inured to such a style of living, would have been ashamed to go out on the street during the daytime in such rags." The part of St Petersburg he is in, however, "was of such a kind that it would have been difficult to surprise anyone by one's manner of dress."[9] All of this gestures to the wretched state which both Raskolnikov and the city share, a state akin to a rotting tomb. As he emerges from his tiny, dank apartment onto the streets, Raskolnikov's rags hang off him like Lazarus' burial clothes (Jn 11:44). Yet this is not a resurrection; it turns out that Raskolnikov is a figure of living death, the city itself his tomb. Finally, the time between Raskolnikov's murder of his landlady and his figural resurrection is four days, the length of time Lazarus spends in the tomb.

There are a number of female characters in *Crime and Punishment* who fulfil roles akin to those of Mary and Martha of Bethany, as well as that of Christ, throughout the novel. Raskolnikov's mother Pulkheria and sister Dunya continually offer love in spite of his coldness and indifference. His mother signs off a letter in the early stages of the novel, "Yours to the tomb," figuring the mourning of Mary and Martha at Lazarus' tomb. It is worth noting that in this letter alone the word love recurs more times than in the rest of the novel. She begins: "you know how I love you; you're the only one we think of, Dunya and I, you're everything

---

8. Dostoevsky, *Crime and Punishment*, 374–5.
9. Dostoevsky, *Crime and Punishment*, 7.

to us, all our hopes and aspirations rolled into one." There is a very real sense in this letter that Raskolnikov is indeed already absent, dead, at least spiritually. His mother asks, "Do you say your prayers, Rodya, the way you used to, and do you believe in the mercy of the Creator and our Redeemer? I fear in my heart that you may have been affected by this latest fashion of unbelief."

Dostoevsky tells us that, upon finishing reading the letter, the tears that have been streaming down Raskolnikov's face turn and become "pale and distorted . . . a nasty, lugubrious, jaundiced smile naked across his lips. He put his head on his thin, threadbare pillow . . . "[10] Here Dostoevsky evokes the imagery of a man lying in a tomb, head on the pillow, a deathly, jaundiced face in contrast to the tearful response to his mother. His mother's fear is that he has given himself over to a form of Western nihilism and unbelief, so that in this way he is in a state of living death, eternal life having forsaken him.

Other women bear narrative resemblances too. The tragic figure of Katerina Ivanova Marmeladov, the wife of the drunk Marmeladov and stepmother of Sonya Marmeladov, is weak throughout the novel, dying of consumption. The father Marmeladov narrates Sonya's entrance into a life of prostitution out of necessity: "And towards six o'clock I saw my little Sonya get up and put on her kerchief and her pelisse and go out and at some time after eight she came back. She came in and went straight to Katerina Ivanova and laid thirty silver rubles on the table in front of her without a word."[11] This is then followed by a mourning scene in which Sonya is shaking violently while Katerina Ivanova wraps her in a woolen shawl around her head and face, laying Sonya down on the bed. Marmeladov describes how he sees Katerina Ivanova "without a word, go to my little Sonya's bed-side, and she stayed there on her knees all the evening, kissing her feet, and would not get up . . . "[12]

Several signs layer over one another here. First, Sonya's entrance into prostitution is figured as an act of sacrifice; the thirty pieces of silver, like Judas' reward for betraying Jesus (see Matt 26:15), are Sonya's reward for handing herself over. Yet Marmeladov is the narrator here, and his impotence is figured as the vehicle for this handing over, precisely in inaction

---

10. Dostoevsky, *Crime and Punishment*, 49.
11. Dostoevsky, *Crime and Punishment*, 23.
12. Dostoevsky, *Crime and Punishment*, 23–24.

rather than action. He simply "lay there tipsy"[13] as all this took place. Sonya's act of sacrifice then blurs the boundaries of activity and passivity, as she actively hands herself over to the darkness of St Petersburg, becoming passive. Just as one might understand Christ's refusal to resist crucifixion as an active passivity, *kenosis* ("self-emptying"), so Sonya's action leads her into the darkness for the sake of her family. The fruits of her father's betrayal keep the family alive at the expense of his daughter. Katerina Ivanova, then, participates in this as the one who mourns Sonya's entrance into death, resembling Mary's anointing of Jesus (Jn 11:2; 12:3).[14]

These various scenes weave the Johannine narrative throughout the novel. One might mention others such as Marmadelov proclaiming, "Behold the man," as he holds Raskolnikov forward in a bar (Jn 19:5), or the various ways Dostoevsky weaves Raskolnikov's sister's and mother's love through the novel.[15] The point to highlight here, however, is that the climax performs the function of retroactive disclosure. This is an important narrative convention as it illuminates what has proceeded in the narrative, but does so with the effect of an "afterwardness" that induces in the reader the experience of the reading of John 11. As we are dragged into the tomb with Raskolnikov, we feel the sweltering humidity of the Petersburg summer, we are stifled by our enclosure in Raskolnikov's inner life, and here in the encounter with John 11 we too are lifted out of the tomb for breath. The effect of this retroactivity, then, is part of Dostoevsky's theological sensibility, but also of his psychological acuity.

Together in the Tomb

As we return to the scene at the high point of the narrative—the reading of John 11—remembering the tomb-like environment of Sonya's apartment, and the deathly figure of Raskolnikov, we might think of this moment as the appearance of Christ to Lazarus in the figure of Sonya. Sonya's act of selling herself into prostitution places her equally in the tomb: not as a murderer like Raskolnikov, but rather as one who has handed her life over for the sake of others; indeed, at the hand of an abusive patriarch.

---

13. Dostoevsky, *Crime and Punishment*, 24.

14. Dostoevsky's moralization of sex work and his playing into nineteenth century noble prostitute narrative tropes is certainly problematic here. For a discussion of this see, De Macedo, "Women in Dostoevsky's Fiction," in *Clinical Lessons on Life and Madness*, 201–21.

15. Dostoevsky, *Crime and Punishment*, 19.

Yet another reading presents itself via Raskolnikov's undoubted affection for Sonya and their shared reading of the Gospel. It becomes clear that, just as Sonya becomes Christ for Raskolnikov, equally Raskolnikov is the same for Sonya.

The scene begins with an extended exchange in which Raskolnikov torments Sonya over her family situation. He begins by bringing up the fact that Katerina Ivanova has been beating Sonya. He then points mercilessly to the situation of the family, utterly destitute due to their father's addiction, and about to be evicted due to a failure to pay rent. Raskolnikov points to Katerina Ivanova's illness and Marmeladov's inability to care for the children and then, gesturing to the situation that Sonya finds herself in as a prostitute living in a hovel of an apartment, he exclaims,

> "But what of the children? Where will you take them if not here, with you?"
> "Oh, I don't know!" Sonya screamed, almost in despair, and she clutched at her head. It was evident that the thought had fleetingly occurred to her on many, many occasions, and that he had startled it to life again.[16]

Raskolnikov knows precisely where to point to Sonya's greatest weaknesses: her impotence to protect her family precisely because of the condition she finds herself in while trying to protect her family. So Sonya is driven to the edge as Raskolnikov points to the nightmare scenario in which her siblings are left orphaned without her support. All she has left to invoke at this limit scenario is God: "'God will look after her, he will,' she said, beside herself." Raskolnikov has been leading Sonya to this point, to the point of belief and unbelief, to the point of total contingency on the existence and goodness of God, for he immediately jibes: "'But there may not be any God,' Raskolnikov replied with a kind of malicious satisfaction, gave a laugh and looked at her."[17]

Dostoevsky sets the scene for the reading of John's Gospel with these two figures in the midst of despair and madness. On the one hand, we have Sonya driven to despair by Raskolnikov's cold, rational push of her belief to the limit. On the other, we have Raskolnikov, whose gaze, in contrast to Sonya's tearful eyes "glittering," is "dry, inflamed, and sharp, his lips were quivering violently." Yet at the edge of his madness he crosses over into a kind of desperation too: "getting down on the floor, [he]

---

16. Dostoevsky, *Crime and Punishment*, 381.
17. Dostoevsky, *Crime and Punishment*, 382.

kissed her foot." Mimicking Katerina Ivanova and Mary, Raskolnikov finds himself in Sonya's suffering. Yet, Sonya "jerked back from him in horror, as from a madman. And indeed, he really did look like a man who was wholly insane."[18]

This scene echoes a theme that runs throughout Dostoevsky's novels of the thinness of the boundary between faith and madness.[19] Raskolnikov's madness is a product of his approach to the limit of a kind of rationality, the rationality of a subject who thinks it can master the world out of its own will and resource, an *übermensch* ("overman") of sorts. This is a concept from Nietzsche, a later writer, often paired in readings of Dostoevsky.[20] The overman embraces fate, embraces the suffering and chaos of the world in order to overcome it and not take recourse in the resources of religion and in order to embrace a vision of a world set aright in the hereafter.[21] The figure Raskolnikov identifies with is Napoleon, a figure of exceptional greatness.

When explaining to Sonya what his gesture of kissing her feet meant, he explains: "It wasn't you I was bowing to, but the whole of human suffering." This theme is further explicated as Raskolnikov tells Sonya of her great sinfulness, the greatness of her sin being that she "mortified and betrayed yourself *for nothing*. Isn't that monstrous? Isn't it monstrous that you're living in this filth which you hate and loathe, while all the time you know . . . that you're neither helping nor saving anyone by it?"[22] What makes Sonya pitiful, then, is that there is no goal to her sinfulness. Her embrace of prostitution and throwing herself into a destitute life for the sake of her siblings is hopeless; it cannot save them. Here, however, Raskolnikov is clearly facing himself: his plans for greatness, after the murder of his landlady to attain the material means to get there, having themselves become futile, his conscience driving him to madness. Both Sonya's sacrificial act and Raskolnikov's utterly selfish act are unable to offer hope to either.

---

18. Dostoevsky, *Crime and Punishment*, 382–3.

19. For a discussion of madness generally in Dostoevsky see, De Macedo, *Clinical Lessons on Life and Madness*.

20. For a collection that discusses the variations on this pairing, see Love & Metzger, *Dostoevsky and Nietzsche*.

21. See in particular the vision of the "eternal return" in Nietzsche, *The Gay Science*, §341.

22. Dostoevsky, *Crime and Punishment*, 383.

Raskolnikov compels Sonya to read John 11 to him, asking for it after seeing the Bible on her bedside table. The Bible was Lizaveta's, whom Raskolnikov has murdered four days prior, and it was given to Sonya as a gift. The coincidence makes Raskolnikov uncomfortable, as he thinks to himself, "I'll be turning into a holy fool myself soon, it's catching." And as he presses Sonya to read, the narrator's voice tells us that Raskolnikov intuits how difficult it is for her to read, "for her to give away and reveal everything that was *her*. He knew these feelings really did constitute, as it were, her most genuine and possibly oldest *secret*," which she has held onto through her wretched life. Yet at the same time he intuits that "she had an agonizing desire to read to him, in spite of all her misery and fear, and that it was *him* she wanted to read to, to make sure that he heard it, and that she wanted it to be *now*."[23] The wavering between fear and desire constitutes the deepest recesses of Sonya's faith, her fear of who she is and her desire to be who she is for others.

Utterly vulnerable to Raskolnikov's attacks, Sonya reads. The narrative breaks as Jesus asks Martha whether she believes he is the resurrection and the life (Jn 11:26–27): "taking a new breath, apparently in pain, Sonya read distinctly and forcefully, as though she herself were confessing her creed for all to hear." Sonya's affirmation quivers precisely on the edge of this desire and fear as the only way to hold poise between the two, and so she "quickly raised her eyes to *him*, but soon mastered herself and began to read on." Toward the end of the narrative, her voice gathers confidence and volume, her voice sounding with "triumph and joy,"[24] as she proclaims the Gospel to Raskolnikov, reciting the final section by heart: the raising of Lazarus from the tomb (Jn 11:38–44). Immediately after her reading, her voice shrivels again. Dostoevsky gives her voice volume, joy, at the moment at which it proclaims that which is not proper to itself: the Gospel. In the reading of the Gospel, the Word communicates in and through the voice of the prostitute.

Exchanging Crosses

In the immediate aftermath of the reading of John 11, Raskolnikov hysterically insists to Sonya that, having left his family, "'You're all I've got now . . . Let's be off . . . I've come to you. We're cursed together, so let's

---

23. Dostoevsky, *Crime and Punishment*, 388.
24. Dostoevsky, *Crime and Punishment*, 390.

take the road together!'"[25] This flusters Sonya, and she is unsure what to make of his mania. He does not confess his crime to her immediately, but he does inform her that he knows who killed Lizaveta and that he will tell her tomorrow.

In his study of Dostoevsky, Rowan Williams points to the significance of the Orthodox practice of exchanging crosses in the novels of Dostoevsky. "Orthodox Christians wear a crucifix around their necks; and the exchange of the crosses is in popular Orthodox practice a sign of committed friendship."[26] When Raskolnikov returns to confess his crime to Sonya, she offers him her cypress wooden cross. She has already exchanged crosses with Lizaveta, and has held onto that cross, but offers Raskolnikov her second one. Raskolnikov does not have a cross, but also does not initially accept Sonya's. Only as he is preparing to confess to the police does he return, saying, "I've come for your crosses."[27] Williams notes that Raskolnikov initially thinks he ought to wear a more extravagant cross, like the one the landlady Alyona wore when he murdered her. This "expresses what Raskolnikov is very slowly trying to assimilate for himself—that he is not an exceptional soul but an ordinary criminal, neither Satanic nor a Napoleonic giant but a plain sinner."[28]

Raskolnikov's acceptance of his guilt is his acceptance of his status as a commoner. This brings us back to where we began with Dostoevsky's political concerns over Russia's integration into Western European forms of life. The explicitly Orthodox practice of exchanging crosses, which binds Raskolnikov to his guilt, to Sonya, and to his punishment in Siberian exile, undoes his relationship to the Western ideals which have him confined in the tomb. This gesture returns him to an Orthodox "way," leading him outside the city, whose fever pitch of deviance has had him in its grasp, into Siberia where there is naught but the land. The triangulation of the relations of responsibility and friendship between Sonya, Lizaveta, and Raskolnikov via the exchange of crosses also returns Raskolnikov to the people, to commonness. The attempt to elevate oneself beyond the people as a figure of exception becomes an inevitably violent act, and it is only in solidarity with others that Raskolnikov can find redemption.

---

25. Dostoevsky, *Crime and Punishment*, 391.
26. Williams, *Dostoevsky*, 151.
27. Dostoevsky, *Crime and Punishment*, 622.
28. Williams, *Dostoevsky*, 152.

Returning to the question of the Johannine structure of the narrative, we begin to see how Dostoevsky attempts to position a liberatory vision of the crucifixion. In John 11:46–53, and 18:1–19:37 we have the account of the conspiracy against Jesus, his betrayal, and his crucifixion. Likewise, from the end of the reading of John 11 in *Crime and Punishment*, Raskolnikov begins the process of confession, of binding himself to others, and of following the path through conviction and death: the death of his old self, the overman murderer and finally, in the Epilogue, his resurrection in a labor camp in Siberia.

Nationalism?

Between the structure of the narrative and the political overtones, then, we are left with several questions. The first of these emerges at the intersection of a form of nationalist and religious piety. How far can we follow Dostoevsky's polemic against Western European ideas to be normative or prescriptive? Indeed, is there not something of the risk of a Russian Orthodox chauvinism here? Certainly many of Dostoevsky's readers think this is the case. Paired with strains of antisemitism, it is hard not to avoid the conclusion that there is something deeply problematic in Dostoevsky's nationalist vision of piety. The political dimensions of the text structure the reading of the Johannine narrative, providing us with something of a contextualized recapitulation of the Gospel narrative in the form of a religious-nationalism.

What might be recovered from Dostoevsky beyond this chauvinism, then? Ironically, perhaps, it might be precisely the formal features of Dostoevsky's narratives that provide a way for his work to remain interesting and useful for us. Mikhail Bakhtin famously articulated Dostoevsky's four major novels as "polyphonic."[29] That is, each of the novels entails the use of multiple voices and perspectives, in often dizzying fashion. Each of these voices has a certain integrity of their own, the author's never quite taking center stage to *resolve* the narrative. The effect of bouncing between voices, being in the middle of a series of intersecting lines of responsibility and cruelty, generates narrative movement in Dostoevsky.

As mentioned several times, the time span of the first half of *Crime and Punishment* is a matter of four days. In those four days, we see Raskolnikov continually sever himself from others, totally caught up in his

---

29. Bakhtin, *Problems of Dostoevsky's Poetics*.

own exceptionality. In the meeting with Sonya, we encounter a voice that penetrates his inner life. In the dim light of a fading candle, "the murder and the prostitute encountered each other in the reading of the eternal book." What is disclosed at this moment is not a *single* authorial voice, but the possibility that the Word might be polyphonic. By way of contrast to Raskolnikov's exceptionality, his insistence upon his Napoleonic or overman-like qualities, both he and Sonya are disarmed as they meet each other in the Word, through each other's words. The Word is then *mediated* in and through the very plurality of the world.

To make one final return to the political, then, I would like to suggest that what is most productive about this moment in Dostoevsky is the way it *decenters* the authority of Peter the Great and his will to order the world out of that absolute authority. The gesture made in the reading of John 11 is that no *single* voice can bear within itself the capacity to witness to the divine voice. It is only in the plurality of voices that God is to be found.

Coda

By way of a coda, I would like to attend for a moment to the situation in which we find ourselves in the present. During the drafting of this essay, Russia invaded Ukraine. It was very tempting for those who had read the great novels of the nineteenth century Russian masters to point to the legacy of Russian nationalism and exceptionalism encased within Slavophilism and Russian Orthodoxy. That maneuver, however, risks obscuring the conditions which have generated this most recent conflict, and in fact runs the risk of imputing to Russia an eternal set of features which put it continually at odds with "the West."

I hope that this essay is not read as an attempt to come to terms with this most recent crisis. But, if perhaps it does illuminate this crisis, I hope it does so at the level of method. I have tried to show how Dostoevsky's narrative is at once a carefully crafted political-theological polemic, but also a *theological* reading of the Gospel according to St John. It performs both at a formal level, encasing political conflict within the shape of the life and death of the Messiah, Jesus. The turn to polyphony, however, means that this is not a shape that can simply be carried forward by *one* authorial voice, *one* nation, or *one* national church. There is something perhaps even antithetical to the kind of violence we are seeing playing out between Russia and the West right now in the formal conditions for human life in the power of the resurrection, on Dostoevsky's accounting. That life, for all Dostoevsky's polemic and chauvinism, is grounded in the *decentered* plurality of voices singing forth like an iconostasis of all humanity.

Bibliography

Bakhtin, Mikhail. *Problems of Dostoevsky's Poetics*. Edited and translated by Carly Emerson. Minneapolis, MS: University of Minnesota Press, 1984.
De Macedo, Heitor. *Clinical Lessons on Life and Madness: Dostoevsky's Characters*. Translated by Agnes Jacob. Oxford: Routledge, 2019.
Dostoevsky, Fyodor. *Crime and Punishment*. Translated by David McDuff. London: Penguin, 2003.
———. *Notes from Underground* and *The Double*. Translated by Jessie Coulson. London: Penguin, 2003.
Frank, Joseph. *Dostoevsky: The Seeds of Revolt, 1821–1849*. Princeton, NJ: Princeton University Press, 1979.
Love, Jeff and Jeffrey Metzger, eds. *Dostoevsky and Nietzsche: Philosophy, Morality, Tragedy*. Evanston: Northwestern University Press, 2016.
Moloney, Francis J. *The Gospel of John*. Sacra Pagina 4. Collegeville, MN: Liturgical, 1998.
Nietzsche, Frederich, *The Gay Science*. Edited by Bernard Williams. Translated by Josefine Naukhoff and Adrian del Caro. Cambridge: Cambridge University Press, 2001.
Williams, Rowan. *Dostoevsky: Language, Faith and Fiction*. Waco, TX: Baylor University Press, 2011.

10

Women in John's Gospel and the Women's Ordination Debate

MURIEL PORTER

Introduction

THE NEW-FOUND RECOGNITION OF the important role women played in the canonical Gospels was a key factor for some of us who, from the latter decades of the twentieth century, agitated for women to be ordained in the Anglican Church.[1] In my activism in this cause in the councils of the church and in my writings from the mid-1980s onwards, I kept on my desk a copy of "Messengers," a 1983 poem by a Swedish woman. Reflecting on Easter, Märta Wilhelmsson notes that it was women who rushed to the disciples, passing on "the greatest message of all"—that Jesus was risen. The poem concludes: "Think if women had kept silence in the churches!"[2]

Like the poet, I too was struck with overwhelming force by the realization that women were the crucial bearers of the Easter message, and particularly by the Johannine account of Mary Magdalene, commissioned by the risen Jesus to be the "apostle to the apostles" no less (Jn

---

1. This essay is focused on the debate in the Anglican Church rather than other churches not only because it is the debate I am most competent to discuss, given my activism within it, but also because it is the church where the debate was most protracted and contentious internationally, particularly in both England and Australia.

2. Wilhelmsson, "Messengers," 47.

20:11–20).³ Scholarly reassessment of Mary Magdalene—for centuries depicted as a repentant prostitute rather than a pre-eminent apostle—was a powerful inspiration to me. So too were the reassessments of the other women around Jesus, and in particular two other women in John's Gospel, Martha and the unnamed Samaritan woman. I am sure these reassessments must have influenced other campaigners as well.

The Women's Ordination Debates

Too often, however, the debates many of us became immersed in, in synods and seminars and publications, focused not on these important biblical examples of women's leadership but rather on refuting our opponents' interpretations of quite different Scriptural texts and associated claims. We pushed back against texts that were claimed to insist that women were to be silent and subservient in the churches. We found ourselves arguing from a defensive position, rather than from the significant New Testament accounts of women in apostolic leadership.

This defensiveness was not a new phenomenon. It had happened in earlier contentious theological debates in the Christian churches. For example, the sixteenth century reformers who argued for the marriage of clergy spent a major part of their theological effort on refuting the traditionalists' defense of celibacy, often centered on 1 Corinthians 7. From Martin Luther onwards, they responded with their own interpretation of that chapter, beginning with what St Paul meant when he wrote, "It is well for a man not to touch a woman" (1 Cor 7:1, NRSV).⁴ There was, however, a different set of biblical texts that offered the reformers unequivocal permission for clerical marriage. In the first letter of Timothy, clergy are expected to be married (1 Tim 3:2, 4 and 12). These verses were only rarely invoked in the debate.⁵

---

3. Lee, *Ministry of Women*, 160.

4. Luther, *1 Corinthians VII*, 11–12. Most scholars today would say that the first verse of 1 Corinthians 7 was a question put to St Paul, rather than a Pauline pronouncement in favour of celibacy: e.g. Murphy-O'Connor, "First Letter to the Corinthians," 804. For a full discussion on the Reformation debate about clerical marriage, see Porter, *Sex, Marriage and the Church*.

5. One exception was the English reformer Robert Barnes (c.1495–1540), who in his work "That by God's Word it is lawful for priests . . . to marry wives," argued that these verses proved that "the conjunction and copulation" between husband and wife was "godly and virtuous." *Supplication*, 17.

In similar fashion, the debate about women's role in the Church too often was consumed by the need to refute arguments offered *against* female leadership rather than to focus on positive biblical evidence. For Evangelical opponents, arguments were almost entirely based on selected Pauline texts about the subordination of women in marriage and in the Church, while for Catholic opponents, they were mostly focused on Jesus' choice of men only as the twelve apostles.[6] In the process, New Testament evidence of women as apostles and as leaders in the early Church was too easily overlooked in debate by most proponents of women's ordination. This was partly because of the way in which the issue of women clergy was debated from the nineteenth century on.

The role of women in the church was a foundational concern in what is usually referred to as first wave feminism in the nineteenth century. The first organized women's movement began with a woman's rights convention held in Seneca Falls, New York, in 1848. The aim of the convention was "To discuss the social, civil and *religious* [my emphasis] rights of woman."[7] The convention's Declaration of Sentiments, modelled on the United States' Declaration of Independence, included a protest that women were excluded from the church's ministry and leadership. The Declaration was largely the work of Elizabeth Cady Stanton, who later in the century was the principal author of *The Woman's Bible*.[8] Five of the twelve resolutions passed by the convention dealt with religious issues directly. The convention's demands were picked up by further conventions as the women's movement it had sparked gained momentum.

From the outset, the movement was widely denounced, particularly by churchmen. As women dared to speak publicly, in one case against slavery in New England, the region's Council of Congregational Ministers drew up a "pastoral letter" telling them to cease this activity, insisting that "the appropriate duties and influence of women are clearly stated in the New Testament." The "power of woman" was, they said, "her dependence, flowing from the consciousness of the weakness which God has given her for her protection."[9]

From the beginning then, women's claim to equality in church and society was challenged by references to New Testament strictures. The

---

6. The major arguments are canvassed in the 1977 *The Ministry of Women: A Report of the General Synod Commission on Doctrine*.

7. Porter, "Christian Origins of Feminism," 214.

8. Porter, "Christian Origins of Feminism," 208–24.

9. Clark & Richardson, *Women and Religion*, 211.

die was cast for generations of women activists, who all too readily fell into the trap of refuting these arguments, rather than focusing on the alternative compelling Gospel evidence. Even *The Woman's Bible*—an examination of Scripture from the female perspective—failed in this regard. Elizabeth Cady Stanton's comments there on the resurrection garden scene in John's Gospel, for instance, fail to mention Jesus' commissioning of Mary Magdalene to preach resurrection to the male disciples.[10]

Though numbers of women like Stanton plundered the Scriptures to find female role models for their growing movement,[11] most were blinded to the Gospel depiction of women as apostles and leaders because of the dominant theological portrayals of key figures as either women of dubious sexual behavior or as domestic figures. This is most notable in the case of Mary Magdalene, who was the victim of a pervasive portrait of her as a penitent prostitute, largely credited to a 591 sermon by Pope Gregory the Great. He conflated Mary Magdalene with Luke's unnamed sinful "woman of the city" who, seeking forgiveness from Jesus, gate-crashed the Pharisee's dinner and bathed Jesus' feet with expensive ointment, wiping them with her hair (Lk 7:36–50). In this conflation, the seven demons of which Mary Magdalene was healed by Jesus (Lk 8:2) became the seven deadly sins.[12] Mary Magdalene became fixed as a holy harlot in Western Christian teaching, such that homes for "fallen" women were named after her. Countless artists have depicted her as the penitent sinner, and countless sermons have named her in this vein. This designation was removed by the Vatican in 1969, but still remains potent in popular imagination. Interestingly, the Eastern Church did not make this conflation, but instead remembered her primarily as the bearer of the Resurrection news.[13] Similarly, the Samaritan woman's story of her numerous husbands and her current non-marital relationship (Jn 4:7–42) meant she was readily depicted as an immoral woman, so diverting attention from her missionary role. Luke's portrayal of Martha as burdened by domesticity (Lk 10:38–42) displaced her Johannine role as a first proclaimer of Jesus as the Christ (Jn 11:27). These are the three women in John's Gospel on whom I will concentrate my discussion here, from a

---

10. Stanton, *The Woman's Bible*. https://archive.org/stream/thewomansbible-09880gut/wbibl10.txt; Brown, "Role of Women," 693.

11. Styler, "A Scripture of their own," 65–85.

12. Winkett, "Go Tell!" 21.

13. Winkett, "Go Tell!" 22–23.

selection of the texts published during the critical years of the women's ordination debate.

The Debate Template

Internationally, pressure to see women ordained was growing in most Western churches in the 1960s, as second wave feminism was gathering momentum. Although biblical scholars like Raymond E. Brown were beginning to publish their findings on the Gospel women from the 1970s,[14] these works did not significantly impact the early ordination debate, given they were available only in scholarly journals. The pattern established in the nineteenth century debates about women's role was firmly entrenched, as was apparent in the first major international Anglican discussion about the possibility of ordaining women at the 1968 Lambeth Conference of Bishops. The conference urged its member churches to study the question, so the following year, the General Synod of the Australian Anglican Church gave its Doctrine Commission the task. Max Thomas, a member of that Commission, later reflected that the Lambeth Conference had, in his words, "a lot to answer for." The bishops had couched the issue in negative terms, he said, looking for theological objections to women priests, for reasons against rather than for, their ordination.[15]

From the late 1960s, under the influence of the changing role of women in general society, churchwomen, particularly those exercising such limited ministry then available to them, were emerging as strong advocates for the churches to open up all their ministries to women. A major Church of England report published in 1972 contained the views of a range of women working as deaconesses and licensed lay workers; 90 per cent of the deaconesses were clearly in favor of women priests, two-thirds of the licensed lay workers also reported in favor, and of the other third, only half were opposed, the other half being neutral on the subject.[16] The report noted that it was clear from the replies that there were women who had a sense of call to the priesthood, not only among some of the women surveyed but from their knowledge of women who

---

14. Brown, "Role of Women."

15. Author interview with Max Thomas (1926–2008, theologian, Bishop of Wangaratta 1975–1985), 15 April 1988, cited in Porter, *Women in the Church*, 67.

16. *Ordination of Women to the Priesthood*, 73.

they knew had experienced a vocation, or who they judged would make fine priests.

In Australia, similar findings came from a 1974 survey done by the Commission on the Status of Women of the Australian Council of Churches (NSW) in response to the wider women's movement: "the revolution in thinking about women today presents a strong challenge to the churches which they cannot afford to ignore."[17] Deaconesses from Melbourne became increasingly involved in the women's ordination debate; Deaconess Elizabeth Alfred agreed to be elected to the 1973 General Synod as a laywoman, even though she believed her deaconess status was in fact ordination. A regional Melbourne bishop, Felix Arnott, later Archbishop of Brisbane, had convinced her to stand for election on the basis that it was the only way the deaconess voice would be heard.[18]

In this context, the Australian General Synod's Doctrine Commission presented its major report to the 1977 General Synod meeting. It concluded that there were no theological reasons why women could not be ordained to the three-fold order of deacon, priest and bishop, and called on the Church to "take the appropriate steps when practicable" to do so.[19] In the light of the thirty years of fierce struggle that followed before this could be achieved, the report was remarkable, despite the "double negative" phrasing it adopted to say that theologically, women's ordination was possible. The General Synod, after an intense and anxious debate, supported the Commission's conclusion, but the majority vote, though comfortable, was short of the high level of support needed to pass future legislation.[20] It would take ongoing debate and multiple attempts to pass legislation before women could be ordained as deacons (1985) and priests (1992) in the Australian Church. It took a reference to the Church's highest court, the Appellate Tribunal, before the way was opened for women bishops in 2007.

17. *Report of the Enquiry into the Status of Women*, 3.
18. Porter, *Women in the Church*, 50, 70.
19. *Ministry of Women*.
20. The Australian Anglican Church's Constitution mandates extremely high bars for legislation concerning "the ritual, ceremonial or discipline of the church," a category that includes matters such as ordination. In this category, the legislation requires three-quarter majorities in each of the three Houses of Synod (laity, clergy, and bishops) for immediate application. Provisional approval requires two-thirds majorities in each House, and then must be ratified either by all the dioceses, or by further two-thirds majorities at a subsequent General Synod meeting. *Synod Process & Elections*, 1–103–4.

The 1977 report, perhaps the crucial step on this journey, was almost entirely defensive in tone, even though by the time of its publication women were ordained by Anglican churches in Hong Kong, the United States and Canada, and New Zealand was about to proceed as well. The report's defensiveness is not surprising. Although eleven of the twelve members of the Doctrine Commission supported the report's conclusion, the odd one out was a highly influential clergyman from the Diocese of Sydney, Canon Broughton Knox, Principal of the diocese's Moore Theological College. He insisted that his reasons for dissent be appended to the report. Max Thomas reflected later that "we let Sydney [Diocese] turn this issue into a political football, which we should not have done."[21] Another member of the Commission, Keith Rayner, later Archbishop first of Adelaide and then of Melbourne, and Australian Primate from 1991 to 1999, has written that the debate at the time was "dominated by what might be termed the Moore College interpretation of the New Testament relating to the meaning of 'church' and the headship of the male in the family." It was, he said, the issues raised by Sydney Diocese that set the agenda, even though the formative work for the Commission's report was done by four theologians supportive of women's ordination—Max Thomas, Leon Morris, John Gaden and Rayner himself.[22]

It seems clear that the other members of the Commission were focused on refuting the views argued by Knox, rather than beginning from first principles. Given most Commission members were also leaders in the national church—they included the then Primate, Archbishop Frank Woods—the Commission members would have been alive to the danger of confrontation with Sydney Diocese, given that diocese's long history of disputation. It is not surprising that they trod cautiously.[23]

The report begins with a section on "Man, woman and God in the Bible," tackling questions raised by the masculine terminology for God in the Scriptures, as well as the maleness of Jesus himself and the twelve apostles. It moves on to discuss the exclusion of women from cultic office in the Old Testament, before tentatively arguing that "we may not conclude from the predominance of masculine language that men have any

---

21. Thomas author interview, 15 April, 1988.

22. Rayner, "The decision-makers," 147.

23. For instance, see Davis, *Australian Anglicans* for an overview of the difficulties created by Sydney Diocese in the development of a Constitution for what became the Anglican Church of Australia; also Porter, *New Puritans*.

natural priority over women."[24] It devotes just one paragraph to women in the Gospels, noting almost in passing that "in some Gospels women are the first witnesses to Jesus' resurrection." The paragraph's main focus is on the dignity Jesus showed women and the fact that he drew on women's experiences in parables. The Samaritan woman is referred to merely in relation to the disciples' surprise that Jesus was speaking to her; Martha is discussed only in the context of Jesus' praise for her sister Mary listening to his teaching rather than helping Martha in the kitchen.[25]

Much more space in the Commission's report is devoted to responding to the various strictures on women in the epistles, obviously because that was where the opposition to ordination was based. It engages in detail with texts dealing with male headship, the relationship of husband and wife including the subjection of wives to husbands, (such as 1 Cor 11 and Eph 5:22), and those requiring female silence in the church (such as 1 Cor 14:34f and 1 Tim 2: 11f.) The report suggests that women's silence in churches was, rather than a universal teaching, "the first-century cultural expression of the requirement that 'all things be done decently and in order' (1 Cor 14:40)."[26] Cautiously and politely, it concludes that "rather than excluding women from ordination the New Testament evidence allied with the changed position of women in society in our day indicates that we must take seriously the possibility that all forms of ministry should be open to women."[27]

In contrast, Canon Knox's dissent was forthright and dogmatic. The report, he said, did not "do justice to the character of Holy Scripture as God's word written," accusing the rest of the Commission of "explaining away" the scriptural material bearing on the ordination of women. God's word makes clear, he insisted, that "in creating humanity God gave a headship to man which he did not give to woman"; "headship and its concomitant of subordination is a principle on which creation has been brought into being." Canon Knox does not at any point discuss Jesus' treatment of women, or the portrayal of the women around Jesus in the Gospels. He concluded: "Till the matter of how headship and subordination in the relationship of men and women should be expressed in our congregations in the culture of today has been investigated and solved in

---

24. *Ministry of Women*, 5.
25. *Ministry of Women*, 6.
26. *Ministry of Women*, 11.
27. *Ministry of Women*, 12.

a way which does not ignore the scriptural teaching of the existence of this principle of relationship, it is premature to conclude that there are no theological reasons debarring women from the ministry of leadership in the congregation."[28]

While it is understandable that those on the Doctrine Commission who sought the ordination of women needed to tread cautiously, given the volatility of the Australian national church, proponents outside the formal structure were not so constrained. The debate template laid down over the decades and reinforced by bodies such as the Commission, however, set the pattern for them as well.

The Movement for the Ordination of Women

The most prominent agitator for women's ordination in the Australian Anglican Church was the Movement for the Ordination of Women (MOW), a separate offshoot of the English movement. Formed in 1984, its most active phase was in the latter half of the 1980s and into the early 1990s, when legislation for women priests was finally passed by the General Synod in 1992. It continues to have a low-key presence in the Diocese of Sydney which strongly opposes women as priests and bishops; it has ceased to exist elsewhere in Australia.

In its early days, MOW was a dynamic force, engaging frequently with an eager secular press. Its national conferences, held regularly, attracted large enthusiastic support, mainly from Anglican women but also from supportive men. How far MOW can take the credit for the successful national legislation—for women deacons in 1985 and priests in 1992—is a moot point, given the issue had been well and truly on foot in the General Synod from the mid 1970s. Archbishops such as Frank Woods and later David Penman of Melbourne, Keith Rayner of Adelaide, and Felix Arnott of Brisbane, had been, and continued to be, key players quite independently of any lobby groups.[29] Deaconesses were also pushing the envelope as we have seen. Leading theologian Dr John Gaden strongly promoted women's ordination on the Doctrine Commission in the 1970s. Given the opposition of conservative Anglo-Catholics and Evangelicals who capitalized on the stringent rules of the national Church's

---

28. *Ministry of Women*, 29–32.

29. Porter, *Women in the Church*, 70, 80–81, 108, 111; Alfred, *Called to Serve*, 47; Felix Arnott address to Brisbane Synod, 13 June 1977.

constitution, though, the issue had hit a stalemate when MOW was formed. So while it is safe to say that the momentum for women clergy was well and truly building before MOW's establishment, MOW was important in the opportunity it gave for lay women to enter the field, the encouragement and support it gave them as they became activists, and the media attention it was able to attract at a crucial time in the debate.

Two major papers on the biblical authority for women clergy were presented at MOW's first national conference in 1985. Stimulating though these were, they both effectively followed the template laid down by the opponents. Gretchen Gaebelein-Hull, an American Presbyterian listed as a lecturer on the authority and authenticity of Scripture, spoke on "Feminism and Biblical Authority"; Catherine Kroeger, listed as a teaching associate in Biblical Greek at the University of Minnesota, addressed the conference on "The Pauline View of Women."[30] Both of these papers engaged principally with the masculine imagery and language of the Old Testament, and the strictures against women in the New Testament epistles that figured so prominently in opponents' arguments.[31] Mary Magdalene, the Samaritan woman or any of the other women around Jesus rated a mention only in passing.

That same year, John Gaden, then the Director of Trinity College Theological School, Melbourne, wrote a discussion paper for the Victorian chapter of MOW. Focusing on the texts about women's silence in the church, he found they related to particular problems "rather than being universally applicable."[32] The patterns of ministry evident in the New Testament writings, he said, show that women served as deacons, prophets, evangelists and teachers in the earliest churches.[33] He dealt at length too with the household codes claimed to require wifely subordination and male headship in both the home and the church. This interpretation, he said, was ruled out by the evidence for the leadership of women in the early church he had already noted.[34]

So far, he was following the template, but he departed from it to connect the early church ministry with Jesus, noting that in all the evidence of ministry in the New Testament, "there is a common focus that

30. Sturmey-Jones and Jones, *Ministry of Women*, ix.

31. Gaebelein-Hull, "Feminism and Biblical Authority," 13–20, & Kroeger, "Pauline View of Women," 21–26.

32. Gaden, *Ordination of Women*, 5.

33. Gaden, *Ordination of Women*, 4.

34. Gaden, *Ordination of Women*, 7–8.

ministry derives from and centers on Jesus Christ."[35] He followed this by referring to St Paul's teaching that "there is no longer Jew or Greek, there is no longer slave or free, there is no longer male and female; for all of you are one in Christ Jesus" (Gal 3:28). That this, he writes, is "no innovation on Paul's part . . . is shown by the fact that the setting aside of traditional sex roles in the call to discipleship goes back to Jesus himself." In particular, he continued, "Jesus sets women free from being defined by their traditional roles and relationships to men both eschatologically (Mk 12:18–27) and in the present."[36]

Dr Gaden commented that "it is not surprising, then, that in all four Gospels the faithful women (Mary Magdalen [sic], in particular) are the first to be charged with bearing the good news of the resurrection." For our purposes, his reference to John's Gospel is worth quoting in full:

> But in John's Gospel, where the idea of a special, differentiated apostolic ministry of Peter and the Twelve is only found in the Appendix (Chapter 21), women are regarded as equal disciples with men in bearing witness to Jesus (4:27–42, cf 1:40–42), in confessing Jesus to be the Christ (11:27, cf 6:68f), in anointing/washing the Lord's/each others' feet (12:1–8, cf 13:1–20), and in representing the new community (19:25–27). Jesus did not draw a hard line between leadership and discipleship, and the New Testament evidence for women leading ministry indicates that the implications of his teaching and actions were not lost on the first communities of Christians.[37]

Here at last is recognition of the significance of the woman of Samaria's witness, Martha's proclamation, Mary of Bethany's anointing, and Jesus' mother's equal role (with the beloved disciple) as representative of the new Christian community. Incidentally, Dr Gaden dated his discussion paper as on "The Feast of St Mary Magdalen [sic], 'the apostle to the apostles', July 22, 1985."[38]

---

35. Gaden, *Ordination of Women*, 7–8.
36. Gaden, *Ordination of Women*, 6–7.
37. Gaden, *Ordination of Women*, 7.
38. Gaden, *Ordination of Women*, 18.

Re-evaluating the Gospel Women

By then, recognition of the significance of Mary Magdalene's role, and that of the Samaritan woman, Martha and the other women disciples, had been emerging in scholarly research for two decades. Australian theologian Dr Kevin Giles' work was part of this recognition. In his study published in 1977, the same year the Doctrine Commission's report came to General Synod, he was clear that "any discussion about the Biblical teaching concerning women and their ministry in the Christian community" had to begin with the Gospels. The "example and teaching of Jesus" should be "key to interpreting the whole Bible," he wrote.[39] Although he does not name Mary Magdalene, he argues that the role of women as proclaimers of the resurrection was critical. "No higher commission could ever be given and it was given by Jesus to women" who were the resurrection's "first heralds." He notes Martha's proclamation of Jesus as the Christ, the Son of God (Jn 11:27), and the evangelistic role of the Samaritan woman (Jn 4:39).[40]

Internationally, American scholar Sandra M. Schneiders built on the work of Raymond Brown. Her article focusing on women in John's Gospel is particularly pertinent.[41] She does more than exegete the stories of the individual women in that Gospel, however. She goes behind the stories, seeing in their portrayal evidence of active, full female ministry in the Johannine community. The Gospel author, she writes, "was someone who had a remarkably rich and nuanced understanding of feminine religious experience"; it was likely that this was "the result of actual experience of Christian women who played prominent roles in the community of the Fourth Evangelist." She writes: "It seems more than likely that real women, actually engaged in a theological discussion, competently proclaiming the Gospel, publicly confessing their faith, and serving at the table of the Lord, stand behind these Johannine characters."[42] She concluded that "if the material on women in the Fourth Gospel were released from the shackles of a male-dominated exegesis and placed at the service of the contemporary Church there is little doubt that it would help to liberate both men and women from any remaining doubt that

---

39. Giles, *Women and their Ministry*, 17.
40. Giles, *Women and their Ministry*, 21–20.
41. Schneiders, "Women in the Fourth Gospel," 35–45.
42. Schneiders, "Women in the Fourth Gospel," 38.

women are called by Jesus to full discipleship and ministry in the Christian community."[43]

She identifies the Samaritan woman as a disciple, and one whose witness to Jesus is apostolic in the Johannine perspective. However, "in the history of exegesis and preaching a great deal has been made of this woman's irregular marital situation, very little of the clear indications of her apostleship, and virtually nothing of the vindication of her role against the implicit disapproval of the male members of the community."[44]

As for Martha, she says that John's Gospel "presents Jesus as addressing the foundational question to a woman and the woman as making, on her own responsibility, the Christian confession." She continues: "If this confession, given during the public life of Jesus, grounds the promise of the primacy to Peter, it is no less significant as foundation of community leadership by a woman."[45]

Mary Magdalene's role as the first witness to Jesus' resurrection is attested by both John and Matthew and there are no scholarly grounds for questioning the authenticity of this tradition, writes Schneiders.[46] She concludes:

> The Mary Magdalene material in the Fourth Gospel is perhaps the most important indication we have of the Gospel perspective on the role of women in the Christian community. It shows us quite clearly that, in at least one of the first Christian communities, a woman was regarded as the primary witness to the paschal mystery, the guarantee of the apostolic tradition. Her claim to apostleship is equal in every respect to both Peter's and Paul's.[47]

Like both Peter and Paul, "she saw the risen Lord, received directly from him the commission to preach the Gospel, and carried out that commission faithfully and effectively."[48] It is a pity that Schneiders' firm conclusion that John's Gospel presents women not only as apostles but also significant leaders in at least the Johannine community did not feature prominently in the contemporary women's ordination debate from the

---

43. Schneiders, "Women in the Fourth Gospel," 44.
44. Schneiders, "Women in the Fourth Gospel" 40.
45. Schneiders, "Women in the Fourth Gospel," 41.
46. Schneiders, "Women in the Fourth Gospel," 43.
47. Schneiders, "Women in the Fourth Gospel," 44.
48. Schneiders, "Women in the Fourth Gospel," 44.

time the article was published; its publication in a scholarly journal, however, meant it did not reach activists on the ground.

A more readily accessible discussion about the role of the women around Jesus had, however, emerged from Elisabeth Moltmann-Wendel in 1980.[49] Her book dedicated whole chapters to Martha and Mary Magdalene, as well as to other Gospel women. This work did not have had the scholarly heft of Schneiders' article but her easy prose and imaginative style opened the material to a wide range of women hungry to know more. She demolishes the general view of Martha as merely the disgruntled housewife of the Lucan story (Lk 10:38–42) and focuses on John's story of Martha the apostle. She describes Martha's recognition of Jesus at Lazarus's tomb—"You are the Messiah, the Son of God, the one coming into the world" (Jn 11:27)—as "a special climax in the New Testament."[50] It was equal to Peter's similar confession in Matthew 16:16: "For the early church, to confess Christ in this way was the mark on an apostle."[51] Martha, she says, is not a woman who keeps silence in the community![52] We must conclude, she adds, "from this story and this confession that Martha is . . . a leading personality, like the apostles in the early church."[53] John, she says, "throws overboard our traditional Christian image of Martha: he restores to life the aggressive, disturbing, sage, active Martha who went against all the conventions: mistress of the house, housewife, apostle, the woman who stands beside Peter in her own right."[54]

Moltmann-Wendel, describing Mary Magdalene as the "first apostle" for her role in the first proclamation of the resurrection, is ferocious in demolishing the portrayal of her as "the great sinner." The "great sinner" of Luke's Gospel and Mary Magdalene "have as much to do with each other as Peter and Judas," she writes.[55] That portrait of Mary, she continues, "was constructed by men, and served to kindle male fantasies."[56] She believes this portrait allowed the church as a patriarchal institution to "live with the fact that a woman was instrumental in bringing it to birth."[57]

49. Moltmann-Wendel, *Women around Jesus*.
50. Moltmann-Wendel, *Women around Jesus*, 25.
51. Moltmann-Wendel, *Women around Jesus*, 24.
52. Moltmann-Wendel, *Women around Jesus*, 24.
53. Moltmann-Wendel, *Women around Jesus*, 25.
54. Moltmann-Wendel, *Women around Jesus*, 26.
55. Moltmann-Wendel, *Women around Jesus*, 64.
56. Moltmann-Wendel, *Women around Jesus*, 67.
57. Moltmann-Wendel, *Women around Jesus*, 75.

Also in the early 1980s, Melbourne biblical scholar Frank Moloney published an engaging and accessible study on the Gospel women. Studying the women in the Gospels and the Pauline letters, Moloney declares "the primacy of women in the order of faith" as a "principle and a conviction of the earliest Church."[58] In his conclusion, he writes: "The use of women in the Fourth Gospel . . . as 'models' of the possibility of a journey of faith . . . shows a clear consciousness of the fact that women are not only the *first* in this area, but they are also *to be followed*. This means that, in the order of faith, women assume the role of leaders."[59]

Even with this groundswell of exegesis of the prominent role of Mary Magdalene and other women in the Gospels, a 1989 study by Ruth B. Edwards, a deacon in the Scottish Episcopal Church and New Testament lecturer and clearly a supporter of women's ordained ministry, was cautious and as much concerned with the Pauline texts as with the Gospels. Similarly, a 1988 report of the House of Bishops in the Church of England agonized over the Pauline texts and their various interpretations, but completely overlooked the evidence of the women around Jesus as portrayed in the Gospels.[60]

I used both Moltmann-Wendel and Moloney as guides when I presented a series of studies on women as disciples for an Australian Broadcasting Corporation radio series, "Sacred Reading" in 1989, when the women's ordination debate in Australia was at its height. The series was published in a small book that same year. In the introduction to the book, I noted how amazed I was when I discovered the extent of the women's role in the Gospels as I prepared the talks. I had known something of the story, but not the significance of women's involvement in the whole story of salvation—from Mary's role in the Incarnation, to the women as witnesses of the crucifixion and of the resurrection. I wrote: "The very Gospel record is thus dependent on their evidence. It is just as well women did *not* remain silent in the churches! Yet we have heard so little about *these* disciples and apostles."[61] By 1989, I had been heavily involved in the debate for five years, but had been engaging mainly from the perspective of that negative template rather than primarily from the Gospel evidence of women's leadership. The preparation of those radio

58. Moloney, *Woman First Among the Faithful*, 82.
59. Moloney, *Woman First Among the Faithful*, 94.
60. Edwards, *Case for Women's Ministry; Ordination of Women to the Priesthood*.
61. Porter, *Beyond the Twelve*, 7.

talks was an epiphany for me, and I recall from then on referring often to the Gospel women disciples and apostles, particularly from John's Gospel, in synod debates and other forums.

Conclusion

Many activists working for the ordination of women were effectively side-tracked by the opponents' template into refuting their arguments rather than promoting the issue from positive Scriptural evidence. It was a tactic not confined to our issue, as the sixteenth century debate about clerical marriage demonstrates. It continues in other areas as well. Margaret Simons, Melbourne journalist and academic, commenting recently about the way opponents of climate change have successfully manipulated that debate over the past few decades, noted that what she has termed "progressives" have been "tricked into spending all their energies in reaction—rather than charting their own path."[62] Mary Magdalene, Martha and the Samaritan woman in John offered us all the evidence we needed to argue for the ordination of women. Had we stood firmly, publicly and predominantly on that ground from the beginning, that long and tortuous debate might have been shorter and sweeter.

Bibliography

Alfred, Elizabeth. *Called to Serve: The Spiritual Journey of Elizabeth Alfred*, Melbourne: privately published, 2001.

Arnott, Felix. Address to Brisbane Synod, 13 June 1977, reprinted in *Church Scene*, 1 July 1977.

Barnes, Robert. "That by God's Word it is lawful for priests ... to marry wives," Supplication. In *The Whole Works of W. Tyndale, John Frith and Dr Barnes*. Edited by John Foxe. London: Short Title Catalogue 24436, 1573.

Brown, Raymond E. "The Role of Women in the Fourth Gospel." *TS* 36 (1975) 688–99.

Clark, Elizabeth and Herbert Richardson, eds. *Women and Religion: A Feminist Sourcebook of Christian Thought*. New York: Harper & Row, 1977.

Commission on the Status of Women. *Report of the Enquiry into the Status of Women in the Church*, n.p. Australian Council of Churches: NSW State Council, 1974.

Davis, John. *Australian Anglicans and their Constitution*. Melbourne: Acorn, 1993.

Edwards, Ruth B. *The Case for Women's Ministry*. London: SPCK, 1989.

Gaden, John R. *For the Ordination of Women: A Discussion Paper*. Melbourne: Education Group of MOW (Victoria), 1985.

---

62. Simons, "News Corp's Shift on Emissions."

Gaebelein-Hull, Gretchen. "Feminism and Biblical Authority." In *Ministry of Women, 'Telling Tales:' Proceedings of the First National Conference of MOW (Australia), Sydney, August 23-25, 1985,* edited by Ruth Sturmey-Jones and Malcolm J. Jones, 13-20. Armidale: MOW Armidale, 1985.

Giles, Kevin. *Women and their Ministry: A Case for Equal Ministries in the Church Today.* Melbourne: Dove Communications, 1977.

Kroeger, Catherine. "The Pauline View of Women." In *Ministry of Women, 'Telling Tales:' Proceedings of the First National Conference of MOW (Australia), Sydney, August 23-25, 1985,* 21-26. Armidale: MOW Armidale, 1985.

Lee, Dorothy A. *The Ministry of Women in the New Testament. Reclaiming the Biblical Vision for Church Leadership.* Grand Rapids, MI: Baker Academic, 2021.

Luther, Martin, *Commentary on 1 Corinthians VII.* In *Luther's* Works, edited by Hilton C. Oswald. St Louis: Concordia, 1973.

The Ministry of Women: A Report of the General Synod Commission on Doctrine. Sydney: General Synod Office, 1977.

Moloney, Francis J. *Woman First Among the Faithful: A New Testament Study.* Melbourne: Dove Communications, 1984.

Moltmann-Wendel, Elisabeth. *The Women around Jesus.* Translated by John Bowden. New York: Crossroad, 1987.

The Ordination of Women to the Priesthood: A Consultative Document Presented by the Advisory Council for the Church's Ministry. Oxford: General Synod, 1972.

Murphy-O'Connor, Jerome. "The First Letter to the Corinthians." In *The New Jerome Biblical* Commentary, edited by Raymond E. Brown et al., 798-815. London: Geoffrey Chapman, 1993.

The Ordination of Women to the Priesthood: A Second Report by the House of Bishops of the General Synod of the Church of England GS829. London: General Synod of the Church of England, 1988.

Porter, Muriel. *Beyond the Twelve: Women Disciples in the Gospels.* Melbourne: Desbooks, 1989.

———. *Sex, Marriage and the Church: Patterns of Change,* Melbourne: Dove, 1996.

———. "The Christian Origins of Feminism." In *Freedom and Entrapment: Women Thinking Theology.* Edited by Maryanne Confoy et al., 208-24. North Blackburn, Victoria: Dove, 1995.

———. *The New Puritans: The Rise of Fundamentalism in the Anglican Church.* Melbourne: Melbourne University Press, 2006.

———. *Women in the Church: The Great Ordination Debate in Australia,* Melbourne: Penguin Books, 1989.

Rayner, Keith. "The Decision-Makers: By What Authority?" In *Preachers, Prophets and Heretics: Anglican Women's Ministry.* Edited by Elaine Lindsay and Janet Scarfe, 146-64. Sydney: University of NSW Press, 2012.

Schneiders, Sandra M. "Women in the Fourth Gospel and the Role of Women in the Contemporary Church." *BTB* 12 (1982) 35-45.

Simons, Margaret. "News Corp's Shift on Emissions Reveals Limitations of Power." *The Age,* 7 September 2021. https://www.theage.com.au/national/news-corp-s-shift-on-emissions-reveals-limitations-of-power-20210906-p58p4r.html

The Standing Committee of the General Synod of the Anglican Church of Australia. *Synod Process and Elections.* Sydney: General Synod Office, 2014.

Stanton, Elizabeth Cady et al. *The Woman's Bible*. New York: European Publishing Company, 1895–1898. Lebanon NH: Northeastern University Press, 1993. The Project Gutenberg Ebook, 2006. https://archive.org/stream/thewomansbible09880gut/wbibl10.txt.

Sturmey-Jones, Ruth and Malcolm J. Jones. *Ministry of Women, 'Telling Tales:' Proceedings of the First National Conference of MOW (Australia), Sydney, August 23-25, 1985*, Armidale: MOW Armidale, 1985.

Styler, Rebecca. "A Scripture of their own: Nineteenth-century Bible Biography and Feminist Bible Criticism." *C&L* 57 (2007) 65–85.

Wilhelmsson, Marta, "Messengers." In *No Longer Strangers: A Resource for Women and Worship*. Edited by Iben Cjerding and Katherine Kinnamon. Geneva: WCC, 1983.

Winkett, Lucy. "Go Tell! Thinking about Mary Magdalene." *FT* 29 January (2002) 19–31.

Part III

Contemporary Readings

11

"Walking on the Sea?"

A Moana Intertextual Reading of John 6 in Light of Climate Change in Pasifika

BRIAN FIU KOLIA

Introduction

THE EVENTS AT THE sea in John 6 are designated as miracle story,[1] and as such the details in the story are imagined by the reader through the lens of fantasy and mystic. However, for islanders and people of the sea and the ocean, or people of the *Moana*,[2] the sea is anything but magical. It is the mother of our existence and the created order, and while we depend on the *Moana* for its resources, the *Moana* also possesses the power to take life and be unforgivingly destructive. The picture of Jesus walking on the sea thus provokes images of the sea which may seem miraculous to some readers, but for those from Pasifika who are losing their lands due to rising sea levels, walking on the sea is not miraculous at all, but a distressing reminder that the sea waters are rising to the feet of the islanders.

In this essay, I seek to re-read John 6:16–21 from a Pasifika perspective of *Moana*, based on the relationship of Pasifika people to the *Moana*. To begin, I will analyze the place of the sea in the narrative, before

---

1. O'Day, "Gospel of John," 595.
2. *Moana* is the word for the "sea" or "ocean" for most people in Pasifika.

providing a survey of some of the images of the sea found in the Hebrew Bible. I will then focus our attention on the events at sea in the story of Jonah, bringing it into an intertextual conversation with John 6:16–21. Finally, I will construct a *Moana* hermeneutic to re-read John 6:16–21 and its implications for climate change in Pasifika.

The Sea in John 6

The miracle in John 6:16–21 takes place at the sea. According to 6:1, the location is the Sea of Galilee or the Sea of Tiberius, the former being the common name used in the New Testament while the latter is the name used later in the first century.[3] Intriguingly, scholars are divided on what sense it was a sea, where it is argued by some that "the Sea of Galilee was an inland sea, [and] . . . was subject to strong winds that could make its waters treacherous."[4] Some have argued from a linguistic point of view suggesting that θάλασσα "usually means a body of salt water, rather than a freshwater lake."[5] Others talk of the sea as symbolic, as Margaret Daly-Denton writes:

> Along with Mark and Matthew, the Fourth Evangelist knows that for the landlocked peasants of Galilee the lake was their 'sea.' The fourfold use of the word *thalassa* in this scene is surely intended to invest the lake with all the mythic symbolism associated with the ocean.[6]

The term θάλασσα thus connotes an image of the "sea" that implicates familiar nuances to ancient readers of the Fourth Gospel. In this essay, I want to extrapolate the nuances of the sea as seen in the Hebrew Bible, as a way of highlighting the chaotic nature of the oceanic waters.

Images of the Sea in the Old Testament

In addition to the familiarity with the various seas mentioned in John 6, readers of the Fourth Gospel would have also been acquainted with images of the sea in the Hebrew Bible. I will draw out some of those

---

3. Kruse, *John*, 160–61.
4. Kruse, *John*, 165.
5. Newman and Nida, *Handbook*, 185.
6. Daly-Denton, *John*, 112.

images that resonate with the events at the sea in John 6.[7] In particular, we can recognize how the changing face of the sea in John 6:18 echoes the chaotic and fluctuating imagery of the sea(s) found in the Hebrew Bible.

Chaotic Seas: Genesis 1

According to John 6:18, the sea is said to "become rough" (NRSV). The Greek word used is διεγείρετο which can also mean "rise up" or "stirred up." The object stirring up the sea is the strong wind, which echoes the רוח (spirit/wind) that stirs up the chaotic waters in Genesis 1:2. So in Genesis 1, one of the elements in the primordial chaos is the waters.[8] God rearranges the waters by injecting a dome that separates the waters above from the waters below. Afterwards, God names the waters below the dome, the "seas" (6:10). In these acts, we see God exercizing authority over creation. It is ironic then that God needs to control the sea by way of reorganizing and naming, as it implies that the waters are indeed chaotic. In the Hebrew Bible, however, God is not in combat with other gods, but with a hostile member of God's created order: the sea. Levenson claims that:

> Here the Sea does not seem to be a many-headed monster whose destruction creation necessitates, but neither is it disenchanted and inanimate... Rather, we have a sense of the Sea as a somewhat sinister force that, left to its own, would submerge the world and forestall the ordered reality we call creation.[9]

The suggestion here is that the creation is "inherently unsafe."[10] God's power is therefore required to restrain the sea from damaging the rest of the created order. God would ultimately reorganize and name the hostile waters.

As God names the sea, "the deity *responds* to the creation" and therefore articulates a course of action and interaction between God and what God created.[11] Moreover, Fretheim argues that "[i]n this process,

---

7. I have also conducted a similar survey of sea imagery in the Hebrew Bible in: *Moana and Qohelet*.

8. Carr, *Formation of Genesis 1–11*, 8.

9. Levenson, *Creation*, 15.

10. Levenson, *Creation*, 17.

11. Fretheim, "Book of Genesis," 344.

naming entails knowledge of and relationship with the thing named."[12] On this point, human beings as stewards to creation must also envisage themselves in relationship to their fellow created beings. It is evident then that the ocean is a capricious force that deserves to be acknowledged with respect, and this informs the way one "responds" to it. Strictly speaking, the ocean is a living being in creation that responds to the way the rest of the created order acts towards it.

Genesis 1 identifies the sea as chaotic and requires order and control to subvert its raging waters. It also supports the notion that the ocean exists in relationship with the rest of creation, where the land inhabits deep within the oceanic waters, only to emerge as a result of God's (re) ordering.[13] This view of the sea seems to generate hermeneutical chaos for ancient readers of the Fourth Gospel who were likely aware of the Genesis 1 primordial portrayal of the sea.

Scholars have identified this as related to the *Chaoskampf* (lit. "chaos-struggle") theme of a war between a warrior god and other deities as found in ancient Near Eastern literature.[14] However, this *Chaoskampf* theme can be problematic, as Peter Trudinger argues:

> In any formulation of *Chaoskampf*, the enemies of God are water-beings. Invariably, the major water-beings, Sea, Rivers, Leviathan, and so on, are presented as villains and suffer defeat. In other words, the *Chaoskampf* pattern precludes any intrinsic value being ascribed to a significant component of Earth community.[15]

Chaoskampf thus leads to a deifying of the sea, projecting it as an antagonist to God. Trudinger prefers an alternative way to perceiving the sea. In his re-reading of Psalm 93, he pushes the reader to view the noise and actions of the water-beings as "mimic[ing] people raising arms then falling prostrate before YHWH; the sound of the rivers and waters, cries of praise."[16] Through this reading, the chaos of the sea is observed not as a spiteful attack by a deified being towards its primary deity, but as a

---

12. Fretheim, "Book of Genesis," 344.

13. Cf. Habel, *Birth*, 98. What should be noted here is that Habel (compared to von Rad) does not perceive the primeval Sea as chaos.

14. For the view connecting the battle to that between Baal and Yam, see Day, *God's Conflict*, 4–7. For the link to Marduk and Tiamat, see Gunkel, *Creation and Chaos*, 11–12, 75–77.

15. Trudinger, "Friend or Foe?," 30.

16. Trudinger, "Friend or Foe?," 38.

reverent response by a water-being to its Creator. From a Pasifika perspective, this reading by Trudinger is preferred as it privileges the *Moana*. In the same vein, I seek to privilege the sea when re-reading John 6:16–21.

Salvific Connotations: Exodus 14

To further draw out the erratic image of the sea, I bring our attention to the events at the Red Sea as told in Exodus 14. There, the sea represents both life and death, namely, life for the desperate Israelites and death for the encroaching Egyptians. Walter Brueggemann claims that "[t]hat single core act of the defeat of the 'horse and rider' becomes the elemental claim from which all else in Israel's doxological tradition derives."[17] In the ensuing chapter, the events at the Red Sea receive triumphant appreciation in the "Song of the Sea" (or the "Song of Moses").

The Song further highlights the image of the sea in creation, particularly God's actions in controlling and manipulating the waters. Brevard Childs contends: "First of all, the poem also describes a double action of the waters. With his breath Yahweh heaps up the waters (v. 8) and with his breath he covers the enemy (v. 10)."[18] The ferocity of the sea as described in Genesis 1 re-emerges here, and accordingly, God is required to control it. While this may speak to God's supreme reign (14:8, 10), it also underlines the power of the sea itself. Indeed, the sea is an aqueous force that humankind cannot control and requires the intervention of God. In this, we see two powers in conflict, analogous to the battle between Baal and Yamm/Nahar as depicted in Canaanite mythology.[19] As we read in Exodus 14 and 15, God emerges victorious. Hence, as Thomas Dozeman asserts, "Exod 15:1–12, 18 is a celebration of Yahweh's salvific power conceived as a holy war event."[20] As it seems, it is not so much a victory against the Egyptians, but a triumph over the sea. At the same time, the safe crossing of the Israelites of the Red Sea provides exodus allusions that "are appropriate for the setting of this miracle in John 6."[21]

---

17. Brueggemann, "Book of Exodus," 799.
18. Childs, *Book of Exodus*, 245.
19. Dozeman, "Song of the Sea," 101.
20. Dozeman, "Song of the Sea," 100.
21. O'Day, "Gospel of John," 596.

Walking on the Sea

The walking of Jesus on the sea provides a number of allusions to similar imageries in the Hebrew Bible. Haenchen et al., provide an overview of these allusions:

> As OT precursors for walking on the sea, one usually cites Job 9:8 ("and trampled the waves of the sea"), Isa 43:16 ("Thus says the Lord, who makes a way in the sea, a path in the mighty waters"), and Ps 77:19 ("Thy way was through the sea, thy path through the great waters"). But only Job 9:8 LXX is a real parallel: the Lord "walks on the sea as on firm ground" (περιπατῶν ὡς ἐπ' ἐδάφους θαλάσσης).[22]

When Jesus "walks" (περιπατοῦντα), we are reminded of Job 9:8 as indicated above; but even more so, given that the root πατέω can also mean to "trample."[23] Similarly, in the doxology in Job 9:8, Job authenticates God's power by referring to God's own walking:

נטה שמים לבדו ודורך על־במתי ים
who alone stretched the heavens and walked on the **back** of the sea.[24]

The NRSV translates במתי as "waves," but it is perhaps better translated as "back." This accentuates the image of trampling if we are to imagine the act of walking on the back. To clarify, David Clines notes the influence of creation mythology in this verse and argues that the word ים is also "the name of the sea-god in Ugaritic literature" and so "[m]ost probably it is the 'back' of the sea-monster rather than the 'waves' of the sea on which God treads."[25] The echoes of the creation mythology and *Chaoskampf* are evident here, and one may imagine Jesus walking on the sea as reflective of a divine warrior trampling on the back of a sea-monster. Ironically, it is not the "sea-monster" that the disciples fear, but the sight of the one trampling the sea-monster![26]

22. Haenchen et al. *John*, 279–80.
23. Louw and Nida, *Greek-English Lexicon of the New Testament*, 208.
24. My translation.
25. Clines, *Job 1–20*, 230–31.
26. Cf. Haenchen et. al., *John*, 280. I say this on the premise that the disciples do not know it is actually Jesus walking on the water, who then responds to them to clarify his identity. Guthrie argues that the idea that "the disciples actually saw Jesus walking on the shore and thought he was on the water must be rejected, because it would give no reason for them to be terrified" (*John*, 1038).

Talanoa with Jonah

Further to the imagery discussed above, I want to bring to focus the events at sea in the story of Jonah. I choose this story in particular as it is a tale that resonates with sea-faring Pasifika people whose encounter with the *Moana* portrays similar experiences. Accordingly, I will analyze John 6:16–21 and its intertextual allusions to the events at sea in Jonah 1. Yet, while intertextuality has been used extensively in biblical studies as a way of analyzing allusions and resonances between texts, Pasifika people have always engaged in intertextual conversations through *talanoa*. According to Jione Havea:

> The word *talanoa* (used in Fiji, Tokelau, Tonga, Tuvalu, and Samoa) refers to three interrelated entities: story, *telling* (of stories), and conversation (around stories and tellings). Story (*talanoa*) needs telling (talanoa) in order for it to come alive; telling (*talanoa*) needs conversation (*talanoa*) in order for the story (*talanoa*) to stay current; and conversation (*talanoa*) is empty without story (*talanoa*) and dead without telling (*talanoa*).[27]

In *talanoa*, one can imagine texts sitting at a *kava* bowl in conversation with one another, engaging in *talanoa* as the conversation twists and turns without any deliberate destination. Accordingly, the intertextuality of *talanoa* is a little more fluid and not restricted by the constraints of Western methodologies.[28] As such, I want to utilize *talanoa* in reading John 6:16–21 *with* Jonah 1, as a way of exploring the allusions between the two texts in a fluid manner, much like the *Moana*/sea that flows through these two stories.

Going Down

In John 6:16, the "disciples went down" while in Jonah 1:3, Jonah "went down" to Joppa. The disciples act on their own intuition by "going down," for those who "had been left alone must now take a decision. They do not stay at the place where the feeding took place."[29] In contrast to Matthew and Mark, John specifies that the disciples are not ordered by Jesus, and

---

27. Havea, "Islander Criticism," 2 (n.2).
28. Cf. Havea, "Sitting Jonah with Job," 94–108.
29. Haenchen et. al., *John*, 279.

so they make the decision to go down themselves.[30] In *talanoa* with Jonah, "going down" also denotes a similar self-initiative, although Jonah's enterprise is regarded as disobedience to God's instruction. Perhaps the disciples' acting without instruction could also be construed as disobedience. Jesus never orders them to go down, but they go down anyway. It is dark, and as Carson notes: "[t]he Sea of Galilee lies about six hundred feet below sea level. Cool air from the south-eastern tablelands can rush in to displace the warm moist air over the lake, churning up the water in a violent squall."[31] With some of the disciples being experienced fishermen, they know the dangers but go to sea regardless. Jonah also knows the dangerous consequences of his actions, but also chooses to go down to the sea.

Get Into a Boat

As Jonah and John engage in *talanoa*, they both find their ventures take place in vessels of the sea. The disciples get into a boat (Jn 6:17), while Jonah finds a ship (Jon 1:3). The disciples' purpose in getting into the boat is not clear but, in *talanoa* with Jonah, it is easy to assume that the disciples, like Jonah, must also be escaping, especially given that, in the previous passage in John 6:15, Jesus also retreats in case the people take him by force and make him king. In this sense, the boat becomes a fugitive vessel in both stories.

The Lord's Presence

It is clear in John 6:16–21 that the disciples do not retreat with their Lord, and so Jesus is clearly not with them. In *talanoa* with Jonah, the presence of God in the story is also an issue as the prophet attempts to evade the divine presence. The plotting of each character's location in John 6:15–17 is intriguing, as Francis J. Moloney describes: "Jesus has returned to the mountain (v. 15), the disciples are at the seashore (v. 16), and the multitude has not moved."[32] The image here that Moloney paints suggests that, as each character is located at their own place, the realms are separated: meaning the disciples, like Jonah, are moving away from

---

30. O'Day, "Gospel of John," 595–6.
31. Carson, *Gospel according to John*, 275.
32. Moloney, *The Gospel of John*, 202.

the divine presence (of Jesus). There is an interesting depiction of the seas in both these stories where it is seen as a place of isolation, a place of retreat, a private place. Ironically, as we see in both these stories, that Jesus ultimately walks on the water to his disciples, while Jonah tries valiantly to avoid the Lord only to be found and swallowed by a big fish.

The Rough Sea and Great Winds

The danger of the sea is seen by some scholars as irrelevant to the story, since Jesus does not actually still the waters.[33] Haenchen et al. argue rightly, however, that "[i]f, however, a storm does not threaten, Jesus' walking across the lake is emptied of any real meaning (he cannot be of help)."[34] The changing face of the sea occurs quite violently in both stories as a result of strong winds, and they both serve as a precursor to what ensues, but, more importantly, to provide meaning to the salvific act that follows. For John, the changing sea-face is followed by the miraculous Jesus walking on the sea. For Jonah, the violent sea waters point to the amazing calm after Jonah is thrown overboard.

Terrified

John 6:19 outlines the disciples' emotions upon seeing Jesus walking towards them: "they were terrified." But what of the sea? It may be easy to ignore the turbulent waves in this episode but in *talanoa* with Jonah, we are reminded that some of the disciples are also people of the sea. Jonah 1:5 reads: "Then the mariners were afraid." Despite spending their daily lives out in the seas, even the mariners fear for their lives. Indeed, despite the fact that some of the disciples are experienced fishermen, they too "became" terrified. While it is easy to attribute their fear to the sight of Jesus walking on the sea, Jonah reminds John in this *talanoa* that the sea plays a vital part in the human fear. John 6:19 does not make it explicit as to why the disciples are terrified, and perhaps too much credit has been given to Jesus for their fear. The text does not say that the sea is calm when Jesus walks on it, so it could well be that the sea waves are still raging and that the roughened seas contribute to their terror. Certainly, the

---

33. See Bultmann, *John*, 215 n. 4 [159 n. 1]; Heitmüller, "Das Evangelium des Johannes," 773; Wendland, *Die urchristlichen Literaturformen*, 276.

34. Haenchen et. al., *John*, 279.

ancient readers of the Fourth Gospel may have pictured the sea with the same terror at its chaotic nature as depicted in the Hebrew Bible.

I Am

The *talanoa* between John and Jonah reaches the issue of identity. The way Jesus identifies himself to his disciples, Ἐγώ εἰμι, has been argued by scholars to echo God's identification as "I am" in Exodus 3:14 and thus is better translated as "I am" than "It is I," as in the NRSV. As a result, Jesus' divinity and association with God is implied through his response. In *talanoa* with Jonah, there may also be a different element to Jesus' response that we may need to consider. When the mariners ask Jonah who he is, he responds by saying: "I am a Hebrew." (Jon 1:9). Yet this is not a divine answer, but a cultural identification. Interestingly, he adds to his identification that he worships YHWH, the God who made the sea. In this instance, Jonah associates himself not only with YHWH, but with the sea. What do the mariners care for his Hebrew heritage in the midst of the aqueous chaos? Their fear is intensified after Jonah mentions his God who created the sea and land (Jon 1:10). Havea makes an interesting point here: "Then they took Jonah, cast him into the sea, and the sea responded by standing back from its raging (1:15)."[35] While Jesus' response of "I am" may be understood in divine terms, Jonah reminds John in this *talanoa*, that Jesus is walking *on* the sea, and that the setting of the encounter *is* the sea. Thus Jesus' identification is also relative *to* the raging sea. For the disciples, the context of their struggle and fear is the sea. Ultimately for them, *sea*-ing is believing!

A Moana Hermeneutic

In order to re-read John 6:16–21, I want to construct a hermeneutic based on the Pasifika term for the ocean and sea: *Moana*. It is a word that is common to many Pasifika people, and for this *talanoa* with John 6, I want to bring my own understanding as a Samoan to the fore. For Samoans, the root word of *Moana* is the word *moa* which means "center" or "middle." The word *moa* also means "heart." The implication here is that the *Moana* is the center or the heart of all existence. Everything is connected through the *moa* (center) as the *Moana* is a multi-laned bridge

---

35. Havea, *Jonah*, 26.

which connects (is)lands. As such, I want to construct a hermeneutic based on the *Moana* as the center (*moa*), so that we privilege the ocean/sea/*Moana* in our worldview. To clarify, let us view how Epeli Hau'ofa privileges the sea/ocean/*Moana*:

> There is a world of difference between viewing the Pacific as 'islands in a far sea' and as 'a sea of island.' The first emphasizes dry surfaces in a vast ocean far from the centers of power. Focusing in this way stresses the smallness and remoteness of the islands. The second is a more holistic perspective in which things are seen in the totality of their relationships.[36]

This second position invites us to include (or perhaps bring back?) the ocean/sea/*Moana* into our worldview. The *Moana* is not only the center of the created order but, in reading, it must also be given space as a central character. Through this perspective, we re-read John 6:16–21 by privileging the sea/ocean/*Moana* in the text that has often been neglected.

Moana Re-Reading of John 6:16–21 and Implications for Climate Change in Pasifika

I would like to use the hermeneutic of *Moana* to re-read John 6 in light of climate change in Pasifika—in particular, the significance of *Moana* in the livelihood of Pasifika peoples but also its destructive force as a result of rising sea levels. The challenge is to provide an alternative way of perceiving the text, from the privileged reading positions that resonate with a lack of care for the ocean and its important place in the created order. This lack of concern must also be subverted in our reading, as this re-reading gives privilege to the sea/*Moana* that is often neglected. I will use some of the implications from the intertextual *talanoa* between John 6:16–21 and Jonah 1, to guide our *va'a* through this re-reading. In effect, I invite *Moana* and its people to the *talanoa*.

Going down – Tulou!

When the disciples go down, it is a detail in the story that does not receive much attention. But from a *Moana* perspective, there is an acknowledgement of the sea taking place, for "going down" implies that

---

36. Hau'ofa, *We are the Ocean*, 31–32.

they are leaving the land and stepping into the waters. It also places the reader in Jonah at the sea at Joppa. "Going down" for Pasifika people also denotes respect. In most Pasifika contexts, when people cross a sacred space, they normally "go down" by lowering their bodies and saying the word *"tulou"* which often means "excuse me." In most cases, "[m]uch of the concern of *tulou* is dealing with those people who have been offended when their space is crossed. An awkward situation becomes apparent."[37] By saying *tulou*, they amend the awkward situation and acknowledge they are crossing a sacred space.[38] Pasifika readers could imagine that when the disciples "go down" they fail to say *tulou* to the sacred sea-space that they are about to cross, for what happens next is the sea responding in anger, much like a person seated may respond to someone who fails to say *tulou* when crossing their space. In the current climate, we see the rest of the world guilty of not saying *tulou* to the sea-space, as large carbon emissions from fossil fuels continue to increase, leading to global warming and subsequently resulting in the *Moana* responding in anger through rising sea levels and tsunamis. The recent COP26[39] in Glasgow saw a huge number of Pasifika representatives pleading with world leaders to "go down" and say *tulou* to the oceans but there appears to be no effort by the world powers to lower themselves to the *Moana*. It is only a matter of time before the *Moana* retaliates.

Boats and Boat People

For Pasifika people, the boat/canoe (Samoan: *va'a*) is never intended for escaping but "for movements along sea routes that connect people of different island locations."[40] This is intriguing because it provides an alternative way of reimagining the *va'a* in John 6:16–21. In the Jonah story, we can focus therefore on Jonah connecting with Tarshish rather than retreating from Nineveh. At the same time, the disciples are connecting with the land of Capernaum, where they may also re-connect with Jesus who has fled earlier. The boat/*va'a* therefore is a vessel that pursues the connection between lands, as Hau'ofa imagines. But without the sea, the *va'a* cannot cross, and hence people cannot connect from one land

37. Kolia, "Lifting the Tapu of Sex," 86.
38. Kolia, "Lifting the Tapu of Sex," 86.
39. 26th UN Climate Change Conference of the Parties.
40. Hau'ofa, *We are the Ocean*, 81.

to another. The sea, therefore, is a critical pathway for boats, while at the same time boats are the bridgeways for people to connect via the *Moana*. In the spirit of *tulou*, boats must also pay respect to the *Moana*, to acknowledge that, at any time, the waves may rise and take life at any moment. In light of climate change, large corporations and governments are guilty of not understanding that large ships may contribute to climate change through the emission of black carbon, through tiny black particles that are produced via the burning of marine fuel. Rather than utilizing the *Moana* as a way of connecting (is)lands, such corporations instead abuse the *Moana*, while at the same time isolating themselves from other lands for the sake of profit.

Lord's Presence: Refuge

While the *Moana* is the center for Pasifika people and a bridge between lands, it can also be a place of refuge, to escape from the erratic commotion of life on the land. The Jonah and John stories both suggest this reason for leaving the land but ironically, while they both escape the land, Jonah and the disciples also meet YHWH and Jesus respectively at sea. The sea, therefore, acts as a space for encountering the divine and, for Pasifika people, the *Moana* has always had the feel of approaching a divine space to confront a creature with reverence, for the *Moana* not only gives life but also takes it. Again, in light of climate change, the worldview of the *Moana* as a creature who offers its resources may enlighten us to tread (not trample) the ocean with care, for the *Moana* can turn any time.

Rough Seas

The signs of the seas and its waves tell a story for Pasifika people. A large portion of Samoan indigenous knowledge is based on observations of the sea/*Moana*. For instance, there is a Samoan proverb, "*Ua sina le galu*" ("The wave whitens"), which refers to a wave that is about to break. What this means is that the conclusion is near, usually in reference to the end of an event or a term. There is also a Samoan expression, "*Ua siisii le tai*" ("the ocean deep rises"), which points to a situation of hostility: in particular, when an argument is heated. But before meanings are drawn from these observations of the sea, they are indeed the realities of the *Moana*. In John 6:16–21, the signs of the *Moana* are evident and, through a *Moana* perspective, these signs must be perceived as a story within a story. Beneath this miracle story lies a reality of a sea-faring region which lives with the effects of the changing and unforgiving sea. These signs almost cost the disciples their lives. For Pasifika people, they also live the same reality.

Terrified

Accordingly, the response by Pasifika people to the ocean is one of awe and respect but can also be that of fear and terror. In light of climate change, rising sea levels and natural disasters such as tsunamis, cyclones and volcanic eruptions, mean that the *Moana* is hardly seen by Pasifika as a white-sanded paradise. Hollywood and mainstream media are guilty of perpetuating this image of the *Moana* as a postcard backdrop. The governments of the Western world, as the wider global community witnessed, ensured that COP26 in Glasgow was ultimately a failure. The two biggest tickets had failed to eventuate: first, the renewing of targets for 2030 so that they align with restricting global warming to 1.5°C and, second, a global agreement on fast-tracking the phasing out of coal. The countries whose livelihoods depended on the *Moana*'s well-being were pleading with the world, yet those developed nations who seem unperturbed by the health of the world's oceans could not come around to committing to the 2030 targets and phasing out coal quickly. They were *not* terrified, because they could not see the realities of the sea. Such attitudes tend to manifest in the way we read the biblical text, and perhaps if we minimize the *Moana*/sea/ocean in John 6:16–21, we may be reading from the privileged positions of First World nations—especially those who fail to see the signs of the sea!

I am

As Jesus identifies himself to his disciples, I cannot help but think that in this instance, he is also outlining the relational dynamic. He is who he is, in relation to the disciples, but also to the sea. While scholars have seen the echoes of Exodus 3:14 in Jesus' declaration, I want us to view Jesus' words through a *Moana* perspective, where the focus is not on his lordship, but on who he is relative to the sea. Jesus does not specify that he is the "Lord" but simply "it is I" (NRSV). In response to the climate crisis, we are also asked to identify ourselves in relation to the sea/ocean/*Moana*. Who are we? The answer to this simple question would determine where we stand on the issue of climate change. For Pasifika people, we are called *Tangata o le Moana* (people of the *Moana*) who migrate from our ancestral homes to other lands and continue to migrate. As such, we acknowledge our heritage in the *Moana* and stand to protect its welfare. Several Pasifika climate activists, such as the Pacific Climate Warriors, consist of diasporic Pasifika peoples in Australia and New Zealand who, despite living outside of Pasifika, continue to fight for climate change and the protection of *Moana*. They identify themselves relative to the *Moana*, and so they stand for climate justice. The challenge for us is whether we recognize ourselves as an ally to climate justice or perpetuate the failure of COP26.

Conclusion

In sum, a *Moana* reading allows us to focus our attention on the neglected voice of the sea/ocean in the biblical text. It is easy for Pasifika people to recognize the prominence of the sea/ocean in their lives because they see the ocean around them. For a number of non-Pasifika people who live inland, there may be less urgency shown towards the sea/ocean. A *Moana* hermeneutic, however, may provide an alternative worldview and reading perspective that seeks to place the *Moana* in the *moa* (center) of our reading of texts where the sea/ocean is neglected, and its significance reduced. The events at sea in John 6:16–21 seem far less miraculous through a *Moana* reading, as the realities of the sea/ocean are restored in the text, to bring out more nuances for a richer and deeper interpretation. As such, a *Moana* reading also brings to light the realities of climate change as felt by those in Pasifika. When Jesus walks on the sea, we are reminded of the people of Tuvalu, Tokelau, Kiribati and the Marshall Islands, who are also walking on the sea: not miraculously, but in terror, as a consequence of rising sea levels. At the same time, walking on the sea is also a sign of resilience for the people of Tuvalu, Tokelau, Kiribati, the Marshall Islands and the rest of Pasifika. Here, the words of Pacific Climate Warrior Brianna Fruean of 350 Pacific, spoken at COP26, speak to this resilient spirit: "We are not drowning, we are fighting!"

Bibliography

Brueggemann, Walter. "The Book of Exodus." In *NIB*, edited by Leander E. Keck, vol. 1. Nashville: Abingdon, 1994.

Bultmann, Rudolf. *The Gospel of John: A Commentary*. Translated by George Beasley-Murray. Louisville, KY: Westminster, 1971.

Carr, David M. *Formation of Genesis 1–11: Biblical and Other Precursors*. New York: Oxford University Press, 2020.

Carson, D. A. *The Gospel According to John*. PNTC. Leicester, UK: IVP, 1991.

Childs, Brevard S. *The Book of Exodus: A Critical, Theological Commentary*. OTL. Louisville: Westminster John Knox, 2004.

Clines, David J. A. *Job 1–20*. WBC. Dallas: Word, 1989.

Daly-Denton, Mary. *John: Supposing Him to Be the Gardener*. EBC. London: T&T Clark, 2017.

Day, John. *God's Conflict with the Dragon and the Sea*. Cambridge, MS: Harvard University Press, 1975.

Dozeman, Thomas B. "The Song of the Sea and Salvation History." In *On the Way to Nineveh: Studies in Honor of George M. Landes*, edited by Stephen L. Cook and Sarah C. Winter, 94–113. Atlanta: Scholars, 1999.

Fretheim, Terence E. "The Book of Genesis." In *NIB*, edited by Leander E. Keck, vol. 1. Nashville: Abingdon, 1994.

Gunkel, Hermann. *Creation and Chaos in the Primeval Era and the Eschaton: A Religio-Historical Study of Genesis 1 and Revelation 12*. Translated by K. William Whitney Jr. Grand Rapids: Eerdmans, 2006.

Guthrie. Donald "John." In *NIB*, edited by D. A. Carson et al., 4th ed. Leicester, UK/ Downers Grove, IL: IVP, 1994.

Haenchen, Ernst et al. *John: A Commentary on the Gospel of John*. Hermen. 2 vols. Philadelphia: Fortress, 1984.

Habel, Norman. *The Birth, the Curse and the Greening of Earth: An Ecological Reading of Genesis 1–11*. EBC. Sheffield: Phoenix, 2011.

Hau'ofa, Epeli. *We are the Ocean: Selected Works*. Honolulu: University of Hawai'i Press, 2008.

Havea, Jione. "Islander Criticism: Waters, Ways, Worries." In *Sea of Readings*, edited by Jione Havea, 1–20. Atlanta: SBL, 2018.

———. *Jonah*. EBC. London: T&T Clark, 2020.

———. "Sitting Jonah with Job: Resailing Intertextuality." *B&CT* 12 (2016) 94–108.

Heitmüller, W. "Das Evangelium des Johannes. Göttingen: Göttingen University Press, 1908.

Kolia, Brian Fiu. "Moana and Qohelet: Futility in Diaspora?" In *Thresholds of Theology in Aotearoa New Zealand*, edited by Jione Havea et al. Lanham, MD: Lexington, forthcoming 2022.

———. "Lifting the Tapu of Sex: A *Tulou* Reading of the Song of Songs." In *Sea of Readings*, edited by Jione Havea, 85–102. Atlanta: SBL, 2018.

Kruse, Colin G. *John: An Introduction and Commentary*. TNTC. Downers Grove, IL: IVP, 2003.

Levenson, Jon D. *Creation and the Persistence of Evil: The Jewish Drama of Divine Omnipotence*. New Jersey: Princeton University Press, 1988.

Louw, Johannes P. and Eugene Albert Nida. *Greek-English Lexicon of the New Testament: Based on Semantic Domains*. New York: UBS, 1996.

Moloney, Francis J. *The Gospel of John*. Sacra Pagina 4. Collegeville, MN: The Liturgical Press, 1998.

Newman, Barclay Moon and Eugene Albert Nida, *A Handbook on the Gospel of John*, UBSHS. New York: UBS, 1993.

O'Day, Gail R. "The Gospel of John." In *New Interpreter's Bible*, edited by Leander E. Keck, vol. 9. Nashville: Abingdon 1995.

Trudinger, Peter L. "Friend or Foe? Earth, Sea and *Chaoskampf* in the Psalms." In *The Earth Story in the Psalms and the Prophets*, edited by Norman C. Habel. EB. Sheffield: Sheffield Academic, 2001.

Wendland, Paul. *Die urchristlichen Literaturformen*, HNT. Tübingen: Mohr-Siebeck, 1912.

12

A Sign of the Times

John's Gospel and the Contemporary Anglican Communion

ALEXANDER ROSS

Introduction

THIS ESSAY WILL DRAW out a distinctively Johannine ecclesiology (that is, study and reflection on the church) of—and for—Anglicanism, with a particular emphasis on the place of sign and symbol in the Gospel of John as it relates to ongoing ecclesial reflection within Anglicanism on its own identity, polity, and contemporary witness. It will be argued that the Anglican tradition has within it the resources as well as the potential to demonstrate an ecclesiology of "sign" as a means to mediate the realities of this age and the age to come: a sign of the kingdom but also a sign "of the times" in the world, and through which the new world will be brought into being; and yet called to hold in reconciling tension the darkness of this age with the light to which the church must testify.

Such an ecclesiology for Anglicanism has potential not only for its own life and self-understanding as a "Communion" but also for the contribution it may make to ecumenism and the ongoing endeavor to give visible expression to Christ's gift of unity to the church, testified to in the Gospel of John, that it may be one in witness to the unity of the Triune God.

The essay will further develop a broader thesis of the author in proposing an alternative ecclesial paradigm for Anglican polity that moves beyond a "hyper-modern" dichotomy of devolved autonomy, on the one hand, and, on the other, centralized authority, both locked in a perpetual contest which plays itself out in the one seemingly neutral ecclesial space. Instead, this thesis envisages an ecclesiology of graced and gifted being, where the church is called to manifest the "communion" it has already been given: that is, to be a "sign" of the reality it expresses within the reality it inhabits.

This essay is broadly structured according to two parts to demonstrate a distinctly Johannine ecclesiology which is both *for* and *of* Anglicanism. The first part engages with recent scholarship in Johannine ecclesiology and builds on this work to propose an ecclesiology *for* Anglicanism: that is, an "ecclesiology of sign" developed through a Johannine lens with particular attention to the prologue of John's Gospel.

The second part of this essay seeks to demonstrate that this "ecclesiology of sign" is authentically *of* Anglicanism. This does not mean, however, that it is derived or distilled from any contrived Anglican way of being church—this would be to set the cart before the horse. Rather, it points to some characteristic notes already existing within the Anglican way which make it well-placed to take up such an ecclesiology and to inhabit it more purposefully. This is explored particularly through the affirmation of ecclesial "provisionality"—a "sign" for others—in Anglican self-understanding and its relationship to the indefectibility of the church which necessitates an attentiveness to both eschatology as well as contemporary witness and ecumenism. The symbolism of living water in John 7 further develops this illustration.

An Ecclesiology for Anglicanism

Throughout this essay, and particularly its exploration of sign and symbol in the Gospel of John and especially in the prologue, I intend to establish how such an ecclesiology might resonate with the broader "Cambridge School" to recover and reassert Augustinian Neoplatonism in the Christian conception of the *saecula saeculorum*: all that was, and is, and is to be.[1] It is important to note the caveat, of course, that I neither as-

---

1. What has been dubbed the "Cambridge School" is Radical Orthodoxy, defined and led by John Milbank, Catherine Pickstock, and Graham Ward. My own research

sume nor seek any kind of "strict" or "pure" Platonism in the Gospel of John, the most that might be claimed being, as C. K. Barrett described, a "popular Platonism" which pervaded the *Sitz im Leben* ("life setting") of the Johannine community who breathed "an atmosphere, absorbed but not understood by many who had not read his works" (rather like what is claimed for Christianity in the West today).[2] Nevertheless, a form of Neoplatonism, particularly of the Iamblichan tradition,[3] is being recovered in Christian theology and commended particularly for the field of ecclesiology, not only by Milbank and those in that school, but also by the most recent scholarship on Johannine understandings of the church.

For my own part, however, this carries forward a wider project to advocate for a paradigm-shift in Anglican Studies away from what I have previously characterized as a "flattened ecclesiology,"[4] predicated on the assumption of a seemingly neutral and level ecclesial "playing field" on which autonomous "national churches" play at being "in communion:" itself a qualitative reflection by degree of the *communio trinitatis* ("communion of the Trinity"). The high-water mark of this is perhaps best articulated in the 1997 "Virginia Report" of the Inter-Anglican Theological and Doctrinal Commission. Despite employing the themes of giftedness and participation which I will come to commend and develop further, the "Virginia Report" nevertheless collapses the ontological distinction between the church and the divine life of the Holy Trinity by positing that the "mission of the Church is to be the icon of God's life."[5] From this it follows that its institutional structures are elevated as "God's gift"[6] which themselves give

---

might be deemed sympathetic towards this movement but without any claim to speak for it or within it.

2. Barrett, *Gospel of John*, 35.

3. That is, the form of Neoplatonism formulated by the Arab intellectual, Iamblichus, 245–325 CE.

4. Ross, *A Still More Excellent Way*, 197.

5. Inter-Anglican Theological and Doctrinal Commission, "Virginia Report," para. 2.17.

6. See for example the extraordinary claim in paragraph 1.14 of *The Virginia Report* that the "instruments of Communion" (which then were considered to be the Primates' Meetings, Anglican Consultative Council, Lambeth Conferences, and the Archbishop of Canterbury) are given by God to "hold us in the life of the triune God" and "are also the structures we seek to share with all those who have been baptized into the life of the Triune God." Canterbury as *alterius orbis papa* (lit. "pope of the other world") indeed!

expression to the fundamental bond of Anglican life which is that unity given in the life of God, Father, Son and Holy Spirit. That life of divine communion is made visible in a characteristic way within the ordered life of the Anglican Communion.[7]

The effect of this "flattened" or "collapsed" ecclesiology is that churches of the Communion are perpetually engaged in a contest which pits autonomy against interdependence as they seek themselves to appropriate and exhibit the divine properties of both unity and truth.

The research of my doctoral dissertation, recently published, sought to point towards a "Still more excellent way. . ." through the examination and proposed recovery of a more authentically "provincial" polity within Anglicanism as just one answer to addressing the underlying ecclesial deficiency of our "flattened ecclesiology."[8] A motivating purpose of this essay is to begin to take up the next task, leaving aside for now the consideration of polity, to pursue instead an alternative through the development of an "ecclesiology of sign" illuminated through the testimony of John's Gospel.

It is in this sense that what is offered here is an ecclesiology "for" Anglicanism: not as one amongst a smorgasbord of legitimate offerings but as the only compelling account for an ecclesial vision and identity which is able to relate Anglicanism to the Christian conception of God, creation, and the Economy of Salvation. This essay is then more broadly concerned to expound that Christian conception of reality as an essential basis for ecclesiology; as it is born out in John's prologue and developed more recently through scholarship on Johannine ecclesiology in conversation with the categories of Augustinian Neoplatonism. These categories include gift and giftedness, participation and exchange, and the denial of any neutral sphere, commonly called the "secular," in which to pursue the task of ecclesiology or any other endeavor.[9] I am also grateful to Fergus King for providing an advance copy of his own contribution to this volume which I have drawn on and engaged with a little.

---

7. Inter-Anglican Theological and Doctrinal Commission, "Virginia Report," para. 3.53.

8. Ross, *A Still More Excellent Way*, 200.

9. Williams, *On Augustine*, 127–8.

Ecclesiology and the "Book of Signs"

The Gospel of John has not been closely associated with the study of ecclesiology: despite its advanced Christology.[10] There is not the practical immediacy paired with applied theological reflection which the Pauline writings offer, perhaps the most obvious starting-point for exploring the very beginnings of the church's own articulation of itself; there is not the well-developed and curated (perhaps too much so?) narrative of the church's apostolic origins offered by the Gospel of Luke and the Book of Acts; and there is not the tantalizing but ever-since confessionally-controversial commission to Peter recorded by Matthew (16:18) which is the only clear use anywhere in the Gospels of the word ἐκκλησία to refer to an enduring and dominically-instituted body (cf. Matt 18:17).[11] Nevertheless, a recent body of work has begun to explore the implications of the Johannine writings for ecclesiology.

Johan Ferreira's 1998 monograph moves beyond social analysis of the dynamics of the Johannine community, as well as ecclesiological readings of John influenced through the lens of Pauline and Early Church reflections of the church, to establish a christological ecclesiology which is more authentically Johannine.[12] Ferreira explores this through Jesus' prayer in John 17 and particularly an exposition of the Johannine concept of "glory" through which the church becomes *Christus Prolongatus* (i.e. an extension of the incarnation), which gives it eschatological and soteriological momentum as it "participates in the glory of Jesus, that is, in the sending of Jesus to save the world."[13]

Sandra Schneiders proposes a narrative exploration of Johannine ecclesiology through a close reading of John 20:19–23 which similarly emphasizes christological participation through the themes of "New Covenant," "New Israel" and "New Temple" whereby the church is understood:

> . . . not as an institution replacing the departed Jesus, nor even as his commissioned representative or agent, but as the ongoing presence and action of Jesus through the world as his corporate

---

10. Lincoln, "Johannine Vision," 98.
11. Alexander, "Church in the Synoptic Gospels," 56.
12. Ferreira, *Johannine Ecclesiology*, 14–15.
13. Ferreira, *Johannine Ecclesiology*, 202.

body, the ecclesial community, which will salvifically reveal him as he revealed God.[14]

Andrew Lincoln, in his entry in the recently published *Oxford Handbook of Ecclesiology* continues this narrative approach to unpack christological participation with soteriological purpose to carry forward the *missio Dei* as characteristic of John's understanding of the church but with an emphasis also on the empowerment and guidance of the Holy Spirit.[15]

However, it is Andrew Byers' research on *theosis* (or "divinization") and participation, effected through "filiation" and "exchange," which most directly engages with the prologue in John's Gospel as both establishing a "participatory anthropology [which] . . . gives way to a participatory ecclesiology"[16] as well as attributing to it a Jewish and Platonist (as distinct from "Hellenist") inheritance,[17] capable of upholding a distinctively Christian understanding of *theosis* consistent with its Alexandrian definition: "Though the Johannine idea of divinity is inclusive of human participation in the Fourth Gospel, divine-human parameters and distinctions are carefully maintained."[18]

This might be compared with the ontological distinctions which enable participation and theurgy (that is, the idea of the collaboration between the divine and the human), within Iamblichan Platonism, which carried over into the church's development of an orthodox articulation of the Triune God. It may also be compared to the soteriological implications of the Incarnation for all creation, carried forth through the church which:

> with its ecclesiastical embodiment of the divine hierarchy, its initiations, and its belief in salvation through sacramental acts, may have fulfilled the theurgical program of Iamblichus in a manner that was never concretely realized by Platonists.[19]

The "gifted gulf" between Creator and creation which enables ontological participation between each other while maintaining their

---

14. Schneiders, "Raising of the New Temple," 355.

15. Lincoln, "Johannine Vision," 116.

16. Byers, *Ecclesiology and Theosis*, 185.

17. For the importance of holding to an integration of this double-inheritance, see Milbank and Riches, "Foreword," v.

18. Byers, *Ecclesiology and Theosis*, 170.

19. Shaw, *Theurgy and the Soul*, 271.

distinctiveness is, for Byers, predicated in Christianity, in continuity with Jewish creation theology, with its emphasis on *creatio ex nihilo* ("creation from nothing") which the Gospel of John expounds in its prologue.[20]

It is this Neoplatonic trajectory into which scholarship around Johannine ecclesiology has been moving that I intend to develop and begin to articulate an "ecclesiology of sign" for Anglicanism—at least—as a first attempt to chart the conceptual contours of a remedy to the "flattened ecclesiology" into which I have previously argued Anglicanism has slumped.

Sign and Symbol in the Gospel of John

"Sign" and "symbol" has, of course, been well developed in narrative criticism of the Fourth Gospel, the "Book of Signs." Dorothy Lee has drawn out the distinction identified by Schneiders between symbol, "the experience of a transcendent reality which has its source firmly located within material reality . . . an epiphany of present reality," and sign as instead "an indication of an absent [reality]."[21] This distinction, however, is not necessarily Johannine and for our purposes the terms may well be used interchangeably, though certainly with an emphasis on the sense attributed by Schneiders to "symbol:" the communication and "real presence" of the reality to which it points and in which it participates. This is guarded, however, by the ontological distinctiveness already described and echoed by Lee: "While it may be possible to articulate the symbol, such articulation cannot be substituted for the symbol itself."[22] So too in understanding and speaking of the church—not least Anglicanism—as sign and symbol of the divine life and mission, the ontological distinction should not be collapsed, as I have suggested it has been through the ecclesiology of the IATDC's "Virginia Report."

Instead, an "ecclesiology of sign" envisages the church as suspended from the divine life and mission through its graced and gifted nature and thereby able, through its institution as and incorporation into Christ's body by the empowerment of the Holy Spirit, to participate in that life and mission. The hermeneutical affirmation which drives Lee's exploration of

---

20. Byers, *Ecclesiology and Theosis*, 171 See particularly the discussion in FN 6, reflecting on Hans Boersma's Heavenly Participation.

21. Lee, *Symbolic Narratives*, 16.

22. Lee, *Symbolic Narratives*, 29.

sign and symbol in the Gospel of John drives this Johannine "ecclesiology of sign" too: form and meaning belong together.[23] If the church is to be a sign of God's love and purpose, that is God's own self, and the final realization of God's sovereign justice, that is the kingdom, then it is—following Ricoeur—"a new semantic reality . . . [whereby] form gives birth to content in the creation of new meaning, as two unlike elements . . . are radically fused. The new meaning created is a symbol of archetypal significance."[24] The church as "sign" mediates this place between Creator and creation, empowered by the Spirit to interpret, each to the other, the utterance of the Incarnation—the Word made flesh—with the groaning of all matter as it waits in hope for the glory which has been (Jn 1:14) and will be (Rom 8:18) revealed.

John's Prologue and an "Ecclesiology of Sign"

A brief exposition here of the prologue of John's Gospel will attempt to situate this "ecclesiology of sign" within the greater Johannine conception of God's life and saving purpose. It will also draw out the biblical foundations for the Neoplatonic lens by which this ecclesiology is subsequently imagined. Fergus King's essay in this volume, "Friends, Foes or Rivals?" outlines a helpful framework for understanding the Johannine revelation of the economic Trinity, "a deity who is engaged in four significant acts," which I intend to take in three parts: 1. God's Creating; 2. God's Redeeming and Sanctifying; 3. God's Loving and Sending.

God's Creating

The first three verses of John's prologue speak to the fundamental relationship between, first, the Word and God (Jn 1:1–2), and then, the Creator and creation (Jn 1:3a).[25] As has been identified earlier through the work of Byers, this is predicated on an assumption of the *creatio ex nihilo* which is challenged by the "conundrum" identified by King of the darkness of verse 5 which, even if a "no-thing" as Miroslav Volf posits, represents at least from the very beginning the presence of "oppositional

---

23. Lee, *Symbolic Narratives*, 29.
24. Lee, *Symbolic Narratives*, 31.
25. Moloney, *Gospel of John*, 4:36.

dualities" in the created order.[26] In other words, if darkness is a "no-thing" and not simply a by-product of creation (and therefore itself creation) then it must logically follow that there is darkness before any "thing" has come into being, that is "in the beginning with God." The "Beginning," therefore, which John's prologue describes is one where God is not all in all—as God shall be (1 Cor 15:28, cf Jn 17:22). Indeed, there is that which is "not-God": darkness. Though neither is this creation. Instead, it is a necessary condition for the work of creation as without the pre-existing darkness there is no "room" for creation to be brought into being and God's creative act could not be a possibility. God's work of creation is the bringing of darkness into light: the light which is itself a participation in the divine life (Jn 1:4). The Word brings about this life and light by grace and gift (Jn 1:16), revealing the motivating purpose of God, which is inherently relational, to be "all in all" that nothing is excluded from participation in that life so that ultimately there is no darkness. Darkness is, as the *Exultet* proclaims, "banished forever." And this purpose is relentless, unceasing, and unstoppable (Jn 1:5).

This affirmation is critical because it means that the whole arc of salvation history is not a return to some original state but a single continuum from "Beginning" to "End" effected by the one who is Alpha and Omega. What of the alternative? If God were "all in all" in the Beginning then creation could only be an "arm"—an extension of the divine, neither gifted nor graced but collapsed instead into the "univocity of being." Furthermore, that the darkness is neither "of God" nor of God's purpose for creation has profound implications for theodicy (that is, the problem of evil and suffering in God's world), encountered so frequently in the practical exercise of the church's pastoral ministry and care.

The other implication is that the darkness cannot be understood as some "neutral space" because it is by definition not "of God" and God is not in it. Although out of that darkness God works creation into the state of giftedness which makes it inherently "good." Therefore there can be no secular (understood as some "neutral" sphere) in all of creation because all that "is" is either God, of God (creation) or not-God (darkness).

---

26. King, "Friends, Foes, or Rivals?"

God's Redeeming and Sanctifying

What then is sin and death but the encroachment of darkness back into the good of creation? The "necessary sin of Adam," to echo again the *Exultet*, is necessary because the gift is freely given and received but so too is it freely rejected, and from that first rejection is opened the means for darkness to be let back in (Jn 1:11). The darkness—sin and death—cannot be created by God otherwise it could be uncreated or destroyed summarily: the "problem of evil" would be no problem for God. Far from being one amongst a range of options, the only solution to the problem is the Incarnation, the Cross, and the Resurrection. Darkness has encroached again into creation—God must enter that creation (the Incarnation) to encounter the darkness (the Cross) and recreate it (the Resurrection) first in Christ, then in all who would participate in that new life (Jn 1:12).

Such a reading of the "darkness" in John's prologue provides an important hermeneutical dimension to the Redeeming and Sanctifying nature of God as being neither a simple reconciliation "of the cosmos from the god from whom it has become estranged" nor an act of "intervention."[27] Instead, the Redeeming and Sanctifying work of God in Christ is a continuation of God's creative action. So too, it is undertaken by the same creative agent, the Word—the Son—through whom all things came into being (Jn 1:3). The story of salvation is in fact the story of creation. Rather than a "rescue mission" and return to the innocence of Eden, it is one continuum from "In the beginning" to the end which is God "all in all" (1 Cor 15:24–28). The end of that giftedness of God's creative work is a *theosis*: light ultimately and finally displacing the darkness so that all that is "not-God" is now bound up with God in the gifted goodness of creation to give and receive God's glory (Jn 1:14). Matthew Levering has followed this "linear" and "participatory" model of history through Augustine's *City of God*: "No more shall we wish to be God by grasping, for we will rejoice in partaking in God by his gift."[28]

God's Loving and Sending

The experience and ethic of this end, according to Augustine, is to receive and return God's love and revelatory gift:

---

27. King, "Friends, Foes, or Rivals?," 4, 5.
28. Levering, "Linear and Participatory History," 194.

> God will be the end of our desires. He will be seen without end, loved without stint, praised without weariness ... There we shall rest and see, see and love, love and praise. Behold what will be, in the end to which there shall be no end! For what other end do we set for ourselves than to reach that kingdom of which there is no end?[29]

If this response is our end, the beginning is marked by God's Love and Sending not as itself responsive, reactive, nor remedial but prior, motivating, and constant. These are characteristics not just of the economic Trinity but the immanent also and their working out through salvation history is necessary because it is of God's very own nature: God loves, and God reaches out in love. The church, certainly for Augustine, stands to mediate, herald, and "with its faith and miracles, anticipates this everlasting peace."[30] The church is a sign of the times as well as to them.

King identifies the gift of the Holy Spirit as effecting the Sending grace of God's work, most notably in the Incarnation.[31] The Spirit does not appear explicitly in the prologue, but in a way—and perhaps ironically — the Spirit becomes in John's Gospel the most "embodied" agent in this soteriological narrative through its unity with, and mission to, the church: the Spirit is sent upon the Son, and then through the Son to the church. It is from this moment that the church is gathered and called out (Jn 1:35–51) and it is from this moment that the church is constituted. The sending of the Spirit through John 14 to 20 is the commission to the church to continue this creative work begun in Christ as itself the "Body of Christ."

The church then is bound up, by the Spirit, with God's purpose to Create, Sanctify and Redeem, Love and Send. This is its missional imperative, its pastoral imperative, its call to holiness and transformation of life, and its expressive and prophetic imperative. The church is not itself God—but neither is it passively groaning with all creation, merely waiting. Rather, it is commissioned and empowered to carry forward what Christ has accomplished. In doing so, it must negotiate its place between Creator and creation: it must mediate its mission. How it does this is its "ecclesiology of sign."

---

29. Augustine of Hippo, *The City of God Against the Pagans* XXII.30.1179, 1182.
30. Levering, "Linear and Participatory History: Augustine's City of God," 177.
31. King, "Friends, Foes, or Rivals?"

An Ecclesiology of Anglicanism

Just as this essay's treatment of an "ecclesiology of sign" *for* Anglicanism has not made any claim of exclusivity to Anglicanism alone, so too in the consideration of how such an ecclesiology might be *of* Anglicanism it is not intended that it be derived from any uniquely Anglican attribute but rather to reveal how Anglicanism is already well-placed to take up such an ecclesiology. To illustrate this I shall briefly reflect on the Anglican ecclesial attribute of "provisionality" and the Anglican approach to holding the dynamic between eschatology and contemporary witness in the exercise of the church's indefectibility. This is explored through the christological symbolism of the church as a running river (Jn 7:37–39).

Embrace of "Provisionality"

A distinctive, though not unique, feature of Anglican ecclesial reflection has been a tendency to emphasize its provisional nature within the One, Holy, Catholic and Apostolic church as well as within the economy of salvation and the coming reign of the kingdom of God.[32] Most explicitly it was articulated by Archbishop Robert Runcie in his address at the opening of the 1988 Lambeth Conference, that "Anglicanism has a radically provisional character which we must never allow to be obscured."[33] Anglicanism exists, then, not for its own sake but as a tangible expression, however elusive, of the church as lived through the mediation of a particular culture, language, history and people—albeit a particularity that is always evolving and opening to greater diversity, not least through the rapid globalization of Anglicanism in the nineteenth and twentieth centuries. An awareness and appreciation of the church's provisionality is essential for an "ecclesiology of sign" as Anglicanism takes hold of this mediating position between church and kingdom. Nevertheless, its provisionality is not that of the "disposable" but is rather "sustained": a reconciling ecclesiology whereby Anglicanism acts something like an ecclesial midwife to gently guide and deliver by its own distinctive touch the coming kingdom.

---

32. For a fuller description see Paul Avis's classic study of Anglicanism which opens with a discussion of this "provisionality," see *Identity of Anglicanism*, 2.

33. *Truth shall make you free. Lambeth 1988 Reports*, 13.

The kingdom is not so overtly a theme of John's Gospel as it is in the Synoptic Gospels; however, the kingdom "born of water and the Spirit"—as Jesus explains to Nicodemus (Jn 3:5)—points toward both a sacramental and ecclesial husbandry. Through this vocation, provisionality as the sign which carries us into, and in the end gives way to, ultimate reality is sustained and secured by the doctrine of the church's indefectibility.

Provisionality and Indefectibility

Indefectibility, the fundamental affirmation that the church will be preserved in truth until the end, has developed within Anglican theology to avoid an overidentification of the church with the kingdom which tends toward a hierarchical and authority-driven ecclesiology in which the church cannot err, on the one hand, and, on the other, an ecclesiology of the "wheat and the weeds" which privileges a "faithful remnant" (necessarily self-defined) and tends toward "de-churching" any who do not fit the narrow boundaries of confessional orthodoxy.[34] Instead within Anglicanism there developed a more nuanced understanding of indefectibility in relation to the church's provisionality from Richard Field's ecclesiology of an "essential church" to William Laud's definition of the "truth of salvation" in which the church will be preserved from error, through to William Palmer's "perpetual visible divine society"; a society brought into the divine.[35] This is followed in the twentieth century by Michael Ramsey's affirmation that the church does not apprehend the truth, but rather it is seized by the truth, ." . .the Truth the divine action which apprehends the Church."[36]

Anglicanism's developed commitment to ecclesial provisionality (although perhaps not as developed as it might be) makes it well-placed to take up an "ecclesiology of sign" as such an ecclesiology necessitates the same dynamic of form and meaning giving way to new reality.[37] Attentiveness to ecclesial provisionality in Anglican self-understanding distinguishes its place amongst those churches of the Reformation while

---

34. For greater discussion of Indefectibility within both the Roman Catholic and Reformed traditions see Soujeole, *Mystery of the Church*, 3:515–625; and particularly within Anglicanism, Avis, *Anglicanism and the Christian Church*, 43–141.

35. See Avis, *Anglicanism and the Christian Church*, 70, 141, 177–8.

36. Ramsey, *Gospel and the Catholic Church*, 126.

37. Williams' ecclesiology of integrating the Church's "ideal" with its provisionality is explored further in Zink, "Living with Difference."

mediating its inheritance from the Roman Catholic communion too.[38] However, such an ecclesiology is also under threat by contemporary local and global movements to narrow Anglican identity around confessional ecclesial statements and commitments which ultimately serve to "de-church" those who do not choose to "re-align" with these new and self-appointed arbiters of Anglican authority and polity. This makes the recovery of an "ecclesiology of sign" not just an abstract theological excursion but an urgent political imperative.

A Particular Symbol

While an "ecclesiology of sign" envisages the church as itself sign and symbol, mediating the present age with the age to come, there is one symbolic image for the church itself which might help illustrate what has been explored so far in relation to ecclesial provisionality and indefectibility. That is, the symbol of a flowing river which is also, appropriately for this volume, one with distinctly Johannine resonances.

If the prologue suggests the symbol of light as a christological basis to locate an "ecclesiology of sign" there is also in John's account of Jesus at the Feast of Tabernacles (7:1–10:2) a suggestion not only of light but also of water, "rivers of living water" (7:38), as a symbol which points not only to the identity of Christ but also a vision of the church. The Feast of Tabernacles, as it had developed by the close of the Second Temple period, was "not only historicized [but] also eschatologized, celebrated in terms of the end time,"[39] and may itself have represented that mediation by ritual and rite of all that was, is and is to be. Having attended the Feast keeping his identity secret (7:10), Jesus' eventual bold self-revelation as the source of living and thirst-quenching water coincides with the eighth day of the Feast, described by Moloney in his reconstruction from rabbinic sources as "almost a feast in its own right," during which the water libations of the previous days would cease and particular invocation made "for a superabundance of rain as a sign of YHWH's special and continuing care for the people."[40] Just as Jesus stands in the midst of the

---

38. This point is made amongst the submissions to the Lambeth Commission on Communion, see "Windsor Reception Report" and, for the Anglican challenge to Roman Catholicism to reflect on provisionality see; Rush, *Catholic Commentary on Walking Together on the Way*, 25–26.

39. Moloney, *Gospel of John*, 4:233.

40. Moloney, *Gospel of John*, 4:234.

Feast on that eighth day and in his own person "transcends the ritual" as himself "the source of living water for *all* who believe in him,"[41] so too does this source and font of life-giving water create a stream "out of the Believer's heart" (7:38) carried forward by the gift of the Spirit (7:39).[42] Again, the Spirit is to chart the current of this ecclesial river from its source to its end.

This flowing river, with its streams and tributaries, might be a helpful illustration of this "ecclesiology of sign" in which to locate Anglicanism. Perhaps an evolution of the old "branch theory," although much more dynamic and inclusive with a strong eschatological dimension, this vision of Christian identity (that is, the church) as being caught up in a great running river nevertheless allows that, in places, it diverges into streams and channels. Still, it runs and rushes onward and constant toward the one confluence, the one mouth, the one end and eternal expanse. The "mysterious personality"[43] of the church persists even amidst the diversions and the possibility of reunion remains not just at its eschatological end but also "on the Way."[44] Of course, such an image still allows for the possibility that particular streams may become so diverted, or dehydrated, that they do not make it to that great delta but even this does not take away from their directional flow. Anglicanism can make no claim to be the whole church, this is its provisionality; but neither is it merely a "component" of the church. Rather, it is caught up in the church's great movement and flow while holding onto the whole of that "mysterious personality." This echoes again Michael Ramsey's affirmation that the church is seized by the truth; just as the current seizes the water. Just as the Holy Spirit seizes the church and moves and channels it through the world. Part of God's good creation but also shaping and shifting that creation as it runs ever onward and brings it to its end.

---

41. Moloney, *Gospel of John*, 4:252.

42. For the problem of whose heart the water flows from, Jesus or the believer, and particularly "the possibility that both Jesus and the believer are intended," see Moloney, *Gospel of John*, 4:256.

43. Soujeole, *Mystery of the Church*, 3:626.

44. For an example of how this imagery might make a practical impact, see the shift in methodology being adopted in ecumenical dialogues: Anglican-Roman Catholic International Commission (ARCIC III), *Walking Together on the Way*.

Conclusion

This essay has begun to sketch an "ecclesiology of sign," both for and of Anglicanism, as a response to the "flattened ecclesiology" into which the various players in contemporary controversies have dug in and deadlocked. The Gospel of John particularly inspires reflection through the prologue's vision of God's Creating, Redeeming and Sanctifying, and Loving and Sending, together with the christological illustration of the church as "living water," to open up an alternative paradigm of graced and gifted *being* as well as *purpose*. Such an ecclesiology is fundamentally premised on the church's vocation to participate in, and bring all creation into participation with, the divine life through the work of creation. The church becomes, therefore, a sign of the kingdom as it carries the world into that new creation. It is also a sign of the times, bearing the realities of this world without being defined by them. Seized by the Spirit, Anglicanism is well-placed, not least by its tradition of theological reflection on ecclesial provisionality, to take up this "ecclesiology of sign" as a bold and transformative vision of the church, for the church.

Bibliography

Alexander, Loveday. "The Church in the Synoptic Gospels and the Acts of the Apostles." In *The Oxford Handbook of Ecclesiology*, edited by Paul Avis, 54–98. Oxford: Oxford University Press, 2018.

Anglican-Roman Catholic International Commission (ARCIC III). *Walking Together on the Way: Learning to Be the Church Local, Regional, Universal*. London: SPCK, 2018.

Augustine of Hippo. *The City of God Against the Pagans*, edited by R. W. Dyson. CTHPT. Cambridge: Cambridge University Press, 1998.

Avis, Paul. *Anglicanism and the Christian Church: Theological Resources in Historical Perspective*. London: T&T Clark, 2002.

———. *The Identity of Anglicanism: Essentials of Anglican Ecclesiology*. London: Bloomsbury, 2007.

Barrett, C. K. *The Gospel According to St John: An Introduction with Commentary and Notes on the Greek Text*. 2nd ed. Philadelphia, PA: Westminster, 1978.

Byers, Andrew J. *Ecclesiology and Theosis in the Gospel of John*. SNTMSS 166. Cambridge: Cambridge University Press, 2017.

Ferreira, Johan. *Johannine Ecclesiology*. JSNT 160. Sheffield: Sheffield Academic, 1998.

Inter-Anglican Theological and Doctrinal Commission. "The Virginia Report." London: Published for the Anglican Consultative Council, 1997.

King, Fergus. "Friends, Foes, or Rivals? John amongst the Philosophers." In *The Enduring Impact of the Gospel of John: Interdisciplinary Studies*, edited by Robert A. Derrenbacker, Jr. et al. Eugene, OR: Wipf & Stock, 2022.

Lee, Dorothy. *The Symbolic Narratives of the Fourth Gospel: The Interplay of Form and Meaning.* NTL. Sheffield: JSOT, 1994.

Levering, Matthew. "Linear and Participatory History: Augustine's City of God." *JTI* 5 (2011) 175–96.

Lincoln, Andrew. "The Johannine Vision of the Church." In *The Oxford Handbook of Ecclesiology*, edited by Paul Avis, 98–118. Oxford: Oxford University Press, 2018.

Milbank, John, and Aaron Riches. "Foreword." In *Theurgy and the Soul: The Neoplatonism of Iamblichus*, by Gregory Shaw, 2nd ed. Kettering, OH: Angelico, 2014.

Moloney, Francis J. *The Gospel of John.* Sacra Pagina 4. Collegeville, MN: Liturgical, 1998.

Ramsey, Michael. *The Gospel and the Catholic Church.* 2nd ed. London: SPCK, 1990.

Ross, Alexander John. *A Still More Excellent Way: Authority and Polity in the Anglican Communion.* London: SCM, 2020.

Rush, Ormond. *A Catholic Commentary on Walking Together on the Way: Learning to Be the Church—Local, Regional, Universal of the Anglican-Roman Catholic International Commission.* London: SPCK, 2018.

Schneiders, Sandra M. "The Raising of the New Temple: John 20.19–23 and Johannine Ecclesiology" *NTS* 52 (2006) 337–55.

Shaw, Gregory. *Theurgy and the Soul: The Neoplatonism of Iamblichus.* 2nd ed. Kettering, OH: Angelico, 2014.

Soujeole, Benoît-Dominique de la. *Introduction to the Mystery of the Church.* Translated by Michael J. Miller. Thomistic Ressourcement. Washington, DC: Catholic University of America Press, 2014.

The Truth Shall Make You Free: The Lambeth Conference 1988. The Reports, Resolutions, Pastoral Letters from the Bishops. London: Church House Publishing, 1988.

"The Windsor Report: Reception Reference Group. Report on Responses." 2005.

Williams, Rowan. *On Augustine.* London: Bloomsbury, 2016.

Zink, Jesse. "Patiently Living with Difference: Rowan Williams' Archiepiscopal Ecclesiology and the Proposed Anglican Covenant." *Ecclesiology* 9 (2013) 223–41.

13

"In Spirit and in Truth"

The Meeting of Lectionary and Liturgy in the Gospel of John

COLLEEN O'REILLY

Introduction

SITTING ON THE RIM of Jacob's well in Samaria, and contrary to custom speaking with a woman whom he has just encountered, Jesus tells her, "God is spirit and those who worship him must worship in spirit and in truth" (Jn 4:24).[1] The first Christians came to understand Jesus' words to be announcing a new "place" for true worship, a "place" now always present because Jesus, the risen Christ, is present everywhere.[2] This essay is concerned with the selection of readings for Holy Communion from the Gospel of John, both at the time of the English Reformation in the sixteenth century and in the twentieth century. Two tables, Attachments A and B, compare the Lectionary of the 1549/1662 Book of Common Prayer (BCP) with the *Revised Common Lectionary* (RCL) 1992 adopted by Anglicans and now widely used by Australian Anglicans, as well as other Churches in Australia and globally.[3] Use of the Fourth Gospel in the readings for celebrations of the Holy Eucharist,

---

1. All scriptural references are from the NRSV.
2. Moloney, *Gospel of John*, 128.
3. Consultation on Common Texts, *Revised Common Lectionary*.

called Holy Communion in BCP, at Christmas and Easter has been expanded in the RCL. In Lent and Holy Week now, John comes to the fore. The development of the three-year cycle for reading the Synoptic Gospels has also allowed for the continuous reading of chapter six of John in Year B, the Year of Mark. These, and other selected readings for use in the pastoral services, give the Fourth Gospel, with its concern for worship, a greater prominence in RCL than in BCP.

Scripture in Early Christian Worship

We know from references throughout the four Gospels that Jesus himself participated in Temple worship and in synagogue gatherings, read from the scrolls, and controversially healed on the sabbath in the synagogues of the Galilee (e.g. Mk 1:21–28; Matt 7:28–29; Lk 4:16–21; Jn 2:13–22).[4] Luke also tells us that, after the Easter events, Jesus' disciples continued to participate in the familiar Jewish worship of the Temple in Jerusalem (Acts 2:46). The Torah was read publicly in Temple ceremonial; synagogue gatherings also centered on readings from the Torah.

Following Jewish practice in the first century CE,[5] the reading of Scripture became central to Christian worship in the early centuries. In his *Apologia,* Justin the Martyr refers to the "memoirs of the apostles or the writings of the prophets" being "read as long as time permits" on Sundays in the Christian assembly (*1 Apol.* LXVII, c. 155).[6] Here is the beginning of the practice of reading from both Jewish and Christian writings when the Church gathers for worship. While the canon of Scripture was finally being settled late in the fourth century,[7] other contemporaneous developments were coalescing to create the earliest lists of readings for use in worship and to create a liturgical calendar of seasons and days to which readings became attached.[8]

Synagogue worship, it seems, read Scripture continuously. The early church initially followed this *lectio continua* approach, although it

---

4. McGowan, *Ancient Christian Worship*, 66–71.

5. For an extensive study of the origins of Christian worship in that of the synagogue, see Fisher, *Jewish Roots of Christian Liturgy*.

6. https://www.newadvent.org/fathers/0126.htm. See White, *Documents of Christian Worship*, 101.

7. Cross & Livingstone, editors, *Oxford Dictionary of the Christian Church*, 279.

8. Cobb, "History of the Christian Year," 403–17; Hope, "Liturgical Books," 66.

is anachronistic to speak of a common lectionary emerging. It seems that the first fixed point of connection between festival and Scripture is the Christian observance of Passover, leading to the development of Easter, and martyrs' feasts in the third century.[9] By the fourth century, the homilies of Augustine of Hippo and Chrysostom of Constantinople show "no sign of a 'lectionary' proper but rather a richer set of norms, still focused on Easter, martyrs' feasts, and now also Christmas and Epiphany."[10] Pilgrimages to sites in the Holy Land where those events were believed to have taken place prompted the development of a liturgical cycle connected to them.[11] Sermons preached by the early Fathers indicate that festivals and days of devotion began to attach readings to them from both the Hebrew Scriptures and the New Testament.[12] It is possible that the Paschal or Easter season read continuously, among other biblical texts, from the Gospel according to John.

As the calendar and the choice of readings developed, appropriate portions were added for the Offices (short services of the Word) at pilgrimage sites. Bishops may well have influenced or even controlled these selections, as the church of east and west created significantly different lectionaries over time. By the beginning of the fifth century, the Armenians had a complete system of readings for the festivals.[13] It is to them that we owe the origins of Ascension and Pentecost as feasts, as well as the individual days of Holy Week, and the fortieth day after Christmas becoming the Presentation of Christ in the Temple.[14]

Scripture in Medieval liturgies

By the Middle Ages, worship had become complex. A plethora of books was needed for the celebration of the liturgies of the Western Church, especially for the Mass. Celebrants' books known as *sacramentaries* provided the collect of the day, the offertory and post-communion prayers, and the eucharistic canon with prefaces for feast days, ordinary Sundays,

---

9. On Jewish influence in early Christian liturgy, see Skarsaune, *In the Shadow of the Temple*, 378–98.

10. McGowan, *Ancient Christian Worship*, 100.

11. See McGowan and Bradshaw *Itinerarium Egeriae* (*Pilgrimage of Egeria*, c. 381–386).

12. See for example Toal, ed., *Sunday Sermons of the Great Fathers*.

13. Senn, *Christian Liturgy*, 114.

14. Senn, *Christian Liturgy*, 157.

and votive Masses. These ranged from weddings and anniversaries, times of illness or affliction, times of epidemic and war, to Masses for good weather and safe journeys, for the sick, and for the dead.[15] In addition, *antiphonaries* contained instructions for singing, though it was not until the tenth century that melodies were written using notes. These music books were often very large so that a group of singers could read and sing together. *Ordines* were books with instructions, called rubrics, for the performance of liturgical rites.[16]

Lectionaries, books with the full text of Scripture portions, were developed to provide *lectors*—readers—with the texts to be proclaimed. This seems unnecessarily complex to those used to one prayer book to accompany one Bible. However, the intention was not complexity but uniformity, and the proper ordering of worship as far as was possible everywhere the Roman Church had jurisdiction.[17] Nevertheless, by the sixteenth century, reformers were agitating for revision of the rites which, as the preface to the 1549 Book of Common Prayer stated, caused "more business to find out what should be read, than to read it when it is found."[18] Central to the reformers' concern was the restoration of greater portions of Scripture, a practice they attributed to the early church, but which had become fragmented by "planting in uncertain stories, legends, Respondes, Verses, [and] vaine repetitions."[19] Commemorations of the saints and other holy figures had become overlaid with stories that were not biblical, and the continuous reading of biblical books interrupted by the frequent insertion of these days into the calendar.

Scripture in Reformation Liturgies

The reformers, principal among them Archbishop of Canterbury Thomas Cranmer,[20] believed themselves to be restoring ancient truths and practices which needed expression in the reformed worship of the Church in

---

15. Cummings, *The Book of Common Prayer*, xviii.
16. Cross & Livingstone, *Oxford Dictionary of the Christian Church*, 79, 1191.
17. Hope, "Medieval Western Rites," 220–40.
18. Cummings, *Book of Common Prayer*, 5.
19. Cummings, *Book of Common Prayer*, 4.
20. Cummings, *Book of Common Prayer*, 5. See also MacCulloch, *Thomas Cranmer*. This comprehensive biography of Cranmer's life sets out the complex development and interaction of his personal and political views over time.

England.[21] Chief among these truths was worship in the local language, no longer in Latin, which was the universal language of the educated of Europe. St Paul, it was argued, would only have used in worship the language that people understood.[22]

As a consequence of this principle, the reading of the Scriptures in English became the new norm. This innovation, when coupled with the development of printing, eventually made the Scriptures accessible to any literate person. A new lectionary, a revised schedule of readings, was developed for inclusion in the Prayer Book of 1549 so that the whole Bible was read frequently when followed daily in morning and evening prayer. The BCP Calendar of Saints' Days, holy days and commemorations was pruned to retain those with certain biblical authenticity, and the seasons of Advent, Lent, Holy Week and Easter retained though now observed in a simpler manner.[23]

The Collect for the Second Sunday of Advent in the 1662 *The Book of Common Prayer* (BCP), an original composition by Cranmer in 1549, is thus:

> O Blessed Lord, who caused all Holy Scriptures to be written for our learning: Grant us so to hear them, read, mark, learn and inwardly digest them that we may embrace and hold fast the blessed hope of everlasting life, which you have given us in our Savior Jesus Christ. Amen.[24]

The imagery of "consuming" the Scriptures and ruminating on them appeared earlier in Cranmer's *Homily on the Reading of Scripture* which ended with an exhortation to read in this way: "Let us ruminate, and, as it were, chew the cud, that we may have the sweet juice, spiritual effect, marrow, honey, kernel, taste, comfort and consolation of them."[25]

21. Cummings, *Book of Common Prayer*, 5.
22. Cummings, *Book of Common Prayer*, 5.
23. Cummings, *Book of Common Prayer*, 5, 219–38.
24. *Book of Common Prayer* 1662. This Collect first appears in 1549 Prayer Book compiled by the English reformers and is the work of its principal drafter, Archbishop of Canterbury, Thomas Cranmer. See MacCulloch, *Thomas Cranmer*, 417.
25. *The Books of Homilies* are authorised sermons issued in two volumes for use in the Church of England, the first being published during the reigns of Edward VI and Elizabeth I. Originally proposed in 1539 as a means of promoting the new theology of the reformers, Book 1 was edited by Thomas Cranmer who wrote at least five of the twelve homilies. Although authorised by the Church's Convocation in 1542, publication did not occur until 1547. Titled in full, *A Fruitfull Exhortation to the Reading and Knowledge of Holy Scripture*, dating would indicate that the imagery in the homily gave

No doubt Cranmer's own commitment to biblical scholarship underpinned his determination to ensure the reading of the whole Scriptures by the whole church. His studies at Jesus College, Cambridge, then only recently established, focused on the Old and New Testaments rather than canon law, the usual area of most postgraduate study at the time.[26] It was the reformers' intention, brought to fruition under Cranmer's leadership, that there should be one book of common prayer for everyone. The existing situation was that a number of dioceses had their own "uses," as the rites were called, and each of the religious orders had their own particular monastic books. The idea of common prayer was prayer-in-common for clergy and laity alike, without distinction, and in every diocese in England.[27]

Cranmer's new lectionary, which has been placed immediately after the Preface and accompanying documents in every edition of BCP since, directed that at morning and evening prayer each day, the Old Testament would be read through annually and the New Testament three times. This provision, in addition to reciting the whole Psalter monthly, meant that the reformers did not, it can be assumed, consider change to be necessary to the lectionary for the celebration of Holy Communion. Cranmer retained the medieval practice of an Epistle and Gospel reading for each Sunday and Holy Day. We do not know why he chose to do so. He had earlier observed that the Lutherans in Nuremberg "in the Epistles and Gospels [they] kept not the order that we do but do peruse every day one chapter of the New Testament."[28] Perhaps he simply preferred the familiar pattern and retained it.

The laity as well as the clergy were now able, if they wished, to pray the daily offices of morning and evening prayer, as well as receiving Communion regularly, thereby hearing a full diet of Scripture.[29] The pattern set by Cranmer was that Holy Communion followed morning prayer, resulting in hearing a reading from the Hebrew Scriptures before Communion. It is hard to know how realistic the expectation of attendance at Morning and Evening Prayer was for the laity, and how well its practice was observed by them in ordinary parish churches. As Charles Sherlock notes,

---

rise to the imagery in the collect. http://www.anglicanlibrary.org/homilies/index.htm.

26. MacCulloch, *Thomas Cranmer*, 22–23.
27. Cummings, *Book of Common Prayer*, 4–6.
28. MacCulloch, *Thomas Cranmer*, 70.
29. Cummings, *Book of Common Prayer*, 4–5.

when people worked the land or carried out a trade, it was possible. The population shifts and changes to living patterns caused by the Industrial Revolution, however, meant that Sunday-only worship became the only realistic option for lay people. This meant they heard only the Sunday Epistle and Gospel readings, leaving large gaps in the Scripture content to which they were exposed. Consequently in 1871 the Church of England attempted lectionary revision to provide for the new situation, producing separate lectionaries for Morning and Evening Prayer, and leaving the readings for the Epistle and Gospel at Holy Communion—which was now a separate service—unchanged.[30]

Cranmer can hardly have appreciated that his Calendar and Order for the reading of Holy Scripture would endure in the English Church, and everywhere else that the English colonized with only the most minor alterations, for more than four hundred years. Cranmer's ordering of the year and the readings held until the revision of worship by the mainstream Western churches, beginning with the Second Vatican Council (1962–1965), and flowing into the liturgical life of Anglicans throughout the world. The outcome of Vatican II was a flourishing of liturgical scholarship among all the major Christian traditions, not only Roman Catholicism.

Scripture in Modern Liturgies

By the mid twentieth century, most Christians, including Anglicans and Episcopalians, attended only one service on Sundays, which by then was increasingly the Holy Eucharist, also called Holy Communion. The nineteenth century Oxford Movement had led to the renewal of Anglicanism by reviving lost or neglected catholic belief and practices neglected or rejected by the sixteenth century reformers.[31] In time this led to the controversial revival of ritual, though much of what was then disputed is now commonplace, such as wafers used for the bread of Holy Communion. In the twentieth century, the parish Communion movement—restoring Holy Communion as the central act of worship every Sunday—sought to reinstate, as was often said, the Lord's people gathered around the Lord's Table on the Lord's Day.[32] Although it can be said to have originated ear-

---

30. Sherlock, *Australian Anglicans Worship*, 47.
31. Cross & Livingstone, *Oxford Dictionary of the Christian Church*, 1205–1206.
32. http://www.parishandpeople.org.uk/story.html.

lier in the century, it gained ground amongst Anglicans during the 1960's when weekly Communion became the new practice in those parishes where previously Morning Prayer, often Choral Mattins at 11am, had been the principal act of worship.[33]

Very few lay people were by then taking part in weekday morning or evening prayer, "daily to be said and used throughout the year," as BCP expresses it. This meant most people were hearing a limited range of Scripture. In the Roman Catholic Church, the Second Vatican Council recognized the same problem with the mediaeval custom of an Epistle and Gospel readings at Sunday Mass. They responded with a new three-year lectionary, with four portions of Scripture for celebrations of the Holy Eucharist. The publication in 1969 of the new *Lectionary* was to be a game changer, not just for Roman Catholics, but ecumenically.[34]

The old pattern of an Epistle and Gospel only in the celebration of the Eucharist for each Sunday or holy day was about to change. The Vatican Council's document on worship, the *Constitution on the Sacred Liturgy*,[35] drew on the same principle that had driven the sixteenth century reformers, giving paramount importance to Scripture. It was a norm that "in sacred celebrations there is to be more reading from holy Scripture, and it is to be more varied and suitable."[36] The whole liturgy was to be in the vernacular, which for the reformers had been an article of faith. The Thirty-Nine Articles stated it to be "repugnant to the Word of God . . . to minister the Sacraments in a tongue not understanded of the people."[37] Neither the English reformers of the sixteenth century nor the Roman bishops gathered in Council in the twentieth objected to worship in Latin when that was understood by those participating.[38] The reality was that increasingly fewer people, including clerics, did comprehend

---

33. George, "Some Aspects of the ethos of Anglicanism," 23. See also Griffith & Radcliff, *Grace and Incarnation,* and Holden, "Parish and Organisational Life," 103.

34. *Ordo Lectionum Missae*, 1969.

35. Abbott, *Documents of Vatican II*, 137–82.

36. Abbott, *Documents of Vatican II*, 149.

37. Article XXIV *Of Speaking in the Congregation in such a Tongue as the people understand.*

38. A celebration of the Holy Communion in Latin, according to 1662 BCP, is held by St Mary the Virgin, Oxford, the University Church, at the opening of each term. Cranmer's revised rites had been issued in Latin translation for use where they would be understood. https://www.universitychurch.ox.ac.uk/content/upcoming-services.

Latin sufficiently to justify its continued universal use to the exclusion of local languages.

The purpose of revision of the lectionary, as set out in the document for reform of the liturgy at the Second Vatican Council, was the opening of the treasures of Scripture "more lavishly, so that richer fare may be provided for the faithful at the table of God's Word."[39] In 1966, observers from non-Roman Catholic Churches were invited to sit with the committee during its discussions implementing the Council's call for a new lectionary. Among them, American scholar Jaroslav Pelikan exemplified reception of the new direction when he wrote that the emphasis on Scripture and on preaching based on the readings, and the simplifying of the liturgical year, are matters "for which all Christians who stand in the heritage of the reformation ought to be grateful."[40] He welcomed the recognition of the paramount importance of Scripture which he observed had not always been obvious in Roman rites. Pelikan's response urged creative and imaginative action in reforming the calendar and lectionary, since he believed the Council's hope to contribute to the unity of all who believe in Christ would then be realized.

Subsequently, by 1969, a Roman Catholic three-year lectionary was devised for Sundays, the original feast day, and for the seasons of the liturgical year, principally Advent-Christmas and Lent-Easter. Sundays after Epiphany and Pentecost were to be "ordinary," that is ordered by number since those seasons varied in length depending upon the day of the week when Christmas Day occurred, and the date of Easter Day, which is decided in the West by lunar calendar and varies each year.

A reading from the Old Testament was chosen to be the first portion of Scripture and selected for its relationship to the Gospel of the day as either typological in prefiguring the Christ revealed in the Gospel, or in terms of prophecy and fulfillment through him. A Psalm, or a portion of one, was chosen as a response to the first reading. In the Easter season, the Hebrew Scriptures were replaced with the Book of Acts, witnessing to the first responses to the resurrection as the infant Church began to form. The second reading was to be from one of the Epistles of the New Testament.

For the first time, each of the Synoptic Gospels was to be given focus throughout a year, beginning each First Sunday of Advent with Year A,

---

39. Abbott, *Documents of Vatican II*, par 51 of the Constitution on the Sacred Liturgy, 155.

40. Pelikan, *A Response*. Quoted in Abbott, *Documents of Vatican II*, 181.

the Gospel of Matthew, followed by Year B, the Gospel of Mark, and Year C, the Gospel of Luke. Readings from the Fourth Gospel were selected for the Christmas and Easter seasons in all three years. Additionally, readings from the Gospel of John were to supplement the cycle in Year B when Mark, the shortest Gospel, was read.

The publication of the 1969 *Lectionary* has proven to be a watershed moment, the importance of which reaches way beyond the original intention of those responsible for its devising. The unforeseen result of the hard work following the Vatican Council was the substantial influence on other Churches' calendars and lectionary revisions. It is hard to imagine that, without the catalyst of the then new Roman Catholic lectionary, other Churches would necessarily have devised such a scheme for themselves.

A radical new practice was being established. With some hesitation at first, but then increasing enthusiasm, other Churches included the new pattern of readings into their revised eucharistic liturgies. Adjustments were required for Anglican and mainline Protestant Churches, but the result was an extraordinary commonality of readings in Western Churches for the first time in four hundred years. American Lutheran scholar, Frank Senn, provides a fuller description of the process of ecumenical adoption of the lectionary including the debates that led to the *Revised Common Lectionary* in 1988, and subsequent adjustments.[41]

The earliest attempts at revising Anglican liturgies along these lines in the 1960's in Australia culminated in the introduction of *An Australian Prayer Book* (AAPB) in 1978,[42] and developed more extensively in the current book, *A Prayer Book for Australia* (APBA) in 1995.[43] Alongside the revision of rites has been revision of the Calendar of the Church Year and the Lectionary which provides the table of readings for Sunday celebrations and weekday prayer. The revised ways of worship are now so long established that only older Anglicans have any memory of the BCP pattern inherited from the sixteenth century reform.

The Liturgical Commission of General Synod, the body responsible for drafting the revised services for 1978 *An Australian Prayer Book* (AAPB), expressed the view that since the "hearing and intelligent understanding of the Scriptures is fundamental to Anglican worship," a fuller

---

41. Senn, *Christian Liturgy. Catholic and Evangelical*, 657–61.

42. Standing Committee of the General Synod of the Church of England in Australia. *An Australian Prayer Book*.

43. General Synod of the Anglican Church of Australia. *A Prayer Book for Australia*.

selection of readings best met this principle.⁴⁴ The new Roman lectionary, coming into use as the Liturgy Commission of the General Synod was working, was followed with few changes. The result was that the publication of the 1978 *AAPB*, the first completely revised prayer book in the Anglican Communion as it happened, provided for a fuller selection of readings for Holy Communion than Anglicans had been accustomed to hearing, in line with the new practice of their Roman Catholic neighbors. The publication of the *Revised Common Lectionary* (RCL) in 1992, during the preparation of the second revised book, *A Prayer Book for Australia* (APBA) 1995, led to its inclusion with only minor amendments.⁴⁵ A similar story exists for prayer books across the Anglican Communion.⁴⁶

John's Gospel in the Liturgy

APBA offers considerably more readings from John's Gospel than Cranmer's lectionary which has eighteen portions of John set for Sundays and other holy days, in an annual cycle, while Saints Days and Commemorations in BCP provide for readings from the Gospel of John on five occasions. In contrast, the selections in the Calendar of Saints days and other commemorations in the 1995 *APBA* provide for readings from John seventeen times, including morning prayer on what is observed as Australia Day, 26 January.⁴⁷

In the revised three-year schema, Year A provides for up to sixteen readings from John, depending on whether the alternative for Easter Day from the Gospel of Matthew is chosen. Similarly in Year C, there is a maximum of fifteen readings, if the Lukan text is not used on Easter Day. Year B is when the Fourth Gospel features more extensively, with

44. *An Australian Prayer Book*, Preface, 12.

45. See Burge, "Readings for Sundays and Holy Days," 99–105.

46. The BCP was translated into the vernacular in many of the countries to which it was exported by the British colonists. For example, it was first translated into Maori in 1830, (http://justus.anglican.org/resources/bcp/Maori/index.htm) and sections were translated into Swahili in 1939 (http://justus.anglican.org/resources/bcp/Swahili/std.html). The BCP was translated into Welsh as early as 1567 (http://justus.anglican.org/resources/bcp/Wales/welsh1567.htm) and a trial liturgical revision was made available in Welsh in 1966. (http://justus.anglican.org/resources/bcp/Wales/HE_Welsh1966.htm). The New Zealand prayer book of 1989 provides substantial material in Maori as well as English.

47. Australia Day commemorates the arrival of the First Fleet of white settlers, convicts and marines at Port Jackson (Sydney Harbour) in 1788.

twenty-five readings to supplement Mark's shorter text, inserted into the Sundays following Pentecost.[48]

Why is there no Year D, a Year of John? The question suggests that the Fourth Gospel is relegated to a secondary role in the formation of the revised lectionary for Sundays and Feast Days, as if somehow judged to be unworthy of its own "year." The use of the Fourth Gospel, however, accords with both ancient practice and Cranmer's own modified tables of readings, while developing it further to make use of even more pericopes. The Gospel of John has a primary place in the RCL. It is read every year at Christmas, every day of Holy Week and at length on Good Friday, as already noted. On Holy Saturday, Easter Day, the Day of Pentecost, Trinity Sunday and All Saints and All Souls, portions of John are annual fare. Essentially the whole Fourth Gospel is covered since there is a continuous reading of John 6:1–69 (all but two verses of the whole chapter) over five Sundays in the Year of Mark, Year B, as already noted.[49]

The use of the Fourth Gospel in Lent is expanded in RCL, and in Holy Week the daily Gospel reading enables a focus on events in the last week of Jesus' life as set out in John's narrative. It provides also a rich diet of readings for other festivals, and particularly Christmas. Whose heart and mind is not lifted beyond shepherds, angels and wise men by the prologue to John's Gospel? There the emphasis shifts from the stories known even in the secular sphere and readily told to children to the central Christian claim that the Word of God, who was in the beginning with God and through whom all things were made, has come to dwell among us (Jn 1:1–14).

John's Gospel in Marriage Rites

Marriage was a contentious matter among the sixteenth century reformers both in England and in Europe. First, there was the assertion that clerical celibacy was not required by Scripture, nor was it to be preferred to marriage. Second, there was dispute over the purposes of marriage. Clerical celibacy was already being discussed in the fourteenth and fifteenth centuries. The Oxford don John Wycliffe (1328–1384) cautiously discussed the issue, though without advocating clerical marriage; his later

---

48. See Appendix.
49. See Loader, "The Role of John's Gospel in the Three Year Lectionary."

followers, the Lollards, questioned clerical celibacy more enthusiastically.[50] In 1518, a very popular and influential essay on marriage, *Encomium matrimonii* by the scholar Desiderius Erasmus,[51] confronted the prevailing view that only the celibate person could truly experience a close and loving relationship with God.

Cranmer himself was twice married. His first marriage, sometime between 1515–1519, while a layman, ended with the death of his wife and child, in childbirth.[52] His second marriage to Margarette took place in Lutheran Nuremberg in 1532 where he encountered former monks and clergy now married to wives, described by one of Cranmer's English companions as "the fairest women of the town."[53] He was a diocesan priest of the Church in England, then still in communion with the Pope, and required to refrain from marrying, the meaning of the promise of celibacy. Celibacy is often confused with the virtue of chastity, refraining from illicit sexual relationships, which is expected of all Christians, married or not. The existing custom, still observed by the Roman and Eastern Churches, is that a married man can be ordained, but an ordained man cannot marry. In the Roman Church, generally, the married man must be widowed, no longer married.[54] Cranmer was breaking canon law and risking popular anger, though the issue of married clergy was a lively one in England as well as Europe and was in fact happening.[55]

---

50. Hornbeck, "Theologies of Sexuality in English 'Lollardy,'" 19. Wycliffe's supposed role as a forerunner of the English Reformation owes more to sixteenth century Reformation polemic, where he was named the "morning star" of the Reformation, than to his teaching. See Margaret Aston, "John Wycliffe's Reformation Reputation," 23.

51. Desiderius Erasmus (1466–1536) is a fascinating character: the son of a priest, a non-person in mediaeval Europe, he was an Augustinian priest who lived outside his community and promoted the humanist ideals of *Devotio Moderna*. His enthusiasm for marriage was, as MacCulloch notes, second-hand (*The Reformation*, 625).

52. The date of the marriage is uncertain, and so is the name of his wife and date of her death. See MacCulloch, *Thomas Cranmer*, 22–23.

53. MacCulloch, *Thomas Cranmer*, 71.

54. In recent times, the Roman Catholic Church has made an exception to its celibacy rule to ordain as priests married Anglican clergy who have converted principally because of their rejection of the ordination of women in the Anglican Church. For example, at the time the Vatican established the Personal Ordinariate of Our Lady of Walsingham, a traditionalist Church of England bishop, John Broadhurst, a married man, was ordained priest in the Catholic Church in 2011: https://www.bbc.com/news/uk-11559782.

55. Porter, *Sex, Marriage and the Church*, 56.

When it came to drafting a wedding service in English, Cranmer not only drew on existing rites, principally Sarum, but presumably brought his own experience to bear on the statement of the purposes of marriage. Perhaps it was from his own experience that he added marriage was "honorable among all men," even the clergy. Just as clerical marriage was contentious, so also was the ordering of the purposes. According to the English reformers, these were the already accepted purposes: first, so that children would be born, second as remedy against the sin of fornication, and third for the mutual society of the two spouses.[56] One Continental reformer, Martin Bucer, favored the companionship of spouses as the primary purpose.[57]

Marriage was considered a sacrament; though not a dominical sacrament instituted by Christ (Baptism and Holy Communion), it was one of the seven defended by Henry VIII (for which he was granted the title Defender of the Faith by the Pope).[58] The freely given consent of the couple to marry each other was all that was necessary for a marriage to have taken place; neither parental agreement nor witnesses were required, though these enabled certainty in the matter.[59] Cranmer's *Form for the Solemnization of Matrimony* in the 1549 BCP referred, in the preparatory address by the priest, to the wedding at Cana in Galilee, attended by Jesus, his mother and his disciples (Jn 2:1–12). While this might seem a convenient story about Jesus celebrating a wedding, it is the first sign of Jesus' identity in John's Gospel. The Scriptures required by the rubrics are Psalms 128 or 67, and selected sentences to be read are provided if there is no sermon following the (unspecified) Gospel, which was presumably that set for the day. The service assumes the context is a celebration of Holy Communion then, or on the same day, since the rubric says, "the newe maried persones (the same daye of their marriage) must receive the holy communion."[60]

---

56. This ordering of marriage's purposes was reversed only in 1995 by the General Synod in Australia with the authorisation of *A Prayer Book for Australia*. See Porter, "Christian Marriage: A Concise History," 158.

57. Whitaker, *Martin Bucer and the Book of Common Prayer*, 2–3.

58. Cross & Livingstone, *The Oxford Dictionary of the Christian Church*, 463.

59. Cross & Livingstone, *The Oxford Dictionary of the Christian Church*, 1055.

60. Cummings, *Book of Common Prayer*, 71.

John's Gospel in Funeral Rites

The one Scripture reading at the Order for the Burial of the Dead in the BCP is the whole of the fifteenth chapter of Paul's first letter to the Corinthians. The burial service was a severe pruning of previous custom. Reacting against the elaborate ceremonies and multiple Masses for the departed to speed their journey from purgatory, the reformers made it possible to take the body, called "the Corps," directly to the grave without necessarily entering the church.[61] Sentences of Scripture were to be read as the procession moved to the place of burial. The first of these was from the story of the raising of Lazarus, with the words of Jesus, "I am the resurrection and the life" (Jn 11:25). Once the "vyle body," that is, the mortal body, was placed in the grave, Paul's lengthy assurance of the truth of resurrection was to be heard by those standing there.

Although John 11:25-26 continues to be the first words of Scripture spoken in Anglican funeral rites, funerals these days frequently include a reading of John 14:1-6 which could be said to be part of a reduced "folk lectionary" which endures even among those with little knowledge of the Scriptures. Some might therefore dismiss its use, but the pastoral challenge in liturgical terms is to begin with what is familiar to people and draw them into the greater story of the Scriptures. That, at least, was the task the reformers set themselves in redrafting the lectionary in the 1540's, and that has continued to be the objective of all revision since.

Conclusion

Far from being overlooked, the Gospel of John is now read more extensively than previously and read in every year at certain times. Sometimes, this accords with ancient practice, such as reading from the Passion in the Gospel of John on Good Friday. The custom was retained in BCP, and the length of the reading extended in RCL. In fact, the Fourth Gospel in the lectionary forms the structure which holds the other Gospels, and indeed the other readings, in place. The Fourth Gospel can be likened to a large, wide, old tree which forms the essential trunk and branches for the whole three-year structure. John can be seen either as of lesser significance, because of not having its own year, but as I have argued here,

---

61. Cummings, *Book of Common Prayer*, xxviii; Duffy, *Stripping of the Altars*, 474-5.

it is substantial in framing the whole. Worship "in spirit and in truth" is the goal of all liturgy and the Fourth Gospel plays an essential role in making true worship possible.

Appendix

Table 1

Readings from the Gospel according to John in the Eucharist	1662 BCP	RCL Year A	RCL Year B	RCL Year C
Advent 3			Jn 1:6–8, 19–28	
Advent 4	Jn 1:19–28			
Christmas	Jn 1:1–14		3rd service Jn 1:1–14	
St John the Evangelist	Jn 21:19–25			
2nd after Christmas			Jn 1:(1–9), 10–18	
2nd Sunday after Epiphany	Jn 2:1–11	Jn 1:29–42	Jn 1:43–51	Jn 2:1–11
3rd Sunday in Lent		Jn 4:5–42	Jn 2:13–22	
4th Sunday in Lent		Jn 9:1–41	Jn 3:14–21	
5th Sunday in Lent	Jn 8:46–59	Jn 11:1–45	Jn 12:20–33	Jn 12:1–8
Monday in Holy Week		Jn 12:1–11	Jn 12:1–11	Jn 12:1–11
Tuesday in Holy Week		Jn 12:20–36	Jn 12:20–36	Jn 12:20–36
Wednesday in Holy Week		Jn 13:21–32	Jn 13:21–32	Jn 13:21–32
Thursday in Holy Week		Jn 13:1–17; 31b-35	Jn 13:1–17; 31b-35	Jn 13:1–17; 31b-35
Good Friday	Jn 19:1–37	Jn 18:1–19:42	Jn 18:1–19:42	Jn 18:1–19:42
Easter Day	Jn 20:1–10	Jn 20:1–18 alt. Matt 28:1–10	Jn 20:1–18 alt. Mk 16:1–8	Jn 20:1–18 alt. Lk 24:1–12
1st Sunday after Easter (BCP). Easter 2 (RCL)	Jn 20:19–23	Jn 20:19–31		
2nd Sunday after Easter Easter 3 (RCL)	Jn 10:11–16			Jn 21:1–19

3rd Sunday after Easter (BCP) Easter 4 (RCL)		Jn 10:1–10	Jn 10:11–18	Jn 10:22–30
4th Sunday after Easter. Easter 5 (RCL)	Jn 16:5–15	Jn 14:1–14	Jn 15:1–18	Jn 13:31–35
5th Sunday after Easter Easter 6 (RCL)	Jn 16:23–33	Jn 14:15–21	Jn 15:9–17 *or* Jn 16:16–24	Jn 14:23–29 *or* Jn 5:1–9
Sunday after Ascension Day Easter 7 (RCL)	Jn 15:26, and 16:1–4	Jn 17:1–11	Jn 17:6–19	Jn 17:20–26
Whit Sunday (BCP) aka Pentecost (RCL)	Jn 14:15–31	Jn 20:19–24 *or* Jn 7:37–52	Jn 15:26–27, 16:4b–15	Jn 14:8–17 (25–27)
Monday of Whitsun Week	Jn 3:16–21			
Tuesday in Whitsun Week	Jn 10:1–10			
Trinity Sunday	Jn 3:1–16		Jn 3:1–17	Jn 16:12–15
9th Sunday after Pentecost [17]			Jn 6:1–21	
10th Sunday after Pentecost [18]			Jn 6:24–25	
11th Sunday after Pentecost [19]			Jn 6:35, 41–51	
12th Sunday after Pentecost [20]			Jn 6:51–58	
13th Sunday after Pentecost [21]			Jn 6:56–69	
One and twentieth Sunday after Trinity	Jn 4:46–54			
The twenty-fifth Sunday after Trinity (or Sunday next before Advent) Christ the King (RCL)	Jn 6:5–14		Jn 18:33–37	

Table 2

Saints Days or Commemorations	BCP	Australian Lectionary
Saint Thomas, apostle. 21 December	Jn 20:24–31	Jn 20:24–29
St John, apostle and evangelist. 27 December		Jn 20:2–8
Australia Day. 26 January		*Morning prayer* Jn 8:31–36a. *alt.*
First Anglican Service at Sydney Cove. 3 February		Jn 6:25–35
Saint Matthias, apostle and martyr. 24 February		Jn 15:9–17
St Mark, evangelist and martyr. 25 April, also Anzac Day	Jn 15:1–11	Jn 15:9–17 or Jn 19:1–12
St Philip & St James, apostles and martyrs. 1 May	Jn 14:1–14	Jn 14:6–14
St Matthias, apostle and martyr 14 May		Jn 15:9–17
St Barnabas, apostle and martyr. 11 June	Jn 15:12–16	
St Peter and St Paul, apostles and martyrs. 29 June		Jn 21:15–22
The Coming of the Light Torres Strait. 1 July		Jn 12:35–47
St Mary Magdalene. 22 July		Jn 20:1–18
St Bartholomew, apostle and martyr. 24 August		Jn 1:45–51
Martyrs of New Guinea. 2 September		Jn 12.20–32
Holy Cross. 14 September		Jn 3:13–17
St Michael and All Angels. 29 September		Jn 1:45–51
St Simon & Saint Jude, apostles and martyrs. 28 October	Jn 15:17–27	
All Saints. 1 November		Jn 11:32–44
All Souls. 2 November		Jn 5:19–29

Bibliography

A New Zealand Prayer Book: He Karakia Mihinare o Aotearoa. Auckland: Collins, 1989.
Abbott, Walter M. *The Documents of Vatican II*. London: Geoffrey Chapman, 1966.
The Anglican Church of Australia. *A Prayer Book for Australia*. Alexandria NSW: Broughton Books, 1995.
An Australian Lectionary. Mulgrave, VIC: Broughton Publishing Trust. Published annually.
Aston, Margaret. "John Wycliffe's Reformation Reputation." *Past & Present* 30 (1965) 23–51.
The book of the common prayer and administration of the Sacraments, and other rites and ceremonies in the Churche: after the use of the Churche of England. London: Edward Whitchurch, 1549, Short Title Catalogue 16267; *The boke of common praier and administration of the Sacraments, and other rites and ceremonies in the Churche of England*. London: Richard Grafton, 1559. Short Title Catalogue 16291; *The Book of Common Prayer and administration of the sacraments and other rites and ceremonies of the Church according to the use of the Church of England . . .* London: John Bill and Christopher Barker 1662, Short Title Catalogue (Wing)B3622.
The Books of Homilies: A Fruitfull Exhortation to the reading and knowledge of holy Scripture. http://www.anglicanlibrary.org/homilies/index.htm
Burge, Evan. "The Readings for Sundays and Holy Days." In *A Prayer Book for Australia. A Practical Commentary*, edited by Gillian Varcoe. Alexandria, NSW: E. J. Dwyer, 1997.
Cobb, Peter G. "The History of the Christian Year." In *The Study of Liturgy*, edited by Cheslyn Jones et al., 403–419. London: SPCK, 1978
.Consultation on Common Texts. *Revised Common Lectionary*. Norwich: Canterbury, 1992.
Cross, F. L. and Livingstone, E. A. *The Oxford Dictionary of the Christian Church*. 3rd ed. Oxford: Oxford University Press, 1997, 1998.
Cummings, Brian, ed. *The Book of Common Prayer: The Texts of 1549, 1559 and 1662*. Oxford: Oxford University Press, 2011.
Davies, J. G., ed. *A New Dictionary of Liturgy and Worship*. London: SCM, 1986.
Duffy, Eamon. *The Stripping of the Altars: Traditional Religion in England 1400–1580*. New Haven: Yale University Press, 1992.
Fisher, Eugene J., ed. *The Jewish Roots of Christian Liturgy*. New York: Paulist 1990.
George, Ian. "Some Aspects of the Ethos of Anglicanism." *St Mark's Review* 143 (1990) 18–25.
Griffith, Bruce D. and Jason R. Radcliff. *Grace and Incarnation: The Oxford Movement's Shaping of the Character of Modern Anglicanism*. Eugene, OR: Pickwick, 2020.
Holden, Colin. "Parish and Organisational Life in the Diocese of Melbourne." In *Melbourne Anglicans: The Diocese of Melbourne 1847–1997*, edited by Brian Porter. Melbourne: JBCE, 1997.
Hope, D. M. "Liturgical Books." In *The Study of Liturgy*, edited by Cheslyn Jones, et al., 65–69. London: SPCK, 1978.
———. "The Medieval Western Rites." In *The Study of Liturgy.*, edited by Cheslyn Jones, et al., 220–40. London: SPCK, 1978.
Hornbeck, J. Patrick. "Theologies of Sexuality in English 'Lollardy *Journal of Ecclesiastical History* 60 (2009) 19–44.

Loader, William. "The Role of John's Gospel in the Three Year Lectionary." https://billloader.com/Johnlect.html

MacCulloch, Diarmaid. *Thomas Cranmer. A Life*. New Haven: Yale University Press, 1996.

———. *The Reformation. A History*. New York: Viking, 2003.

McGowan, Andrew B. *Ancient Christian Worship. Early Church Practices in Social, Historical and Theological Perspective*. Grand Rapids: Baker Academic, 2014.

McGowan, Anne and Paul F. Bradshaw. *The Pilgrimage of Egeria: A New Translation of the "Itinerarium Egeriae" with Introduction and Commentary*. Collegeville, MN: Liturgical 2018.

Moloney, Francis J. *The Gospel of John*. Sacra Pagina 4. Collegeville, MA: Liturgical, 1998.

Ordo Lectionum Missae, editio typica. Vatican City: Typis Polyglottis Vaticanis, 1969.

Porter, Muriel. "Christian Marriage: A Concise History." In *Marriage, Same-Sex Marriage, and the Anglican Church of Australia: Essays from the Doctrine Commission*, edited by The Doctrine Commission of the Anglican Church of Australia, 155–66. Mulgrave, VIC: Broughton, 2019.

———. *Sex, Marriage and the Church: Patterns of Change*, Melbourne: Dove, 1996.

Skarsaune, Oskar. *In the Shadow of the Temple: Jewish Influences on Early Christianity*. Downers Grove, IL: IVP, 2002.

Senn, Frank C. *Christian Liturgy. Catholic and Evangelical*. Minneapolis, MN: Fortress 1997.

Sherlock, Charles. *Australian Anglicans Worship. Performing APBA*. Mulgrave, Victoria: Broughton, 2020.

St Mary the Virgin, University Church. "Upcoming Services." https://www.universitychurch.ox.ac.uk/content/upcoming-services

Standing Committee of the General Synod of the Church of England in Australia. *An Australian Prayer Book for Use Together with the Book of Common Prayer, 1662*. Sydney: Anglican Information Office, 1978.

Toal, M. F., ed. *The Sunday Sermons of the Great Fathers: From Pentecost to the Tenth Sunday after Pentecost*. Chicago: Henry Regnery, 1959.

White, James F. *Documents of Christian Worship: Descriptive and Interpretive Sources*. Louisville, KY: Westminster John Knox, 1992.

Whitaker, E. C. *Martin Bucer and the Book of Common Prayer*. Great Wakering, Essex: Alcuin Club, Mayhew-McCrimmon, 1978.

14

Encountering God

Preaching an Incarnate Word

RAEWYNNE J. WHITELEY

> "In the beginning was the Word . . . And the Word became flesh and lived among us" (Jn 1:1; 14)[1]

Introduction

SHADOWS LENGTHEN AS THE words echo through the chapel. The purity of a single voice singing "Once in Royal David's City" blossoms into a feast of carols and lessons, which reach a climax in the final reading from the Gospel according to John: "In the beginning was the Word, and the Word was with God, and the Word was God." The words hardly vary, whether read from the King James Version at the Festival of Nine Lessons and Carols from Kings College in Cambridge or a more recent translation from the Bible beside your bed. In a few short verses, they give us a glimpse of eternity before bringing us firmly back down to earth, the Word become flesh and living among us, or as Donne put it, "immensity cloistered in [Mary's] dear womb."[2]

---

1. The English translation used in this essay is the NRSV.
2. Donne, "Annunciation" and "Nativity." https://shakespeareauthorship.com/xmas/donne.html.

The Gospel of John is one that is both familiar and unfamiliar to us. We see "John 3:16" written on banners at sports matches, hear John 14:1–6 read at funerals, and readily quote "love one another as I have loved you," but it is the stories in the Synoptics, from the baby in a manger to the parables of lost sheep, coins, and children, and of course the Good Samaritan, which most readily come to mind when we think of Jesus. John tends to fade into the background, in part, I suspect, because the lectionary has us read it piecemeal rather than offering it to us regularly, week by week.[3] And so we tend not to have a clear sense of the overall sweep of the Gospel, let alone the ways in which each part fits in the overall story. Added to this is the narrative style of John in which long dialogues intertwine word and event,[4] so that we rarely get a whole narrative unit at one sitting. This practice of breaking the text into "manageable" pieces means that words often come adrift from their setting, and so many hearers have no real sense of what John "is all about."

As preachers, we have our own preconceptions: those seemingly endless weeks about bread in Year B of the Revised Common Lectionary, the readings from the farewell discourses which sometimes feel like an intrusion into the joy of resurrection in the weeks after Easter, and, of course, the Christmastide poetry of the prologue which puts the poverty of our own language into sharp relief. None of them is particularly easy to preach, and so it is with some trepidation that I address the question of how to preach this Gospel.

In answering this question, this chapter will explore not only the content of our preaching, but how the Gospel of John might itself inform how we understand the preaching act, and how our preaching might be shaped by the Gospel.

Beginning at the Beginning: What is John about?

John is unique in the way he begins his Gospel. The writers of Matthew, Mark, and Luke are explicit in announcing their purposes as they begin their Gospels: an account of the genealogy of Jesus the Messiah (Matt

---

3. As O'Reilly points out elsewhere in this volume, the lectionary does have us read significant parts of the Gospel of John over the course of three years, particularly when saints days and commemorations are included; however, we do not experience the same sort of immersion that occurs when we read from the same Gospel week after week.

4. O'Day, *Word Disclosed*, 6.

1:1) leading to his birth, the good news of Jesus Christ (Mark 1:1), and a well investigated orderly account (Luke 1:1-4), and in Matthew and Mark these announcements also make a claim for Jesus' identity. These purposes form a lens through which we read the whole of each Gospel respectively.

In John, by contrast, it is not until the end of chapter 20 that we hear an explicit statement of purpose: "written so that you may come to believe that Jesus is the Messiah, the Son of God, and that through believing you may have life in his name" (Jn 20:31, echoed in 21:24-25). This does seem a little late in the story.

But what if the purpose of John's account is, as in the other Gospels, right there from the very beginning? In that case, those haunting words of the prologue do not simply set the scene; they tell us what this Gospel is all about: the Word made flesh in whom we encounter the fullness of the glory of God.[5]

Words and the Word, or What are we Doing When we Preach (1)?

"In the beginning was the Word." These words hark back to Genesis 1, placing the Word with God at the beginning. Hearing that "all things came into being through him," one cannot help but make a connection between the Word and God's words which spoke creation into being.[6] The identity of this Word remains ambiguous throughout through the prologue, until finally in verses 14-18 it becomes clear that this Word is God's Son; it is not until verse 34 that John the Baptist names Jesus as God's Son, and in so doing, links him with the Word.[7]

However, the Word incarnate in Jesus Christ is not the only word in John. Outside the prologue, λόγος is used to refer to the words of anyone: God, Jesus, prophets, and ordinary human beings. And the web of meaning becomes even more complex as the phrase "word of God"

---

5. As Morris notes, "In one short, shattering expression John unveils the great idea at the heart of Christianity—that the very Word of God took flesh for our salvation" (*John*, 102); see also Kittredge, *Conversations in Scripture*, 19.

6. In the Hebrew Scriptures, the expression דבר יהוה refers to the word of God involved at creation and speaking to human beings through the prophets (Kysar, *John*, 40); in the Septuagint, λόγος is used to refer to this spoken word of God (Ford, *Gospel of John*, 29); see also Edwards, *Discovering John*, 103.

7. Jesus' identity is a constant focus in this Gospel, as Kysar notes (*John*, 15).

comes into common use in Acts and the Epistles. While today we often use that phrase to refer to Scripture, in the New Testament (before the Bible as we know it had come into being) it tends to be used of preaching (e.g. Acts 6:4; 2 Tim 4:2). So we end up with a fourfold λόγος: the Word of God incarnate, words spoken by God, the word of God preached, and ordinary human words.

As preachers, we stumble into the midst of this web of words. We are very aware of the hard work that goes into preparing a sermon, and know how much we ourselves are in the words; we pray that God is with us in the preparing and the preaching. But there are times when God seems to be particularly present, such as when our hearers hear things we never said, or hear us speaking a word that seems to directly address their lives even when we are not aware of their situations. That is when we are particularly aware that the words we preach are not ours alone; they are also in some sense God's words.

Karl Barth expressed this tension between the word of God and our human words in the preaching act in terms of two principles:

> Preaching is the Word of God which he himself speaks, claiming for the purpose the exposition of a biblical text in free human words that are relevant to contemporaries by those who are called to do this in the church that is obedient to its commission. Preaching is the attempt enjoined upon the church to serve God's own word, through one who is called thereto, by expounding a biblical text in human words and making it relevant to contemporaries in intimation of what they have to hear from God himself.[8]

While Barth's principles are useful in describing the presence of both the divine and the human word in preaching, they do little to speak of the relationship between the two. A number of attempts have been made to speak of this in terms of double agency: the way in which divine and human activity coexist. However, such arguments all too easily result in the subordination of one to the other[9] or the distancing of God from the preaching event.[10]

---

8. Barth, *Homiletics*, 44.

9. E.g. Thiemann defines double agency in terms of the utterance of one speaker taken as the enacted intention of another; thus the preacher's words are the enacted intention of God and the preacher becomes the mouthpiece of God (*Revelation and Theology*, 106).

10. Wolterstorff's exploration of a metaphorical understanding of God's voice with

It is more fruitful, I would suggest, to consider the incarnation to be the fundamental paradigm for the relationship between divine and human words. In response to Christological controversies of the fifth century, the council of Chalcedon defined the nature of the relationship between the divine and the human natures of Jesus Christ as "recognized in two natures without confusions, without changes, without division, without separation; the distinction of natures being in no way annulled by the union, but rather the characteristics of each nature being preserved and coming together to form one person and subsistence."[11] Here the divine and human coexist with neither subordination nor separation.

In order to speak of how the incarnation might shed light on the preaching event, we must briefly step outside the frame of reference of John's Gospel—John seems to have little interest in *how* the divine and the human are related—and draw on the Synoptic accounts of Jesus' birth, where the process of the incarnation is described in terms of the action of the Holy Spirit (Matt 1:18; Luke 1:35). This moment of *epiclesis* (i.e. calling down of the Spirit) prefigures that of the Eucharist, wherein the Holy Spirit is invoked on the bread and wine so that while they retain their form and substance, they simultaneously become bearers of Christ's body and blood. Whilst John may not typically be thought of as expressing such a sacramental theology (given the absence of an explicit proto-Eucharist in John's account of Jesus' last night with his friends before he dies), there are echoes of it in Jesus' long discourse in John 6.[12]

Furthermore, John's emphasis on the Holy Spirit being sent upon the disciples and guiding them into truth (14:16–17, 26; 15:26–27; 16:13; 20:2) together with his linking of truth and Jesus' words (e.g. 1:14, 17; 17:17) suggest the idea that the Holy Spirit might work in preaching similarly to its work in the sacrament, enabling human words to remain fully

---

his distinction between deputized discourse, where someone does something in the name of someone else and with their authority, and appropriated discourse, wherein one person claims another's speech for him or herself, seems to place God at one remove from the preaching event. Either the preacher's words are done in God's name by virtue of ordination, or God takes credit for the preacher's words (*Divine Discourse*, 13, 42–54).

11. Bettenson, *Documents*, 51.

12. As Moloney notes, the language of 6:25–59 points forward to the place where we (together with the original hearers) encounter the flesh and blood of Christ, that is, in the Eucharist (*John*, 223). Lee argues that there is a sacramental nature to John's theology which arises from his incarnational theology (*Hallowed*, 47).

human while simultaneously being the (preached) word of God.[13] Thus, through the action of the Holy Spirit, the divine and human are heard as a unified voice in the preaching event, neither overwhelming nor displacing the other.

When it comes to the practice of preaching, this comes as both challenge and relief. Our humanity as preachers is an essential part of our preaching. We cannot simply wait for the inspiration of the Holy Spirit to do our work for us; the preacher's involvement in material life, and hence the preacher's own work of preparation, are an essential part of that material through which God is made present and speaks, as are our own character and experience, which contribute to the authority and credibility of what is heard. The simple act of climbing into a pulpit does not bestow on us an infallibly divine voice: as a partner with the divine, the preacher is invited to rediscover the importance of prayer, of openness to the Holy Spirit in preparation, and a need to "hallow" this preparatory time rather than letting it be pushed aside by the more "urgent" demands of ministry. In choosing to speak through us (as fallible human beings), God becomes vulnerable, relying on us to submit to the divine calling to preach, to the divine word in Scripture, and to the divine inspiration of the Holy Spirit. As we partner with God, we trust that God will be at work in and be heard through us.

When God Shows up, or What are we Doing When we Preach (2)?

However, the significance of the incarnation is not fully comprehended by the word λόγος. Christ is, in his incarnation, the model for the sacramental principle, that by which divine grace is primarily mediated to humanity by means of earthly, material, historical realities.[14]

---

13. This is more explicit elsewhere in the New Testament: in Mark 13:7 and Luke 12:12, the disciples are promised that the Holy Spirit will give them words to speak; in Acts, the Holy Spirit is frequently identified as enabling preaching. See further discussion in Rice, *Embodied Word*, 93–94, 126–8.

14. Crockett, *Eucharist*, 215. Macquarrie, e.g., speaks of Christ as the primordial sacrament ("Incarnation as Root of the Sacramental Principle," 34), arguing that the Eucharist "enshrines as its core and inner meaning a making-present of Christ and his grace. It incorporates the recipient into the body of Christ and conforms his existence to the pattern of Christ" (*Principles*, 469). See also Rahner, *Theological Investigations* 4:96, 175; 5:205.

One of the traditional definitions of the sacraments focuses on their function as means of grace "in which [God] doth work invisibly in us, and doth not only quicken, but also strengthen and confirm our Faith in him."[15] What makes sacraments distinctive is not simply that they are vehicles or instruments through which God ministers grace, but that they are sure and effectual means, that is to say, through them, God may reliably be encountered, and we may with certainty expect to receive the grace of Christ in his death and resurrection. Macquarrie suggests that such an encounter happens not only in the sacraments but in the word, as "the divine presence is focused as to communicate itself to us with a directness and intensity like that of the incarnation itself, which indeed is re-presented in the proclaiming of the word."[16] Brown and Loades add to this understanding by drawing attention to the way in which the preached word, like the sacraments, enables us to participate in, to become one with, Christ:

> Whether within the biblical text or beyond, words can and do thus function sacramentally, despite all their apparent clash and dissonance. For it is precisely through meditation upon such images that our participation in the Word made flesh is most effectively deepened. Chewing the Eucharistic elements and chewing the words should thus not be seen as opposed activities. Words, no less than the Word himself, can be fully sacramental. The divine Poet whose Word shaped the language of creation also thereby made possible the words—the human poetry—that describe that creation, and it is these words that enable us to participate in the Word as their source and ours.[17]

This sacramental understanding of the word preached not only evokes and nourishes us in faith; it is (at its best) a place in which God self-communicates, a locus of God's presence, where we may encounter God in Christ—which returns us to John's Gospel and its story of the Word made flesh in whom we encounter the fullness of the glory of God.

---

15. "Of the Sacraments," Article 25 of the Thirty-Nine Articles, *Book of Common Prayer*, 621.

16. Macquarrie, *Principles*, 447.

17. Brown & Loades, "Introduction: The Divine Poet," 19–20.

Ink into Blood: How then Do we Preach?

If our hearers are to encounter God in and through our preaching, then our sermons must be more than simply educative or entertaining. T. S. Eliot famously said that the poet's task was to turn blood into ink,[18] and John's Gospel is itself poetic, his language a "beautiful but often rocky country of sharp light, wild sounds, and sodden earthy smells."[19] Brouwer turned Eliot's phrase on its head, arguing that it is the purpose of speaking literature to turn ink back into blood;[20] that is the purpose not only of literature but of preaching. In the sermon, we bring the λόγος of God back into conversation with our own incarnate lives, and we do this through our words.

Our words are a primary way that we think and how we describe what we know. We use them to construct meaning and to reconstruct it; they are how we communicate not only what is, but what might be. The words we use when we preach shape not only what people understand, but what they experience. Thus, when the language of our preaching is predictable and pedestrian, we implicitly suggest that nothing out of the ordinary might be expected in the time and place of this sermon. However, if our language is vivid and descriptive, if it creates space for possibility, then our hearers may just be able to imagine that God is indeed present among them.

This is the type of language used so often in John, replete with images, metaphors, and multiple layers of meaning. The poetry does not end with the prologue. A spring of water gushing to eternal life, birth from above, a sheepfold, and a house with many rooms; each of these images, and many others, drawn from the everyday lives of Jesus' hearers, draws them in and opens them to new ways of knowing God.

While those metaphors may be somewhat abstract, at least to our ears, John's Gospel is full of earthy, everyday details: the panic when you run out of wine at a party, the stench of a four-day-old corpse, 153 fish, Peter's shame. We know these things, or things very like them, and hearing things we know disposes us to look for God active in our everyday stuff of our own lives.

If the incarnation is about God taking on human flesh, then incarnational preaching must reflect real human life. Using language that is

---

18. Eliot, *Use of Poetry*, 154.
19. Herrstrom, *The Book of Unknowing*, "Beforehand."
20. Quoted in Bartow, *God's Human Speech*, 63–64.

sensory, that describes the look, sound, smell, feel, or taste of something, allows our hearers to experience something of the reality of what we are describing. The smell of dust on the disciples' feet, the coolness of the water, the roughness of the towel, the rising heat of embarrassment, the gaping silence until Peter finally blurts out, "Lord, are you going to wash my feet?," invite the hearers to meet Christ in that scene. And using sensory language might just jar people enough to re-hear the stories like the wedding at Cana, Nicodemus' night-time visit, and the woman at the well that have been rubbed smooth by their familiarity.

This is no less true when we preach on those "manageable pieces" of the discourses in John 6 and John 13–16 and the prayer of John 17. These words are not spoken in isolation; they belong to a particular time and place when God became flesh. This makes it particularly important that our preaching grounds them in that story, in the real life of their original setting, so that a connection can be made to real life in our setting.

It can be tempting to limit our incarnational language to the world of the text. Often sermons begin well, but end up with broad banalities. However, attention to the detail of our experiences can allow our hearers to recognize their own experiences, and make connections. The cardboard boxes that provide the only mattress for someone sleeping rough, the tears running down the cheeks of an elderly woman, the incessant parroting of "are we there yet?" speak of real life, and if real life makes it into the pulpit, then maybe God might make it into our real lives. We might indeed encounter God.

And that, of course, is one of the major themes of the Gospel. We are led towards Jesus by John the Baptist, who declares him to be "the Lamb of God who takes away the sin of the world" (1:29); a day later, John is pointing out Jesus to his own disciples (1:35–36). They turn to follow Jesus, who invites them to "come and see" (1:39), words which are echoed when Thomas demands to see the risen Christ's wounds as proof that it is truly he who is risen (20:24–29). A similar echo can be heard from Jesus' call to Philip (1:43) to his final words to Peter by the lake (21:19, 22). In between, John tells us about the wedding at Cana, the woman at the well, the night time meeting with Nicodemus, the healing at the pool of Bethzatha, the man born blind (9:1–38), the conversation with Martha and raising of Lazarus, and the appearance to Mary Magdalene in the garden, each of these encounters unique to this Gospel. Time after time, people are transformed by meeting Jesus, their Lord and their God (20:28).[21]

And that is the point. The Gospel of John begins with the Word made flesh, in whom we encounter God. And it ends with Simon Peter, the one who had denied him. Three times Jesus asks, "Simon, do you love me?" And three times, he answers, "Yes, Lord," and it is only the third time that he is named by the new name that Jesus had given him, Peter, the rock. And Jesus says, "Follow me." To encounter Jesus to become his follower, is to be transformed.

That is the hope when we preach the Gospel of John: that people will hear, will encounter God, and through that encounter will be transformed.

A Sermon John 14:23-29[22]

As last words go, the ones spoken by Jesus to his disciples the night before he died, four generous chapters in the Gospel of John, are unusually long and unusually labored. Reading them is like reading the will of your great-great-grandfather, or one of the letters written in the trenches during the First World War. They are words spoken to close friends, giving them advice on how to survive the difficult days ahead, preparing them for life without him. We read them after his death, and it is too late to argue, too late to ask questions: we have just these words, the only tangible legacy of a crucified Savior.

At the time, though, the disciples were there. Together in a quiet room, he washed their feet, spoke quietly with them, and sent Judas the betrayer out to do his treacherous work. They were full of questions. "Where are you going?," "Why can't we come with you?," "Why are you leaving us alone?"

Jesus' answers, no more satisfactory to them then than to us today, were about love, and denial, and glory, and betrayal, and death. And a promise that he would continue to love them and reveal himself to them. Which is what prompted Judas—not Iscariot, the betrayer, but another one with the same name—to ask, "How will you reveal yourself to us?"

And Jesus answered, as we heard in our Gospel reading, "Those who love me will keep my word, and my Father will love them, and we will come to them and make our home with them. Whoever does not love me does not keep my words."

---

21. For further exploration of the way in which these encounters result in participation in the life of God, see Schneiders, *Written That You May Believe*.

22. This is the author's own.

It wasn't a very satisfactory answer.

Because what it sounds like Jesus is saying is that we have to earn his love. It sounds like God's love is conditional. It sounds like God's love is only for those who keep the rules. Which, of course, is what some people would like us to believe. It's so much easier that way. Do this, and this, and this, and God will love you; do that, and that, and that and God will not.

So, is that right? Is it true? Does God only love the people who "get it right" whatever "right" might be?

Many of us spent our childhoods trying to win the approval and, if we are honest, the love, of our parents. It's a hard habit to break: many of us continue to do it as adults, even when our parents are no longer with us. Is our relationship with God just the same thing writ large? Are we doomed to be forever rebellious teenagers? Is Christian faith ultimately just a matter of obedience and reward, like much of the rest of our lives?

"If you love me, you will keep my words."

Obedience and legalism are out of fashion these days; in fact they've been out of fashion on and off for the last two thousand years, ever since Jesus began railing at the scribes and Pharisees for keeping the details of all 633 commandments in the Book of the Law and ignoring the spirit of them.

We value activism, idealism, individualism. And yet, we still tend to see obedience as a way to get approval, whether it's obedience to our parents' expectations, obedience to our employers, or obedience to the lifestyle expectations of the world around us. Talking about obedience might be out of fashion but we still carry an ambivalent allegiance to it.

"If you love me, you will keep my words."

So back to the question. Is God's love only for those who keep the rules? No, but it's a paradoxical no.

Because God loves us. If Scripture says nothing else, it's that God loves us, unconditionally and without limits.

The stories of the Old Testament resound with God's love. From the very beginning creation is presented as the loving act of God, one where God not only creates human beings, but everything we need to survive. And in every new circumstance, the love of God is at work. Whether it's putting a mark of protection on Cain so that he will not be killed for his crimes, or providing food in the desert, or safety from attacking armies, God's love is at work.

It's no different when we get to the New Testament. "For God so loved the world that he gave his only Son," writes John, a Son whom we know as Jesus, who healed the sick and raised the dead and in the end died for our sake. God loves us. And nothing can separate us from that love.

And it's only because God loves us that we can love God. It is only because God loves us that we can even know God. So no, God's love is not only for those who keep the rules, God's love is not dependent on us.

And yet neither does God force God's love on us. There is no divine rape of humanity. God's love comes to us as an invitation, a gift, something which we are free to accept or refuse, something which we can respond to or ignore.

God loves us and invites us into a relationship of mutual love. And when we open ourselves to that love, if we allow ourselves to respond to that love, God sweeps us up, embraces us, with love. We are caught up into the life of God, the boundaries of heaven and earth become blurred, and God's love spills over and into and through us. It's grace all the way.

And if we open ourselves to God's love, if we love God, then we will keep the words of Jesus, not as a matter of duty but as a matter of inevitability. Because when Jesus is talking with the disciples that last night before he died, the only two commands he gives are to wash one another's feet, and to love one another.

Keeping Jesus' words isn't about rules; it's not about placating or impressing God, it's about love. It's about being people, being a community, that is characterized by the very love of God flowing through us, a community characterized by love and by humble service. And it's grace all the way.

It's grace all the way. That's the paradox. God's love is not bound by our keeping the rules, but when we allow God's love to flow through us we can't help but keep the rules—the rules of love.

So why do we so easily turn to a rule bound faith? I suspect, at least in part, that it's because we don't always find it easy to receive. Our lives are built on self-sufficiency and independence.

It's hard to let go of control. We find it uncomfortable to accept a position of humility which would allow us to love one another, not at a distance, but up close, close enough to wash one another's feet, close enough to experience love and denial and glory and betrayal and even death, and to experience the resurrected life of Christ welling up within us the love of God, Father, Son and Holy Spirit, overflowing and transforming our lives.

Here, today in the Eucharist, in this bread and this wine, God offers us not just a sign of that all-embracing love; God offers us God's very own self. As we receive and welcome it, the love of God will spill over and through us, and from us into our community and our world.

It's grace all the way: grace upon grace.

Bibiography

The Book of Common Prayer and Administration of the Sacraments and Other Rites and Ceremonies of the Church According to the Use of the Church of England [1662]. Cambridge: Cambridge University Press, 1920.

Barth, Karl. *Homiletics.* Translated by Geoffrey W. Bromiley and Donald E. Daniels. Louisville, KY: Westminster John Knox, 1991.

Bartow, Charles L. *God's Human Speech: A Practical Theology of Proclamation.* Grand Rapids, MI: Eerdmans, 1997.

Bettenson, Henry Scowcroft. *Documents of the Christian Church.* 2nd ed. London: Oxford University Press, 1963.

Brown, David and Ann Loades. "Introduction: The Divine Poet." In *Christ the Sacramental Word,* edited by David Brown and Ann Loades., 1–25. London: SPCK, 1996.

Crockett, William R., *Eucharist: Symbol of Transformation.* New York: Pueblo, 1989.

Donne, John. "Annunciation" and "Nativity." https://shakespeareauthorship.com/xmas/donne.html

Edwards, Ruth B., *Discovering John: Content, Interpretation, Reception.* 2nd ed. London: SPCK, 2014.

Eliot, T. S. *The Use of Poetry and the Use of Criticism: Studies in the Relation of Criticism to Poetry in England.* 2nd ed. London: Faber & Faber, 1964.

Ford, David. *The Gospel of John: A Theological Commentary.* Grand Rapids, MI: Baker Academic, 2021.

Herrstrom, David Sten. *The Book of Unknowing: A Poet's Response to the Gospel of John.* Eugene, OR: Wipf & Stock, 2012. https://search-ebscohost-com.ezproxy2.commonawards.org/login.aspx?direct=true&db=nlebk&AN=906731&site=ehost-live.

Kittredge, Cynthia Briggs. *Conversations with Scripture: The Gospel of John.* Harrisburg, PA: Morehouse, 2007.

Kysar, Robert, *John, the Maverick Gospel.* 3rd ed. Louisville, KY: Westminster John Knox, 2007.

Lee, Dorothy A. *Hallowed in Truth and Love: Spirituality in the Johannine Literature*: Eugene, OR: Wipf & Stock, 2011.

Macquarrie, John. "Incarnation as Root of the Sacramental Principle." In *Christ, the Sacramental Word,* edited by David Brown and Ann Loades, 29–30. London: SPCK, 1996.

———. *Principles of Christian Theology.* 2nd ed. New York: Charles Scribner's Sons, 1977.

Moloney, Francis J. *The Gospel of John.* Sacra Pagina 4. Collegeville, MN: Liturgical Press, 1998.

Morris, Leon. *The Gospel According to John.* Grand Rapids, MI: Eerdmans, 1971.

O'Day, Gail. *The Word Disclosed: Preaching the Gospel of John*. St Louis, MI: Chalice, 2002.

Rahner, Karl. *Theological Investigations* (23 vols). Baltimore: Helicon 1961.

Rice, Charles L. *The Embodied Word. Preaching as Art and Liturgy*. FRP. Minneapolis, MN: Augsburg Fortress, 2010.

Schneiders, Sandra M. *Written that you may believe: Encountering Jesus in the Fourth Gospel*. 2nd ed. New York: Crossroad, 2003.

Thiemann, Ronald F. *Revelation and Theology: The Gospel as Narrated Promise*. Notre Dame, IN: University of Notre Dame Press, 1985.

Wolterstorff, Nicholas. *Divine Discourse: Philosophical Reflections on the Claim That God Speaks*. Cambridge: Cambridge University Press, 1995.

———. "Sacrament as Action, Not Presence." In *Christ the Sacramental Word*, edited by David Brown and Ann Loades, 103–22. London: SPCK, 1996.

15

From Text to Life

A Pastoral Reading of the Gospel of John

GARY HEARD

Introduction: Purpose of Pastoral Theology[1]

PASTORAL THEOLOGY IS AT the same time one of the oldest practices of faith and one of the newer disciplines in theological education. It is grounded in the belief that God is active—and revealed—in the historic circumstances of human affairs. Pastoral readings are grounded in the belief that the biblical documents are, amongst other things, born of theological reflection upon human history from the beginning and, from the inside, stories of faith related out of the lived experience of human life. This experience has been honed in the context of community—a resource for the practice of theological reflection through the centuries.[2] The pastoral theologian is also aware that the context out of which these reflections emerge can often be discerned through the text itself, as well as through the thoroughgoing research of other disciplines.

---

1. This section draws heavily on my unpublished doctoral thesis: Heard, "Out of Time," esp. 213–20 and 239–45.

2. An artificial distinction is often drawn between historical/traditional theology and practical pastoral theology. Both are grounded in experience. The scriptural texts are reflections on and articulation of the experience of the historical people of God, shaped, honed and refined through communal reflection. They are in no wise abstract constructs on the nature of God.

It thus seeks to pay diligent attention to the text in order to "hear" what is implicit. In the same way that one might read through meeting minutes of an organization and gain insight into the challenges being faced, so the text of Scripture can provide insight into the community being addressed and the type of response which the author is seeking to elicit.

While the pastoral endeavor seeks to develop a rich and deep understanding of the context which the text seeks to address—in order to identify and expose the theoretical underpinnings which shape the approach—pastoral theology is not primarily curative nor prescriptive but is, rather, descriptive in its practice and formative in its purpose. This reflects the conviction that every practice is embedded in theory,[3] and, conversely, that a theoretical and articulated response reflects practical purposes. A pastoral reading is not looking for trite answers to contemporary problems, nor is it seeking to recite old solutions without reference to either the present or historical context. In that sense, pastoral/theological reflection is a process rather than a product,[4] in which the historical traditions are brought into meaningful engagement with present circumstances. The result is that "theology is revitalized in the practical and direct response of theologians to pain, yearnings, and possibilities of the cultural-historical currents of a time and a people."[5]

In this case, the reflection commences in the historical context and terms of the Fourth Gospel, with subsequent consideration of the implications for the present time. Arguably a reversal of the usual process of theological reflection (which usually commences with a contemporary experience or issue), pastoral theology ultimately begins with the search we all make for meaning in life, taking with complete seriousness the struggles we engage in to understand ourselves, our culture, and the functioning of nature and society; and the connections between them.[6]

From Text to Life

A robust pastoral theology, therefore, demands a thorough exegesis of the text and a solid grounding in historical and systematic theology. It brings these insights into conversation with a rich description of the

---

3. Browning, *Fundamental Practical Theology*. 5.
4. Graham et al., *Theological Reflection: Methods* 5.
5. Parks, "North American Critique," 102.
6. Deeks, *Pastoral Theology*, 67.

experience of life in the present context. In relation to a reading of the Gospel of John, it seeks both to bring the Evangelist's community life to the text and through the text back to the life of the community.[7] In this context, a pastoral reading of the Fourth Gospel invites attention to the context which the Evangelist is addressing. Recognizing that this is the subject of some debate, and aware of the variety of responses which have been formulated through research, the pastoral theologian seeks to read the text of the Gospel with a pastoral ear, noting the concerns which are addressed, and the way in which the writer seeks to address them. Out of this reflection we will move to consider present implications of the text.

A Unique Contribution

Pastoral theology[8] can be defined as the place where contemporary experience and the resources of the religious tradition meet in a critical dialogue that is mutually and practically informing.[9] One aspect of the uniqueness of practical theology is that it is informed by a variety of disciplines, including many of the social sciences—for example, psychology, sociology, anthropology, history, and their various offspring. It is this capacity to draw on the insights of a wide range of disciplines, as it responds to the realities of context, that makes practical theology a unique discipline, one which is able to cross boundaries and open up otherwise closed conversations. Practical theology, due to its different angle of vision, provides another understanding of God and the world.[10]

The pastoral theologian is also aware of the dangers of interpreting the text to the immediate concerns of the present day.[11] The important first step in a pastoral reading of the Gospel is to develop an understanding of the community to which the writer is addressing the text and the

---

7. The word "community" is used in the general sense of the audience of the Fourth Gospel and not in terms of a sectarian community, cut off from the wider community and the rest of the church (see Porter, *Johannine Social Identity*, 228–35).

8. Or "practical theology": the terms are often used interchangeably.

9. Woodward et al., *Blackwell Reader*. xiii.

10. Paver, *Theological Reflection*. 140.

11. Coakley laments the often shallow nature of theological reflection which accompanies pastoral theology, and challenges pastoral theologians to a more constructive engagement with systematic theology and other disciplines. See "Can Pastoral Theology Be Saved?"

way in which that text would be received and heard before considering how the insights gained apply to a contemporary context.

While the systematic theologian is aware of the way in which the Fourth Gospel contributes to the development of the thinking of the church through the centuries, particularly in relation to the way in which it impacted credal formulations, and the biblical scholar is similarly aware of the contribution of the Fourth Gospel to the development and clarification of the understandings, priorities and challenges facing the early church, the pastoral theologian is aware that the Evangelist is addressing a community in formation, not only theologically, but in dealing with a range of issues particular to the time and context, but also with an eye to the ongoing implications for the present time. The pastoral theologian will, therefore, be aware of both communal and individual implications, as well as reflecting on the ongoing implications for the life of faith.

The focus on the Fourth Gospel often falls upon its Christology, given the high formulations which open the Gospel (1:12, 18), and the seven signs which appear through the Book of Signs (1:18–12:50), as well as its contribution to the shape of the credal formulations which followed in the ensuing decades.[12] Moloney underlines this by stating that "Johannine Christology is not an end in itself. It is in service to the author's major concern: theology."[13] And yet the pastoral theologian is also aware that the Evangelist has another end in mind—he is writing to and for an audience in formation which is seeking to discover what it means to live faithfully as followers of Jesus in its own time and place. We note further evidence of this in the narratives in the Book of Acts and the writings of Paul (e.g. Acts 10; Gal 2). These provide insights into the early church as it moves through a significant transition from its beginning amongst primarily Jewish followers of Jesus before expanding also through the Gentile world, raising questions and posing challenges which are not only theological, but pastoral[14]: this outlines the situation out of which the Fourth Gospel emerges.

While the early church's theological formulations were undoubtedly fluid, as early Christians sought to proclaim and explain the life, death and resurrection of Jesus, there were also doubtless practical concerns facing the church, both internally and in relation to external relationships, as

12. For a reception history study of John, see Edwards, *John*.

13. Moloney, *Love in the Gospel of John*. 54.

14. This strong pastoral focus is highlighted in John 10:118 in which Jesus articulates his relationship to his followers using explicit pastoral imagery.

the community transitioned through different phases of its early life. The difficulty in identifying the specific context to which the Evangelist was writing does represent a challenge, but the literary structure and concerns addressed internally provide a framework for understanding that the Gospel is directed at key spiritual needs and pastoral concerns of its time and context.[15]

Life Revealed in/by the Text

The first part of the Gospel addresses a succession of encounters with individuals from diverse backgrounds before shifting focus to Jesus' relationship with the disciples in the farewell discourse (Jn 13–17) which is part of the Book of Glory (13:1–21:25). Following the prologue and opening narrative, we encounter a series of pericopes in the "Cana to Cana" cycle (2:1–4:54),[16] for example, which engage with Jewish characters such as Jesus' mother (2:1–12) and Nicodemus (3:1–11), and with heterodox Jews and Gentiles, such as the Samaritan woman (4:1–42) and the royal official (4:43–54). Following the cycle is the story of a man suffering long-term illness (5:118), a man born blind (9:1–41) and two sisters at the death of their brother (11:1–44, 12:1–8). These narratives are often interspersed with dialogues addressing Jesus' identity (e.g. 3:12–21; 5:19–47; 9:39–41; 11:25–27). This intertwining of Christology and pastoral concerns is a mark of the Book of Signs.

In fact, before we encounter the narratives directed at human relationships, the first hints that the Gospel exhibits a pastoral focus occur in the prologue which, whilst representing an elevated Christology, alerts the pastoral reader to a parallel focus. Noting that the opening of the Gospel draws upon the integration of two traditions of thought, combining Hebrew narrative with Hellenistic philosophy, the reader is invited to consider reasons for this apparently intercultural engagement.[17] One does not need to read much further to note the enigmatic insertion at verse 13 ("children born not of natural descent, nor of human decision

---

15. Culpepper identifies a range of issues, including those raised in the epistles (*Gospel and Letters of John*, 42–61).

16. Moloney, *John*, 63–65.

17. The background of thought found in Hellenistic Judaism is itself indicative of the blending of Hebraic and Hellenistic thinking in almost all forms of Jewish experience; see Hengel, *Judaism and Hellenism*.

or a husband's will, but born of God"[18]) which seems initially to interrupt the flow of the text,[19] and which suggests diversity in the readership, alerting the pastoral reader to a potential focus in the Gospel.[20] It is possible to consider that the terms, "born not of natural descent, nor of human decision, or a husband's will, but born of God," may be read as referring to those who are children of God either by their Jewish heritage, by conversion into Judaism, by answering the call of Jesus in his ministry, or by those responding to the call without having met Jesus during that ministry: something that the reader will be alert to as the Gospel unfolds. One notes that this latter designation reflects the affirmation of Jesus to Thomas—"blessed are those who have not seen and yet have believed" (20:29)—who are to be considered as equals in the community. That the prologue makes mention of this diversity is significant in shaping the way in which we encounter the Gospel message. That this is so closely intertwined with a uniquely Johannine Christology suggests a relationship between the two which needs to be considered as one continues to read through the narrative, particularly in the "Cana to Cana" cycle.

While there are continuing debates about the date and context into which the Fourth Gospel is written,[21] these verses on their own provide evidence to suggest that the community has a significant component of both followers of Jesus who are not Jewish ("born of natural descent") and who are likely second-generation Christians or later, both Jewish and Gentile.[22] Noting that the Fourth Gospel reached its final form after the death of Peter (foreshadowed at 21:14), suggests that the church has either moved or is moving through the process of migrating from being a community which knew Jesus as he walked and taught, and were alive at the time of the crucifixion. The shift towards a community for whom encounter with Jesus came through proclamation rather than partnering with Jesus on the journey, coupled with a growing distance

18. English translations are from the NIV.

19. This verse can be seen as the center of a chiastic structure; e.g. Culpepper, *Gospel and Letters of John*, 111–20, and Brown, "Believing in the Gospel of John," 9–11.

20. With this in mind, the pastoral reader then considers whether these themes recur at any stage throughout the Gospel.

21. Academic dating places John normally around the 90's or turn of the century CE (Moloney, *John*, 1–6), although a minority argue for an earlier dating. For a wide range of possible dating, see Kruse, *John*, 16–17.

22. Kysar notes that the Gospel is directed towards a community comprised of Christians of a mixed background, though frames their struggle as a dispute with the local Jewish synagogue (*John: The Maverick Gospel*, 21–23).

from Jerusalem and its Temple roots, raises important questions and challenges for those whom the Evangelist seeks to address.[23]

A Mixed Community

With this alert at the beginning of the Gospel, our eyes are opened to discern what the consequences of a mixed community might mean. Just as, in the early church, the post-resurrection community had to wrestle with such questions as the place of circumcision and the type of foods which could be eaten (e.g. Gal 5:2-6; 1 Cor 8:1-13; Acts 15), the Fourth Evangelist seems to be guiding the community towards wrestling with new sets of questions, without the benefit of living disciples who had walked with Jesus and who had heard much more than the Gospels were able to convey (20:30; 21:25). Thus the Fourth Gospel provides a framework which encourages its audience to reframe or leave behind previous understandings of the life of faith, particularly those shaped by the Temple (destroyed by the Romans in 70 CE). The first step in this process is reflected in the attitude expressed by John the Baptist whose followers needed to be pointed to a greater authority on more than one occasion (1:15; 3:22-30; 5:33-38; 10:40-42). These reminders have a pastoral purpose for a group of people in transition,[24] and serve as a warning to future readers to be prepared to engage with issues and responses for which they require grace and openness.

Some Examples

As a brief overview, we first note the focus of the encounter with Nicodemus (3:1-11) whose reappearance at the burial creates both a sense of continuity and discontinuity with Temple Judaism (19:38-42). In the initial encounter, the conversation with Nicodemus reflects the distinctions outlined in 1:13—children "born of natural descent" over against those "born of God." This liberation of God's elect from being restricted to those born into Israel's covenant or joined by later decision is underlined in 3:16, declaring that *whoever believes* is incorporated

---

23. On the Diaspora Jewish context of John, see Keener, *Gospel of John*, 1.175-80.

24. This stands in contradistinction to Smith (*Future Directions*, 56) who argues that the Gospel is the theology of a people under siege, placing the focus of struggle to internal tensions which are compromising their witness.

into the promise of God, a point reinforced in the following verses. This encounter broadens the understanding of the covenant community that birth into a Jewish family is not enough, a point which is reinforced in 8:31, where authenticity as a disciple is dependent upon holding to the teaching of Jesus which sets free (8:32). That this statement is directed towards (potential) Jewish followers suggests they would be freed from the limitations of Temple worship, and sets the framework for the implications of the coming of the Spirit. The Evangelist takes this authority of Jesus' teaching further in the declaration that Jesus is greater than Abraham (8:58), arguably invoking the Abrahamic promise to be a father of many nations (Gen 15:5–6). While some authors point to elements in the Gospel which are negative towards the Jewish people,[25] it is arguable that "the gospel of John does not oppose . . . Jewishness but the response of unbelief,"[26] noting that there are Jewish followers of Jesus amongst the leaders in the synagogue (12:42). The text seems to take this further insofar as Jewish followers, representing the majority of Gospel characters, are actively affirmed.

The same point is apparent where the Gospel turns its attention to the Samaritan community through the engagement with a Samaritan woman at Jacob's well (4:1–42). The culmination of the narrative is a declaration which liberates true worship from both the Jewish community expectations and those of its Samaritan counterpart: "*Yet a time is coming and has now come when the true worshipers will worship the Father in the Spirit and in truth*" (4:23). The encounter ends with a declaration of faith for the whole world, not only Jews and Samaritans (4:42), continuing the theme of a community of faith which is not only ethnically diverse, but in which all are accepted as equals, with Christ as "the Savior of the world."

This cycle of the Gospel concludes with Jesus' return to Galilee where the reader is conditioned to expect rejection and unbelief (4:44). Instead, an encounter with a royal official results in a miracle and a believing household. (4:53). In this way, the Gospel affirms the place of Jewish and Gentile believers in the ongoing community of faith, and alerts the reader to the source of the first two signs of the Gospel narrative—both occurring in Cana—as emanating from two actions: the instruction of Jesus' mother which marks the beginning of Jesus' public ministry against

---

25. See e.g. Reinhartz, "Jews of the First Gospel."
26. Culpepper, *Document of Faith*, 112.

his apparent intentions (2:5), and the request from a member of the royal household (4:47), both of which deliver above expectations.

What marks all of these encounters is a lack of condemnation from Jesus, replaced by an inclusive and instructive approach. John 3:17 serves as a critical reminder not only in relation to the diversity of encounters which follow in the Gospel, but to the church through the ages—a reminder that has not often been upheld by the church. Too readily has the church moved to condemn those regarded as sinful as a first point of proclamation, something seen most recently in relation to matters of human sexuality and gender identity, which are not isolated incidents in church history. The Johannine declaration that "God did not send his Son into the world to condemn the world, but to save the world through him" (3:17) is a strong pastoral injunction which ought to shape evangelistic endeavors—a key thrust of the Gospel (20:31). Jesus' encounters with people from diverse backgrounds and experience in the Fourth Gospel exhibit a lack of condemnation, where most people initially feel or are at risk of rejection. This attitude is practically and repeatedly expressed as a reflection of the Gospel's Christological underpinnings and applies not just to the evangelistic outlook of the Gospel, but also to its pastoral purpose. In this view, all are welcomed as equals, regardless of their beginnings.[27]

This sense of inclusiveness *as equals* in the Christian community, regardless of heritage, is not only reinforced throughout the Gospel narrative; it has opened the door for the community to address and respond to questions which heretofore have not been faced by the early church or addressed by Jesus in his ministry. The dual reflection at the end of John 20 and 21 underlines that the Gospel is not a closed book on understanding the call of Jesus for the church and its mission,[28] reflecting a point which is made earlier in the Gospel: *"I have much more to say to you, more than you can now bear. But when he, the Spirit of truth, comes, he will guide you into all the truth. He will not speak on his own; he will speak only what he hears, and he will tell you what is yet to come"* (16:12–13). In this way, the beginning and end of the Gospel point to a community of mixed engagement with Jesus during his ministry, transitioning in leadership,

---

27. This same attitude is further illustrated in the story of the woman caught in adultery (Jn 7:50—8:11), even though it is clearly a later addition to the Fourth Gospel (see Moloney, *Gospel of John*, 259–65).

28. On the complex relationship between John 20 and 21, see e.g. Lee, "Witness," esp. 91.

and facing questions about authority and direction in this changing community. From a pastoral perspective, this embracing of diversity is an important reminder to all communities of faith going forward.

The Call for Unity amidst Uncertainty

While there is no doubt about the Christological focus and intent of the Gospel, the pastoral focus—which is grounded in Christology—comes to the fore in the farewell discourse (13:1—17:26). While some may lament the lack of focus on discipleship in published research,[29] it is likely that this is due to a focus on a search for individualized actions and commands, rather than the corporate emphasis which underpins the approach of the whole Gospel, or its focus on attitudes rather than actions which is at the heart of the discipleship teaching. The farewell discourse—like the prologue itself—opens with its focus on Jesus' relationship to the Father, which becomes the basis for the relationship of the disciples, first of all to Jesus, and then to one another (13:1–3). Even the clearing of the temple at the opening of Jesus' ministry is depicted as an invitation to recovery of the temple purpose and the inner meaning of Jesus' own identity and remains devoid of condemnation (2:13–16). Where there is conflict with the Jewish leaders, Jesus' response is reflective of this: "But do not think I will accuse you before the Father" (5:45).

The rationale for this discourse becomes obvious when the focus of the Gospel shifts to the prayer of Jesus (17:1–26). It is possible that there are tensions in the community which inhibit the ability of the church to share the message of Jesus and to "have life in his name" (20:31). The new commandment to love one another is related quite strongly to its evangelistic purpose: "By this everyone will know that you are my disciples, if you love one another" (13:35), evidence that these transitions in the community may be creating tensions which impinge upon the mission of the church.[30] It is reasonable to assume that the need for this commandment and the prayer for unity is included because there are tensions in the community which undermine the ministry of the community and which suggest conflict within. Why pray for unity and call the community to love one another if this is already taking place?

---

29. See, e.g., Segovia, "Peace I leave with you," 77.

30. For a recent study of mission in the Fourth Gospel, see Gorman, *Missional Theosis*, and King, *Missional Introduction*, 113–26.

But we do not have to wait until John 15 for this to become evident. The focus of the Gospel shifts in John 13, when it first turns to Jesus' last evening with the disciples. Here the call for unity resonates most strongly, grounded in the servant attitude which Jesus demonstrates in the washing of feet, which is set as a prefiguring of the crucifixion and an example for the leaders to follow. That the prime focus falls on Peter suggests that this call to servanthood is directed primarily, though not exclusively, at the leaders of the community. One could also conclude that the enigmatic comment "Those who have had a bath need only to wash their feet; their whole body is clean" (13:10) is a reference, not only to the cleansing power of Jesus' death and the unity it engenders, but also to the insufficiency of baptism without servanthood.[31]

John 14 reinforces the diversity of the Christian community. Coloe suggests that the reference to "in my Father's house" is to the household of God, where there are many rooms—which she sees as referring to a lived sense of community.[32] The description of Jesus as "the way" (14:7) suggests a pattern for living and loving, which has already been expressed in the earlier narrative—an inclusive narrative where the marginalized are welcomed and included as equals, a community in which the Spirit rests on all believers (7:37-39)—a community in which disciples are instructed to wash one another's feet (13:14) and in which the Spirit of truth abides (14:16-18). Of note is that the command to love as it appears in the Synoptic Gospels does not appear here (cf. Mk 12:39-41/par.; Lk 10:25-28). The love command refers to loving Jesus and his commands, and loving one another,[33] although the Gospel itself gives remarkably few commands about what to do or not to do.[34] This ultimately points the reader towards the role of the Spirit in guiding the community into truth. Remarkably, as the narrative reminds the community, it will be led into new territory, where the community seems to be instructed to not only look back to the teaching of Jesus (14:26), but also to look forward and let the Spirit guide (14:16-17; 15:26; 16:12). As a message to a community in

---

31. For a study of this episode and its place within the Johannine community, see esp. Thomas, *Footwashing*, 126-85.

32. Coloe, "Sources in the Shadows," 72. See also Coloe, *Dwelling in the Household of God*, 145-66.

33. Nevertheless, John's Gospel has a strong ethical focus, often portrayed through narrative rather than specific instructions; see the collection of essays in Skinner & Brown, eds., *Johannine Ethics*.

34. Koester, *Word of Life*, 188.

transition, a community where leadership is moving to followers who are "born of God" and who believe without seeing (20:29), it is remarkably liberating.

In this context, the prayer of Jesus for his followers underlines the importance of maintaining unity and love amidst this time of change. It also underlines the reality that the challenges being faced have been unable to be addressed earlier—thus the need for the Spirit to come and to guide the community into truth—nor to be included in the stories of Jesus, as suggested by 21:25. The unity of all believers, regardless of when and how they come to believe, is affirmed again in 17:20–22. The call to peace, and the declaration of peace amongst believers is made into the context where there are unknowns which will be addressed in the power and under the guidance of the Spirit (16:33). It is a community where questions of organization remain open,[35] and where the equality of all members regardless of their beginnings in the faith is underlined and reinforced on numerous occasions. The call to love one another (13:34) reinforces that all are equal, an injunction which is reinforced in increasing measure through the Gospel (15:12; 17:11, 20–21). It calls into being a community whose mission is not to be marked by an attitude of condemnation.

The post-resurrection appearances of Jesus serve to reinforce the message of equality and uncertainty. Jesus' response to Thomas' declaration of faith affirms the position of post-resurrection believers in the community of faith: "Because you have seen me, you have believed; blessed are those who have not seen and yet have believed" (20:29). The discourse between Jesus and Peter (21:15–19) which restores the failed disciple and points not only to his death but the ambiguity about the continuing presence of the "disciple whom Jesus loved" (21:20–23) leave the future open to the reader of the Gospel.

Conclusion: Looking Forward

As we read the Gospel from the vantage point of the twenty-first century, there are pastoral calls which need to be heeded afresh. The Evangelist provides ample evidence that there are no second-class Christians in the community of faith. Regardless of background and culture, each is accepted as equal on the same journey towards wholeness. That the Gospel

---

35. Koester, *Word of Life*, 203.

concludes by using Peter as an example of one needing to learn and grow is a strong concluding statement of this value.[36] That misunderstanding is a mark of almost every encounter in the Gospel and is met by Jesus without condemnation should stand as a mark of the continuing faith community. Those condemned by religious people as sinners become proclaimers of the Gospel (John 9). Jesus declares himself as the one who comes that they may have life to the full (10:10). Consider, among the encounters with Jesus recorded in this Gospel, who might be included, welcomed, and celebrated as a member of our faith communities today!

The contention of this work is that there is a strong pastoral purpose to the Gospel for a community in transition—a community which is composed of believers of diverse backgrounds who are confronting questions that had hitherto not been envisaged in the teachings of Jesus. While we may be uncertain of the precise date and geographical context into which the Gospel is composed, it is evident that the leadership of the community is in transition beyond a time where there are those who have a lived experienced of Jesus of Nazareth, and includes believers not only of Jewish background, but from Samaritan and Gentile communities. The open-ended role of the Spirit and the focus on the call to unity serve to underline the tensions and challenges facing the community in this environment, calling the church community to unity with—and love for—one another as they seek to address the challenges. The "high Christology in which Jesus seems to be hardly human at times"[37] actually serves to elevate Jesus above the conflicts and debates which characterize the Gospel focus. The Johannine Jesus is not shown as taking sides in community debates but rather in elevating thinking to a new plane, thereby inviting the community to follow in this way.

The pastoral message of this Gospel retains its power and relevance today. Think of the way in which Jesus responds to those who live through failed marriages and through adultery, to those excluded because of their social or physical status, as well as to women and to people of power, and ask whether the church has upheld this commitment to equality which is evident in this Gospel. When we turn our attention to new questions and challenges beyond what the Gospel envisages, how open has the church remained to consider these in the light of Jesus' non-condemnatory

---

36. It is also noted that other leaders in the community are identified for their misunderstanding: Nicodemus (3:3–10), Martha (11:21–27), and Mary Magdalene (20:11–18).

37. Culpepper, *Gospel and Letters of John*. 48–50.

approach? Recent history and contemporary experience as the church has grappled with same sex relationships and gender identity—to name just two contemporary issues—has demonstrated much more of a closed mind than an openness to what the Spirit might be leading us into and has stretched and strained the unity of God's people, not to mention the impact on the church's evangelistic mission.

There is not just a single purpose for the writing of this Gospel, but an intertwining of purposes, whereby diversity of the community is affirmed, authority is shared as equals guided by the Spirit in love, and where Christology serves at least in part as a paradigm for relating as community in order that the mission of the community is not compromised but strengthened by demonstrated love for one another. To reframe Moloney's conclusion, Johannine Christology is not an end in itself; it serves as a paradigm for the attitudes which Jesus expects of the church and which will strengthen its mission and evangelistic purpose: a community which is inclusive, built on equality of all members, lacking a condemnatory spirit, grounded in love, and open to a future which is in many ways unknown, but for which the Spirit will resource them on the journey.

Bibliography

Brown, Sherri. "Believing in the Gospel of John: The Ethical Imperative to Becoming Children of God." In *Johannine Ethics: The Moral World of the Gospel and Epistles of John*, edited by Sherri Brown and Christopher W. Skinner, 3–24. Minneapolis, MN: Fortress, 2017.

Browning, Don S. *A Fundamental Practical Theology*. Minneapolis: Fortress, 1991.

Coakley, Sarah. "Can Pastoral Theology Be Saved?" ABC Religion and Ethics. ABC, June 20, 2021. https://www.abc.net.au/religion/can-systematic-theology-become-pastoral-again-and-pastoral-theol/10095582.

Coloe, Mary L. *Dwelling in the Household of God. Johannine Ecclesiology and Spirituality*. Collegeville, MN: Liturgical, 2007.

———. "Sources in the Shadows: John 13 and the Johannine Community." In *New Currents through John: A Global Perspective*, edited by Francisco Lozada and Tom Thatcher, 69–82. Atlanta, GA: SBL, 2006.

Culpepper, Richard A. *The Gospel and Letters of John*. Nashville, TN: Abingdon 1998.

Culpepper, Alan R. "The Gospel of John as a Document of Faith in a Pluralistic Culture." In *What Is John?*, edited by Fernando F. Segovia, 107–28. Atlanta, GA: Scholars, 1996.

Deeks, David. *Pastoral Theology: An Inquiry*. London: Epworth, 1987.

Edwards, Mark. *John*. BBC. Oxford: Blackwell, 2004.

Ferreira, Johan. *Johannine Ecclesiology*. Sheffield: Sheffield Academic, 1998.

Gorman, Michael, *Abide and Go: Missional Theosis in the Gospel of John*. Didsbury Lectures 2016; Eugene, OR: Cascade Books, 2018.

Graham, Elaine et al. *Theological Reflection: Methods*. London: SCM, 2005.

Heard, Gary D. *Out of Time, Out of Place: Pastoral and Theological Implications for Parents of Extremely Premature Infants*, 2011. https://repository.divinity.edu.au/entities/publication/1a4a2ab2-0b82-4c2c-94f7-91318eb50deo.

Hengel, Martin. *Judaism and Hellenism. Studies in their Encounter in Palestine during the Early Hellenistic Period.* WUNT 10. 2 vols. Translated by John Bowden. Eugene, OR: Wipf & Stock, 1973, 2003.

Keener, Craig S. *The Gospel of John. A Commentary*. 2 vols. Peabody, MS: Hendrickson, 2003.

King, Fergus J. *A Missional Introduction to the New Testament*. IICM. North Augusta, SC: Missional University Press, 2021.

Koester, Craig R. *The Word of Life: A Theology of John's Gospel*. Grand Rapids, MI: Eerdmans, 2008.

Kruse, Colin G. *John*. London: IVP, 2017.

Kysar, Robert. *John, the Maverick Gospel*. Louisville, KY: Westminster John Knox, 1993.

Lee, Dorothy A. "Witness in the Fourth Gospel: John the Baptist and the Beloved Disciple as Counterparts." In *Creation, Matter and the Image of God. Essays on John*, 91–110. Adelaide: ATF, 2020.

Moloney, Francis J. *The Gospel of John*. Sacra Pagina 4. Collegeville, MA: Liturgical, 1998.

———. *Love in the Gospel of John: An Exegetical, Theological, and Literary Study*. Grand Rapids, MI: Baker Academic, 2013.

Parks, Sharon Daloz. "The North American Critique of James Fowler's Theory of Faith Development." In *Stages of Faith and Religious Development: Implications for Church, Education, and Society*, edited by James W Fowler et al., 101–15. New York: Crossroad, 1991.

Paver, John E. *Theological Reflection and Education for Ministry: The Search for Integration in Theology*. EPPET. Aldershot, England: Ashgate, 2006.

Porter, Christopher A. *Johannine Social Identity Formation after the Fall of the Jerusalem Temple: Negotiating Identity in Crisis*. BIS 194. Leiden: Brill, 2022.

Reinhartz, Adele. "The Jews of the Fourth Gospel." In *The Oxford Handbook of Johannine Studies*, edited by Judith M. Lieu and Martinus de Boer, 121–37. Oxford: Oxford University Press, 2018.

Segovia, Fernando F. "'Peace I leave with you; my peace I give to you.' Discipleship in the Fourth Gospel." In *Discipleship in the New Testament*, edited by Fernando F. Segovia, 76–102. Philadelphia: Fortress, 1985.

Skinner, Christopher W. and Sherri Brown, eds. *Johannine Ethics: The Moral World of the Gospel and Epistles of John*. Minneapolis: Fortress, 2017.

Smith, D. Moody. "Future Directions of Johannine Studies." In *Life in Abundance: Studies of John's Gospel in Tribute to Raymond E. Brown*, edited by John R. Donahue, 52–62. Collegeville, MN: Liturgical, 2005.

Thomas, John Christopher. *Footwashing in John 13 and the Johannine Community*. JSNTSup. London: Bloomsbury, 1991.

Woodward, James et al. *The Blackwell Reader in Pastoral and Practical Theology*. Oxford.: Blackwell, 2000.

16

Losing Ourselves to Gain Ourselves for Justice

An Address on John 17:20–26[1]

GARRY WORETE DEVERELL

FIVE YEARS AGO, TWO hundred and fifty Aboriginal and Torres Strait Islander leaders gathered at Uluru to sign a "Statement from the Heart,"[2] which called upon the Australian people to join with them in working toward a "makaratta" or treaty between our peoples,[3] built upon truth-telling and a constitutionally recognized Indigenous "voice" to the national parliament. Two days ago, at a ceremony on Gadigal land in Sydney,[4] nine national religious leaders signed a resolution

---

1. This address was preached at St Paul's Cathedral, Melbourne, as part of the observance of Reconciliation Week, 7th Sunday after Easter, 2022.

2. The "Statement from the Heart" was issued in 2017 by delegates to the First Nations National Constitutional Convention, held over four days near Uluru (sometimes called the "heart of Australia") on Pitjantjatjara country in Central Australia. The Statement is "an invitation to the Australian people from First Nations Australians. It asks Australians to walk together to build a better future by establishing a First Nations Voice to Parliament enshrined in the Constitution, and the establishment of a Makarrata Commission for the purpose of treaty making and truth-telling." https://ulurustatement.org/the-statement/

3. Makarrata "is a complex Yolngu word describing a process of conflict resolution, peacemaking and justice." https://www.abc.net.au/news/2017-08-10/makarrata-explainer-yolngu-word-more-than-synonym-for-treaty/8790452. The Yolngu are the people of north-east Arnhem Land in the Northern Territory.

4. "Gadigal" refers to the area now comprising the city of Sydney: "The original

calling upon the national parliament to work towards a referendum on the "voice" as soon as possible. The religious leaders represented Buddhists, Jews, Hindus, Sikhs and Muslims. I'm grateful to God that there were also Catholics, the Uniting Church, the National Council of Churches and, yes, even Anglicans. Chris McLeod, our national Aboriginal bishop, represented the Primate, Archbishop Geoffrey Smith, on this occasion.[5]

One of the pleasing things about this ceremony was the fact that none of the nine religious leaders gave a speech. Rather, they listened. They listened to an oration from Rachel Perkins, an Arrernte and Kalkadoon woman,[6] a prominent filmmaker, and the daughter of Charlie Perkins, the man whose 60s activism played a key part in the recognition of mob[7] as human beings in the 1967 referendum. Ms Perkins used her oration to call for unity—amongst mob, in the general community, and in the faith communities—unity in supporting the Statement from the Heart and the call of the religious leaders for a referendum on an Indigenous voice to parliament. For this is the only way, she argued, that we are ever likely to see something like justice arrive in our nation, the nation of Australia, for Aboriginal and Torres Strait Islander people.

It goes without saying, perhaps, that you only have to call for unity if unity isn't actually there. And it isn't. Demonstrably. None of the communities Ms Perkins was addressing can claim to be agreed, even within themselves, on either the Statement from the Heart or the urgency of a referendum. I can tell you, with some authority, that Aboriginal and Torres Strait Islander communities are not agreed. Many mob do not even know what the Statement from the Heart actually says. And the same is surely true with the Anglican community. Perhaps even more so. The

---

Aboriginal inhabitants of the City of Sydney local area are the Gadigal people." https://www.cityofsydney.nsw.gov.au/history/aboriginal-histories.

5. To change the Constitution to create a First Nations Voice to Parliament, a referendum would be required; to be successful, a referendum must be supported by a national majority of voters, and a majority of voters in the majority of Australian states (that is, in four of the six states). The successful 1967 referendum amended the Constitution to allow the Commonwealth to make laws for Aboriginal people and include them in the census. https://www.aph.gov.au/About_Parliament/Parliamentary_Departments/Parliamentary_Library/FlagPost/2017/May/The_1967_Referendum.

6. The "Arrernte" are the people upon whose lands the colonial settlement of Alice Springs was built; the "Kalkadoon" are people from the Mount Isa region of Queensland.

7. "Mob" is an Aboriginal English word meaning "kin," "tribe," or "clan."

ministry conference I attended during the week made it quite clear to me that a voice for Aboriginal and Torres Strait Islander people—indeed, even as simple a matter as listening to the mob who are part of us, who live and work in our midst—is really the very last thing on our ecclesial mind. The very last. What seems to be uppermost in our Anglican minds are things like the intrusion of the state into our affairs and, you guessed it, sex (who can have it, and what kind). Which, on my most buoyant days, attracts little more than a gentle eye-roll but, on others, a feeling of deep despair at just how tone-deaf and narcissistic we have become. Honestly!

That's why I really feel for the Jesus of John's Gospel, whose earnest prayer for unity appears in today's lections. Let's listen in to his prayer once more, the prayer he offered, according to John, just before he was arrested and crucified:

> I ask not only on behalf of these, but also on behalf of those who will believe in me through their word, that they may all be one. As you, Father, are in me and I am in you, may they also be in us, so that the world may believe that you have sent me. The glory that you have given me I have given them, so that they may be one, as we are one, I in them and you in me, that they may become completely one, so that the world may know that you have sent me and have loved them even as you have loved me. (Jn 17:20–23 NRSV)

Now there's a few things in this passage which require clarification. First, when Jesus prays for "those who will believe in me through their word," the "their" in this sentence is the disciples, the apostles, who will go out to preach. "Those who will believe in me through their word" are, therefore, the Christian communities these apostles will found and, ultimately, everyone who decides to become a Christian because of the apostolic witness. So that's us, my friends. Jesus is praying for us. Not for someone else, some historical community on the other side of the globe. For us. For *our* conflict-ridden community.

A second and crucially important clarification. When Jesus says that he has given us his "glory," the glory already given him by his Father, he is not talking about fame and fortune, or even about victory or success in any conventional sense. For when John talks about glory, in this his gospel, he is in fact talking about crucifixion and the sacrificial pouring out of one's life for others. Allow me to quote from an earlier passage, that scene at which Judas leaves the supper to betray Jesus to the authorities:

> So when he had dipped the piece of bread, he gave it to Judas son of Simon Iscariot. After he received the piece of bread, Satan entered into him. Jesus said to him, "Do quickly what you are going to do." ... So, after receiving the piece of bread, he immediately went out. And it was night ... When he had gone out, Jesus said, "Now the Son of Man has been glorified, and God has been glorified in him. If God has been glorified in him, God will also glorify him in himself and will glorify him at once." (Jn 13:26–27, 30–32)

And an even earlier passage, in chapter 12:

> "Very truly, I tell you, unless a grain of wheat falls into the earth and dies, it remains just a single grain; but if it dies, it bears much fruit. Those who love their life lose it, and those who hate their life in this world will keep it for eternal life ... Now my soul is troubled. And what should I say—'Father, save me from this hour'? No, it is for this reason that I have come to this hour. Father, glorify your name." Then a voice came from heaven, "I have glorified it, and I will glorify it again." ... Jesus said, "This voice has come for your sake, not for mine. Now is the judgement of this world; now the ruler of this world will be driven out. And I, when I am lifted up from the earth, will draw all people to myself." He said this to indicate the kind of death he was to die. (Jn 12:24–25, 27–28, 30–33)

I share these passages at length to convey the sense in which John uses the concept of "glory." For him, the pinnacle of Christ's glorification by the Father is not, in fact, his resurrection or ascension to the Father. It is his crucifixion—that moment when he surrenders himself entirely to his Father's will out of love for the people to whom he was sent. So let's be clear, let's make no mistake. When Jesus talks about glory, he is talking about sacrificial, cruciform, love. A love that bears fruit only at great personal cost. The cost, even, of death. So, this is what Jesus prays for us: that we might live into his cruciform glory; that we might suffer and, perhaps, even die, for the sake of the world and our fellow Christians; that we might be as one in such love that the world might know and learn of God's love by the way we pour out our own lives for others.

A third clarification, if you will indulge me. When Jesus talks about unity as "oneness," he is not talking about "uniformity." He is not talking about us all becoming carbon-copies of each other in body or mind, and thus simply *unable* to disagree with each other. No. The model Jesus uses for "oneness" is not the cookie-cutter but the circular reciprocity of the

Father, the Son and the Holy Spirit. In this earliest example of what will become trinitarian thinking, John has Jesus pray that we might indwell each other—as the Father does the Son, and the Son the Father—not to the point where we simply *become* each other, without any hint of differentiation. (For the Father is NOT the Son and the Son is NOT the Father). Each comes to "indwell" the other, rather, in something of the manner that dancers and jazz musicians do, by their intuition about where the other is going next, and their choice to cooperate with each other out of a deep and abiding care and respect. That is why the Cappadocian fathers of the church called the Trinity a circle-dance: a mutual yielding and cooperation of each with the other, even as the possibility for dissension and disagreement remains forever at hand. It is also what we Aboriginal people call "country"—the biospheric dance of plants, animals, and humans, of star-, land-, and sea-scapes—that simultaneously begins and ends all forms of life in an infinite coinherence of past, present, and future. The availability of these realties to human imagination and culture we call "dreaming," not because they are made up, but because they constantly precede and exceed our pretensions to mastery, just as they interrupt and reorder what we foolishly mistake as unassailably good, urgent, or true.

This, then, is what Jesus prays for the church. And, if I may speak quite personally again, it is why I remain a Christian even though many of my fellow-Christians regularly wound and drive me crazy. It is why I am a Christian even though the church has never come to terms with its leading role in the attempted genocide of my people. It is why I remain a Christian even though the church remains racist. It is why I remain a Christian even when mob are ignored and rendered invisible by our Councils and theological colleges. It is why I am a Christian. Why? Because I believe in the sacrificial love of Christ for sinners as the only hope for us all. The *only* hope. The only *hope*. For I, too, regularly hurt my kin. I, too, am blind to the sufferings of others and too much centered in my own hurts and fears. I, too, am in desperate need of grace: the undeserved favor that is offered to us all for the making of the church, and of a society, and of an ecology that is finally reconciled, made one, whole and at peace.

That is not to say that we are equal in our sacrificial callings. We are not. It is incumbent upon the more powerful partner to do the lion's share of the work to close the yawning gap between us, whether that gap be economic, cultural, or theological. So let's call a spade a shovel. The social and economic rules in this commonwealth, the cultural assumptions of this colony, and the theological imagination of this colonial church, are all those of white people, of colonists whose forebears are in Europe. If you are not from Europe, or your forebears were not—and especially if you are Indigenous to this country, with its 300 clans or nations—the only way to survive is to adapt to the colonial rules and imagination. Doing so is enormously costly and regularly depletes and exhausts the personal and economic resources available to those of us who would really prefer to live from and to country. Yet colonists do it with relative ease, and white people assume that there is no other way to live. The playing field is, therefore, deeply and structurally uneven. The fight is fixed, the mare has been hobbled, the dice have been loaded. And this is especially the case if you are "the wrong kind of black." So, if we are really the church, if we are to take Christ's call to sacrificial love seriously, it is incumbent upon the strongest to do most of the sacrificing. Which, let's be honest, is deeply counter to everything we are taught from an early age in this colony.

Let me conclude with this. If we are ever to be reconciled, if we are ever to come to terms with the hurt and the injustice we render, one to another, in this colony called "Australia," we must discipline ourselves to live into the prayer of Christ to his Father. If there is ever to be something like justice, we must be prepared to put aside all our many forms of cheap and trivial grace, our many band-aid solutions and duct-tape fixes. Instead, if we are colonists, we must learn what it means to love at great cost, to embrace genuinely cruciform solutions to end our cultural and economic warfare against the last and the least. If Christ, whom we claim to worship, was willing to give himself entirely for our salvation—to pour out his life even to death, for the sake of all this world's most little and vulnerable ones—what prevents us from so giving *ourselves* for this great work? What? What precisely? Is it the fear of losing ourselves? Losing our treasured control? Losing our sense of moral and intellectual superiority, our sense of being on the side of the angels? Is it a fear of losing what we believe is rightfully ours to possess?

Please, friends, don't be afraid. Listen to the wisdom of country once more, the wisdom which Christ embraced and shared with his disciples: "Very truly, I tell you, unless a grain of wheat falls into the earth and dies, it remains just a single grain; but if it dies, it bears much fruit. Those who love their life lose it, and those who hate their life in this world will keep it for eternal life." In reality, there is nothing to lose, my friends, nothing but fool's gold and false promises. But look at what you can gain! Justice for the vulnerable, peace for the troubled, a home for the exiles. And friends,

friends who love you and have your back. A community in which you can laugh, and cry, and dance, and sing. A communion of all creatures which includes the plants and the animals, the waterways, the starry host and the earth itself. A veritable body for Christ, who fills and embraces all that is alive. So, please, don't be afraid to lose all you have for the sake of justice. For you will receive back a hundredfold everything you ever could lose.

Contributors

Dr Peter Campbell is the Registrar, Trinity College Theological School, University of Divinity, and Honorary Research Fellow, Melbourne Conservatorium of Music, University of Melbourne. His PhD examined Australia's Intervarsity choral movement and he has written extensively on aspects of Australian music history. Peter is a singer, chorister, and composer who has performed across Australia, Britain, Europe, and North America. He has recently published *The Triumphs of our Fleur-de-Lys: 150 Years of Trinity College, Melbourne*. Melbourne: Melbourne University Press, 2022.

The Rev'd Canon Dr Robert ("Bob") Derrenbacker Jr is Dean of the Theological School at Trinity College, University of Divinity, where he also serves as the Frank Woods Associate Professor in New Testament. He earned a PhD in New Testament at the University of Toronto and was ordained in the Anglican Diocese of Toronto. He has published and presented his research widely on the Gospels, authoring numerous articles and a monograph: *Ancient Compositional Practices and the Synoptic Problem*. Leuven/Dudley, MA: University of Leuven Press, 2005. In the past, he has held faculty positions in New Testament at Tyndale Seminary (Toronto) and Regent College (Vancouver) and was President of Thorneloe University, a small Anglican college in Sudbury, Ontario, Canada.

The Rev'd Dr Garry Worete Deverell is Lecturer and Research Fellow in Indigenous Theologies at the University of Divinity. A trawloolway man from northern lutrawita (Tasmania), he is an Indigenous theologian and the author of *Gondwana Theology: A Trawloolway Man Reflects on Christian Faith*. Melbourne: Morning Star, 2018, and *The Bonds of Freedom: Vows, Sacraments and the Formation of the Christian Self*. Milton

Keynes: Paternoster, 2008. With years of pastoral and parish work, he is also an experienced academic: a graduate of the University of Tasmania, the MCD, and Monash University where he completed his doctoral studies in theology and liturgy. In the past, he held a Turner Fellowship at Trinity College Theological School, University of Divinity, and also serves as an Associate Priest at St Paul's Cathedral, Melbourne.

Dr Katherine Firth, whose doctoral study was in musicology and literature, manages the academic program at International House, the University of Melbourne. She is Lecturer in Research Education and Development at La Trobe University and a professional librettist and translator. She is also the external member of the Academic Committee of Trinity College Theological School. She has previously collaborated with Andreas Loewe on a theological commentary on Bach's John Passion — *Johann Sebastian Bach's St John Passion (BWV 245): A Theological Commentary with a New Study Translation by Katherine Firth*. Leiden: Brill, 2014, and a Lent Book, *Journeying with Bonhoeffer: Six Steps on the Path to Discipleship*. Melbourne: Morning Star Publishing, 2019.

The Rev'd Dr Gary Heard is the Spiritual Care Coordinator at Bethesda Health Care in Perth, Western Australia, and the Woodbridge Adjunct Professor in Pastoral Theology at Trinity College Theological School, University of Divinity. Having completed an honours degree in New Testament, he moved into a doctoral thesis in pastoral theology. For several years, he was Deputy Chair of the Human Research Ethics Committee at the Royal Women's Hospital, Melbourne. Over the last three decades, he has combined pastoral leadership in Baptist Churches with study, teaching and administration in theological colleges, and in chaplaincy roles in various community contexts.

The Rev'd Dr Fergus J. King is the Farnham Maynard Lecturer in Ministry Education and Director of the Ministry Education Centre at Trinity College Theological School, University of Divinity. He is a graduate of St Andrews and Edinburgh, with a DTh from the University of South Africa. He is also Professor of New Testament Mission (Sociocultural Interpretation) at the Missional University, based in North Augusta SC. He is a member of the International Association for Mission Studies, the FBS, and the SNTS. Ordained in the Scottish Episcopal Church, he has worked in Anglican churches in Tanzania, England, and Australia. He is

Canon and Canon Theologian of the Diocese of Tanga (Tanzania). He is the author of *Epicureanism and the Gospel of John*. WUNT 537. Tübingen: Mohr Siebeck, 2021.

The Rev'd Dr Scott A. Kirkland is the John and Jeanne Stockdale Lecturer in Practical Theology and Ethics at Trinity College Theological School, University of Divinity. He was ordained to ministry in the Anglican Church in 2022. He is the author of *Into the Far Country: Karl Barth and the Modern Subject*. Philadelphia: Fortress, 2016, and with John C. McDowell, *Eschatology*. Grand Rapids, MI: Eerdmans, 2018. He is currently the co-editor of the series *Dispatches: Turning Points in Theology and Global Crises*. Philadelphia: Fortress, 2017–. He is currently completing a monograph on Fukuyama's end of history thesis and involved with Christopher Porter in an international research project: "Figuring the Enemy."

The Rev'd Dr Brian Fiu Kolia is a second-generation Australian-born Samoan. He is an ordained Minister of the Congregational Christian Church of Samoa, and a Lecturer in Hebrew Bible at Malua Theological College. He is an Adjunct Faculty member at Trinity College Theological School, University of Divinity. He holds a PhD in Hebrew Bible from the University of Divinity, Melbourne, Australia. His research interests are in diasporic theory, critical race theory, decolonising methodologies, Hebrew Bible and biblical hermeneutics, as well as cultural and Indigenous knowledge.

The Rev'd Professor Dorothy A. Lee FAHA is the Stewart Research Professor of New Testament at Trinity College Theological School, University of Divinity. Her areas of speciality include the Gospels, and feminist studies and spirituality in the New Testament. She is a member of the Doctrine Commission of the Anglican Church, the CBAA, SNTS, SBL and FBS, and an Anglican priest and Canon of St Paul's Cathedral, Melbourne. She has published widely in the Fourth Gospel and is working on a monograph on Johannine themes with Zondervan and a study of animals in the New Testament. Her most recent publication is *The Ministry of Women in the New Testament: Reclaiming the Biblical Vision for Church Leadership*. Eugene, OR: Baker Academic, 2021.

Dr Tamara Lewit is an Honorary Fellow in the School of Historical and Philosophical Studies at the University of Melbourne, and a Fellow of the Society of Antiquaries, London. She specializes in the study of wine production from the first to the seventh centuries CE, including production in early monasteries and on Church estates. Her recent publications include "'*terris, vineis, olivetis* . . . :' Wine and Oil Production After the Villas." *PCA* 10 (2020) 119-217, and "The Early Church and Community Resilience in the Late Antique Levant: An Archaeological Perspective." In *Place, Spirituality, and Wellbeing: A Global and Multidisciplinary Approach*, edited by V. Counted et al. Switzerland: Springer, 2022. She is currently working on the production of wine in fifth to sixth century monasteries of the Levant.

The Rev'd Professor Mark Lindsay FRHistS is the Joan F.W. Munro Professor of Historical Theology at Trinity College Theological School, University of Divinity. A priest in the Anglican Diocese of Melbourne, he has taught in universities and seminaries across Australia, and in England. With a particular interest in Barthian and post-Holocaust theology, he has published three books on Karl Barth, and a fourth on the doctrine of election — *God Has Chosen: The Doctrine of Election Through Christian History*. Downers Grove, IL: IVP, 2020. He is currently writing a major biography of Markus Barth.

The Very Rev'd Dr Andreas Loewe FRHistS is Dean of St Paul's Anglican Cathedral Melbourne, a Fellow and Lecturer in Music History at the Melbourne Conservatorium of Music, Faculty of Fine Arts, the University of Melbourne, and an Adjunct Member of Faculty of Trinity College Theological School, University of Divinity. His doctoral studies were in Church history. He has previously collaborated with Katherine Firth on a theological commentary on Bach's John Passion — *Johann Sebastian Bach's St John Passion (BWV 245): A Theological Commentary with a New Study Translation by Katherine Firth*. Leiden: Brill, 2014, and a Lent Book, *Journeying with Bonhoeffer: Six Steps on the Path to Discipleship*. Melbourne: Morning Star Publishing, 2019.

The Rev'd Professor Francis J. Moloney SDB, AM, FAHA is a Senior Professorial Fellow at Catholic Theological College, University of Divinity. He joined the Salesians of Don Bosco in 1959 and was ordained priest in 1970, studying at Melbourne University, the Salesian Pontifical

University and Pontifical Biblical Institute, both in Rome, and the University of Oxford (DPhil). He was the Foundational Professor of Theology at Australian Catholic University and Professor of New Testament Studies and Dean of the School of Theology and Religious Studies at The Catholic University of America. He is the author of more than forty books, many focusing on the Gospel of John and the Johannine writings. A significant collection of his many articles and essays is published in *Johannine Studies (1975–2017)*. WUNT 372. Tübingen: Mohr Siebeck, 2017.

The Rev'd Dr Colleen O'Reilly AM recently retired as the Chaplain to Trinity College, Melbourne, having been in parish ministry, both lay and ordained, since 1982. She was instrumental in setting up the movement for women to be ordained in the Anglican Church in Australia and a co-founder of the journal *Women-Church*. Unable to be ordained within the Diocese of Sydney — though she was teaching theology with the Uniting Church — she moved to Melbourne where she was Associate Dean and Director of Research in the Melbourne College of Divinity, the precursor to the University of Divinity. She was ordained in the Diocese of Melbourne and worked thereafter in parish ministry. A past President of the Australian Academy of Liturgy, her doctoral studies focussed on the convergence of ritual and pastoral care. She is a member of the General Synod Liturgy Commission.

The Rev'd Dr Christopher A. Porter is Postdoctoral Research Fellow at Trinity College Theological School, University of Divinity. He works on the Fourth Gospel with a particular emphasis on the intersection of theology and psychology. Trained in Psychology, he brings a Social Identity framework to the consideration of the biblical text and theology. Currently, he is working on an introduction to Social Identity Theory; theological approaches to social identity formation in the Fourth Gospel; a reception history of the Christology of the Fourth Gospel; narrative identity construction and Christian formation; and socio-cognitive approaches to religious animus and enmity. He has recently published *Johannine Social Identity Formation After the Fall of the Temple in Jerusalem. Negotiating Identity in Crisis*. BIS. Leiden/Boston: Brill, 2022.

Dr Muriel Porter OAM is a Melbourne journalist, author and historian. An Honorary Research Fellow of the University of Divinity, she is a member of the Adjunct Faculty, Trinity College Theological School,

University of Divinity. Through her decades-long involvement in both the General Synod of the Anglican Church of Australia and Melbourne Diocesan Synod, and through her writing, she was a leader in the struggle to see women ordained as priests and bishops in the Anglican Church of Australia. She has published numerous books on the contemporary Australian religious scene including, most relevantly for her essay, *Women in the Church: The Great Ordination Debate in Australia*. Ringwood, VIC: Penguin Books, 1989.

The Rev'd Dr Alexander Ross is a parish priest in the Diocese of Melbourne and a member of the Adjunct Faculty at Trinity College Theological School, University of Divinity. He was formerly Associate Dean and Bye-Fellow of Emmanuel College, Cambridge. An alumnus of Trinity College Theological School, he completed graduate study at the University of Oxford before undertaking doctoral study at the University of Cambridge as a Commonwealth Scholar under the supervision of former Archbishop of Canterbury, Rowan Williams. His doctoral dissertation was published in 2020 as *A Still More Excellent Way: Authority and Polity in the Anglican Communion*. London: SCM, 2020.

The Rev'd Dr Raewynne Whiteley is the newly appointed Warden of Wollaston Anglican Theological College, Perth, Western Australia, University of Divinity. She completed a PhD in Practical Theology (Homiletics) at Princeton Theological Seminary and has taught homiletics and theology in diocesan theological education programs, as well as serving as Canon Theologian of the Diocese of Long Island. Prior to her current appointment, she was Deputy Director of Discipleship and Lay Ministry in the Diocese of Southwark. She is a member of the Academy of Homiletics and has published in the area of homiletics, including *Steeped in the Holy: Preaching as Spiritual Practice*, Lanham, MD: Cowley, 2008.

www.ingramcontent.com/pod-product-compliance
Lightning Source LLC
Chambersburg PA
CBHW061428300426
44114CB00014B/1597